An anthology of Aquinas's writings requires no apology. A deeper and more extended knowledge of his thinking is needed today, but few people have the time to peruse the more than one hundred works he left as his legacy to mankind when he died at the age of forty-nine.

I have tried to provide a Reader that brings to the general public a broader representation of his interests, his arguments, and his thinking on a wider variety of topics than I have found available in the English translations already published. And so within this one book I hope to give a sense of the total Aquinas: theologian and philosopher, man of faith and of reason.

That is why there are translations not only from the strictly theological treatises, but from the hitherto unpublicized commentaries on the Scriptures; not only from his own specialized philosophical debates, but from his commentaries on Aristotle's philosophical works; not only from these Aristotelian commentaries, but from commentaries on Neoplatonic works as well; and finally, not only from his religious prose, but also from his religious poetry.

This Reader opens upon a serious section on Metaphysics, and something should be said to justify this. The passages in this section have been placed chronologically so that one can easily recognize the early and continued presence of Aquinas's central philosophical distinction between the essence or nature of a thing and its existence (*esse*). The emphasis on this metaphysical insight is justified by the fact that all later sections of the book may be said to hold their unity as Thomistic thought by the implicit or explicit presence of this same insight. Awareness of this principle is a necessity for feeling at home in any work of St. Thomas.

A glance at the Contents shows that the problems that interest contemporary man—the problem of love, of knowledge, of freedom, of God, of religious life—were of intense interest to Thomas Aquinas. The method followed here is to set forth Aquinas's view of reality and then to see this view affecting his discussion of all human concerns.

Mary T. Clark, Editor

AN AQUINAS READER

Edited, with an Introduction by
MARY T. CLARK

HODDER AND STOUGHTON
LONDON · SYDNEY · AUCKLAND · TORONTO

ACKNOWLEDGMENTS

To Pierre Conway, O.P., for selections from his unpublished translations of Prologues from the Commentaries on the works of Aristotle.

To F. R. Larcher, O.P., for selections from his unpublished translation of the work *On the Perfection of Religious Life*.

The Editor expresses gratitude to Professor Harold Cannon of Manhattanville's Department of Classics for generously checking her translations and to Rev. Norris Clarke, S.J., for examining the texts; to Mary Louise Birmingham for helpful criticism.

To Magi Books, Inc., for selections from the Aquinas Scripture Commentaries (ASC); Vol. 1, *Commentary on St. Paul's Epistle to the Galatians;* copyright © 1966 by F. R. Larcher; Vol. 2, *Commentary on St. Paul's Epistle to the Ephesians;* trans. Matthew L. Lamb; copyright © 1966 by Magi Books, Inc.

CONTENTS

MAN AS MORAL

MAN AS RELIGIOUS

BIBLIOGRAPHY

AN AQUINAS READER

INTRODUCTION

An examination of all the passages will show that the essential Aquinas is existential. This statement is not intended as paradox but as fact. Each creature has its own being; at the same time it is related not only to other beings but to God. These relationships are so essential to creatures that we may rightfully call them the necessary conditions of their existence. Such basic and indispensable relationships may never be looked upon as "accidents" in the Aristotelian way of classifying relations as "accidents." By looking at finite things without their ontological relationships, Aristotelians could see nature apart from God. It was this ancient view of nature that Augustine repudiated. Aquinas never returned to it, even when he accepted insights from Aristotle. Although it was Augustine who emphasized that without God nature cannot be itself, it was Thomas Aquinas whose metaphysical analysis made clear that the "act of existing" cannot come from anyone less than God and that when a finite man is recognized as receiving existence from God, his possibilities for change become infinite. This does not make the relation of nature to God intrinsic so that the relationship to God as giver of existence (First Cause in the language of physics) should enter into the definition of the thing caused. But this does make the relationship to God an inevitable consequence of being created or called by him.

No, the creature is itself, robustly real, a center of autonomy. And yet St. Thomas is quick to tell us that the creature's kind of being—finite being—provides it with an open, dynamic relationship to Absolute creative Being. This relationship is not only the source of all existence but the source of all development. And if this is what is meant by nature in process, a philosophy of existence is open to it.

But instead of using the word "process" to denote the ongoing and dynamic character of finite reality, Aquinas used the word "participated" to indicate that nature was "becoming," was dynamically open to the transcendent.

By revealing the essence/existence (*esse*) structure of creatures within a framework of existential relationship to God,

Aquinas was able to retain the Platonic insistence upon
exemplary causality (that all sensible reality is a reflection or
imitation of intelligible reality, its exemplar or idea) as well
as the Augustinian doctrine of creatures as images of God, a
teaching taken from Genesis. Not all philosophy students
have realized that by not remaining on the level of Aristotle's
distinction between substance and accident—by going deeper
through distinguishing essence from existence—Aquinas has
escaped from the Aristotelian categories of substance and the
nine accidents of quality, quantity, relation, etc. Existence as
infinite becomes the exemplar of all finite participants. But
the latter do not merely image their exemplar in some extrinsic fashion. The image theory that Plato had related to
the forms and that Augustine related to the divine ideas was
transposed by Aquinas into a doctrine of participation
whereby creatures have an intrinsic, limited sharing of
"existence" with all the perfection that existence brings with
it. In this framework "to image" now means "to be" after
the manner of the Supreme Exemplar—to be spiritual, to be
unified, to know, to live, to be free. This is imaging God in
existence, in action. It follows, moreover, that human evil is
rooted in unlikeness to God.

What Aquinas did was identify a central perfection—*esse*—
in which all things participate. He then showed that the having of existence requires an efficient and formal exemplary
cause, and since man is among these existents, his exemplar
would be personal, unparticipated being, and all things are
like God insofar as they have existence. This existence is, of
course, the most intrinsic of all perfections. Without existence, there is nothing real. Because of this existential situation, which is echoed in the intellect's orientation toward
Absolute Being in its life of knowledge, we may gain some
positive knowledge of God by knowing creatures inasmuch
as the possession of existence is the foundation for an analogy
between finite beings and Infinite Being.

By his metaphysics of an existence common to all and
unique to each, Aquinas like Augustine saw man as radically
existing "toward God" (*ad Deum*), and because he shares
existence with all creatures, man is horizontally related to all
as man-in-the-world. For the being (*esse*) by which each

one is subsistent, distinct, unique is that being whereby it is united to all. Personal uniqueness in this perspective is not opposed to human community. Therefore the Thomistic metaphysics of reality may never be rightly classified as a doctrine of isolated substances or as a system of static concepts without doing violence to the Thomistic texts. With this in mind we present here rather full texts from a wide choice of works so that it may become readily apparent that not only in metaphysical topics but also in his treatment of God and man-in-the-world as well as in his discussion of man as ethical or religious, the essential Aquinas is existential.

Life

To know St. Thomas is to know the medieval mind at its finest, its most powerful, and, indeed, its most modern. For he is timeless and timely, a man for all ages. His thought has influenced such diverse artists as Dante and T. S. Eliot and James Joyce, such different theologians as John Courtney Murray and Karl Rahner, such unlike philosophers as Edith Stein and Jacques Maritain, such a political figure as Eugene McCarthy. Modern man is more rooted than he realizes. And if, as John H. Randall says in *Studies in Civilization,* the first modern philosopher is not Descartes but Aquinas, we may justly say that at least some of our roots are within the fertile ground of Thomistic thought. And for that reason we owe it to ourselves to know something of this remarkable man.

We tend to think of Thomas Aquinas as a teacher. It seems pretty remarkable to me that anyone, especially a teacher, could produce some one hundred works of closely textured, carefully reasoned, and invariably creative thinking during forty-nine years of life! His, to be sure, was an age without the distractions of communications media and without the contemporary clamor for speakers on panels and convention platforms. Probably the most disturbing element to one's own study was the scholarly pursuits of others in the same field who were following an opposing tradition of thought.

In a real sense Aquinas's work was his life, for his life was an interior one, a life of the mind and the spirit. And yet it was an exciting life: the imprisonment for a year; the darling of at least one Pope; a center of controversy in university life and philosophical thought; an intellectual innovator not wholly appreciated by his own fellow Dominicans nor by Church authorities, somewhat like Pierre Teilhard de Chardin in our own era; a precursor of the ecumenical movement to end the East-West split; an explorer of original sources with even more urgency than that of today's theologians and philosophers; a seminary reformer; a *peritus* at Church Councils and General Chapters; a professor at three universities— surely he fulfilled a long life in a short time!

Honorius III was Pope and Frederick II was Emperor when Thomas was born in the county of Aquino near Naples about the year 1225, youngest son of a Norman mother, Teodora D'Aquino, second wife of Landolfo, a Lombard who had at least eight children. At the age of five Thomas was escorted to the Abbey of Monte Cassino as a Benedictine oblate and there he remained until obliged to leave the politically endangered abbey when he was fourteen, but not before he had experienced his own authentic attraction toward religious life. Matriculation at the Imperial University in Naples introduced Thomas to two future forces in his life—Aristotle and the Dominicans. His instructor in natural philosophy, Peter of Ireland, was a careful commentator of Aristotle, and we may credit him with making Aquinas dissatisfied with the paraphrasing method of his future teacher, Albert the Great. To this university where the Dominicans taught theology came the Dominican master general, Jordan of Saxony, and it is quite possible that young Thomas was among the students listening to his preaching. But we know that with the advice of another Dominican, John of San Giuliano, Thomas at seventeen became a Dominican novice. Fearful of family opposition, his superiors planned that Thomas would go from Naples to Rome and then to Paris. Before this was accomplished, the brothers of Aquinas, instigated by their mother, overtook the travelers and kidnapped Thomas, taking him to Roccasecca, the family castle. There they detained, distracted, disturbed, and finally tempted him through a woman—so the story goes—to forsake his religious vocation. With a firebrand he frightened his tempters out of the room and set to work to deepen his knowledge of Scripture, to study Peter Lombard's *Four Books of the Sentences,* and even to produce after reading Aristotle a brief treatise called *Fallacies.*

The rock-fastness of Aquinas's commitment to God brought release after a year, and with his detainment counting for the vocation trial period known as the "novitiate year," Aquinas soon reached Rue St. Jacques in Paris for a three-year stretch of early theological studies. There followed four more years of seminary study at Cologne under Albert the Great, who had accompanied him from Paris, a period during which Aquinas was ordained at the Cologne Cathedral. Here at Cologne Aquinas's great gifts of mind were discovered when, quite by accident, Albert read an extremely subtle and original commentary on *The Divine Names* in the handwriting of Aquinas. At Paris once again for four years of advanced theological studies, Aquinas was successively Bachelor of the Bible and Scripture lecturer, completing his work leading to the Master of Theology degree by 1256. That his appointment, as well as Bonaventure's, as university master awaited Alexander IV's intervention in 1257 is part of the complex situation that catapulted Thomas Aquinas into the center of controversy—academic, ecclesiastical, philosophical, theological.

And so it was that Aquinas's first intellectual assignment was conditioned by the transitional status of the thirteenth century, which was witnessing the rebirth of the evangelical spirit that grew into the two great mendicant orders, Franciscan and Dominican. These orders, very much in the spirit of the Vatican II document on the *Church and the Modern World,* were sending out their friars on the medieval highways and byways to meet the people wherever they clustered. And since education had traveled, through the gradual development of cathedral schools into universities, from the country to the city, the Franciscans and Dominicans went on foot to Paris and other cities. As mendicants they looked upon their poverty not with a pharisaically "see how holy we are" complex, but as preparation for alacrity in moving quickly wherever the Gospel needed preaching. Their riches were their relevancy. In this spirit Bonaventure and Thomas Aquinas made themselves relevant to the university, although this required the possession of manuscripts! Now at this very time the diocesan priests who taught under the administration of the bishop at the University of Paris had gone on strike in public protest over existing university conditions. The conflict that was precipitated when the mendicant friars replaced them at the university lasted through the next decade and invited Aquinas to his first dialogue.

The secular priests had immediately challenged the right of mendicant friars to do any teaching at the university. At a deeper level, this was a revelation of their failure to understand the changes taking place in the Church of their day, for they were resisting the new Christianity emerging from a review of the nature and structure of the Church, to which there corresponded the change from the monastic to the mendicant mentality. Such inflexibility inevitably spawned a depreciation of the value of religious life itself. The bitterness of the opposition to the mendicant friars' right to teach and to religious life was expressed by a secular master at Paris, William of St. Amour, in a work, *Contemporary Dangers*. In his answer, *An Apology for Religious Orders*, Aquinas shows himself completely aware of the Parisian academic *lebenswelt*, plagued as it was by growing pains. Although at Rome in 1256 William was condemned, he continued his struggle against the mendicants, and during Aquinas's absence from the university, in a renamed and revised copy of his early work, William renewed the attack, but not without some effect upon university morale. The Franciscan Thomas of York wrote a defense of religious life that was attacked in 1269 by Gerald of Abbeville in a pamphlet called *Against Christian Perfection*. Not only did Bonaventure answer this new attack, but its title also accounts for the name given by Aquinas to his second attempt to dialogue with these unwilling listeners: *On the Perfection of Religious Life*. In it Aquinas discusses the value of the three religious vows of poverty, chastity, and obedience. The discussions resulting from this treatise are synthesized in a work *Against the Dangerous Doctrine Drawing Young Men Away from Religious Life*. The calm serenity of these works gives witness to Thomas's skill in speaking persuasively to protagonists of another view—always with the hope of arriving at mutual understanding.

It was, however, endemic to Aquinas to talk *to* those who disagreed with him rather than to refute them. This dialogical attitude was as natural to Thomas as it is to our century and characterized not only his manner of carrying on an argument but the style of his own summas and treatises as well as his techniques as commentator.

And because Aquinas freely and fully dedicated himself to the intellectual interests of his age, the story of his life is a tale of encounters with Parisian professors, questioning bishops, disciples of Mohammed and Greek Orthodox teachers, classical and contemporary thinkers, patristic and avant-garde theologians.

In any age when the Church is attempting to renew her self-understanding there will be a concern for Christian unity in response to Christ's appeal "that all may be one." And so it should come as no surprise that in order to reconcile Rome and Constantinople, mediation was attempted by a Greek bishop of southern Italy, who wrote a work *Against the Errors of the Greek Church*. Thomas reviewed this book at the request of Urban IV. Another attempt to find common ground with Greeks, Armenians, and Mohammedans is the letter to the *Cantor of Antioch*, in which moral and philosophical reasons on behalf of the Catholic faith are offered. It is noteworthy also that as the *peritus* of Urban IV, Aquinas was directed to bring together the various comments of the Greek and Latin fathers upon the Four Gospels. The result was a continuous commentary by twenty-two Latin and fifty-seven Greek fathers edited under the title *Catena Aurea*. These writings and a major one, the *Summa of Christian Teaching* (*Summa Contra Gentiles*), were intended to promote Christian unity. And Thomas's own theological thought, deeply influenced as it was by the Eastern Christian mystic Dionysius the Pseudo-Areopagite, had its part in making him receptive to Eastern orientations. After all, it was a Greek father of the Church, Maximus the Confessor, who had led the way in blending Eastern and Western mentalities. Symbolic indeed was Thomas Aquinas's last trip, taken for the purpose of attending at Lyons the Church Council called to promote unity of faith between East and West.

Through his various *Commentaries* Aquinas appears as a

student who aims to discuss with rather than to triumph over a deeply respected author. He therefore seeks to understand the basic principles that structure the author's thought processes. If he finds these principles to be intellectually viable he will ignore many of the conclusions with which he may not agree and stoutly declare himself in fundamental agreement with the author. By empathy he discovers the developments that the historical positions allow and at times credits the author with these positions. The ecumenical endeavor of Aquinas the commentator in dealing with such radically contradictory texts as those of Boethius, Dionysius, Aristotle, and Proclus is paramount in the whole project. So when we hear Aquinas accused of being unhistorical in his handling of the texts we should remember that an author is judged by his aim. In the case of Aquinas the aim was philosophical understanding for the promotion of intellectual harmony rather than historical scholarship. Aquinas sensed that mental rapport, common ground, was the prerequisite of any dialogue that hopes to arrive at consensus.

And yet Aquinas's conviction that every man should be allowed to speak for himself made him dissatisfied with the translations that ushered Aristotle into thirteenth-century Europe. Because these works had gone from Greek to Syrian to Arabic to Latin, it was doubtful that they could be called original texts or first sources. Aquinas secured a Greek expert, William of Moerbeke, to translate Aristotle's original Greek texts into Latin. Anyone studying the record of Aquinas's commitments would readily acknowledge that there was absolutely no time for him to be his own translator, and it was necessary to have the work in Latin if the commentary was to be read by students at the University of Paris, where all the teaching took place in Latin. This itself was a step in the direction of authentic texts. And Aquinas, as a matter of fact, had a keen historical sense. He was the first to declare, in 1268, that the work *On Causes,* which was circulated in Europe as part of the Aristotelian corpus, was actually the *Elements of Theology* written by Proclus. If he had discovered this before writing his *Commentary on Dionysius' Divine Names* he would have realized that in that work Dionysius is quoting directly from Proclus and could not therefore be the first-century disciple of St. Paul he was reputed to be. Perhaps Aquinas felt at home in his dialogue with Dionysius precisely because of the Neoplatonic spirit the latter shared with Augustine, whom Aquinas revered. Because Peter Lombard's *Sentences* are said to be 80 percent from Augustine, Aquinas does not profoundly disagree; but his *Commentary* is a very interesting dialogue and at times reveals disagreement with contemporaries such as Albert and Bonaventure.

Now the very fact that translation schools were set up at Toledo and Sicily signals the eagerness of medieval scholars to learn from Mohammedans and Jews. And learn Aquinas did. First from Avicenna, who opened up a new stream of Platonism and Neoplatonism with its great philosophic contributions—the notion of "going forth and return" of the universe, procession and conversion, and especially "participation," the theory that lower things in the world of the "many" share in the perfection of the one ideal form that they more or less remotely resemble. Aquinas was never *completely* to reject this, inasmuch as he accepts its implication that all sensible and finite beings come from one supreme source of reality. And in fact the novel Thomistic theory of analogy/causality presupposes the notion of "participation." If Aquinas gained greatly from reading the philosophical works of Avicenna with his insistence that "existence" was not included in "essence," there was never total agreement. This made dialogue necessary. It was somewhat the same with Moses Maimonides. From him Aquinas was happy to borrow profusely in the question of demonstrating God's existence, but he could not agree with Moses that the various attributes of God were merely synonyms. This required discussion. At the suggestion of a former Dominican master general, St. Raymond of Penafort, Aquinas devoted his first *Summa* (*Summa Contra Gentiles*, translated in this book as *Summa of Christian Teaching*) to a reasoned discussion with those who did not accept the Catholic faith—pagans, Jews, Greek schismatics, but especially Mohammedans, with whom Aquinas was forced to keep to the philosophical level, as in most of the first three books. Some historians also think that the opuscule *Power of God* is structured to deal with questions raised by Avicenna.

When in 1266 Aquinas began his *Summa of Theology,*
he already had at hand many of the Greek-Latin translations
of Aristotle's works. The importance of this lies not merely
in all that they could contribute to this major *opus* of synthe-
sizing the insights available from the greatest thinkers of
West and East, but above all because they provided Aquinas
with the primary sources he needed to meet the greatest test
of his intellectual life. This was to be the encounter with
Siger of Brabant, a Belgian priest-professor in the University
of Paris Arts Department who was strenuously teaching the
Averroistic version of Aristotle. According to this version:
1. there was only one intellect or soul, common to all men
(monopsychism, a position not explicitly stated in Aristotle's
On the Soul), with the inevitable conclusion that Aristotle
(who for Siger was equivalent to "philosophy") taught that
man was mortal, although the opposite was held by the Christian faith; 2. the material world was eternal; 3. the will is a
passive power, merely activated by knowledge; 4. there are
many intermediaries between God and man, making the doctrine of divine Providence an unreality.

It was because such positions were being inferred from the
Arabian Aristotle that the Aristotelian works had been forbidden in 1210, the *Physics* and *Metaphysics* banned in 1215.
Although the record shows that the whole of the Aristotelian
corpus was to be found in the Paris Curriculum in 1255, the
prohibition was renewed by Urban IV in 1263.

When Thomas returned to the University of Paris in 1269
for his second professorate, he was deeply disturbed to find
Siger of Brabant imposing his Averroistic interpretations of
Aristotle upon the Parisian students, who could not read the
original texts and whose undeveloped minds ill prepared them
to detect sophistry. So began the most delicate and demanding
of all the Thomistic dialogues, and this time it was not with
a dead authority but with a colleague very much alive, who
insisted not merely on Aristotelian principles but on the conclusions and interpretations drawn by Averroes. Aquinas the
man of faith, fortified by years of concentration on Aristotle,
just having written his great theological witness to the
inner harmony of faith and reason, faces Siger the rationalist, leader of the "heterodox Aristotelians," or "Latin-

Averroists" as they were once called. The argument was forced to be philosophical. It was not enough to insist with the Catholic Siger that from Scripture we derive teachings quite opposed to those of Averroes. Siger admitted this. But he did not particularly care, adding that a position arrived at philosophically could be true even when it contradicted what Christians believed. Both could be true. This is referred to in many histories as the "double truth theory."

Aquinas's task was clear. To converse with such an avowed Aristotelian he must dissociate Aristotelian principles from Arabic interpretations and then demonstrate that conclusions in perfect harmony with Christian beliefs were derivable from Aristotle's principles. He would then go on to indicate, as far as the actual text warranted, that Aristotle had himself drawn such conclusions. This is precisely what he did in that powerful work *On a Common Intellect,* where he proved that Aristotle attributed to each man his own intellect. Within the year, the teaching of Siger, defender of Averroistic Aristotelianism, was condemned by Stephen Tempier, Archbishop of Paris. There was at the same time some questioning of Aquinas about his doctrines, which many of his day failed to distinguish from Siger's. In an effort to clarify his position, Thomas wrote *On the Eternity of the World against the Grumblers,* wherein he pointed out that Aristotle never really demonstrated but merely presupposed the world's eternity. Thomas further claimed that neither the world's eternity nor its noneternity is philosophically demonstrable, and it is intellectual honesty to admit this. Believers in the Bible have learned from Genesis I that the world began in time. Thomas hastened to complete his own work called *The Soul,* which was directed against the Averroistic interpretations of Aristotle's treatise on this same topic. If F. van Steenberghen is right, the conversation that Aquinas kept up with his university colleague led Siger to modify some of his original positions. But this did not keep back the falling of the final blow against Averroism, a blow struck by the same Stephen Tempier who this time included twenty Thomistic propositions among the 219 theses condemned at Paris in 1277. In the autumn Siger was summoned before the French Inquisitor, Simon du Val, and from there he proceeded to the Papal

Court of Orvieto to plead his cause. There he was absolved
of formal heresy but directed to remain in Orvieto, where
one day his mentally deranged secretary stabbed him to death.

The condemnation of Averroism in 1270 did not mean for
Aquinas the end to controversy. We must remember that
while he was in open forum confronting the liberals of his
day—those whom Renan called the thirteenth-century Parisian freethinkers—he himself was opposed by the conserva-
tives of his day, the Franciscans and secular priests who
called themselves "Augustinian." They feared that Aristotelian ideas would destroy the purity of Christian faith. Between
1270 and 1272 Aquinas devoted himself to instructing these
"Augustinians" by writing *On the Virtues in General, On
Hope,* and *On the Cardinal Virtues.* These works should have
calmed their fears.

Anyone who fears that Aquinas might be too slavish a student of Aristotle should read his work *On Truth*—one of his
earliest—concerned with knowledge and reality and God's
being and action. There one sees him coming to grips in a
profound and original way with contradictory and comple-
mentary, ancient and modern currents of thought—Augustinian, Aristotelian, Arabic, Neoplatonic. This was in fact the
first of the sixty-two *disputed questions* that admirably reveal a philosopher at work, developing through dialogue.
These regular discussions throughout the university year provided one of the best opportunities for living dialogue between faculty and students, faculty and their colleagues. In
addition, there were twelve holiday debates, impromptu inquiries similar to our open question periods.

Serenity, intellectual poise, and respect for the opinion of
others characterize Aquinas's dialogues with his pagan and
Jewish predecessors and colleagues, and these qualities doubtless have their source in an utter at-homeness with Scriptural orientations that provided him with a happy combination of sureness and freedom. Never, from the beginning of
his intellectual life until the last two years as professor at the
University of Naples, did Aquinas cease to meditate on and
comment on the Holy Bible. And by this drinking from the
same source that nourished Augustine, and, like him,
enamored of that New Wisdom binding together faith and

reason, Aquinas thought of himself as Augustine's collaborator, never his opponent. Thus the fears of the so-called Augustinians were groundless.

Whereas today the Church is passing through a phase that some refer to as a deinstitutionalizing process, the thirteenth century was caught up in a reverse movement. The mendicant friars—Franciscan and Dominican—dramatize the back-to-the-Gospel movement that characterized the spiritual renaissance of the high Middle Ages. As the first years of the divine romance passed with the death of Francis and Dominic, both religious orders were faced with the need to institutionalize the spirit of the Order. As a son of St. Dominic, and a brilliant one, Thomas Aquinas was given an active part in the shaping of the Dominican life-style to bring the Dominican ideal into structures that would preserve it for the future. In his day the training of priests had been carried on with a minimum of long-range planning. Aquinas gave his attention, therefore, to seminary reform. As early as 1259 Thomas Aquinas attended his Order's General Chapter at Valenciennes, where he helped to formulate the plan of studies for Dominican religious. It was decided that the seminary program would in the future include a philosophy course. Thomas saw philosophy as desirable, not detrimental to Christian believers.

At the 1260 Provincial Chapter at Naples Thomas Aquinas was named preacher-general, and many sermons survive from this period of preaching at Orvieto and Viterbo, close to the papal court, first of Urban IV, later of Clement IV. A wider responsibility for shaping Dominican religious life came with his appointment in 1267 as definitor for the Roman Province while he continued to teach theology, this time at the University of Bologna. He therefore represented the Roman Province at the Parisian General Chapter in May of 1269, where weighty intellectual and apostolic issues were up for decision. He remained on at Paris as second-time professor of theology for the next three years and took final leave to attend his last General Chapter at Florence in 1272. Although there was a request for his return to the University of Paris, he was assigned to the University of Naples, where he spent the last year and a half of his life teaching theology and writing the *Summa* and various opuscules and commentaries.

On December 6, 1273 Thomas Aquinas put down his pen and declared: "I cannot; such things have been revealed to me that all that I have written seems to me as so much straw." Summoned to Lyons by Gregory X to attend the Church Council that aimed at reunion with the Greek Church, Aquinas in weakened health took to the road but fell ill on the way. Taken from his sister's house to the Cistercian monastery of Fossanuova, he died listening to the Canticle of Canticles. As he received the last rites he prayed: "I receive Thee, ransom of my soul. For love of Thee have I studied and kept vigil, toiled, preached, and taught. . . ." The year was 1274.

And he could have added, "and prayed." Many in the Catholic world have studied the thought of Thomas Aquinas, often, alas, in forms he would have repudiated, but many more have sung his prayers: the *Adoro Te*, the *Pange Lingua*, which includes the *Tantum Ergo*. These come from the Office, Mass, Sequence, and hymns for the Feast of Corpus Christi, first celebrated in 1264. It is said that Urban IV agreed to establish this feast to honor Christ's presence in the Blessed Sacrament at the urging of Thomas Aquinas. This he asked for when, upon being offered the Cardinal's hat, he refused it and then was told that he might ask for anything else within the Pope's power.

And so we see that Aquinas's career in higher studies ended where it had begun—at the University of Naples. His religious life likewise ended where it had begun—in a monastery. Famous as a Dominican and as a master at Paris, Aquinas was to be at home in all religious orders whose rationale he had so ably argued, and at all universities dedicated to free inquiry.

The University of Paris requested that his body be sent there, but it remained for a time at the Cistercian monastery. Later his bones were taken to the Dominican house in Toulouse, whence during the French Revolution they were removed to the Church of St. Sernin in Toulouse.

In 1324 Bishop Stephen Bourret of Paris reversed the condemnation of his predecessor. The Thomistic doctrines were removed from the list of Averroistic propositions condemned. The reversal had come when Aquinas's teachings were re-evaluated and his personal life examined. In 1323 the Church raised up Thomas Aquinas as a scholar-saint.

The significance of his scholarship is more obvious in the twentieth century than it was in the nineteenth. He had welcomed and worked with Aristotle's world view. The admission of all of Aristotle's works into Christian thought was an admission of "all the natural values of human social activity." In a sense this was a rejection of that type of Platonic other-worldliness that implied repudiation of "this world"; and because it was an option for a thoroughgoing Incarnationism, it was an acceptance of human values without a forsaking of Platonic transcendence, which reached its true realization in the One Exemplar—the God-man, source, norm, and end of human history. In this sense Aristotle assisted Thomas to be more Christian, not less so.

And so if Catholic thought in modern times was considered to be excessively other-worldly, we should remember that Thomism did not penetrate and influence the modern centuries. Only in the twentieth century, with the Neo-Thomistic revival originally stimulated during the pontificate of Leo XIII, did Thomas Aquinas re-enter the universities and then only, very often, in the sketchy form of manuals, somewhat distorted by an imposed thesis format, shorn of his intellectual *lebenswelt*, pulled out of perspective. From the time of Scotus and Ockham, through Nicholas of Autrecourt, Luther, Hobbes, Hume, and Montaigne, the scope of reason had been narrowed to confine itself eventually to the sensibly empirical. If the Scholastics did have too restricted a conception of human experience, the principles of Thomism that effectively united this-world values with other-worldly values could have provided built-in correctives operating in the course of time. Instead, religious reaction to wholesale empiricism showed itself in an overstress of ultimates. Christians concerned themselves not with men but with souls. But because Aquinas offered a robust and buoyant philosophy of reality in opposition to the philosophy of signs and symbols (which short-circuited this world to arrive immediately at the next) favored by other medievals, there is ample reason for honoring him today as one whose existential realism makes him not only a scholar-saint but a saint of the secular—one who saw the sacred value of time, of this world.

Aquinas would be pleased also to have us recognize in him an upholder of unity—the ecumenical unity of East and West, the historical unity of time and eternity, the religious unity of created and Creator. It was on behalf of such unity that Aquinas made and used his fruitful philosophical distinctions. This unity of mankind, he would be the first to realize, is more than a theological task, more than an economic or political achievement; it is in fact a work of love. But then Thomas Aquinas's total theological framework was grounded not on static ideas but on a movement of exodus and apocalypse, outgo and return through the dynamism of love—the divine love of Creation and Redemption initiating that human love that reaches God by participating in the power of the Resurrection.

Editor's Note: When not otherwise indicated, the translations have been made by the Editor from the Parma edition, or the Leonine edition where this exists.

Author references found in each sectional Introduction refer to books listed in the Bibliography at the end of the book.

BRIEF CHRONOLOGY OF THE LIFE
OF THOMAS AQUINAS

1225   Born at castle of Roccasecca near Naples.

1230   Enters Monte Cassino as Benedictine oblate.

1239   Leaves Monte Cassino.
Goes to University of Naples for undergraduate arts studies.

1244   Receives Dominican habit at Naples.
On way to Parisian House of Studies seized by brothers at Tuscany, imprisoned at Roccasecca; resisted temptations to give up vocation.

1245   Returns to Dominican House at Naples.
Travels to Paris for early university studies at St. Jacques with Albert the Great.

1248   Goes to Cologne for theology under Albert the Great.
Is ordained sometime between 1248 and 1252 at Cologne Cathedral.

1252   Returns to Paris for graduate studies.
Biblical Bachelor (1252–54).
Sententiary Bachelor (1254–56) and lecturer on Scripture.

1256   Promoted to master of theology by papal dispensation four years before required age.
1257–July 1259: first Parisian teaching period in theology.

1259   Attends General Chapter at Valenciennes; revises Dominican Plan of Studies.
Italian period: called to Papal Court at Anagni, Orvieto, Rome, Viterbo.

1260   Named preacher-general of Dominicans.

1265   Made regent master in Dominican House of Studies at Rome.

1267 Made definitor of Roman Province, theology master at University of Bologna.

1269 Attends General Chapter at Paris.
      January 1269–May 1272: second Parisian teaching period in theology.

1272 Attends General Chapter at Florence.
      Returns to Naples as Master of Theology at the University and Dominican House of Studies.

1273 Has heavenly revelation on December 6 while celebrating Mass in chapel of St. Nicholas: ". . . such things have been revealed to me that all that I have written seems to me as so much straw."

1274 Summoned in January to Church Council at Lyons by Gregory IX.
      Falls ill on journey, stops at sister's house, then taken to Cistercian monastery of Fossanuova.

1274 Dies on March 7 at age of forty-nine.

1277 March 7: Stephen Tempier, Bishop of Paris, condemns 219 statements, including some of Thomas's.
      Robert Kilwardby, O.P., Archbishop of Canterbury, condemns philosophic positions that include Thomas's.

1278 General Chapter of Dominicans upholds Thomas's teaching.

1282 General Chapter of Franciscans prohibits reading of *Summa of Theology* in Franciscan schools.

1284 John Peckham, Archbishop of Canterbury, censures Thomist statements.

1323 At Avignon, July 18, Thomas Aquinas canonized by Pope John XXII.

1324 Stephen Bourret, Archbishop of Paris, revokes the 1277 condemnation of Thomist theses by the former Bishop of Paris.

The following two charts show the philosophical and intellectual influences on Aquinas.

CHART I.

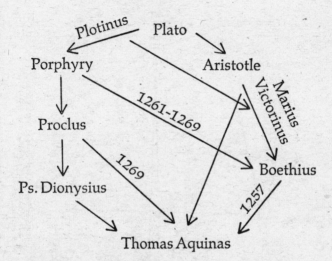

Adapted, with permission, from:

C. Fabro, *La Nozione Metafisica Di Partecipazione Secondo S. Tommaso D'Aquino*, Rome, Societa Editrice Internazionale.

In Chart I we see at a glance the major philosophical influences undergone by Aquinas. It is obvious that Neoplatonic influences predominate, directly through Porphyry as well as indirectly through Neoplatonic interpretations of Aristotelian texts as well as through Boethius, who inherited a Western Christian Neoplatonism from Marius Victorinus. We note a direct and full knowledge of Aristotle, but much indirect knowledge of Plato as well as the possibility that there was access to the *Timaeus, Phaedo,* and *Meno* that existed in Latin.

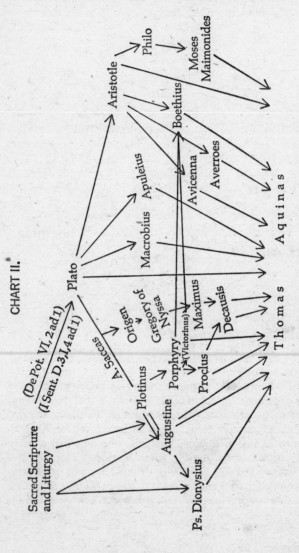

CHART II.

Sacred Scripture and Liturgy

Ps. Dionysius

Augustine

Plotinus

A. Saccas

Origen

Gregory of Nyssa

Plato

(De Pot. VI, 2 ad 1)
(I Sent. D. 3, 1, 4 ad 1)

Macrobius

Apuleius

Aristotle

Philo

Moses Maimonides

Boethius

Avicenna

Averroes

Porphyry
(Victorinus)

Maximus

Decausis

Proclus

Thomas Aquinas

Adapted, with permission, from: C. Fabro, *La Nozione Metafisica Di Partecipazione Secondo S. Tommaso D'Aquino*, Rome, Società Editrice Internazionale, pp. 118-119.

Chart II has assembled the main intellectual influences upon Aquinas. By now historical studies have sufficiently advanced to make it pure folly to identify Thomism with Aristotelianism or with any previous philosophy. The chart indicates that Aquinas had access to Neoplatonism through Augustine, Boethius, Proclus, Dionysius the Pseudo-Areopagite, Maximus through Scotus Erigena's translation, and to John Scotus Erigena himself. By studying the Greek fathers, Aquinas met other sources of Neoplatonism. The link through Augustine has long been known. The enormous influence of Scripture has not been unknown in the scholarly literature, but has been largely ignored in popular works. For all these elements to mingle harmoniously each had to be greatly modified.

REALITY

The crucial metaphysical question that today is associated with the name of Heidegger was the question raised by Aquinas: Why is there something rather than nothing? Neither Plato, for whom matter always existed, nor Aristotle, for whom the world of becoming was eternal, answered this question. To give more than a likely account of creation was to exchange myth for metaphysics. This Aquinas did by proposing the distinction between existence and essence to explain the absolute beginning of being and to show the structure that made possible the multiplicity of finite things.

Thomas used the traditional formulas of metaphysics in a way that was new for his time. When the scholar comes across such terms as act/potentiality, being, *id quod est* (that which is), *quo est* (that by which it is), and participation, he correctly recognizes the influence of Aristotle, Plato, and even Boethius and Plotinus. But he would be mistaken if he were to identify the thought of Thomas with that of his predecessors, since Thomas uses the formulas in a thoroughly original way.

Take the idea of *participation* as it turns up in Thomistic texts. Thomas was more convinced than Plato that participation helped us to appreciate what is going on in the created universe; he was in deep agreement with Bonaventure that whoever denies the "ideas" denies the Word of God. But participation for Aquinas is not in ideas or forms as with Plato. It is closer to the Neoplatonism of participation in the "infinite," yet even here the difference is great. Whereas for Plotinus there was participation in the One, for Aquinas it was in *esse* or be-ing that things participated. Nor with Aquinas does participation signify a shadowy or unreal existence; the act of being (*actus essendi*) really belongs to the finite thing. In this insistence upon the "ontological consistency" of beings we experience the influence not of Neoplatonism but of Aristotle, for whom things really possessed their own constitutive and operative principles.

Once again, however, influence must not be mistaken for identity. For while it is true that the act/potentiality structure was used by St. Thomas to compare and contrast existence and essence with form-matter composition, he nevertheless expressed the real distinction between existence and essence, as the texts show, in terms of participation. It will ever remain Aquinas's neatest accomplishment to have discovered the complementarity of the two greatest minds of classical Greek philosophy to the point of teaching that the Platonic philosophy of participation in being becomes viable only within an Aristotelian philosophy of the experience of becoming, made possible by "potentiality," the basis of change and of continuity. Aristotle's passive potentiality, aptly applied to the explanation of physical change, was transformed by Aquinas into a metaphysical complexification and multiplication. As the source of different *kinds* (species) of things, potentiality is called "essence;" as a source of a thing's specific activities, it is called "nature." Because essence, which limits the infinite riches of existence to being *this* rather than *that* thing, refers to a concrete reality as its foundation, there is just as much scope for an evolution of essences as there is for a scientifically demonstrated evolution of things.

At times students of Aquinas fail to grasp the mutual working relation in the existence/essence composition. For example, each has its own contribution to make: the act of existing (*actus essendi*) is limited by the essence-recipient, whereas the essence becomes real through the act of "to be" that it receives. Like prime matter, essence is called potentiality. But since neither prime matter nor essence is absolute non-being, they might be spoken of as "imperfect act" within the spirit though not the letter of St. Thomas's metaphysics. Aristotle even spoke of a certain yearning or desire of matter for substantial form so that when we call potentiality imperfect act we are only referring to that reality or dynamism that might be operative in any material thing wherein potentiality is never found alone. This view of matter was somewhat validated by Aquinas on the metaphysical plane when he spoke of the principles of created being—matter, form, essence, existence—as participating in the act of "esse" or to-be. By thus deepening the metaphysical analysis to include existence Aquinas is perhaps making explicit what his philosophical predecessors had glimpsed—the causal contributions made by matter and form and the yearning for perfection or reality. In fact, the very gradation of participation in existence becomes with Aquinas the basis for the hierarchical world structure as well as the point of departure for the necessary inference to Unparticipated Being or God. Thus the famous Thomistic theory of analogy and causality presupposes the theory of participation. That is why we may call the "analogy doctrine" the semantics of the metaphysical distinction between essence and existence, recalling that this distinction is meaningless apart from the causality of participation taken over from Neoplatonism and adapted to the only dualism that was important to Aquinas—a Creator-creature dualism that is no conceptual superstructure but an existential exigency for any dialogue of love.

In studying Thomistic metaphysics it is far too easy to get bogged down in a dead-end dispute about the real distinction between essence and existence. Taken by itself, this distinction does not interest Thomas Aquinas and should not be isolated from his total teaching. Like his medieval colleagues, Thomas was primarily concerned with the real distinction between God and man. Man's metaphysical composition of essence/existence radically distinguishes him from God, whose simplicity is rooted in his unlimited act of existing, which is his very Essence.

But if finite being is therefore only an imperfect image of Infinite Being, it is nevertheless an image, because there is some analogy between creatures having existence and the Creator, who is Existence: All things are alike in sharing an ever-varying relationship between each one's essence and existence and all are proportionately dependent upon God, whose relation between his essence and existence is one of identity: His Essence is to exist. Since the pure perfections that are present in creatures can be attributed in an eminent degree to God, an analogy that is true to the Thomistic texts is not one of "proper proportionality" alone, as Father Klubertanz has ably argued, but a rich combination of proportionality and attribution. This means that things not only resemble God because they have an essence/existence structure, but they also image God by participating in the perfection of being. In the Thomistic doctrine of participation creatures have an intrinsic, limited sharing of "being" that determines their specific perfections and their possibilities for development in perfection. In this analogy of attribution or likeness in perfection to God, the likeness is intrinsic to the creature, and because analogy is rooted in the act of being (*actus essendi*), imaging God is an active process.

In man this process is personal. The more perfect personal action is, the more is humanity renewed, improved, and increased qualitatively. Since this process touches upon what is most intrinsic to man and the source of his reality—namely, his participation in existence—man's possibilities are as infinite as the One who is the Ground of his existence.

And so Thomistic metaphysics clues us in on what the eye does not observe—the existential grounding of the process of knowing and loving and choosing with which we are all familiar. In this perspective we come to see that man does not abstract, conceptualize, possess, or grasp the Absolute or the truth—he is awakened by the Absolute, becomes aware within the horizon of the Absolute, and responds to truth, to goodness, to love, the authentic presence of the Absolute. Corresponding to this vocation of man to commune with the Absolute in and through human actions are certain "psychological conditions." Although intentionality and tendency are primarily ontological, in the psychological order they express participation in being (*esse*): the presence in this or that reality of a force or perfection surpassing it and drawing it beyond itself. Intentionality, a word associated by many with Husserl, signifies "to tend to something else." Such is the condition of human knowledge, the condition of human desire. The relation of finite conscious being to Absolute *Esse* is implicit in the very act of knowing, the very act of loving, of choosing. For the finite act of "to be" is the intentional presence of God in the creature and simultaneously "the act that is the creature itself." This metaphysical analysis reveals the relative perfection of the concrete individual as well as its insufficiency. God is there, present as the giver of perfection, of reality, of existence, as well as the promise of fulfillment.

Existential metaphysics is not rationalist metaphysics, and

so an existentialist metaphysician does not regard God as a *deus ex machina,* a stopgap God, but as lord of reality and of history, the ground of all things that are and are becoming. Yet human insufficiency has the important function of differentiating man from God while it alerts man to look beyond himself for happiness, to discover that he is not yet wholly himself and that he becomes himself by relating to others. Not that man is a "part" of the world as an organic whole, yet man recognizes that what many refer to as "others" are really integral to himself. As a participant in existence, in history, each man is horizontally related to all other participants as well as vertically related to God as the common source of their existential "uniqueness." On the psychological level men feel urged to relate themselves precisely because of a prior network, so to speak, of ontological relationships that as persons it is their vocation consciously to assume. The notion of "being," therefore, far from excluding that of relation, requires it, since it is in the metaphysical analysis of concrete being that we discover its absolute dependence upon God and its relative dependence upon others. Thomist "be-ing" is neither a concept nor static nor unrelated; the metaphysics that studies concrete being is not rationalist but existential, a metaphysics with built-in respect for the richness of the reality it studies, the mysterious rather than the problematic aspect of the real, and the consequent impossibility of speaking definitively about the natures or possibilities of things.

Aquinas's key notion of participation in *esse* designates not merely a complex of conceptual relations or conditions of intelligibility but total dependence in a threefold order of causality—exemplary, efficient, and final—of all creatures upon their Creator.

This participation in existence is a gift whose intelligibility is found only in God's freedom. When we face this fully, we are facing the mystery of love, the mystery that underlies the universe. All nature and most especially all persons are an epiphany of this love, and man's power to respond to this love is what the gift of charity is all about. But since all love begins with thanksgiving, and the prephilosophical awareness of creaturely indigence is pretty universal, we may not rule out the possibility that charity accompanies man's inarticulate, groping gratitude toward God.

In any case the possibility of union between finite and infinite being is grounded in the Thomistic actualist conception of being as a dynamic tendency toward the Absolute. Thus finite being expresses in a paradoxical unity at once the finite individuality and the absolute value of being. Apparently, every man knows whatever he knows under the influence of the dynamic infinity of being as true, and every man desires under the influence of the same dynamic infinity of being as good, stirred thereto by the loveliness of the finite forms of beauty.

More has been written about the distinction between essence and existence than about their inseparability. Yet it is by following this latter clue that man's access to reality through rational judgment is assured. There is no conceptualization that is divorced from realization, and realization is achieved under the influx of a judgment of existence. The works of Joseph Maréchal and of André Marc should be consulted by those who wish to see how the Augustinian approach to metaphysical experience from within the life of the mind finds a place within the Thomistic analysis of the metaphysical conditions for knowledge. For St. Thomas there is no subject/object dichotomy as there was to be for Descartes. Because being is the formal object of human knowing, no thinking takes place that is not thinking of something. Knowing intends something to be known; consciousness is always consciousness *of* something. There is no subject knowing without an object known, with the result that an analysis of knowing involves the known; but just as there is no essence that does not exist, neither does any conceptualization take place except under the dynamism of absolute being. When "intentionality" is seen to be present in all consciousness, and existence in all judgments, we have a "critical epistemology" that preserves knowledge from being mere logic and allows experience to be really human experience, i.e., meaningful by relation to absolute truth and goodness.

It is easier today with the widespread knowledge of existentialism for the general public to grasp what St. Thomas meant by distinguishing essence from existence. As Father

D'Arcy in his book *St. Thomas Aquinas* puts it: the existentialists' "very errors have called attention to the importance of the distinction of essence and existence, and have shown how earthquaking can be the misapprehension or misapplication of these two principles, once thought to be so esoteric and abstract."

In this section on Metaphysics we present a sampling from almost every type of work written by Thomas Aquinas, because in these texts spanning Thomas's lifetime of teaching the omnipresence of the real distinction between essence and existence as the exigency of the status of creatures participating in an existence not self-given is serious evidence of the fundamental importance of this distinction in all Thomistic thinking about man and his world.

This is why the specifically metaphysical texts are here placed in chronological order with their approximate dates of composition, a method not followed in the other sections. They are an impressive witness to the centrality and the continuity of the famous existence/essence distinction. It is also through this historical presentation of the texts that we may examine the variety of reasons put forward by Aquinas to demonstrate the need to admit this distinction. But it is especially here that we recognize the role of essence as denoting the measure of participation in reality or existence as communicated by the living Creator-God. For even when Thomas discusses God within a metaphysical framework, his one God is recognizable as the God of Genesis, not as a Greek philosophical god.

Thus we have a symphony of three movements—Aristotelian, Neoplatonic, Biblical—potentiality, participation, Creation—where all is harmonized within a metaphysical synthesis that distinguishes Creator from creature in order to relate them through a continual communication of existence as an ultimate principle of reality and of perfection and of progress.

In each text we should also try to be aware of the one with whom Aquinas is conversing. Thomas left us no "Confessions," no "Journal," but he reveals his own mind to us in and through the dialogue with colleagues and predecessors.

In the *Commentary on Sentences* he is often found in dialogue with his contemporaries, Albert and Bonaventure. The very style of the Thomistic Commentary, criticized by some as unhistorical, is forged in the interest of dialogue, for the commentaries do not so much represent mere "benevolent interpretations" of predecessors as a staking out of common truth-territory. In the discussions with the Moors represented by the *Summa of Christian Teaching* (*Summa Contra Gentiles*) Thomas has substituted the spirit of colloquium for the crusading spirit. We must be sensitive then to the fact that it is only after he has transferred new meaning into old terms that Aquinas asserts his agreement with Aristotle or Plato or Dionysius. And in a sense Aquinas is acting as historian of philosophy through his various commentaries. In his commentaries on the works of Dionysius and on the *Causes* we hear the opinions also of Plato, Proclus, and the Neoplatonists; in the commentaries on the *Physics, Metaphysics, Ethics, Soul, Politics,* etc., we hear Aristotle arguing with his predecessors, while in a work like Aquinas's *On a Common Intellect* we are in the presence of Averroes, at least as he appears to Aquinas, and in the discussion of *esse* as outside the essence we overhear a conversation with Avicenna. Neoplatonists are heard from through the fathers, and in his theological works Aquinas collaborates with Augustine and other Latin theologians as well as with the Greek fathers, especially after the research Aquinas had done for his *Catena Aurea*.

1. GENERAL METAPHYSICAL TEXTS: PARTICIPATION, BASIS OF ANALOGY/CAUSALITY

Being, its meaning, and the real distinction between essence and existence.

In this section the dates of the works are given, as far as they can be determined, so that a student may recognize the presence of the same metaphysical principles from the beginning to the end of St. Thomas's life. The chronological problem of many of these works remains open to research and discussion. For detailed state of the question, consult I. T. Eschmann, O.P., "A Catalogue of St. Thomas's Works" in E. Gilson, *The Christian Philosophy of St. Thomas Aquinas*, New York; Random House, 1956.

On Being and Essence	1250–56
Commentary on Sentences	1253–59
On Truth	1256–59
Commentary on Boethius's *Goodness of Substances*	1257–58
Commentary on Dionysius' *On the Divine Names*	c.1260
Summa of Christian Teaching	1259
(*Summa Contra Gentiles*)	1261–64
On the Power of God	1265–67
Summa of Theology	1266–68
(*Summa Theologiae*)	
On Spiritual Creatures	1266–69
Commentary on Physics	1268
Commentary on Metaphysics	1268–72
On the Soul	1269–70
Summa of Theology	1269–70
On Separated Substances	1269–73
Compendium of Theology	1269–73
Debated Questions	1269–72
(*Quaestiones disputatae*)	
Commentary on St. John's Gospel, Prologue	1269–72
On Evil	1269–72
Commentary on The Causes	1271–72

The Meaning of Being   1. *On Being and Essence*, c. 1
                                      1250–56

We should be aware that we speak of *being* in itself in
two ways, as the philosopher [Aristotle] declares in *Metaphysics* V, 1017:22. In the first sense, being is divided among
ten categories; in the second sense it refers to the truth of
statements. There is this difference: In the second sense anything about which we can make an affirmative statement is
called "being," although it may not refer to anything real.
In this way, we call privations and negations "beings" since
we state that affirmation is opposed to negation and that
blindness *is* in the eye. But in the first sense we can only use
the word "being" of that which exists in reality. In this sense
of the word, therefore, blindness and such things are not
beings. So the word "essence" is not taken from being in the
second sense. For as the case of privations makes clear, in
that sense we speak of some things as beings when they have
no essence. Essence is derived rather from being in the first
sense. That is why the commentator [Averroes] says in the
same passage that "being" in the first sense of the word signifies the essence of a thing. And since "being," in this sense,
as we said, is divided into the ten categories, "essence" must
refer to something found in all natures and through which
various beings are placed in various genera and species. Thus
humanity is the essence of man, and so forth. . . . Essence
signifies that through which and in which a being has its act
of existing (*esse*).

Now, being is predicated absolutely and primarily of substances; it is predicated secondarily and in a qualified manner
of accidents. Thus essence is truly and strictly in substances,
but in accidents only in a certain qualified way.

Real Distinction Between Es-   2. *On Being and Essence*, c. 4
sence and Existence

The essence of a composite substance therefore differs
from that of a simple substance in that the essence of the
former is not form alone but comprises form and matter,

whereas the essence of a simple substance is form alone. And two other differences arise from this. The first is that the essence of a composite substance because of its designated matter can be signified as a whole or as a part, as was said. And so the essence of a composite thing is in no way predicated of the composite thing itself, for we cannot say that man is his essence. But the essence of a simple thing, which is its form, can only be signified as a whole, since there is nothing receptive of form outside the form, and so the essence of a simple substance, however grasped, is predicated of the substance. And therefore Avicenna says that the essence of a simple substance is the simple substance itself because there is nothing else to enter into the essence. The second difference is that the essences of composite things as received in quantified matter are multiplied according to its multiplication, and that is how some things are the same specifically but differ numerically. But there can be no multiplication of a simple substance since its essence is not received in matter. And so there cannot be found many individuals of the same species in these substances, but there are as many species among them as there are individuals, as Avicenna explicitly says.

Hence, substances of this kind, although they are forms without matter, have not that absolute simplicity that would make them pure act, for they have a mixture of potentiality, as is clear from the following: for whatever does not belong to the notion of essence or quiddity (whatness) is something added to it from outside as in composition with the essence, since no essence is understandable apart from what belongs to it. But every essence or quiddity is understandable without any knowledge of its existence; for I can understand what a man or what a phoenix is, and yet not know whether it exists in nature. Hence it is evident that existence is other than essence or quiddity, unless perhaps there is something whose essence is its very existence. And this would have to be unique and primordial since a thing is multiplied only through the addition of some difference, as the nature of genus is multiplied into species or as the nature of species is multiplied in different individuals by the forms being received in different matters, or by one being absolute and the other being received in something, just as, if there were a separated heat, it would then be in virtue of its very separation different from a heat not separated. But if we posit that which is existence-only so that it is subsistent existence itself, this existence will not assume any addition of a difference because it would then not be existence-only but existence-and-an-added-form; and much less would it assume any addition of matter, because it would then be not subsistent existence, but material. And so there can be but one thing that is its own existence. And so in anything else, its existence is other than its quiddity or nature or form. Therefore with spirits, their acts of existence must differ from their forms; and hence it is said that a spirit is form-and-existence.

But everything belonging to a being is either caused by the principles of the being's nature, as the ability to laugh in man, or comes to it through an extrinsic principle, as light in the air from the influence of the sun. But existence itself cannot be caused by the very form or quiddity of a thing; I mean that it cannot be caused as by an efficient cause, since then something would be its own cause and bring itself into existence; but this is not possible. Therefore everything that is such that its existence is other than its nature must have its existence from another. And because everything that exists through another is led back to that which exists through itself as to its first cause, there must be one thing which is the cause of existence in all things because it alone is the act-of-being; otherwise there would be an infinite series of causes, since everything which is not existence-only would have a cause of its existence, as was said. Hence it is evident that a spirit is form-and-existence, and that it has its existence from the first being, which is existence-only, and this is the first cause, which is God. But everything that receives anything from another is in potentiality to the act received. Therefore it is necessary that the essence itself, or the form, which is the spirit, be in potentiality relative to the existence that it receives from God, and that that existence be received as act. And so potentiality and act are found in spirits, but not, however, matter and form, unless equivocally. On this account likewise, to suffer, to receive, to be a subject and all such things that apparently are associated with being material, belong equivocally to intellectual and to corporeal substances, as the commentator [Averroes] says in *De Anima* III. And since, as was shown, the quiddity of a spirit is the spirit itself, its quiddity or essence is identical with it while its existence received from God is that by which it subsists as a reality among realities. And so such substances are said by some to be composed of that-which-is and that-by-which-it-is (*quod est et quo est*), or of that-which-is and existence (*quod est et esse*), as Boethius says.

And since we place potentiality and act in spirits, it is easy to see how there can be a multitude of spirits; this would be impossible if there were no potentiality within them. And for this reason the commentator says in *De Anima* III that we could not discover multiplicity in separated substances if the nature of the possible intellect were unknown. Therefore these are distinguished from one another by their degree of potentiality and act, so that the superior spirit closer to the first being has more act and less potentiality, and so of the others. And this holds for the human soul, which has the lowest rank among intellectual substances. Therefore its possible intellect is related to intelligible forms just as prime matter, the lowest rank in sensible existence, is related to sensible forms, as the commentator says in *De Anima* III. For this reason also the philosopher likens it (the possible intellect) to a tablet on which nothing is written. And so in comparison with other intelligible substances it has more potentiality. It is thus brought so very close to material realities that the material reality is led to participate in its existence, so that from soul and body there results a single existence in a single composite, although the soul's existence is not dependent on the body. And so after that form-which-is-the-soul there are other forms having more potentiality and closer to matter insofar as their existence is not without matter. In these also we find an order and gradation down to the primary forms of elements, which are closest to matter. And so they have no operation except that of those active and passive qualities and all others by which matter is disposed to form.

Real Distinction Shown By Distinction of Concepts

3. *Commentary on Sentences* I, d. 8, q. 1, a. 1 1253–59

Since in everything that exists, there must be considered its quiddity, by which it subsists in a determined nature, and its act of existence, in virtue of which it is said of it that it is in act, the name "thing" is imposed on the thing from its quiddity, as Avicenna says . . . whereas the name "being" or what is is imposed from the very act of existence itself. Now, since in any created thing its essence differs from its *esse,* that thing is properly named from its quiddity and not from its act of existence, as man is named from humanity. In God, however, his act of existence itself is his essence; and so the name that is taken from the act of existence names him properly and is his own proper name, just like the proper name of man that is taken from humanity.

Commentary on Sentences I, d. 8, q. 5, a. 2

. . . It does not therefore seem that soul has matter, unless matter is regarded equivocally.

Others say that the soul is composed of *quo est* (that whereby it is) and *quod est* (that which is). "That which is" differs, however, from matter; because "that which is" refers to the supposit itself having *esse;* however, matter does not have *esse,* but only the composite of matter and form; whence matter is not "that which is," but the composite; whence in all those things composed of matter and form there is also a composition of *quo est* and *quod est.* In composites of matter and form, however, the *quo est* can be spoken of in three ways: The *quo est* can be named "form" as the part that gives *esse* to matter; also, the very act of being can be called *quo est,* namely, *esse,* just as that whereby one runs is the "act of running"; in addition, we may call *quo est* that very nature that arises from the union of form and matter, like humanity (this is mainly done by those, among whom is Avicenna, who call quiddity form, positing form as the whole, not as a part). It does not belong, however, to the meaning

of quiddity or essence that it should be composed; it follows
that we can find and know a simple quiddity not arising from
the composition of matter and form. If, however, we find any
quiddity not composed of matter and form, that quiddity
either is its own *esse* or not. If that quiddity is its own *esse*,
this will be the essence of God himself, who is his own *esse*,
and it will be wholly simple. Indeed, if it is not its own *esse*, it
must have acquired *esse* from another, just like every created
quiddity. And because this quiddity does not subsist in matter, it, unlike composed quiddities, does not need to be in
another, but on the contrary it must be in itself; and thus the
quiddity itself will be "that which is" and its *esse* itself will
be "that by which." And because everything that is not from
itself is with respect to such a quiddity a possible, a quiddity
of this kind that has its to-be from another will be a possible
with respect to its *esse* and in respect to that from which it
has to-be which has no potentiality; and so in such a quiddity
will be found potentiality and act, and according to its quiddity it is "possible," whereas its *esse* is its "act." And in this
way I see composition of potentiality and act in angels, composition of the *quo est* and *quod est;* and in the same way
with the soul, whence angel or soul can be called quiddity or
nature or simple form insofar as their quiddity is not composed of diverse things. Nevertheless, there is a composition
of these two, namely, of quiddity and *esse*.

Real Distinction Between God *Commentary on Sentences* II,
and World Shown By Partici- d. 1, q. 1, a. 1
pation

I answer that it must be said that "first" is spoken of in two
ways: namely, absolutely first and first in some genus or order. If it is used the second way and thus according to many
genera, there are many causes: 1. first principle, as materially
first, which prime matter is; 2. formatively first which *esse*
is, and so of others; 3. by descending further to the various
kinds of things, there are found various first principles in
different things according to the same kind of cause, just as
the first matter of liquids is water; of dry things, earth; and
of animals, seed or menstrum. But it is impossible for the

absolutely first to be other than one, and this is evident in a threefold way: first, from the very order of the universe, whose parts are found to be mutually ordered as though parts of a complete animal that they mutually serve. However, such coordination is unusual without someone intending it. Therefore there must be an ultimate highest good desired by all; and this is the Principle. This appears in another way from the nature of things. For in all things there is found the nature of the being in which there is more or less dignity; so among those things of nature there are some that are not the *esse* that they have; others are existing by their quiddity being known, which is false, since the quiddity of anything can be known without knowing whether it is. Therefore it is necessary that they have *esse* from another, and we must arrive at that other whose nature is its own *esse*. Otherwise we would proceed to infinity, and that other is what gives *esse* to all. Nor can there be more than one, since being is one in all by analogy, for unity in the caused requires unity of cause *per se* (this is the way of Avicenna, *Metaph.* VIII). The third way is from the immateriality of God himself, for it is necessary that the cause moving the heavens be a force not in matter, as in *Phys.* VIII it is shown.

In those matterless things, however, there cannot be diversity, except that the nature of one exists more completely in act than the nature of another. Therefore it is necessary that what is full perfection and purity of act be that unique one from which proceeds all that is mixed with potentiality: because act precedes potentiality and decreased perfection, as is shown in *Metaph.* IX.

About this, however, there are three errors.

For some, like the first Naturalists, did not posit anything but a material cause—whence each one proposed one of the many material principles and called it absolutely first. Some indeed proposed along with a material cause an acting cause, calling two contraries the first agent (namely, Empedocles, *Phys.* VIII), such as friendship and strife, and this agreed with the opinion of Pythagoras, who divides all beings into two orders, reducing one order to good and the other to evil. From thence spread the infection of the Manichean heresy of the two gods, one the creator of the good, the invisible, the incorporeal, the god of the New Testament; the other, creator of the visible, the corporeal, the god of the Old Testament (from Augustine, *Morals of the Catholic Church,* c. 10). A third error came from those who proposed an agent and matter, but an agent not as the principle of matter, although there is such an agent: and this is the opinion of Anaxagoras and of Plato (in the *Phaedo,* the *Timaeus,* and more clearly in the *Parmenides*), except that Plato superadded a third principle, namely, the ideas separated from things that he called exemplars. One was not the cause of another, but through these three the world and the things from which the world is made were caused.

Real Distinction Shown By   *Commentary on Sentences* II,
Distinction of Concepts   d. 3, q. 1, a. 1

Nevertheless we do suggest a certain composition in angels; just what kind we shall now investigate. . . . The act of existence (*esse*) by which a thing is said to be in actuality is found to be diversely related to different natures or quiddities. There is one kind of nature whose act of existence does not belong to its very intelligibility. And this is evident from the fact that this nature can be understood while at the same time it is not known whether it exists or not, as in the case of a phoenix or an eclipse, or anything of this world. . . . Another nature is found, however, whose very act of existence is related to its intelligibility; indeed, the act of existence itself is its nature. Now this kind of act of existence does not acquire its *esse* from another, because what a thing has from its own quiddity, it has of itself. But everything that is not God has received its *esse* from another. . . . Therefore in God alone his *esse* is his quiddity or nature; in all other things their *esse* is outside their quiddity, which receives the *esse.* And since everything that does not possess something of itself but receives it from another is possible or in potentiality with respect to what it receives, therefore the quiddity in this case is like a potentiality and its received *esse* is like an act. Hence as a result there is found in such a being a composition of act and potentiality. And if such a potentiality is called "matter," the being will be composed of matter and form, although here the term "matter" is used in a completely equivocal manner (for the wise man is not concerned with names).

Participation/Causality   *On Truth*, q. 21, a. 2, c.
                                      1256–59

. . . The nature of the good is found in the act of existing (*ipsum esse*). So, just as there can be no being not possessing the act of existing, every being is necessarily good from the very fact that it has existence. . . . And hence it follows that the good and being are convertible. . . .

On Truth, q. 21, a. 5, c.

In agreement with three authorities we must state that creatures are good only by participation and not by their essence. The authorities are Augustine, Boethius, and the author of *The Causes,* who declares that God alone is pure goodness. They arrived at the identical conclusion, however, by different arguments.

To make this point clear we should reflect . . . that goodness, just like the actuality of being, is divisible into substantial and accidental. Yet there is a difference: We call something absolutely a being by reason of its substantial act of existing, but not by reason of its accidental act of existing. When anyone receives substantial existence, because generation is a motion directed to existence, we say that he is generated without qualification, whereas when accidental existence is received, we speak of a qualified generation. It is the same with corruption, i.e., the loss of existence. But it is wholly opposite with the good. When considering substantial goodness, we speak of a thing's being somewhat good, but in referring to accidental goodness we say something is unqualifiedly good. So we do not speak of an unjust man as simply good but only good in his way, i.e., insofar as he is a man. But we call a just man good without qualifying this.

And for this reason: Something is called "being" only when considered absolutely, in itself, whereas it is called "good" . . . in relation to other things. Now, a thing is fully established to subsist in itself by its essential principles, whereas only by means of accidents added to the essence is it established as it should be in relation to all things outside itself, since the actions whereby a thing is somehow united to another come from the essence through powers distinct from it. So anything reaches its goodness absolutely only when it is complete in both its essential and its accidental principles.

Any perfection reached by a creature through its essential and accidental principles together is present in God in its fullness through his one simple act of being. His essence is his wisdom, his justice, his power, and the like—all of these being distinct in us from our essence. Thus in God absolute goodness is itself identical with his essence, whereas with us it is found only in conjunction with things added to our essence. Therefore, entire or absolute goodness increases and decreases and disappears completely in us, but not in God. Yet our substantial goodness always remains. Apparently this is what Augustine meant by saying that God is good essentially, whereas we are good by participation.

There is yet another divergence between God's goodness and ours. When a nature is considered absolutely, goodness is not understood as essential, but only when it is considered in its act of existence. For example, humanity has no property of good or goodness unless it is existing. Yet the divine nature or essence is itself its act of being [*actus essendi*], but the nature or essence of any created thing is not its own act of being but participates in being from another. So in God the act of being is pure, since God is his own subsistent act of being (*esse*); whereas in the creature the act of being is received or participated. So that we should allow for absolute goodness to be attributed to a creature by reason of its substantial existence, yet the fact is that the creature has goodness by participation inasmuch as it has a participated existence. Yet God is essentially goodness because his essence is his existence. Apparently the philosopher in *The Causes* means this when he says that only the divine goodness is pure goodness.

An additional difference is found between the divine goodness and the creature's goodness. Goodness has the function of a final cause. But God has this inasmuch as he is everything's ultimate end as well as First Principle. Accordingly, no other end is characterized as an end except in relation to the First Cause, inasmuch as a secondary cause only influences the effect under the influence of the First Cause, as is explained in *The Causes*. So, likewise, good, qualified as end, cannot be said of any creature without presupposing the relation of creature to Creator.

Even if the creature were its own act of being, as is God, the creature's act of being would still not be characterized as good except by reason of its relation to its Creator; and by that fact, it would still be called good by participation and not absolutely through its essential principles. But the divine act of being is characterized as absolutely good in itself, even when nothing else is presupposed. It is evident that this is what Boethius meant.

Participation/Causality Indicative of Real Distinction Between Essence and Existence   *Commentary on Boethius's Goodness of Substances* 1, 2 1257–58

Every mind grasps those things that are most common, such as being, one, and good. And thus Boethius discusses here, first, some notions dealing with being; second, some dealing with one or unity, from which come our notions of the simple and the composite, as witnessed in the statement: "In every composite, the *esse* is one thing, the thing itself is another." Third, he discusses some notions dealing with good, such as "all diversity is discord."

In discussing being, moreover, he argues that *esse ipsum* (being itself) is somehow common and undetermined. That which is determined is twofold: in one way as a subject possessing *esse*, in another way as a predicate, as when we say of man or anything else not merely that he is, but that he is something, for instance, white or black. He first proposes notions understood through a comparison of *esse* to *id quod est*; second, he proposes notions understood through a comparison of "that which is absolutely" (*quod est esse simpliciter*) to "that which is something" (*id quod est esse aliquid*) as when he says, "Nevertheless there is a difference" between "to be something in that which is" (*esse aliquid in eo quod est*) and "to be something" (*esse aliquid*).

About the first he suggests two things: First, he proposes the difference between *esse* (*quod est esse*) and "that which possesses *esse*" (*id quod est*); second, he shows the difference: "The thing itself is not yet *esse*." In other words, as he put it, to possess being (*id quod est*) is not to be being itself (*esse*). These are two distinct notions. Nor is all this to be referred to existent things themselves, of which he has not yet spoken. He is here referring to a way of thinking or to intentions. Moreover, by *esse*, one meaning is signified; by *id quod est*, another is signified, just as "to run" signifies something different from what "that which runs" signifies; for "running" and "being" signify abstract concepts such as whiteness, whereas "that which is" (*quod est*), i.e., being (*ens*) and running (*currens*), signify concrete realities, as white describes a concrete reality. Next, when he says, "The thing itself is not yet *esse*," he indicates three differences. The first of these is due to the fact that *esse* itself is not signified as the subject itself of being, just as "to run" is not signified as the subject of running. Whence, just as we cannot say that "to run" itself runs, so we cannot say that the *esse* itself is. But just as the thing is signified as if it were the subject of being, so that which runs is signified as the subject of running, and likewise just as we can call that which runs a runner because he runs insofar as he undergoes running and participates in it, so we can call that-which-is a being because it is a being insofar as it participates in the act of being (*actum essendi*). This is expressed by "The thing itself is not yet *esse*" (*Ipsum esse nondum est*), since *esse* is not attributed to it as to a subject of being "but that-which-is has taken on the *form* of being," i.e., it has received the act of being and thus "it is and exists," i.e., it subsists in itself. For being is not predicated properly and essentially except of substance, which subsists. He proposes a second difference when he says: "That which is can participate in something" (*Quod est participare aliquo potest*), and this difference comes from what participation implies; for to participate is to take a part, as it were (*partem capere*). And so when anything receives particularly what belongs to others universally, it is said to participate in it, just as man is said to participate in animal because man does not have the function of an animal according to its generic totality. Thus man is said to participate in animality inasmuch as he does not possess the animal mode of being in the same way as do those who constitute the entire community of animal being, and likewise does Socrates participate in man; in much the same way also does an accident participate in a subject, and matter in form. For the substantial or accidental form that in itself has a common essence is determined to this or that subject, and likewise an effect is said to participate in its cause, especially when its power does not equal that of its cause, for example, when we say that air participates in the sun's light because air does not receive light in the same brightness it has in the sun.

I shall pass, however, to the third way of participating, since it is impossible according to the first two ways for absolute *esse* to participate in anything; for it cannot participate in the way that matter participates in form or accident participates in a subject because, as was said, *esse* itself signifies something apart. Nor can it participate as a particular participates in a universal, for those things spoken of as a part can participate in something as whiteness in color, but being itself (*ipsum esse*) is present in all things: whence others participate in it but it does not participate in anything else. But that-which-is, a being (*ens*), although this is a most common expression, is nevertheless referring to something concrete and so it participates in being itself (*ipsum esse*) not as the more common is participated in by the less common, but it participates in *ipsum esse* as the limited participates in the unlimited. By *id quod est* he is therefore saying this: that a being is able to participate in some way; but *ipsum esse* can participate in no way at all, and this proves what was said above, namely, that the thing-which-is is not yet *esse* (*ipsum esse nondum est*). However, it has been shown that *id quod est* cannot participate in any other way; whence it follows that participation is proper to something when it already is. From this we see that that-which-is has received *ipsum esse*, as was said. So it remains that *id quod est* can participate in something; *ipsum esse* cannot participate in anything.

. . . Next, when he says, "in every composite it is one thing to be and another to be something," he is proposing notions of the composite and the simple that are relevant to unity. We should reflect that what was previously said about the difference between the to-be and that-which-is was according to the mode of knowing: Here, however, he indicates how it is applied to things. First, he shows this in regard to composite things; second, in regard to simple things such as: In every simple thing its to-be and that-which-it-is are one. Therefore we must first consider that just as *esse* and "what is" differ in simple things as mental intentions, so in composite things they really differ, and this is clear from the premises; for, as was said above, that which is itself to-be neither participates in something so that its essence might be composed of many nor has it anything extra added to it so that there is a composition of accidents within it; and therefore *ipsum esse* is not composite. Hence the composite thing is not its *esse,* and therefore he says that "in every composite the *esse* is other than the composite which participates in *ipsum esse.*" . . . And so if some forms are without matter so that each is simple as lacking matter and consequently quantity, the disposition of matter, nevertheless, although every form is determinative of its to-be, none of them is its to-be (*esse*), but is as one having to-be (*esse*). Suppose in accord with Plato's teaching we posit that immaterial form to subsist that is the idea and essence of material men, and another form that is the idea and essence of horses. It will be evident that the subsisting immaterial form, although it is a certain determination of species, is not itself common to-be but participates in it. And this is likewise the case when we posit those immaterial forms of higher rank that are the essences of sensible things, as Aristotle wished: For each of them insofar as it differs from the others is a certain special form participating in *ipsum esse* (to-be itself). And so none of them will be truly simple. That alone, moreover, will be truly simple that does not participate in *esse,* not inhering in anything, but subsisting. Only one can be this way, because if *ipsum esse* (to-be itself) had nothing other added to it beyond "that-which-is-to-be" (*id quod est esse*), as was said, it is impossible for that-which-is-itself-to-be to be multiplied by anything differing from it; and since it has nothing beyond itself added to it, it consequently is not receptive of any accident. However, this simple and sublime one is God himself.

On Evil, As Not Participating the Good   *Commentary on Dionysius' On the Divine Names*, c. IV, lect. 14 a.   ca. 1260

Whence if evil has no cause per se but only *per accidens*, it follows that evil has no essence, and this is what he adds as though concluding that evil itself is not anything, if evil is taken as something subsisting in itself as evil. Moreover, everything that is totally of some kind is essentially such, just as when something is totally good, it is the essence of goodness; for if it participates in good, it must be divided into the participating and the participated. If therefore nothing is essentially evil, that which is evil is not totally evil, but participates in good; and it is according to that participating in the good that the whole *esse* of that which is called evil exists.

So then through this he has clarified what evil is. For evil cannot be a subsisting essence as the good is the essence of goodness; rather, an evil thing is good through its essence but evil through the goodness it lacks—which it ought to have but has not.

Existence Itself Unparticipating   *Summa of Christian Teaching* I, 23   1259

It necessarily follows from this truth that nothing exists accidentally in God nor is there anything in him other than his essence.

For existence itself is unable to participate in anything outside its essence; but that which exists is able to participate in something else. For there is nothing more formal nor more simple than existence. And so existence itself cannot participate in anything. Now, the divine substance is existence itself. Therefore there is nothing in him that is not of his substance. And so no accident can be in him. . . .

Existence Never in a Genus   *Summa of Christian Teaching*
                                    I, 25

It necessarily follows that God is not in any genus. . . .
Anything is put in a genus by its *whatness*, for genus is
predicated of what a thing is. But the *whatness* of God is his
very being. Now, nothing is put in a genus in respect to its
existence, because *existence* (*esse*) would then be a genus
signifying being itself. It therefore follows that God is not
in a genus.

The philosopher proves that being cannot be a genus in
this way. If being were a genus, in order to restrict it to a
species we would have to discover a difference. But no difference participates in the genus so that, for instance, the
genus is comprised in the notion of the difference, for in
this way the genus would appear twice in the definition of
the species; but the difference should be something over and
above what is comprised by the notion of the genus. But if
being can be predicated of everything, when it is predicated,
there is nothing over and above being. And so no difference
can contract being. Consequently, being is not a genus, and
thus it necessarily follows that God is not in a genus.

And so it is also clear that God cannot be defined inasmuch
as every definition is made up of genus and difference.

Creatures Do Not Participate   *Summa of Christian Teaching*
in God's Existence   I, 26

Things do not differ from one another by having existence,
since they all agree in that. If things do differ from one another, therefore, this must come from the fact that the act of
existence is possessed by specifically different natures. Things
differ, therefore, by reason of their different natures receiving
existence diversely in proportion to each nature. Now, the
divine act of existence is possessed by no other nature but is
itself the very nature or essence of God. And so if the divine
act of existence could be identified with the act of existence
of all things, all things would coalesce together into the absolute unity of one single being. . . .

Participation/Causality   *Summa of Christian Teaching*
                                      I, 28

Anything has excellence or perfection as derived from its act of existence, for no perfection would be added to a man from his wisdom unless he actually is wise, and so with the others. Accordingly, the measure of anything's excellence is in proportion to its being, for anything is said to be more or less excellent insofar as its act of existence is proportioned to some kind of excellence, of greater or less dignity. And so if there is anything to which belongs the whole power of being (*tota virtus essendi*), no perfection belonging to any other being can be lacking to it. But anything that is its own act of existence possesses the total power of being, just as were whiteness to exist in separation from all things, nothing of the power or perfection of whiteness would be lacking to it, for a particular white thing lacks something of the power of whiteness because of some defect in the subject receiving the whiteness, since the subject receives it according to its own capacity and not according to the whole power of whiteness. And so God who is his own act of existing . . . has existence according to the whole power of being itself; therefore no perfection found in anything can be lacking to him.

And just as all perfection is present in anything insofar as it is, so likewise every defect is present in anything insofar as it is not in some way or other. And just as God has being totally, so is nonbeing totally lacking to him, since nonbeing is eliminated in the measure that anything has being. All defect is therefore removed from God so that he is wholly perfect.

But those things that only exist imperfectly do so not because of any imperfection in absolute being itself, for they do not exist according to the whole power of being but because they participate in being in a particular and very imperfect way.

Only Creatures Participate in   *Summa of Christian Teaching*
Existence   II, 52

. . . Being (*esse*) insofar as it is being cannot be varied;

but it can be diversified by something outside (*praeter*) being (*esse*), as the existence of a stone is different from the existence of a man. A being that is only subsistent being can be but one. Now it was previously demonstrated that God is his own subsistent being (*esse*), and so besides him there can be nothing that is its own being (*esse*). Therefore in every substance other than God the substance itself has to be distinct from its being (*esse*).

. . . It is impossible that there should be two *esses* absolutely infinite; for an *esse* that is absolutely infinite comprises every perfection of being (*essendi*); and thus, if such an infinity were present in two, we could find nothing whereby (*quo*) one differs from the other. Now, subsistent being (*esse*), because it is not limited by any recipient, has to be infinite. And thus there can be no more than the first subsistent being.

. . . Being itself (*ipsum esse*) belongs to the first agent by nature, for the *esse* of God is his substance. . . . Whatever belongs to anything, however, by its own nature, does not belong to others except by way of participation, as heat belongs to things other than fire. *Ipsum esse* or being itself belongs to all things other than the first agent by participation. But whatever belongs to anything by participation is not its substance. Therefore it is impossible that the substance of anything other than the first agent should be being itself (*ipsum esse*).

And so God is properly named (Ex. 3: 14) "who is" because to him alone it is proper that his substance be not distinct from his being (*esse*).

Existence is to Essence as Act is to Potentiality
Summa of Christian Teaching II, 53

Whatever participates in anything is compared to that which is participated as potentiality to act, since the participator is made to be actually what it is by that which is participated. Now, it was previously shown that only God is essentially being (*esse*), whereas all other things participate in being (*esse*). Therefore every created substance is compared to its existence as potentiality to act.

Aristotelian Terms Adjusted   *Summa of Christian Teaching*
to Existential Participation   II, 54
Analysis

Now, composition of matter and form is not of the same
nature as the composition of substance and being (*esse*), although both compositions result from potentiality and act:

First, inasmuch as matter is not a thing's very substance or
else all forms would be accidental, as the early natural philosophers held; but matter is a part of substance.

Second, inasmuch as being (*esse*) itself is the proper act,
not of matter, but of the total substance: for being (*esse*) is
the act of whatever we can speak of as existing. But the
whole and not matter is said to exist. Therefore we cannot
say that matter *is* but that the substance itself is.

Third, because the form is not being itself (*esse*), but they
are related in a certain rank; for form is related to being
(*esse*) as *light* to *illuminating,* or as *whiteness* to *being white.*

Fourth, because being (*esse*) is related to the form itself
as act. For in things made up of matter and form, the form
is called the principle of being because it perfects the substance whose act being is, just as transparency in relation to
air is its principle of being light, since it makes the air the
proper subject of light.

And so in those things made up of matter and form, neither
matter nor form, nor even being itself may be referred to as
that-which-is. But the form may be spoken of as that
whereby-it-is insofar as it is the principle of being; but the
whole substance is *that-which-is,* and being (*esse*) is that
whereby the substance is spoken of as a being.

But in intellectual substances which, as we saw, were not
made up of matter and form and wherein the form itself is
a subsistent substance, the form is *that-which* is, and being
is the act whereby it *is.*

Therefore there is only one composition of potentiality
and act in them, one, namely, of substance and being (*esse*),
which some speak of as *that-which-is* and *being* or of *that-
which* is and whereby it *is.* . . .

Evolution in Philosophic   *On the Power of God,* q. 3,
Awareness of Existence   a. 5, c. and ad. 1   1265–67

The ancient philosophers who studied nature followed the order of human knowledge. Just as human knowledge comes to the intellect from the senses, the early philosophers first concentrated on the sensible realm and gradually ascended to the intellectual one. And since they encountered accidental forms among the objects of sense and not substantial forms, these early philosophers stated that all forms are accidental and that matter alone is a substance. And because substance is a sufficient cause of those accidents derived from within the substance, the early philosophers taught that matter was the only cause and so the cause of everything observable in the sensible world; and thus they were forced to conclude that there was no cause of matter and hence absolutely to deny the existence of any efficient cause. Later philosophers, however, became somewhat aware of substantial forms, yet, wholly absorbed in observing particular forms, they did not arise to the knowledge of universals; and so they proposed certain active causes to change matter to this or that form, but not to give being to things as things; they called these causes mind (*nous*), attraction and repulsion, responsible, as they put it, for adhesion and separation. In their opinion, all things did not come from an efficient cause, and matter pre-existed the activity of any efficient cause. Afterward, philosophers like Plato, Aristotle, and their disciples proceeded to study universal being, and so they alone proposed a universal cause of things from which everything came into existence, as Augustine states (*City of God,* 8: 4). This agrees with the Catholic faith and may be proven by the following three arguments:

First, if in many things we find anything common to all, we must conclude that this thing is the effect of one cause, since it is impossible that anything common to many should be caused by each thing, simply because each differs from the other, and diversity of causes produces diversity of effects. As soon as we discover that being (*esse*) is common to all things that are in themselves distinct from one another, it necessarily follows that their being must come not from themselves but from the action of some cause. This is apparently Plato's argument, inasmuch as he required that every multiplicity be preceded by unity in reality as well as in number.

The second argument is that whenever anything is discovered to be in many things in various degrees by participation, it must come to those in which it exists imperfectly from that one wherein it exists most perfectly. For wherever there are positive degrees so that more or less can be attributed to this or that one, it is always in reference to one thing that they more or less approach; for if each one were in itself competent to have it, no reason would exist why one should have more of it than another. Hence fire, which is the ultimate in heat, causes heat in all hot things. Now there is one most perfect and most true being, and this follows from the fact that there must be an altogether immovable and absolutely perfect mover, as philosophers have shown. From this being, therefore, all less perfect beings must get their being. This is the argument of the philosopher (*Metaph.* 2: 1).

The third argument rests upon the principle that whatever exists through another is related to that which exists of itself. And so if there were any independent heat, it would be the cause of all hot things, which have heat by participation. But there is a being that is its own being; and this comes from the fact that a being that is pure act without any composition is required. And so all other beings that are not their own being but have being by participation must proceed from that one being. This is Avicenna's argument (*in Metaph.* 8: 6; 9: 8). It is thus proven by reason and held by faith that everything is created by God.

1. Although the first cause or God does not enter into the essence of creatures, nevertheless the being in creatures is unintelligible except as caused by the divine being, just as no proper effect can be known except in relation to its proper cause, which produced it.

Existence Extrinsic to Essence   *On the Power of God,* q. 5,
a. 4, ad. 3

If we are discussing substantial existence (*esse*), then existence is spoken of as an accident in the way of analogy, not as though it were in the genus of accident but because like an accident it is not part of the essence (for it is the act of the essence). . . .

Real Distinction Indicated by   *Summa of Theology,* I, q. 3,
Being Caused   a. 7, ad. 1   1266–68

Anything whose source is God resembles him, as caused things resemble the First Cause. But it is essential for any caused thing to be a composite in some way, since its existence at least differs from its essence, as will be shown later (q. 4, a. 3).

Existence as Act Indicates   *Summa of Theology,* I, q. 4,
Real Distinction   ad. 3

We must say that existence (*esse*) itself is the most perfect of all inasmuch as it is related to everything as act, since nothing has actuality except insofar as it exists. Therefore existence (*esse*) itself is the actuality of all things, even of forms themselves.

Existence as the Source of   *Summa of Theology,* I, q. 4,
Value   a. 3

. . . Moreover, from what was previously shown (q. 3, a. 4), that is, that God is subsistent existence itself (*ipsum esse subsistens*), it follows that he possesses within him all perfections. . . . Since God is therefore subsistent existence itself (*ipsum esse subsistens*), nothing belonging to the perfection of being (*essendi*) can be absent from him. But the perfections of all things belong to the perfection of being (*essendi*) inasmuch as all things are perfect insofar as they in some way have existence (*esse*). Thus God does not lack the perfection present in everything.

Real Distinction Stated   *Summa of Theology*, I, q. 4,
                                     a. 3, ad. 3

Those things that agree in form are said to be alike. But
there is nothing that can agree in form with God, for in all
things except God alone, essence differs from existence. And
thus no creature can be like God.

Participation and Imaging   *Summa of Theology*, I, q. 4,
                                       a. 3, ad. 3

A creature's likeness to God is not asserted by reason of
agreement in form in respect to the same genus or species
but only by analogy, because God is essential existence (*esse*),
whereas all other things are beings by participation.

Meaning of Being   *Summa of Theology*, I, q. 4,
                              a. 1, ad. 1

Being signifies that something properly exists in actuality,
as asserted in a. 3: Every being insofar as it is a being exists
in actuality.

Causing Requires God's Per-   *Summa of Theology*, I, q. 8,
sonal Presence   a. 1

God is present in all things not, certainly, as part of their
essence nor as an accident but as an agent is present to that
upon which it acts. For an agent by its power must have contact with and be immediately united to that in which it acts;
and it is therefore proven in *Physics* VII that what is moved
and the mover must be united. Now, inasmuch as God by his
own essence is being (*esse*) itself, his proper effect must be
created being, just as to set on fire is the proper effect of fire.
But God causes this effect within things not only when they
originally begin to exist, but as long as they continue in existence, just as the sun causes light in the air as long as the
air remains illuminated. And so as long as anything has being,
God must be present within it in a way appropriate to its
being. But being is intimate to everything and very funda-

mentally present in all things, since it is formal in relation to all that is found in anything, as we say (q. 7, a. 1). It is necessary, therefore, for God to be present in all things, and intimately so.

Summa of Theology, I, q. 8, a. 2

. . . God is present within all things as causing their being, power, and action, and thus he is in every place as giving it existence and locale; and this is to be everywhere. . . . Again, everything located somewhere is in place insofar as it fills a place. But not as a body does God fill a place inasmuch as a body is spoken of as filling a place to the extent that it excludes the copresence of another body. But because God is in a place, others are not excluded from there, for by the very fact that he gives existence to all the things that fill every place, he himself fills every place.

Natural Knowledge of Subsist-   *Summa of Theology,* I, q. 12,
ent Being Unavailable to Par-   a. 4, c. and ad. 3
ticipants

By its nature our intellect naturally knows those natures existing in individual matter only, and then only when they are abstracted from this by attentive intellectual action, and thus through the intellect these objects can be understood as universal; this is beyond sense power. Now, by its nature the angelic intellect knows those natures that are not in matter, but this goes beyond the intellectual power of our soul in its present state of life as united to the body. Consequently, to know self-subsistent being is natural only to the divine intellect and is beyond any created intellect's power inasmuch as no creature' is its own existence because it has participated existence. And so no created intellect can see God's essence unless God unites himself by grace to the created intellect as intelligible to it.

ad. 3. Since the sense of sight is entirely material, it cannot increase in immateriality. But because our intellect or the angelic intellect is naturally superior to matter, it can be raised above its own nature to a higher degree of immateriality. This is evident in the fact that sight cannot know abstractly what it perceives concretely, for it never perceives nature except as this particular nature, while our intellect can know abstractly whatever it knows concretely. Now, although it knows things having a form present in matter, yet it analyzes the composite into these two elements and reflects upon the form as separated. Although the angelic intellect also naturally knows the concrete in any nature, it is nevertheless able to know existence as separated, inasmuch as it knows that the thing itself is other than its existence. And therefore inasmuch as the created intellect is naturally able to know the concrete form and the concrete being abstractly by a sort of analysis into parts, it is capable by grace of being elevated to know separate subsisting substance as well as separate subsisting existence.

Participation in Being, Foundation of Relationship to God   *Summa of Theology* I, q. 44, a. 1 and ad. 1

Everything existing in any way comes from God. For whatsoever is present in anything by participation has as its necessary cause that being to which this thing essentially belongs, just as iron is made hot by fire. Now, it was previously shown (q. 3, a. 4) when speaking of the divine simplicity that God is a being essentially self-subsisting, and it was shown (q. 11, a. 3, a. 4) that subsisting being necessarily is unique, just as, if there were a subsisting whiteness, it would be unique inasmuch as whiteness is multiplied by its recipients. And so with the exception of God all beings are not their own being but are beings by participation. And thus it is necessary that all things differentiated by diverse participation in being so that they are more or less perfect are caused by one first being who most perfectly has being.

And thus Plato said (*Parmen.* 26) that unity must precede multiplicity; and Aristotle said (*Metaph.* 2: 4) that the greatest in being and the greatest in truth is the cause of every being and every truth, just as the greatest heat is the cause of all heat.

ad. 1. Although the relation to its cause does not enter into the definition of anything caused, yet this is a consequence of its essence, since if anything has being by participation, it follows that it is caused. And so such a being cannot exist without being caused, just as a man cannot exist without having the capacity for laughter. But inasmuch as "to be caused" does not enter into the essence of being as being, it is therefore possible for us to discover an uncaused being.

Real Distinction Indicated by Finitude   *Summa of Theology*, I, q. 50, a. 2, ad. 4

. . . we must say that every creature is simply finite insofar as its existence (*esse*) is not absolutely subsistent but limited to some nature to which it comes . . . its existence (*esse*), however, is finite because it is determined to some special nature.

Spiritual Substances: Real Distinction Shown by Participation   *On Spiritual Creatures*, a. 1, c. and ad. 8   1266–69

There are many conflicting opinions concerning this question [whether a spiritual substance is made up of matter and form]. Some state that a created spiritual substance is a composite of matter and form; yet some deny this. And so that we may not begin ambiguously to study this truth, we should consider the meaning of the term "matter." Now, it is clear that because potentiality and act are divisions of being (*ens*) and because every genus is divided into potentiality and act, the term "prime matter" is usually used to signify that which is in the genus of substance as a kind of potentiality taken as excluding every species and form, even privation, and is nevertheless a potentiality capable of receiving both forms and privations, as Augustine clearly indicates in *Confessions* 12: 7, 15 and in *Literal Commentary on Genesis* 1: 14, and the philosopher in *Metaph*. 7: 3, 1029a20.

Now, if matter is so understood in its proper and usual sense, matter cannot be within spiritual substances. . . .

Nevertheless, if we use the terms "matter" and "form" to designate any two things related to each other as potentiality and act, there is no difficulty in saying (to avoid a terminology dispute) that matter and form exist in spiritual sub-

stances; for in any created spiritual substance two elements
are found, with one related to the other as potentiality to
act. This is evident from the following, for it is clear that the
first being who is God is infinite act possessing within himself the total plenitude of being not restricted to any generic
or specific nature. And so his very existence must not be one
that enters some nature that is not its own existence, because
it would thus be limited to that nature. And so we say that
God is his own existence (*esse*). But of no other being can
this be said. For just as many separate whitenesses would be
meaningless (for if there were any "whiteness" separated
from any subject and recipient, there would be only one
whiteness), so a self-subsisting existence would be impossible
unless it were only one. Consequently, everything existing
after the first being, inasmuch as it is not its own existence,
receives existence in something by which the existence itself
is restricted; and so in any created object the nature of the
being participating in existence is other than the participated
existence itself. And since a thing participates in the first act
by likeness to the extent that it has existence, the participated
existence must always be related to the nature participating
in it as act is related to potentiality. Therefore, in the world
of physical objects, matter does not in itself participate in
actual existence, although it participates in it through form;
for the soul entering the matter makes the matter itself actually exist, as the soul does to the body.

And so in composite things we observe two kinds of act
and two kinds of potentiality. Primarily, matter is as potentiality in relation to form, and form is its act. Second, if the
nature is comprised of matter and form, the nature is as
potentiality in relation to existence itself to the extent that it
can receive it. And so when the basis of matter is withdrawn,
should there be any form of a determinate nature subsisting
in itself without matter, it will still be related to its own existence as potentiality is related to act. But I am not speaking
of potentiality that is separable from its act, but of that
potentiality that is always accompanied by its act. And this is
how the nature of a spiritual substance not composed of matter and form is a potentiality in relation to its own existence;
and hence in a spiritual substance there is a composition of

potentiality and act and, therefore, of matter and form, only if every potentiality is called matter and every act is called form; but according to the common use of the terms we are not speaking properly here.

ad. 8. To be composed of "that-which-is" (*quod est*) and of "that-by-which-something-is" (*quo est*) is not identical with being composed of matter and form. For although form can be spoken of as "that-by-which-something-is," yet matter cannot properly be spoken of as "that-which-is" because it only exists potentially. But "that-which-is" is something subsisting in existence, and with regard to corporeal substances this is the very thing that is composed of matter and form, while in regard to incorporeal substances it is the simple form itself. But "that-by-which-something-is" is participated existence itself, since everything is insofar as it participates in existence itself. And so Boethius likewise uses these words in this sense in *Goodness of Substances,* stating that in the case of beings other than the First, "that-which-is" and "existence" (*esse*) are not identical.

Heavenly Bodies: Participation Denoting Real Distinction — *Commentary on Physics* VIII, lect. 21, 1153–54   1268

One cannot say that a heavenly body is a subsistent form, inasmuch as it would then be an intellect in act, and would be neither sensible nor quantified. Consequently it is composed of matter and form and of potentiality and act, so that potentiality for nonbeing is somehow within it.

But if we allow that a heavenly body is not composed of matter and form, it must be admitted, nevertheless, that potentiality for nonbeing is somehow within it. For every simple subsistent substance must either be its own existence or participate in existence. But there can only be one simple substance that is its own subsistent existence, just as there could be only one whiteness if it were subsistent. And so every substance that comes after the first simple substance participates in existence. But everything that participates is composed of the participant and the participated. So in every simple substance subsequent to the first simple substance, there is potentiality for being.

He [Averroes] was taken in, moreover, through the equivocal meaning of potentiality; for often potentiality is predicated as related to an opposite. But this meaning cannot apply to heavenly bodies and separated simple substance, for Aristotle recognized in them no potentiality for nonbeing because simple substances are forms only and existence does belong to forms independently (*per se*)—for a heavenly body's matter is not in potentiality to another form. For just as a heavenly body is related to its own structure of which it is the subject as act to potentiality, and yet it cannot not possess such a structure, so also the matter of a heavenly body is related to its form as potentiality to act, and yet it is not in potentiality to a privation of this form or to nonbeing. For not every potentiality is of opposites, or the possible would not be a result of the necessary, as is said in *On Interpretation*, 13: 22 b 22.

His position is also opposed to what Aristotle intends when in *On the Heavens*, I, he utilizes in a demonstration the statement that a heavenly body has the potentiality or power to exist always. So when he says that in a heavenly body there is no potentiality for existence, he cannot avoid inconsistency. For this is both clearly false and opposed to Aristotle's intention.

Let us inquire whether Averroes entirely refutes Alexander, who says that a heavenly body receives eternity from another. His refutation would certainly be adequate if Alexander had argued that a heavenly body has within itself potentiality for being and nonbeing, acquiring eternal existence from another. And I am supposing here that he did not intend to exclude God's omnipotence, by which anything corruptible can become incorruptible. For this is beside the point here. Allowing for his intention, Averroes still reached no conclusion opposed to that of Alexander, who never held that eternity was acquired by a heavenly body from another so that it itself has any potentiality for being and nonbeing but so that it did not get its existence from itself. For everything that is not its own existence participates in existence from the First Cause, which is its own existence. So that even Averroes allows in *De Substantia Orbis* that God causes the heaven not only as to its motion but likewise as to its substance. This could only be the case because it holds existence from him. But from him it holds only eternal existence. It holds its eternity, therefore, from another. And Aristotle's words also agree with this in *Metaph.* 5: 1015 b 9–10 and above at the outset of Book 8, where he states that there are some necessary things having a cause for their necessity. In view of this, what Alexander intends as the solution is evident, namely, just as any heavenly body has from another its motion, so likewise from another does it hold existence. Thus, inasmuch as eternal motion shows the infinite power of the mover but not of the mobile object, its eternal duration shows the infinite power of the cause from which it holds its existence.

Transcendental Unity and Real Distinction by Being Caused *Commentary on Metaphysics* IV, lect. 2, 556–58 1268–72

But we should observe that Avicenna had a different opinion about this; for he stated that being and one are not terms signifying a thing's substance but what is added to it. He spoke of being in this way because in the case of anything deriving its existence (*esse*) from something else, its existence must differ from its substance or essence. But the term "being" designates existence itself, and so evidently being or existence is something added to a thing's essence.

In a similar way he spoke of "one" inasmuch as he believed the one interchangeable with being to be identical with the one that is the principle of number. And the one that is the principle of number must designate a reality added to the substance, or else number inasmuch as it is composed of units would not be a species of quantity, which is an accident added to substance. He spoke of this kind of one as interchangeable with being not in the sense that it designates the very substance of a thing or being, but because it designates an accident found in every being, as the capacity for laughter is found in every man.

But he seems to be mistaken about the first point. For although a thing's existence is other than its essence, it should not be understood to be something added to its essence as an accident is added, but something which with the essence constitutes a thing's principles. And so the term "being," which is attributed to a thing by reason of its very existence, designates the same thing as the term that is attributed to it by reason of its essence.

Commentary on Metaphysics
XII, lect. 1

Being means something having existence (*habens esse*).

God's Being as Pure Act Distinguished from Participants in Being   *On the Soul*, a. 6, c. and ad. 2
1269–70

The act of existing (*actus essendi*) is the highest act in which all things can participate, but the act of existing itself does not participate in anything at all. And so if there is a being that is itself a subsisting act of existing (*ipsum esse subsistens*), as we call God, we say that it does not participate in anything. But this is not the case with other subsisting forms, which necessarily participate in the act of existing itself and are related to it as potentiality to act. And therefore inasmuch as there is some potentiality in these forms, they can participate in something else.

Being Has a Perfect and Imperfect Sense   *Summa of Theology* I–II, q. 2, a. 5, ad. 2   1269–70

"Being" taken simply, as including all perfection of being, surpasses life and all that follows it; for thus being itself includes all these. And in this sense Dionysius speaks. But if we consider being itself as participated in by this or that thing, which does not possess the whole perfection of being, but has imperfect being, such as the being of any creature, then it is evident that being itself together with an additional perfection is more excellent. Hence in the same passage Dionysius asserts that things that live are better than things that exist, and intelligent things better than living things.

Plato and Aristotle Agree on Participation   *On Separated Substances,* c. 3   1269–73

After considering these matters, it is easy to see where Plato's position on immaterial substances both agrees with and differs from that of Aristotle.

First of all, Plato and Aristotle agree about the way these exist. Plato maintained that all inferior immaterial substances are one and good by participation in the primary substance, which is essentially one and good. Now, the participant in something receives that in which it participates from the participated, and the participated is to this extent its cause, as the air has light, which it is participating from the sun, which is thus the cause of its illumination. So, with Plato, the highest good accounts for each immaterial substance being one and good. Likewise, Aristotle had this opinion, since as he himself put it, "Whatever is most being and most truth is the cause of being and truth in all other things" (*Metaph.* 1: 1, 993b, 24–31).

Second, Plato and Aristotle agree upon their natural condition, inasmuch as both maintained that these substances are utterly without matter although not without the composition of potentiality and act. For whatever is received as participated must be the act of the participating substance itself. And so because Plato maintained that all substances below the highest, which is one and good in itself, are participants, they are necessarily composed of potentiality and act. This is also Aristotle's position, since he maintained that the nature of the true and the good is attributed to act (*Metaph.* 11: 7, 1072a, 24–28). And so the first truth and the first good must be pure act. And anything less than this must have some addition of potentiality. . . .

Pure Act Can Only Be "Existence"   *Compendium of Theology,* ch. 11   1269–73

God's essence cannot differ from his existence. In a being whose essence differs from its existence, *what* it is must be distinguished from that *whereby* it is. For a thing's essence enables us to say what it is, whereas its existence enables us

to say that it is. Thus any definition signifying an essence
clarifies what the thing is. But because there is no composition in God, as previously shown (ch. 9), what he is cannot
be distinguished from that whereby he is. God's essence is,
therefore, nothing other than his existence.

We have also shown that God is pure act with no addition
of potentiality. His essence must therefore be the ultimate
act within him, since any act referred to the ultimate act is
in potentiality to that ultimate act. But the ultimate act is existence itself (*ipsum esse*), for because all motion is an
emergence from potentiality to act, that toward which all
motion inclines must be the ultimate act, and this must be
what all desire, inasmuch as all natural motion inclines toward what is naturally desired. This is existence. Hence the
divine essence or pure and ultimate act must be existence itself (*ipsum esse*).

Participation Causality

Debated Questions XII, q. 5,
a. 5   1269–72

I answer that it must be said that the opinion of Avicenna
was that one and being always predicate an accident. This,
however, is not true, because one as converted with being
signifies the substance of a thing and likewise being itself; but
one taken as the principle of number signifies an accident.
Therefore it should be known that anything whatever that
is in potentiality and act is put into act through that which
participates a higher act. Through this, moreover, something
is especially put into act because it participates through likeness the first and pure act. The first act, however, is *esse*
subsisting through itself; whence anything receives fulfillment
because it participates in *esse;* whence *esse* is the fulfillment
of every form, because through this is fulfilled that which
possesses *esse,* and when it is in actuality, it possesses *esse;*
and there is no form except through *esse,* and so I say that
the substantial *esse* of a thing is not an accident, but the
actuality of any existing form whether nonmaterial or material. And because *esse* is the fulfillment of all things, thence
it is that the proper effect of God is *esse,* and no cause gives
esse except insofar as it participates in the divine operation;

and so, strictly speaking, it is not an accident. And what Hilary says, I say. What is broadly called "accident" is everything that is not part of the essence; and this is *esse* in created things, because in God alone *esse* is his essence.

Existence and Participation

Debated Questions II, q. 2, a. 3 (1)   1269–72

There are two ways of predicating anything of a reality: either essentially or by participation. For we predicate light of a shining body by participation, but if there were any separated light [self-existent], we would predicate light essentially of this. Therefore we have to assert that being is predicated essentially only of God, inasmuch as the divine existence (*esse*) is an existence (*esse*) that is subsistent and absolute. But being is predicated of every creature by participation, since no creature is its own existence (*esse*) but is something having existence (*esse*).

We also say that God is good essentially, since he is goodness itself, but we say that creatures are good by participation, since they have goodness. Now, anything and everything insofar as it exists, is good. . . .

Now, whenever something is predicated of a reality by participation, there must be within this latter something other than that in which it participates. Hence in all creatures the creature itself that has existence (*esse*) is other than its act of existence (*esse*).

And Boethius means just this when he states in *Goodness of Substances* that in all existing things, with the exception of the First Being, *esse* and *quod est* are distinct (*aliud*).

But we should realize that something is participated in two ways. In one way as when it is present in the very substance of the participant, as the genus is participated by the species. But in this way *esse* is not participated by the creature. For whatever is present within the substance of anything is included in its definition. But because being is neither a genus nor a species, being is not included in any creature's definition. So being is participated in as something not belonging to the thing's essence, and thus the question whether-something-is is distinct from the question what-something-is.

Therefore, since anything that is extra with regard to a thing's essence is spoken of as an accident, the existence (*esse*) implied by the question whether-something-is is an accident. And so the commentator in *Metaphysics* 5 says that this proposition: "Socrates exists" is an example of accidental predication as implying a thing's entity or a proposition's truth.

Yet it is true that this term being (*ens*), inasmuch as it signifies the thing having this kind of existence (*esse*), signifies the essence of the thing and is divided into the ten categories—not univocally, however; for *esse* does not belong to all in the same way (*ratio*), but belongs to substance per se, to the others differently.

So that if in angels there is a composition as of essence and existence (*esse*), this is not a composition as of parts of the substance, but as of the substance itself and that which adheres to the substance.

Existence, Not an Accident *On the Power of God,* q. 5, a. 4, ad. 3

When we speak of *esse* as an accident, we do not mean that it is within the category of accident, at least when we speak of the existence (*esse*) of a substance (since it is the "act" of the essence), but merely that it is spoken of as accident by likeness to it inasmuch as just as an accident is not part of the essence, neither is existence (*esse*).

Debated Questions II, a. 2, a. 3 (1), ad. 2

Existence (*esse*) is an accident not as though related to the substance *per accidens,* but as the actuality of every substance.

Thus God who is his own actuality is his own existence (*esse*).

Existence and Essence Con- *On the Power of God,* q. 3, a.
created 3, ad. 2, ad. 17

2. Since existence (*esse*) is attributed to the quiddity (essence), not only the existence (*esse*) but the very quiddity is

said to be created, since it is nothing before having existence (*esse*), except perhaps in the Creator's intellect, where it is not a creature but the creative essence itself.

17. At the same moment that he gives existence (*esse*), God makes that which receives existence (*esse*), so he has no need of causing from pre-existing things.

The Unparticipating One Is   *Commentary on St. John's*
Lord of All   *Gospel,* Prologue 1269–72

For in these four ways the ancient philosophers arrived at the knowledge of God. But some through the authority [government] of God arrived at knowledge of him, and this is the most efficacious way. For we see those natural things acting on account of an end, pursuing certain useful ends; and since they lack intellect, they cannot direct themselves unless they are directed and moved by some other, by intellect, and this is because the very motion of natural things toward a certain end indicates the "to be" of something higher by which natural things are directed and guided to the end. And therefore when the whole course of nature deliberately proceeds and is directed toward an end, we are obliged to affirm something higher that directs this; and since God is the helmsman, this is God: and this authority of guiding is manifest in the Word of God when he says, *Lord.* Whence in Ps. 88: 10, is said: "You have power to rule the seas; the motions, however, of its waves you mitigate," as though saying: You are Lord and you govern the universe.

John shows that he has this knowledge of the Word when he says (below, 1, 1): *He came unto his own,* namely, into the world: because the whole world is his own. Others in truth came to the knowledge of God from his eternity: for they saw that whatever is in things is mutable, and inasmuch as the higher rank anything holds in the scheme of things, so much the less mutable it is. For example, lower bodies are mutable according to substance and according to place: celestial bodies, higher, are immutable according to substance; however, they move only according to place. According to this, therefore, evidently it can be gathered that the first principle of all things, supreme and higher, is immutable and eternal. And the Prophet of the Word implies this eternity when he says "sitting," i.e., presiding for eternity without any changing, Ps. 44: 6: "Thy seat, O Lord, in the age of ages."

Heb. 8: "Jesus Christ, yesterday, today, and forever." John shows this eternity, saying: *In the beginning was the Word.*

Some, moreover, came to the knowledge of God from the position of God himself; and these were the Platonists. They considered that everything that is by participation is led back to something that is through its essence as to the first and highest, just as all things that are hot by participation can be led back to fire, which is hot through its essence. Since therefore all things that exist participate in *esse* and are beings by participation, it is necessary that there be something at the utmost peak of all things, which is itself *esse* through its own essence, and his position is revealed when it is said "above the lofty Throne," which, according to Dionysius, refers to the divine nature. Ps. 112: 4: "The Lord high above all nations."

This is what is its own "to be" by its own essence, and this is God, who is the most sufficient, the noblest, and the most perfect Cause of total *esse*, from whom all things that exist participate in *esse*.

Lucifer and Participation   *On Evil,* q. XVI, 3   1269–72

I answer that it must be said that various authorities seem to incline toward this: that the devil sinned by seeking unauthorized equality with God. However, it cannot be that he should desire divine equality absolutely, for equality is a certain recognized relation of each extreme. The reason for this is clear. First, indeed, on God's part, not only is it impossible for anything to be equal to him, but also this is contradictory to the structure of his essence. For through his essence, God is *ipsum esse subsistens* (subsistent being itself): nor is it possible that there should be two of this kind, just as there cannot be two separated ideas of man, or two individual whitenesses standing. And so whenever anything is from another, it follows that what is, as it were, participating *esse*, cannot be equal to that which is essentially the *esse* itself.

Nor because of his own structure can the devil be unaware of this, for it is natural to intelligence, even separated intelligence, that it understands its own substance. So naturally it knows that its *esse* was participated from something higher, because a certain natural knowledge in it was not yet corrupted through sin. And so the result is that his understanding could not conceive of his own equality with God as possible. Moreover, no one tends toward that which he knows is impossible, as is said in *De Caelo et Mundo,* IV, 33; and so it is impossible that the movement of the devil's will should tend toward seeking divine equality, absolutely.

Second, this is apparent on the ambitious angel's part. For the will always desires something good either for itself or for another. However, the devil is not said to have sinned because he wanted divine equality for another (for he could without sin want the Son to be equal to the Father), but because he sought divine equality for himself. For the philosopher says in *Ethic.* 9: 4 that everyone seeks good for himself. If, however, another were to be made, he would not care what happens to him. Thus it is clear that the devil did not desire a situation that would change his identity. If, however, he were equal to God, even if this were possible, he would not be himself; for his species would be changed if raised to a higher rank of nature. And the result is that he could not desire absolute equality with God. And, likewise, he could not desire what was not absolutely subject to God. Then because this is impossible, neither could it occur to him as possible, as was previously clarified, then also because he himself would cease to be if he were not totally subject to God. And whatever else can be said that refers to natural rank, his evil could not consist in this, for evil is not found in those things that are always in act, but only in those things in which potentiality can be separated from act, as was said in *Metaph.* 9: 22. All angels, however, are so established that if something belongs to their natural perfection, they will hold it immediately from the principle of their creation: Nevertheless they were in potentiality to supernatural good, which through the grace of God they were able to pursue. And the result is that the devil's sin would not be in anything pertaining to the natural order, but to something supernatural. Therefore the devil's first sin was in this: that in pursuing supernatural happiness, which consists in the full vision of God, he did not raise himself to God as if desiring along with the holy angels the final perfection from God's grace, but he willed to pursue it through the power of his own nature (not, however, without God working in nature, but without God conferring grace). And so Augustine, in the book *On Free Choice*, assigns the devil's sin to the fact that he delighted in his own power, and in *Commentary on Genesis* 4 Augustine says that if the angelic nature turned to itself, often the angel would take more delight than in that by whose participation it is blessed, and swelling with pride, would fall. And because to have final happiness through the power of his own nature, and not from the grace of someone higher, is proper to God, it is clear how much for this reason the devil sought equality with God and how much for this reason also he sought not to be subjected to God so that evidently he would not need his grace beyond the power of his own nature. And this agrees with the preceding article above, where it was said that the devil did not sin by desiring anything evil, but by desiring something good, namely, final happiness, not according to due order, that is, not as pursuing it according to the grace of God.

Neoplatonic Participation   *Commentary on The Causes,*
                                       lect. IX   1271/2

Therefore the First Cause is cause of all knowing and of power and of all *esse;* therefore it follows that by it all things are caused. He proves, moreover, that it is the cause of all these, by the fact that what is the principle and the most excellent in any rank is cause of all that follows in that rank; but the First Cause has a more excellent knowing than all knowing and more excellent power than all power and more excellent *esse* than all *esse*. It is therefore the cause of all knowing and of all power and *esse,* and from this it follows that it is the Creator of the intelligence and of the soul and of nature and of the rest.

. . . And this is the second way in which something can have the property of not being in another, just as if whiteness were to be existing in separation from its subject, although for it this is not possible, it would evidently be individual in this way; and this is the way with separate substances, which are forms having *esse,* and with the very First Cause, which is itself subsistent being (*ipsum esse subsistens*).

2. SPECIAL ASPECTS

Aristotle on Metaphysics   *Commentary on Metaphysics,* Prologue

1. As the philosopher teaches in his *Politics,* whenever several things are ordered to one, it is necessary that one of them be regulating, or ruling, and the others regulated, or ruled. This, indeed, is evident in the union of soul and body—for the soul naturally commands, and the body obeys. Likewise, among the powers of the soul, the irascible and concupiscible powers by a natural order are ruled by reason. But all the sciences and arts are ordered to one thing, namely, to the perfection of man, which is his happiness. Hence it is necessary that one of them be the ruler of all the others, and, as such, rightly deserving of the name of "wisdom," it being the part of the wise man to order others.

2. Now, what this science is, and with what things it is concerned, may be considered if one diligently looks into how someone is suitable for ruling. For, just as in the aforesaid book the philosopher says that men of strong intellect are naturally the rulers and lords of others, while men who are of robust body, but lacking as to intellect, are naturally servants, so that science should be the natural ruler of others which is, of all, the most intellectual. This is the science treating of the most intelligible things.

3. The "most intelligible things" may be taken in three ways. First, from the order of intellection. Those things from which the intellect receives certitude are seen to be more intelligible. Hence, since the certitude of science is acquired by the intellect through causes, the knowledge of causes is seen to be in the highest degree intellectual. Hence too, the

science considering first causes is seen to be in the highest degree the regulator of the others.

4. Second, by comparing intellect to sense. Sense being the knowledge of particular things, the intellect is seen to differ from it as comprehending universals. Hence that science is in the highest degree intellectual that is concerned with principles in the highest degree universal. These, indeed, are being, and those things that follow on being, such as one and many, potency and act. Such things should not remain wholly undetermined, since without them a complete knowledge of what is proper to some certain genus or species cannot be had. Nor again should they be treated in some one of the particular sciences—since every genus of being, to be known, requires these, there would be a same reason for treating them in every particular science. Hence it remains for such things to be treated in some one common science, which, as being intellectual in the highest degree, is the regulator of the others.

5. Third, from the knowledge itself of the intellect. Since each thing has intellectual power by virtue of being immune from matter, those things must be in the highest degree intelligible that are in the highest degree separated from matter. For the intelligible and the intellect must be proportionate, and of one genus, the intellect and the intelligible in act being one. But those things are in the highest degree separated from matter which abstract, not only from signate matter [matter signed by quantity], "as in the case of natural forms taken universally, concerning which natural science treats," but entirely from sensible matter. And this not only according to notion, as in the case of mathematical things, but also according to being, as is the case with God and the intelligences [angels]. Hence the science treating of these things is seen to be intellectual in the highest degree, and the ruler, or mistress, of all.

6. Now, this threefold consideration should be attributed, not to different sciences, but to a single science, for the aforesaid separated substances are the universal and first causes of being. And it belongs to the same science to consider the proper causes of some genus, and the genus itself—just as natural science considers the principles of natural body.

Hence it necessarily pertains to the same science to consider separated substances and being in common, the latter being the genus of which the aforesaid substances are the common and universal causes.

7. From this it is clear that, while considering all the three aforesaid things, this science nevertheless does not consider any one whatever as subject, but solely being in common. For the subject in a science is that whose causes and passions [properties] we seek, and not the causes themselves of the genus in question. Rather, the knowledge of the causes of some genus is the end to which the consideration of the science attains.

8. Now, although the subject of this science is being in common, the whole is yet said to be concerning things separated from matter as to being and notion. This is by reason of the fact that not only are those things said to be separated as to being and notion that can never be in matter, such as God and the intellectual substances, but also those that may be without matter, as is the case with being in common. This would not occur if they were to depend upon matter as to being.

9. According to the three aforesaid, therefore, from which the perfection of this science is derived, it obtains three names. It is called "divine science" or "theology" insofar as it considers the aforesaid substances; it is called "metaphysics" insofar as it considers being and those things that follow upon it (for these "transphysical" things are encountered following the procedure of resolution, as the more common come after the less common). But it is also called "first philosophy" insofar as it considers the first causes of things. Thus, therefore, it is evident what the subject of this science is, and what its relation is to the other sciences, and how it is named.*

* Translated by P. H. Conway, O.P., and R. F. Larcher, O.P. (ASC 1).

Commentary on The Causes,
Prologue

Relation of philosophy to its order of learning

1. As the philosopher says in *Ethics* X, the final happiness of man consists in the best activity of man's highest power, that is, of the intellect with respect to the best intelligible object.

2. Since an effect is known through its cause, it is plain that the cause is by nature more intelligible than the effect—even though at times, so far as we are concerned, effects are more known than causes, due to the fact that it is from particulars, falling under the senses, that we acquire the knowledge of universal and intelligible causes.

3. Hence it is necessary that, absolutely speaking, the first causes of things be by nature the greatest and best intelligible things, since they are beings in the highest degree, and true in the highest degree, being, as they are, the cause to other things of their being and truth, as is evident from the philosopher in *Metaphysics* II—even though the first causes of this sort are less known, and later known, so far as we are concerned.

4. For our intellect is related to them as is the eye of the owl to the light of the sun, which light, because of its exceeding brightness, it cannot perfectly perceive.

5. Therefore it is necessary that the final happiness of man that he is able to have in this life consists in the consideration of the first causes—since that little that can be known of them is more lovable and noble than all that can be known of lower things, as is evident from what the philosopher says in *Parts of Animals* I.

6. To the extent that this knowledge is perfected in us after this life, to that extent is man constituted perfectly happy, according to the words of the Gospel, "This is eternal life, that they may know thee, the true and living God" [John 17: 3].

7. Hence the principal goal of the philosophers was that, by means of all they considered in things, they might arrive at a knowledge of first causes. For this reason they ordered the science of first causes last, intending to devote the final period of their life to its consideration.

8. First, they would begin with logic, which sets forth the method of the sciences; second, proceed to mathematics, which even children can master; third, to natural philosophy, which, because of experience, requires time; fourth, to moral philosophy, of which a young man cannot be a suitable hearer. Last, however, they devoted themselves to divine science [metaphysics], which considers the first causes of things.*

Early Errors in Metaphysical   *On the Power of God,* q. 3,
Analysis   a. 6

The ancient philosophers who studied material things observed only the material principles of nature and so fell into the error of supposing that all natural things are uncreated. Because they thought matter and conflict to be the principles of nature, they came to hold two first principles of things by three wrong ways of considering contraries. The first was to consider only the point of specific difference between contraries, ignoring their generic unity from the fact that contraries are in the same genus. And so they found a cause for that wherein they differed, not for what they had in common. Thus, as explained in *Physics* 1: 4, they proposed two first contraries as two first principles to account for all contraries. Empedocles, one of these, looked upon the first contraries as the two first active principles, namely, attraction and repulsion; and it is said (*Metaph.* 1: 4) that he was the first to propose the two principles, good and evil. Their second mistake was to judge two contraries to be equal, whereas one contrary must always imply privation of the other and thus be perfect while the latter is imperfect, the former good and the latter less so (*Phys.* 1: 2). Consequently they looked upon good and evil as distinct natures, inasmuch as they seemed to them to be the most generic contraries. This was

* Translated by P. H. Conway, O.P., and R. F. Larcher, O.P.

why Pythagoras said that all things were divisible into two genera, good and evil; in the genus of good things he classified all perfect things such as light, males, repose, and so forth, whereas in the genus of evil he classified darkness, females, and so forth. Their third mistake was to consider things in relation to themselves or to one another but not as related to the order of the universe. Thus whenever they discovered any one thing to be harmful to another or imperfect when compared with perfect things, they proclaimed it as simply naturally evil and not originating from the cause of the good. And so Pythagoras classified women as being imperfect in the genus of evil. This likewise was the source of the Manichean judgment that corruptible things as less perfect than incorruptible ones are the product not of the good God but of a contrary principle, and the same holds for the visible when compared with the invisible, and the Old Testament when compared with the New, a position strengthened by observing that some good creatures like man are harmed by some visible and corruptible creatures. But impossibility lurks in this error, for everything is derived from one First Principle, which is good. We may prove this now by three arguments.

The first argument: Whenever various things have any one thing in common, in respect to that common thing they must be referred to one thing, since either one must be the cause of the other or they both must come from a common cause, inasmuch as it is impossible for what they have in common to be rooted in the properties in which they differ. . . . Now, all contraries and different things existing in the world have some one thing in common, either the specific or generic nature or at least the common principle of being, and therefore they must all have one principle as the cause of being in all. But being as being is a good, evidenced by the fact that everything desires to be, for the good is defined as that which is desirable. And so above the whole variety of causes we must suppose one first cause, just as above those contrary agents in nature the natural philosophers supposed one primary agent, namely, the heaven, as cause of all lower motion. But since variety in position is found in this heaven, and from this variety the contrariety of lower bodies is de-

rived, we must come to a first mover that is moved neither
per se nor accidentally.

The second argument: Every agent acts insofar as it is in
actuality and thus perfect in some way. Now insofar as anything is evil it is not in actuality, since we call evil what is in
a state of potentiality, without its proper and due act. But
insofar as anything is in actuality, it is good, because this
gives it perfection and entity as well as essential goodness.
Hence nothing acts insofar as it is evil but everything acts
insofar as it is good. In both ways, then, that position holding
evil to be the creative principle of evils is insupportable. This
argument coincides with what Dionysius says (*On the Divine
Names* IV): that only by the power of good does evil act,
and evil is beyond the scope of intention and generation.

The third argument: If different beings were to be derived
exclusively from contrary principles without these being derived from one supreme principle, it would be impossible for
them to belong to the same order except by accident, because
if many things are coordinated there must be one coordi-
nator, unless this happens by chance. Now, we notice corruptible and incorruptible things, spiritual and bodily, perfect
and imperfect altogether in one order. Thus the spiritual
things move the bodily, as is evident in man, at least. Also,
corruptible things are governed by incorruptible things, as we
see in the alteration of elements by heavenly bodies. Nor
may we say that this happens by chance, for then it would
not be a question of always or for the most part, but only in
a few cases. So all these different things must be derived
from one First Principle whereby they are coordinated, and
on this account the philosopher concludes (*Metaph.* 12: 10)
that there is one ruler of all.

Meaning of Existence   *On the Power of God* VII, 2,
                                    ad. 9

What I mean by existence (*esse*) is the most perfect of all,
and this is apparent from the fact that actuality is always
more perfect than potentiality.

Notice that no form at all is considered as actual unless
some existence is understood as present, for humanity or

fire can be viewed as existing within the potentiality of matter or within an agent's power or even within an intellect, but it is made to be *actually existing* only by having existence (*esse*).

So obviously this existence (*esse*) is the
actuality of all acts
and therefore the perfection of all perfections.
Neither may we think that this existence (*esse*) has anything added to it so that this "something added" would be more formal than it and would determine it as act determines potentiality; for this kind of existence (*esse*) is essentially other than what it is "added" to in order to be thus determined [*esse* belongs to an utterly different order from that of essence], and nevertheless it cannot happen that what is thus added to existence (*esse*) is anything extraneous to it, because there is nothing that can be extraneous to existence (*esse*) except, obviously, nonbeing, but then nonbeing can be neither form nor matter; and therefore existence (*esse*) is determined by something other, not as potentiality is determined by act but rather as act is determined by potentiality.

For even when forms are defined, we add the respectively proper matter of each in that place where the "difference" is usually mentioned, as, for example, we say that the soul is the act of "a physical organic body," and it is in this way that this existence (*esse*) differs from that existence (*esse*), for it is the existence (*esse*) of this or that nature.

What "Is" Principally Signifies   *Commentary on Interpretation* I, lect. 5, 20–22

So that we may grasp what Aristotle is stating, we should realize that he has just declared that the verb does not signify that a thing exists or does not exist; and neither does "being" (*ens*) signify that a thing exists or does not exist. So when he states "it is nothing," he means that it does not signify that a thing exists. Certainly this is most evident in the expression "being" (*ens*), since "being" is only "that which is." And so we notice that it signifies both a thing when saying "that which," and existence (*esse*) when saying "is." Should the word "being" (*ens*), which signifies a thing having existence, signify principally existence (*esse*), doubtless it would signify that a thing exists. But the word "being" (*ens*) does not signify principally the composition involved in saying "is"; but inasmuch as it signifies the thing having existence, it signifies with composition [co-signifies]. This signifying with composition is insufficient with respect to truth or falsity; for the composition in which truth and falsity are involved can be understood only when connecting the extremes of a composition.

If instead of what Aristotle states we say "nor would 'to be' itself," as in our texts, the meaning is sharper. For through the verb "is," Aristotle demonstrates that no verb signifies that a thing exists or does not exist, since "is" used by itself does not signify that anything exists, although it signifies existence. And since "to be" itself is apparently a sort of composition, so also the verb "is" signifying "to be" can appear to signify the composition in which there is truth or falsity. To obviate this Aristotle adds that the composition signified by the verb "is" cannot be grasped without the composing thing. This is because any comprehension of the composition which "is" signifies rests upon the extremes, so that without them, no understanding of the composition is complete and so cannot be true or false.

Hence he states that the verb "is" signifies with composition inasmuch as it does not signify composition principally but consequently. It primarily signifies that which is understood absolutely in the way of actuality; for "is," strictly speaking, signifies "to be in act," and hence signifies in the manner of a verb. But the actuality that the verb "is" principally signifies is the actuality of every form in general, whether substantial or accidental. So that when we want to signify that any form or act is actually in some subject we signify this through the verb "is," either absolutely or relatively; absolutely, according to present time, relatively, according to other times; and on this account the verb "is" signifies composition, not principally, but consequently.

All Creatures Participate in Existence   *Debated Questions* III, q. 8, a. 20 (1)

If by matter we mean anything in any way in potentiality,

and if by form we mean every kind of act, then we must argue that the human soul, as well as any created substance at all, is comprised of matter and form. And this is because every created substance is comprised of potentiality and actuality, for it is clear that only God as existing by essence is his own existence (*esse*), inasmuch as his existence (*esse*) is his very substance. And this cannot be asserted of any other being, since there can only be one subsistent existence (*esse*).

Every other being must then be a being by participation, so that within it the substance that participates in existence (*esse*) is other than the existence itself (*esse*), which is participated.

But every participant is related to that in which it participates as potentiality to actuality. Consequently, every created substance is comprised of potentiality and act, i.e., of *quod est* and *esse* as Boethius states in *Goodness of Substances,* just as any white thing is made up of "that which is white" and "whiteness."

. . . Potentiality and act are first principles within the order of substance, whereas matter and form are first principles within the order of changeable substance. So it is unnecessary for every composition in the category of substance to be one of matter and form; only in changeable substances is this necessary.

Creatures Related to God

Summa of Theology I, q. 4, a. 2, c

In God are all the perfections of all things. And so because no excellence in any genus is wanting to him, he is declared to be totally perfect. Two reflections point to this.

First, inasmuch as any perfection present in an effect must exist in the producing cause, either formally the same when the agent is univocal, or when equivocal, present to a greater degree—as whatever is generated by the sun's power is likewise in the sun. It is clear then that an effect pre-exists in an efficient cause; but since matter as matter is imperfect, while an agent as agent is perfect, to pre-exist within the potentiality of a material cause is to pre-exist more imperfectly, whereas to pre-exist virtually in the efficient cause is to pre-exist more perfectly, not more imperfectly. Dionysius refers to this point when he says of God: "It is not that he is this and not that, but that as the cause of all, he is all."

Second, God, as we have proven, is being itself, subsistent in itself. Therefore within himself he must include the whole perfection of being. For evidently, no hot thing has the whole perfection of heat because it does not participate in heat to its full perfection, for if this heat were self-subsisting, it would lack no power of heat. Consequently, because God is subsistent being itself, he lacks nothing of the perfection of being.

Now, to the perfection of being belongs all the perfections of all things, for it is precisely insofar as they have some kind of being that things are perfect. Therefore, no perfection belonging to anything is wanting to God. This line of thought is referred to also by Dionysius when he states that God does not exist in some particular way but embraces within himself all being, absolutely, without limitation, universally; and he then adds, "he is very being to subsistent things."

Individuation   *On Spiritual Creatures,* VIII,
                                      Responses and ad. 4

There have been various opinions about this question. Some have declared that all spiritual substances are specifically the same, while others maintain that all angels in the same hierarchy or order are in one species. Yet others asserted that all angels are specifically different from one another, and to me also this seems true.

The *first* reason is drawn from the type of substance they are. For we must necessarily say that they are either simple forms subsisting apart from matter, as previously explained, or that they are forms made up of matter and form. Now, if an angel is a simple form separated from matter, we cannot even conceive several angels of one species, for any form at all, no matter how inferior or material, remains specifically one form when established as abstract either in actual being or in the intellect. For when whiteness is taken as something subsisting in separation from every subject, we cannot have many whitenesses because we know that this whiteness does not differ from that whiteness except by being in this or that subject. Likewise, given an abstract human nature, there could only be one. But if an angel is a substance made up of matter and form, we must then say that the matters of various angels are in some way distinct. Now, matter can be distinguished from matter in two ways: one according to matter's proper character, i.e., according to its relationship to various acts; for, according to its proper character, matter is in potentiality, and since potentiality is referred to by relation to act, any distinction among potentialities or matters is made from the viewpoint of the order of acts. And so the matter of inferior bodies, which is a potentiality to actual being, differs from the matter of heavenly bodies, which is a potentiality to place. The second way matter can be distinguished, however, is based upon quantitative division insofar as matter existing under these particular dimensions is distinguished from that existing under other dimensions.

The first distinction of matter causes generic difference since, as the philosopher states in *Metaphysics* 5: 28, a generic difference among things is based upon matter. The second distinction of matter, however, causes difference among individuals within the same species. But this second distinction of matter cannot be found among different angels inasmuch as angels are immaterial and wholly lacking quantitative dimensions.

Hence, the only remaining alternative is that if there are many angels and these are composed of matter and form, the distinction of matter is present in them according to the first manner so that they differ not only specifically but also generically.

ad. 4. In regard to the fourth objection, we must say that just as a form within a subject or matter is individuated by being in this particular thing, so a separated form is individuated by being of such a nature as not naturally to exist in anything. For just as actual being in this particular thing excludes the commonness of a universal that is predicable of many individuals, so does being unable to exist in some subject. Therefore, just as this particular whiteness is not prevented from including many individuals because it is whiteness (which pertains to its specific character) but because it is in this particular subject (which pertains to its individual character), so the nature of this particular angel is not prevented from being in many because it is a nature in a given order of things (which pertains to its specific character), but because this nature has no natural capacity for being received in a given subject (which pertains to the character of an individual).

Souls Substantially Differentiated

Summa of Christian Teaching
II, 81

. . . And we must first realize that each of those things that have to be adapted and proportioned to each other derives from its own cause simultaneously its multiplicity or unity. So that if the being of one thing depends upon another, so does its unity or multiplicity, or else the latter depends upon another extrinsic cause. Hence, form and matter should always be mutually proportioned and naturally adapted, so to speak, since the proper act is produced in its proper matter. That is why with respect to multiplicity and unity, matter and form must always agree with each other. Therefore, if the form's being depends upon matter, so will its multiplication as well as its unity. But if such is not the situation, then the form must be multiplied according to the multiplication of the matter, i.e., along with the matter and proportioned to it, yet not so that the unity or multiplicity of the form itself depends upon the matter. But we have seen that the human soul is a form that does not in its being depend upon matter. Consequently, souls are multiplied according to the multiplication of bodies, but the latter will not be the cause of the multiplication of souls. And therefore it does not follow that the plurality of souls ceases with the destruction of bodies, as the first argument concluded.

From this we clearly perceive the answer to the second argument. For not all difference of form causes difference in species but only that difference with regard to formal principles or otherness with regard to the form's intelligible essence, for it is obvious that the form of this or that fire is essentially distinct, yet neither the fire nor its form is specifically different. Hence, a multiplicity of souls separated from their bodies comes from the substantial difference of the forms, because this soul's substance is different from that soul's substance. Yet this difference results not from any difference in the essential principles of the soul itself, nor from any difference with regard to the soul's intelligible essence, but from difference in the *commensuration of souls to bodies,* inasmuch as this soul is adapted to this and not to that body, and that soul to another body, and so in all other instances. And these adaptations remain in souls even when the bodies have perished inasmuch as their substances endure, not depending upon bodies in their being. For souls are as substances the forms of bodies or else they would be united to their bodies only accidentally so that from the union of soul and body would arise something not essentially one, but only accidentally one. But souls have to be adapted to bodies *as forms.* Evidently this is the reason for these different adaptations remaining in separated souls and this explains, therefore, their permanent multiplicity.

The "Existence" of Accidents   *Debated Questions* IX, q. 2, a. 2, c and ad. 2

A distinct *esse* means a distinct, ultimate, complete subject or person. But Christ is only one person. In him, therefore, is only one *esse.*

. . . *Esse* can be used in two ways, as is clear from the philosopher in *Metaphysics* 5 and from a certain Gloss of Origen on St. John's Prologue.

It is used in one way as a verbal copula to signify a composition of any assertion made by the mind; so this *esse* does not refer to the nature of things but is used by the mind in its act of composing and separating, and such *esse* is attributed to everything that can be contained in a proposition, whether this is a being (*ens*) or a privation of being (for we say that there *is* blindness).

Esse is used in a second way as referring to the act of being insofar as it is a being (*ens*) and by means of this act a thing is called being in the nature of things. And in this way *esse* is attributed to those things present within the ten categories so that what is called being by such *esse* is divided according to the ten categories.

But in two different ways such *esse* is attributed to anything. In one way so that it refers to whatever truly and properly has *esse* or exists, and in this way it is attributed only to substance that subsists in itself (per se), whence that which truly exists is called substance in *Physics* I. Anything not subsisting in itself but only in another and with another—whether this be an accident, a substantial form, or any part at all—does not have *esse*, so that it truly is, but *esse* is rather attributed to it.

In another way *esse* refers to that by which anything is, just as there is said to be whiteness not because it subsists in itself but inasmuch as by it something exists as white.

Properly and truly, therefore, *esse* is attributed only to whatever subsists in itself. To this thing a twofold *esse* is attributed. One *esse* comes from those factors from which the unity of the being arises, and this is the person's proper, substantial *esse*. The other *esse* is attributed to the person in addition to the factors comprising it, and this is an added or accidental *esse*, as we attribute "to be white" to Socrates when we say "Socrates is white."

Since then we presuppose in Christ only one subsistent being within whose unity the humanity is present, it is necessary to assert that inasmuch as there is one person of both natures, there is in Christ only one substantial *esse* that is properly attributed to the person. From the person itself and not from the natures Christ has unity. But if the humanity were supposed as separated from the divinity, then the humanity would have its own *esse*, one other than the divine *esse*. For only because a thing is not subsistent through itself does it not have its own *esse*, just as if a box would be a natural individual, the entire whole would have only one *esse*; and yet any part separated from the box would have its own *esse*.

And so it is clear that in this second way of using *esse* we have to assert that there is one substantial *esse* in Christ so that *esse* belongs properly to the person, although there is in him a multiple, accidental *esse*.

obj. 2. Like *esse*, action is attributed to the person. But the unity of the person does not prevent there being many actions

in Christ. So the unity of the person does not prove that there
is only one *esse* in Christ.

ad. 2. The person's action does not come from the integrity
of its unity but comes as a consequence of its unity; so we
find many actions of one person through the various principles of action present in the person, just as man acts with his
tongue and hand. But *esse* is the basis for the person's unity,
so that multiple *esse* is prejudicial to the being's unity.

Unity Not an Addition to Being

Summa of Theology I, q. 11, a. 1, c and ad. 1

Because one means "undivided" being, oneness is not a
reality added to being, but merely expresses the negation of
division. This is precisely why "one" is convertible with being. For every being is either simple or composite. But anything simple is undivided, both actually and potentially, while
anything composite only has being when its parts are together
and compose it, whereas while its parts are divided, it has no
being. So it is clear that a thing's being consists in indivision,
and thus everything protects its unity as it protects its being.

ad. 1. Some identified the one-convertible-with-being with
the one-that-is-the-principle-of-number and came to opposite
opinions. Pythagoras and Plato, realizing that the one-
convertible-with-being added no reality to being but rather
signified the substance of being as undivided, considered that
this also applied to the one-that-is-the-principle-of-number.
And because unities make up number, they concluded that
numbers were the substance of all things. But Avicenna, on
the contrary, thinking that the one-that-is-the-principle-of-
number added reality to the substance of being (or else number composed of unities would not be a kind of quantity),
considered that the one-convertible-with-being added reality
to the substance of beings, as white adds reality to man. But
this is clearly untrue, because everything is by its substance
one. For if by anything other than its substance a thing were
one, this other would have to be one by something other, and
so forth unto infinity. So we must stay with the former assertion and state that the one-that-is-convertible-with-being does
not add reality to being, whereas that one-that-is-the-

principle-of-number adds reality to being and belongs to the genus of quantity.

Goodness and Its Cause   *On Truth,* q. 21, a. 4, c

Opinions on this question have varied. For minor reasons some foolishly asserted that God enters substantially into all things. Some among these, David of Dinant, for example, equated God with prime matter. Others taught that God is the form of all things. Now, the error of this false opinion is quickly seen, for in speaking of God all men know that he is the efficacious principle of all things because everything must come from one primary being. But according to the philosopher's teaching, the efficient cause does not coincide with the material cause inasmuch as they have opposed characteristics. A thing is an agent insofar as it is in actuality, whereas it is characteristic of matter to be in potentiality. Whereas the efficient cause and the form of its effect are specifically the same since every agent effects something like itself, they are not the same numerically, because the maker and what is made cannot be identical. It clearly follows that the divine essence is neither any creature's matter nor its form so that the creature can be said through it to be good formally as through an intrinsic form.

But every form is a certain likeness to God.

And so the Platonists stated that all things are formally good through the first goodness, not as through an intrinsic form but as through a separated form. To understand this position we should remember that for Plato whatever is separated in thought is in reality also separated. So that because man can be known apart from Socrates and Plato, he taught that man exists apart from Socrates and Plato. He called this "man-in-himself" or the "form-of-man" and asserted that Socrates and Plato are called men through participation in this man. Again, just as he considered man as common to Socrates and Plato and all others like them, so he considered good as common to all good things and understandable independently of this or that good. So he stated that good is separate from all particular goods, and this he called "good in itself" or "the idea of the good." All things are called good, he said, through participation in it. This is declared by the philosopher.

Yet as Plato discussed them, the idea of good does differ from the idea of man, in that the idea of man does not extend to all things, whereas the idea of good does and extends even to other ideas. For the very idea of good is itself a particular good. And thus it was necessarily stated that the very good-in-itself is the universal principle of all things; and this principle is God. From this teaching it followed that all things are called good through the first goodness, or God, just as Socrates and Plato (according to Plato) are called men through participation in man as separated and not through any humanity intrinsic to them.

In a way this Platonic view was adopted by the Porretans. They claimed that we predicate good of any creature either absolutely, as when we say, "Man is good," or in a qualified way as when we say, "Socrates is a good man." Any creature is called good absolutely, they asserted, not through its intrinsic goodness but through the first goodness, whereas a creature is called a good this or that through a created goodness, since for Plato, particular created goodnesses are like particular ideas. But the philosopher argues in many ways against this. He argues that the quiddities and forms of things are within particular things themselves, not separated from them, and this he proves in many ways. He also argues more precisely that even should ideas exist, they have nothing to do with good, since good is not predicated univocally of good things, and in the case of nonunivocal predication, Plato did not refer to a single idea. This is the way the philosopher argues against him in the *Ethics*.

In regard to the present issue, the fact that every agent effects something like itself reveals the falsity of the aforementioned position, so that if the first goodness is the efficient cause of all "good," it must impress its likeness upon whatever is made, and thus everything will be called good because of an intrinsic form or its inherent likeness to the highest good as well as because of the first goodness considered as the exemplar and efficient cause of all created goodness. Plato's opinion is in this sense tenable.

We therefore assert in accord with the general opinion that

all things are good formally by a created goodness as through an intrinsic form, but by the uncreated goodness as through an exemplary form.

Analogy   *Commentary on Sentences* I,
                              d. 19, q. 5, a. 2, c and ad. 1

There is one divine being (*esse*) by which all things exist as by an efficient and exemplary principle; yet a different existence (*esse*) is present in each different thing by which this thing formally exists.

ad. 1. There are three ways in which anything is predicated analogically: first, according to concept alone, not according to real being (*esse*), and this happens whenever one concept is predicated of many things as cause and effect while being present in only one. Hence the concept of health is said of animal, urine, and food in diverse ways, according to cause and effect, not as really existing diversely inasmuch as the reality of health exists only in the animal. The second way of predicating is according to real being and not according to concept, and this happens when many things are considered as equal within the concept of some common attribute, although this common attribute in regard to real being does not exist in one common way in all. It is in this way that all bodies under the one concept of corporeity are considered alike. So the logician, concerned only with concepts, asserts that the term "body" is predicated univocally of all bodies, although in corruptible and in incorruptible bodies, this nature's manner of being is diverse. Thus for the metaphysician and the natural philosopher who study things from the viewpoint of their actual being, neither the term "body" nor anything else is predicated univocally of corruptible and of incorruptible beings. . . . The third way of predicating is according to both concept and real being, and this happens when there is no equality either in concept or in existence, as being is predicated of substance and of accident. And in these instances the nature in common must have some manner of real existence in each of the things of which it is predicated, yet differing according to greater or less perfection. And in like manner I assert that truth and goodness

and all attributes like them are predicated analogically of
God and of creatures. It is necessary therefore that all such
attributes exist according to real being both in God and in
creatures, yet according to greater and less perfection. It
follows from this that truth in God differs from truth in creatures because it does not exist in the same manner in both.

Participation, Basis of Anal-   *Commentary on Sentences*
ogy   III, d. 2, q. 1, a. 1, ad. 3

There is a twofold likeness between the creature and God.
One is by participation in some divine good, as, for instance,
all participate in life from him as living. And so the rational
creature possessing existence, life, and knowledge is most
nearly like God. The second kind of likeness is by proportionality, as when a likeness is found between God and fire
because God consumes evil just as fire consumes a body. . . .

Creatures Are "Like" God   *On Truth,* q. 2, a. 11

We must assert that we may not predicate anything univocally of the creature and God, for in univocal predication the
intelligible nature that the name signifies is common to each
thing among those of which that name is predicated univocally (in one way). Hence there is an equality among
things of which the name is univocally predicated, although
one may be prior to another in actual existence. For example, all numbers, considered conceptually as numbers, are
equal, but one number may in fact be prior to another.

Now, no creature, regardless of how much it imitates God,
can ever reach the point of having anything in common with
God according to the same quality. For those attributes that
are common to different things according to the same quality
are common to these according to the quality of substance or
quiddity, but in the order of real existence, they are distinct.
But whatever is in God *is* his own proper act of existing; for
just as in him essence is identical with the act of existing, so
likewise in him science is identical with his act of knowing.
Therefore, because one thing's act of existing can never be
communicated to another, the creature cannot attain the
possession of anything in the same quality that it exists in

God, just as it cannot attain to the same way of existing. Likewise in our own case: If man and the act of existing as man did not differ in Peter, we could not predicate "man" univocally of Peter and Paul because of their different acts of existing.

We cannot say, on the other hand, that whatever is predicated of God and creature is predicated purely equivocally, since if no real likeness of creature to God existed, his essence would not be the likeness of creatures and then he would not know creatures through knowing his own essence. In that case also we could not know God by knowing creatures, nor among the names appropriate to creatures would any one of them be more predicable of him than others, inasmuch as when no likeness is present as in equivocals, any name will do. So we must state that the name "knowledge" is predicated of God's Knowledge and of ours neither wholly univocally nor purely equivocally, but by analogy, which merely means according to a proportion.

Now, there are two kinds of proportional agreement producing a twofold community of analogy. A certain agreement is present among things mutually proportioned to each other by having a definite distance or other relation, as two with one by being the double of one.

Often between two things having no proportion to each other there is a mutual agreement in regard to a likeness of two proportions to each other, as six is like four inasmuch as six is the double of three, just as four is the double of two. The first kind of agreement is one of proportion, the second of proportionality. Thus by the first kind of agreement, something is predicated analogically of two things mutually related, as is being of substance and accident through the mutual relation of substance and accident, and as healthy is predicated of urine and of animal insofar as urine has a certain relation to the animal's health. But often a term is predicated analogically according to the second kind of agreement, as the term "vision" is used of corporeal vision as well as of intellectual vision because intellect is in the soul as sight is in the eye. Because the first kind of analogical predication requires a definite relation between the things possessing something by analogical community, by this way of analogy, nothing can be predicated of God and creature.

But there are two kinds of predication by proportionality: 1. Sometimes the term predicated includes within its primary meaning something with respect to which there can be no likeness between God and creatures, even proportionally. This is so with regard to all that is predicated of God symbolically, as when he is called lion or sun or the like, since matter that cannot be attributed to God is included in the definition of such terms. 2. Often, however, the name predicated of God and creature implies nothing in its principal signification that could interfere with the aforementioned agreement between the creature and God.

This is the situation with all those terms whose definition implies no imperfection and no dependence upon matter for their being, as with terms like "being," "good," and so forth.

Only Analogical Likeness   *On the Power of God,* q. 7, a. 7

I answer that it is impossible for anything to be predicated univocally of God and a creature; this is obvious for the following reasons. Every effect of a univocal agent is equal to the agent's power, and no creature's power, being finite, can be equal to the first agent's power, which is infinite. Wherefore it is impossible for a creature to receive a likeness to God univocally. Again it is clear that although the form in the agent and the form in the effect have a common *ratio,* the fact that they have different modes of existence precludes their univocal predication: so, although the material house is of the same kind as the house in the builder's mind, since the one is the exemplar of the other, nevertheless, *house* cannot be univocally predicated of both, because the form of the material house has its being in matter, whereas in the builder's mind it has immaterial being. Hence granted the possibility that goodness in God and in the creature be of the same kind, nevertheless *good* would not be predicated of God univocally, since that which in God is immaterial and simple is in the creature material and complex. Moreover, being is not predicated univocally of substance and accident, because substance is a being as subsisting in itself, while accident is that whose being is to be in something else. Wherefore it is evident that a different relation to being precludes a univocal predication of being. Now, God's relation to being is different from that of any creature's: for he is his own being, which cannot be said of any creature. Hence in no way can it [being] be predicated univocally of God and a creature, and consequently neither can any of the other predicables among which is included even the first *being*, for if there be diversity in the first, there must be diversity in the others; wherefore nothing is predicated univocally of substance and accident.

Others, however, took a different view, and held that nothing is predicated of God and a creature by analogy but by pure equivocation. This is the opinion of Rabbi Moses, as his writings show. This opinion, however, is false, because in all purely equivocal terms that the philosopher calls equivocal *by chance*, a term is predicated of a thing without regard to anything else; whereas all things predicated of God and creatures are predicated of God with some regard to creatures or vice versa, and this is clearly admitted in all the aforesaid explanations of the divine names. Wherefore they cannot be pure equivocations. Again, since all our knowledge of God is taken from creatures, if the agreement were purely nominal, we should know nothing about God except empty expressions to which nothing in reality corresponds. Moreover, it would follow that all the proofs advanced about God by philosophers are sophisms: for instance, if one were to argue that whatsoever is in potentiality is reduced to actuality by something actual and that therefore God is actual being, since all things are brought into being by him, there will be a fallacy of equivocation; and likewise in all other arguments. And again the effect must be in some way like its cause, wherefore nothing is predicated equivocally of cause and effect; for instance, *healthy* of medicine and of animal.

We must accordingly take a different view and hold that nothing is predicated univocally of God and the creature, but that those things that are attributed to them in common are predicated not equivocally but analogically. Now, this kind of predication is twofold. The first is when one thing is predicated of two with respect to a third; thus being is predicated of quantity and quality with respect to substance. The other is when a thing is predicated of two by reason of a relationship between these two; thus being is predicated of substance and quantity. In the first kind of predication the two things must be preceded by something to which each of them bears some relation; thus substance has a reference to quantity and quality, whereas in the second kind of predication this is not necessary, but one of the two must precede the other. Wherefore since nothing precedes God, but he precedes the creature, the second kind of analogical predication is applicable to him but not the first.

3. AQUINAS ON HIS PREDECESSORS

Aristotle Not Fundamentally   *Commentary on the Soul* I, 8,
Opposed to Plato   107

When he had set forth Plato's view, Aristotle went on to refute it. Here we note that frequently it is not exactly Plato's own meaning that Aristotle criticizes in Plato, but the surface sense of his words. He is forced to this by Plato's faulty method of teaching by the use of symbols and by giving a meaning to his words quite other than their literal sense, as when he refers to the soul as a circle. So when he criticizes Plato, Aristotle is frequently arguing precisely against this literal sense.

Aquinas Modifies Platonism   *Commentary on The Causes,*
          lect. 6

According to the Platonists, the prime cause is in fact above being, inasmuch as the essence of goodness and of oneness that the prime cause is—surpasses separated being itself, as was stated. But in truth the prime cause is above being [transcends being], inasmuch as it is infinite be-ing (*esse*) itself.

Aquinas Reconciling Augus-   *On Spiritual Creatures,* a. 10,
tine and Aristotle   ad. 8

But Augustine, going along with Plato as far as the Catholic
faith permitted, did not admit the species of things with
their own subsistence [the world of forms] but rather admitted ideas of things in the divine mind, declaring that
through these we form judgments of all things by an intellect
illumined by divine light, not so as to see the ideas themselves, which would require our seeing the essence of God,
but through what these supreme ideas impress upon our
minds. For Plato taught that the sciences were related to the
separate species, not so that the latter could themselves be
seen but that by participating in them, our minds would have
knowledge of things. And so when commenting on this passage, "Truths are decayed from among the children of men"
(Ps. 11: 1), Augustine said that just as many likenesses
shine forth from one mirror, so many truths are produced
in our minds from the one primary truth.

Aristotle, however, took another way. First of all, he
showed in many ways that there is something stable in sensible realities; second, that sense judges truly concerning the
proper objects of sense but is mistaken about the common
objects of sense and more mistaken about things accidentally
perceived; third, that there is an intellectual power above the
sense, and this judges of truth not through intelligible things
existing outside but through the light of the agent intellect
by which things become intelligible.

Now, there is no great difference between saying that intelligible things themselves are participated in through God and
saying that the light that makes them intelligible is participated
in through God.

Aquinas Interprets Augustin-   *Summa of Theology* I, q. 84,
ian Illumination   a. 5, c

When the question is raised: Does the human soul know
all things in the eternal exemplars? we answer that a thing is
known in another in two ways. First, when the object itself
is known as we see the images of things reflected in a mirror.

Second, a thing is said to be known in another as in a principle of knowledge, as we may say that we see in the sun whatever we see by the sun. And in this way we must assert that the human soul knows all things in the eternal exemplars inasmuch as we know all things through participation in these exemplars. For the intellectual light that is in us is nothing other than a participated likeness of the uncreated light in which the eternal exemplars are present. Hence it is written (Ps. 4: 6, 7): "Many say: Who showeth us good things?" and the Psalmist answers: "The light of Thy countenance O Lord is signed upon us," as though he were to say: "By the seal of the Divine light in us, all things are made known to us." Yet for us to know material things, in addition to our intellectual light we require intelligible species derived from things. So this kind of knowledge is not had merely by participation in the eternal exemplars, as the Platonists held, claiming that the mere participation in ideas sufficed for knowledge. So Augustine declares (*Trinity* IV, 16): "Although the philosophers by convincing arguments prove that all things occur in time according to the eternal exemplars, were they able to look at the eternal exemplars or to discover from them how many kinds of animals there are and each one's origin? Did they not search for this information from the history of times and places?"

But that Augustine did not think all things to be known in their eternal exemplars or in the unchangeable truth, as though the eternal exemplars themselves were seen, is clear from what he says (*Eighty-three Questions*), i.e., that not each and every rational soul can be declared worthy of that vision, namely, of the eternal exemplars, but only those holy and pure, like the souls of the blessed.

GOD AND THE WORLD

It is especially in his discussion of God as known by human reason that Aquinas boldly opposed Aristotle. For Aristotle the material world was uncaused. And he had taken a strange delight in scoffing at Platonic exemplarism or the influence of a transcendent extrinsic formal cause of the world. Aquinas in fact tended to correct Aristotle's theological thinking with Plato's help.

Yet the reader who has studied both Plato and Aristotle will realize that, in giving the central position to existence, Aquinas is departing from both these masters. The departure is not arbitrary. It is in keeping with the Neoplatonic tradition as it took shape after Plotinus's death. Although in the triad set forth by Plotinus—the One, the *Nous,* the World Soul—the Supreme One was considered to be beyond being, which was present only on the level of *Nous.* Porphyry did in fact speak of being as the First Principle. And in the fourth century the Christian Neoplatonist Marius Victorinus in his work on the Trinity spoke of the Father as being. Perhaps the rather prevalent notion that Aquinas's metaphysics was derived from Avicenna and/or Exodus is itself to be explained by the obscurity that has surrounded both pagan and Christian Neoplatonism. There is many an Augustinian text that indicates that Augustine thought of God as *esse,* but that he did not work out the metaphysics of existence on the finite level.

Many avenues of Neoplatonism opened out to Aquinas. There were translations by John Scotus Erigena of the works of Dionysius the Areopagite and Maximus the Confessor and Gregory of Nyssa. Aquinas often refers to John Damascene. He became familiar with the Greek fathers when he edited the *Catena Aurea,* a string of selections from the patristic commentaries on the New Testament. But the commentaries Aquinas wrote on the works of Boethius assure us of his contact with this Western form of Christian Neoplatonism. And if Boethius, who wrote a work on the Trinity, had at hand the Four Books on the Trinity written by Marius Vic-

torinus Afer, this would represent a direct contact with a
thoroughly orthodox Christian Neoplatonism. He would see
that Neoplatonism need not take the form of Scotus Erigena's
Division of Nature. And when Aquinas read Boethius's *De
Trinitate* (which he commented on, really treating only questions raised by the work), he would be having indirect contact with the Christian Neoplatonism of Victorinus wherein
esse or *be-ing* was the most accurate name for God the
Father. And is it likely that Augustine, who wrote a *De
Trinitate,* did not study that of Victorinus? All I can say now
is that research in this area is still in process.

And so when St. Augustine and St. Thomas sought to understand their faith, they may have been directly or indirectly
in contact with Victorinus, first Christian Neoplatonist of the
West.

Yet it is not fully established whether Victorinus himself
depended for his view of *esse* upon Porphyry, who modified
Plotinus to speak of the One as Being, or whether he depended upon a fourth-century Neoplatonic commentary on
the *Parmenides,* or whether Porphyry authored the anony-
mous commentary, as P. Hadot suggests. In any case, with
Porphyry the second hypostasis is already equal to the One,
and in correcting the Arian Candidus (who may be fictitious),
Victorinus shows that *vivere* (living) and *intelligere* (knowing) are implicit to *esse,* not subordinate.

The notion of *esse* as the source of all perfections is the
foundation stone of Christian Neoplatonic participation/
metaphysics, as indeed it is of the philosophy and theology of
St. Thomas Aquinas. As the Father's self-revelation is for
Victorinus both life and wisdom, so for Aquinas our world
manifests the living God, and the incarnation of wisdom
unites us to him.

All the fathers are not equally careful with Neoplatonic
participation theories. But it seems fairly certain that competent Christian Neoplatonic theologians preceded St. Augustine's contact with Plotinus. When Augustine read Plotinus,
he immediately interpreted the triad there as the trinitarian
God of Scripture. Origen had handled "participation" without perfectly orthodox results. But Gregory of Nyssa sees no
impossibility in the Son both coming from the Father and

being his equal. Gregory emphasized a unified view in his explanation of the natural man's relation to God and the baptized man's relation to God: both are God's gift inasmuch as human existence as well as Christian existence are "by participation." The former is participation in created natural existence, the latter in created divine existence. Participation means "not having something by nature but as received from above" (from that which is of absolute value). In this way it is clear that the participant is really distinct from the participated and that God as infinitely good is the foundation for man's infinite perfectability, his unlimited growth in moral goodness.

Which then is more essential to Aquinas's philosophical synthesis—the distinction between the intelligible and sensible world, or the distinction between the uncreated and the created world? In my judgment the latter is more essential. And so we can conclude that the philosophy of St. Thomas Aquinas is more Neoplatonic than Platonic, and, what is more, rather Biblical than Aristotelian.

And although the distinction between God and the world, between nature and grace is made by participation mediated in one case through the eternal Word and in the other through the Word incarnate, that which participation more profoundly aims at and achieves is the wondrous mystery of unity.

Other Plotinian doctrines mark Thomistic natural theology. There is the negative way of speaking of God, as when all imperfections or mixed perfections are denied of him. At one point Thomas states that only when we admit that we really know nothing of the greatness of God do we have a glimmer of true knowledge of God. Aquinas's conception of God as Being allowed for both God's transcendence and his immanence by power, presence, and essence wherever there are things receiving existence. But how can man by natural powers know in any positive way such a transcendent God? The perfections we discover in creatures, says Aquinas, are necessarily in the creative source, at least virtually, but also formally in an eminent way. In this question Aquinas will not accept Moses Maimonides' answer that qualities such as truth, goodness, beauty, knowledge, and love are mere synonyms for one another, all identical with the Godhead. No, Aquinas steers a careful course between agnosticism and anthropomorphism. We affirm that God is good, but not in the limited way that sensible things are good. So if we are thinking of finite goodness we must negate goodness of God. The two previous judgments give rise to a higher affirmation, which does justice to both: God is supergood (we say that God is good but in a more eminent way than man is good). The goodness of God is here raised to the level of infinite existence—it becomes unknowable to our finite minds but it is true that God is good in a way that surpasses any experience of goodness we have had. This is positive knowledge. Aquinas never claims that it lets us know all about God, but what there is of knowledge is certain. Since this knowledge is based upon a likeness between God and creatures through existence, it is called knowledge by analogy. By it we become aware also of God's providence. Because such knowledge as we have of God philosophically is dependent upon the metaphysical analysis of created or finite being, we have placed the texts on uncreated being and created being in the same section.

Often readers (and commentators, alas) take Thomas's thought less seriously than they take what are now nothing more than the quaint illustrations that he uses in developing his thought. The editor, for example, finds his discussion of providence profound but—not only as a woman but as a person—finds Thomas's illustration silly. And she suspects that he would rejoice to live in an age that had gone beyond the limitations of his natural sciences and his society. No one should cling to the examples of medieval physical science made use of by Aquinas merely to illustrate a point already argued. It should also be noted that the outdating of Thomistic "natural science" does not outdate Thomistic metaphysics, which is an analysis of the structure of created being as created. As long as finite being is with us, the Thomistic analysis will be worth listening to. Metaphysicians work at a deeper level in asking the question "Why?" than scientists do when they ask the question "How?"

And perhaps this is the place to say that Thomas Aquinas never claimed that the five ways for trying to prove God's

existence, placed as they are in the *Summa* immediately after
the declaration that God's existence is not self-evident to us,
were "his proofs." He places them under the authority of
pagan philosophers and of some Christian predecessors.
Sillem's book is of great help here. The fact that there is
only *one* God seems to emerge when God is seen as *esse* or
being. Long before Thomas wrote the *Summa*, he had written at Paris the little metaphysical masterpiece *On Being and
Essence*. There Thomas argued, as Aristotle never did:

> Therefore everything that is such that its existence
> is other than its nature must have its existence from
> another. And because everything that exists through
> another is led back to that which exists through it-
> self as to its first cause, there must be one thing
> which is the cause of existence in all things because
> it alone is the ACT-OF-BEING.

Since no other being has its existence by its own essence,
neither can it cause existence in another; therefore, wherever
there is anything at all, God must be *present* as the giver of
existence, actively giving it, dynamically developing it in and
with the natural forces of the agent or person. (This is the
natural presence of God within us, which grounds the life of
grace—consciousness and communication.)

Now in positing his immovable First Mover as a thinking
thought, Aristotle had guaranteed the purity of the highest
act by enclosing it in the splendor of divine isolation. Aristotle's God is not merely "separated" as ontologically distinct
from all else, but as ontologically absent from all else. The
only kind of presence he can fittingly exercise in things is the
desire that they experience for him, and this keeps matter
and form moving. This desire is not present in the unmoved
mover. It is quite otherwise in Thomas Aquinas's world. The
relation of things to God is defined there in the order of
existence. This results in a depth of dependence. Neither
Aristotle's language nor Plato's can express this. Perhaps the
reason why so many of Aquinas's contemporaries missed the
originality of his contribution was that they did not speak the
language of existence.

The fact that existence or being is the bond uniting all things in the world to one another and to God makes the universe of St. Thomas a religious universe. In their very existence, which after all seems a common enough characteristic, things resemble their cause. Herein lies the true meaning of the proofs for the existence of God as understood by Thomas Aquinas—we come to him-who-is by starting with those objects or subjects of which it can be said that they *are*. Such a proof is a posteriori, it is empirical when empirical is not restricted to describing one type of experience: sensible only.

> . . . from what has already been proved, God is Being itself, of itself subsistent (*ipsum esse per se subsistens*). Consequently, he must contain within himself the whole *perfection of being*.

Therefore, to say that God is infinite being is not to say that he is an abstraction or some physical force, but it is to say that he is personal being. And so when God is creatively present within all things, God is consciously and lovingly present. Man participates more fully in being than animal structures or plant structures do. And so to be human is to have personal being, as our experience reveals. One of the privileges of personal being is to come by any number of ways to self-knowledge. And when the self is truly known, there is knowledge of God's existence.

Uncreated Being: God

Created Being: Nature

I. UNCREATED BEING: GOD

1. HIS EXISTENCE

Theism Undemonstrated *Summa of Christian Teaching*
I, 10, 11, 12

Any attempt to prove God's existence seems useless to those
people who claim that there can be no argument about a
self-evident and indemonstrable truth when the contrary is
an intellectual impossibility. . . .

Their conviction comes from custom. From childhood men
are accustomed to hear and call upon the name of God.
Now, custom becomes second nature, especially when it has
influenced us from an early age; doctrines early imparted
come to be accepted without question. Moreover, what is
evident in itself can be confused with what is evident to
us. . . .

There are others who also declare that any attempt to
prove God's existence is useless, but for very different reasons. Affected by the weakness of the arguments often offered, they declare that this truth cannot be discovered by
reason. According to them, an act of faith in divine revelation is needed.

Demonstration *Summa of Theology* I, q. 2,
a. 2

There can be two procedures in demonstrating anything:
one is through the cause, and is called proof for-the-reason-
that; this kind of demonstration begins with what is prior in
reality. The other takes place through an effect, and is called
a proof insofar-as; and this kind of argument begins with
what is first apparent. When any effect is better known to us
than its cause, we proceed from knowing the effect to knowing its cause. Beginning with an effect, we can demonstrate
the proper cause of its being as long as the effect is more
evident, since if the effect exists, the cause must pre-exist,

inasmuch as every effect depends upon its cause. And thus insofar as God's existence is not self-evident to us, it can be demonstrated by us by beginning with those of his effects that are known to us.

Summa of Theology I, q. 3,
a. 4, ad. 2

Existence can be understood in two senses, one signifying the actuality of being and the other signifying the affirmative judgment made by the mind, which joins subject to predicate. In the first sense, God's existence can be known no more than his essence can; but in the second sense we may be able to know that the proposition we form, namely, that he exists, is true.

Concerning Self-Evidence of   *Summa of Christian Teaching*
God's Existence   I, 11

Nor does it result, as the first argument claimed, that as soon as the significance of the word "God" is understood, we know that God exists. First, because not all know, even those who agree that there is a God, that God is that reality than which no greater can be thought, since there were many ancient thinkers who asserted that this world is God. Nor from the significance of the word "God" as taught by Damascene can such conclusions come. Second, because even allowing that everyone understands this word "God" as signifying something than which no greater can be thought, it does not follow that something than which no greater can be thought does exist in reality. For a thing exists just as its name signifies. Now, from the fact that we understand intellectually what the word "God" is intended to signify, nothing follows except that God is in the intellect. Therefore it will not follow that the reality than which nothing greater can be thought is elsewhere than in the intellect. And hence it does not follow that there exists in reality something than which no greater can be thought. And so this is no argument against those who state that God does not exist, since no matter what is said to exist either in reality or in the intellect, nothing prevents someone from thinking of some greater thing, unless it be stipulated that there is in reality something than which no greater can be thought. . . .

Again, just because we may think that God does not exist, we may not conclude that we can therefore think of something greater than God. For we can think that God does not exist not because of any imperfection in his being or any uncertainty connected with it, since his being is in itself supremely evident, but because of the weakness of our intellect, which can know him not in himself but in his effects, and thus by reasoning it comes to know that he exists.

And this also answers the third argument. For just as it is self-evident to us that a whole is greater than its part, so to those who see the very essence of God, it is most evident that God exists, since his essence is his existence. But since we cannot see his essence, we come to know his existence not in himself but in his effects.

God's Existence Known Not Merely by Faith
Summa of Theology I, q. 2, a. 2, ad. 1

Our position is also challenged by some whose opinion would render useless the efforts of those trying to prove that God exists. For they assert that by reason we cannot discover that God exists, and that such knowledge is had only through faith and revelation.

Some were moved to assert this because of the poor arguments used by some people to prove God's existence.

Quite possibly but falsely, this error might be grounded upon the statements of some philosophers who demonstrate that essence and existence are the same in God, namely, the answer to the question, "What is he?" is the same as the answer to the question, "Is he?". Certainly we cannot by any reasoning process come to the knowledge of *what* God is. It will appear therefore impossible to prove by reason *whether* God is.

Again: If, according to the philosopher's system, we must begin with a name's significance to prove whether the thing exists, and since according to the philosopher (*Metaph.* 4) *a name's significance is its definition,* without knowledge of the divine essence or quiddity, we shall have no means to prove God's existence.

Again: If the principles of demonstration are made known to us originally through the senses, as is shown in the *Posterior Analytics* I: 18, whatever is beyond sense and sensible objects is apparently unprovable. But such is God's existence. Therefore it cannot be proven.

The error of this view is first seen by the art of demonstration, from which we learn to conclude causes from effects; second, by the very order of the sciences, for if no substance beyond sensible substance can be an object of knowledge, there will be no science above Physics. . . . third, by the efforts of the philosophers who have tried to prove God's existence; fourth, by the truth of the Apostle who asserts (Rom. 1: 20): "the invisible things of God are clearly seen, being understood by the things that are made."

Nor should we be affected by the contention of the first argument that essence and existence are the same in God. For this should be referred to the existence by which God subsists in himself, and of this kind of subsistence we are ignorant as we are of his essence. But it does not refer to the existence signified by intellectual judgment, for we can prove the existence of God in this way as when by demonstrative arguments our intellect is led to form the proposition affirming that God exists.

In addition: We need not use the divine essence or quiddity as the middle term when we argue to prove God's existence, as supposed by the second objection; but in the place of the quiddity as middle term we take his effects, as is done in a posteriori reasoning, and from these effects we get the significance of this word "God," for all the divine names are derived either from the difference between God's effects and himself or from a certain relationship between his effects and God.

Likewise it is obvious from the fact that, although God transcends all sensible things and senses, yet his effects, from which we derive the proof of his existence, are sensible things. And so our knowledge originates from the senses, even when it is knowledge of things transcending them.

The fact that God exists and similar truths about him that

are knowable by strict reasoning are not articles of faith but preambles to them. Just as grace presupposes nature, and perfection presupposes the capacity for perfection, so faith presupposes natural knowledge. Yet nothing stops any man from accepting as an article of faith something that can be scientifically known and proven, although perhaps not by him.

Causes   *Commentary on Metaphysics*
                                            V, 1, 2

Aristotle names the kinds of causes and reduces them to four types. He notes first that cause means the immanent matter within which anything comes to be and that exists within it. This he says in order to emphasize its difference from privation or a contrary state from which something is said to originate but that does not stay within, as when something white is made from something black or nonwhite. But whenever any statue is fashioned from bronze or a cruet from silver, these materials are within the product, for bronze is not eliminated by statue nor silver by cruet. These things are material causes.

Second, cause refers to the form or structure or type of a thing. Such is the formal cause, and it brings about an effect in two ways: either as an intrinsic form (when it is called a specific form), or as the extrinsic form after whose likeness the thing is fashioned, and in this way the exemplar of a thing is called its form, which accounts for Plato saying that ideas were forms. The genus and species of anything that the definition of its nature states is determined by the form. Hence the form that is what the Aristotelian "what it was for it to be" means is that which determines *what* a thing is, for the definition, although it includes the material parts, emphasizes the form.

Third, cause signifies the first principle of change and of rest when it is the moving or efficient cause. Aristotle speaks indiscriminately of change and rest, for natural motion and rest are related to the same cause as are violent movement and forced rest. He cites two instances: of the adviser whose counsel causes a certain policy, and of the father who is cause of his child; these include the two principles of efficient motion, namely, will and natural determinism. Generally speaking, all makers are causes of what is made, and all changers of changing things. That is rightly classified as an efficient cause when it makes anything in any way in regard to substance or accidents. Aristotle links maker with changer; the former is the cause of a thing, the latter of its becoming.

Fourth, cause signifies the aim, that for the sake of which something is. Health, for example, is the cause of going for a walk. The question, "Why?" expects a cause. And this involves not only the ultimate aim for which the efficient cause acts but likewise all the intervening means.

Causes of Becoming and of Being · *Summa of Theology* I, q. 104, a. 1

An effect depends upon its cause only insofar as that is its cause. We should note that a cause may be a cause of the coming of the effect and not directly of its existing. We can find examples both in artificial and natural events. A builder causes the construction of a house but not the house that endures; that is caused by the consistence of the components. Any efficient principle that is not the cause of a natural form in itself is the cause of a becoming; it is not the direct cause of the resulting thing. With two things specifically identical, one cannot be the direct cause of the other's specific form, since they are therein identical. But one may be the cause of the other's coming to be in this or that definite matter, as when one man generates another. In other words, it is the cause of a becoming.

But whenever an effect comes from any cause different in nature, the latter may then be the cause of form itself and not merely of its coming into such matter. In that case it will be the cause of a being, not merely of a becoming. Just as the becoming of a thing must end when the action of its cause ceases, the being of a thing cannot endure when the action of its cause has ceased.

Need for Principal Cause · *Compendium of Theology*, 3

Since anything moved by another is a sort of instrument, all things in motion would be instruments if there were no first mover. Moreover, if there were an infinite series of movers and things in motion and yet no first mover, all these infinite movers and things moved would be instruments. Even without any specialized knowledge we can realize what is ridiculous in the notion of any instrument that is not put into motion by a principal: This would be like saying that a saw or ax but no workman was at work in the making of a bed or chest.

Meaning of Motion   *Summa of Christian Teaching*
                              I, 13

It should be noticed that Plato, who speaks of movers in motion (*Phaedrus,* 245c; *Laws,* 893b–896b) understands the term *motion* in a wider sense than does Aristotle, who keeps to its restricted sense of a potential act of a subject in potentiality, which applies only to quantified and material reality (*Physics,* 201). Whenever Plato speaks of anything not a body moving itself, for him this motion includes such actions as understanding and thinking. In other places Aristotle likewise speaks this way, as when he speaks of the first mover moving itself by understanding and willing and loving itself (*De Anima,* 433b15). There is no contradiction here, for it comes to the same thing whether with Plato we come to the first being, which moves itself, or with Aristotle to the first being, which is wholly immutable.

Infinite Series Impossible   *Summa of Christian Teaching*
                                       I, 73

An infinite series of efficient causes in essential subordination is impossible. The causes that are essentially needed to produce any definite effect cannot therefore be multiplied infinitely, as though a block could be lifted by a crowbar, which in its turn is levered by a hand, and so on to infinity.

But an infinite series of causes accidentally subordinated is not considered impossible as long as the totality of causes thus multiplied are assembled as one cause, with their multiplication as incidental to the causality at work. A blacksmith, for example, may operate with many hammers because one after another breaks in his hand, but that any one particular hammer be used after another particular one is incidental.

It is appropriate to divine providence to utilize things according to their manner of being. The action of anything follows its form, which is the principle of action. Now, a voluntary agent acts through no definite form, inasmuch as the will acts when a form is apprehended by the intellect, since the apprehended form objectively moves the will. But there is no definite form of any effect in the intellect, which naturally understands a multitude of forms, and thus the will can produce a plurality of effects. It is not, therefore, appropriate for divine providence to exclude freedom of the will.

The Five Ways Philosophers Have Proven God's Existence

Summa of Theology I, q. 2, a. 3

God's existence can be proven in five ways. First and most obvious is the way that begins with "change." It is obvious that some things in the world are undoubtedly in the process of changing. But anything undergoing change is being changed by something else. This is the case with anything in the process of changing, because it does not yet possess the perfection toward which it is changing, although it is capable of it; whereas anything causing change must already have the perfection it is causing, for to cause a change is to bring into existence what previously was capable of existing, and only something that already exists can do this (just as fire as actually hot causes wood, capable of being hot, to become actually hot, and in this way causes the wood to change). Now, the same thing cannot be simultaneously both actually and potentially x; but it can be actually x and potentially y (the actually hot cannot be simultaneously potentially hot, although it can be potentially cold). Therefore, whatever is in the process of changing cannot cause its own changing; it cannot change itself. Anything in the process of changing is therefore being changed by something else. Moreover, if this something else is in the process of changing, it itself is being changed by another thing, and this by another. Now, the changing has to stop somewhere [i.e., there must be something unchanging], or else there will be no first cause of the changing and, consequently, no subsequent causes; for only when acted upon by the first cause do intermediate causes produce any change (if the stick is not moved by the hand, nothing else is moved by the stick). And so we have to come to some first cause of changing that is not itself changed by anything else, and this is what everyone understands by God.

The second way is derived from the nature of causation. In the sensible world we find causes in an order of succession; we never see, nor could we, anything causing itself, for then it would have to pre-exist itself, and this is impossible. Any such succession of causes must begin somewhere, for in it a primary cause influences an intermediate, and the intermediate a last (whether the intermediate be one or many). Now, if you eliminate a cause, you also eliminate its effects, so that you cannot have a last cause or an intermediate one without having a first cause. Without an origin to the series of causes, and hence no primary cause, no intermediate causes would function and therefore no last effect, but the facts seem to contradict this [the effects are present]. We must therefore suppose a First Cause, which all call "God."

The third way is drawn from the existence of the unnecessary and the necessary, and proceeds as follows. Our experience includes things certainly capable of existing but apparently unnecessary, since they come and go, coming to birth or dying. But if it is unnecessary for a thing to exist, it did not exist once upon a time, and yet everything cannot be like this, for if everything is unnecessary, there was once nothing. But if such were the case, there would now be nothing, because a nonexistent can only be brought into existence by something already existing. So that if ever there was nothing, not a thing could be brought into existence, and there would be nothing now, which contradicts the facts. And so not everything can be an unnecessary kind of being; there must exist some being that necessarily exists. But a thing that necessarily exists may or may not have this necessity from something else. But just as we must begin somewhere in a succession of causes, the case is the same with any succession of things that necessarily exist and receive this necessity from others. Hence we are compelled to suppose something that exists necessarily, having this necessity only from itself; in fact, it itself is the cause why other things exist.

The fourth way is supported by the gradation noticed in things. There are some things that are more good, more true, more noble, and so forth, and other things less so. But such comparisons denote different degrees of approach to a superlative; for instance, things are hotter and hotter the closer they approach what is hottest. There is therefore a truest and best and most noble thing, and so most fully existing. Now *when many things share some property, whatever possesses it most fully causes it in others:* "Fire," to use Aristotle's example, the hottest of all things, causes all other things to be hot. There is, therefore, something that causes in all other things their being, their goodness, and any other perfection they possess. And this we call "God."

The fifth way is taken from the ordered tendencies of nature. A direction of actions to an end is detected in all bodies following natural laws even when they are without awareness, for their action scarcely ever varies and nearly always succeeds; this indicates that they do tend toward a goal, not merely succeeding by accident. Anything, however, without awareness, tends to a goal only under the guidance of someone who is aware and knows; the arrow, for instance, needs an archer. Everything in nature, consequently, is guided to its goal by someone with knowledge, and this one we call "God."

God Is To-Be
Summa of Theology I, q. 3, a. 4, c

Not only is God his own essence . . . but he is also his own existence (*esse*). There are numerous ways of showing this. First, whatever anything has in addition to its essence has to be caused either by the principles establishing that essence (as a property necessarily found with the species—for example, the capacity for laughter in man—is caused by the principles establishing the species), or by some extrinsic agent, as warmth is caused in water by fire. And so if a thing's existence is other than its essence, this existence must be caused by the thing's essential principles or by some extrinsic agent. But nothing having a caused existence can be its own sufficient cause of existing, and so it is impossible for anything's existence to be caused by the essential principles that compose it. Thus anything whose existence is other than its essence must have its existence caused by another. But this cannot be the case with God, inasmuch as he is spoken of as the First Efficient Cause. It is therefore impossible for God's existence to differ from his essence. Second, existence is that which brings into actuality every form or nature; for goodness and humanity are said to be actual only when they are said to be existing. So existence must be related to essence, if the latter is really distinct from it, as act to potentiality. Since God is without any potentiality, essence consequently does not differ from existence in him. His essence is therefore his existence. Third, inasmuch as that which has fire, yet itself is not fire, is on fire by participation, so that which has existence but is not existence is a being by participation. But, as previously shown, God is his own essence; and so if he is not his own existence, he will not be essential being but participated being. He will not therefore be the first being, a position involving absurdity. God is therefore his own existence and not merely his own essence.

God Is Unique *Compendium of Theology*, c. 15

It is clearly conclusive that there can be only one God. If there were many gods this name would be given them either univocally or equivocally. If equivocally, it is useless to continue the discussion, for there is nothing to prevent others from using the word "god" for what we call a stone. If they are called gods univocally, this must be because they are the same in genus or in species. But we have just proven that God can neither be a genus nor a species grouping many individuals under him. Consequently, a number of gods is impossible.

Moreover, whatever individuates a common essence is not multiplied. Although many men can exist, this particular man can only be one. If any essence, therefore, is individuated through itself, it cannot be multiplied. But the divine essence is through itself individuated, inasmuch as God's essence is not distinct from his existence, since we have proven that God is his essence. So there cannot be more than one God.

We also have the following reflection. It is possible to multiply any form in two ways: first, by specific differences as with a generic form (in this way is color differentiated into various species of color); second, by the subjects in which it inheres, for example, whiteness. So any form that does not exist in a subject and cannot be multiplied by specific differences is not able to be multiplied at all. Hence there could only be one whiteness if it were to subsist outside a subject. But the divine essence is existence itself (*ipsum esse*), which admits of no specific differences, as we saw (c. 13). And so because the divine essence is a self-subsistent quasiform, inasmuch as God is his existence, there cannot be more than one divine essence. So a multiplicity of gods cannot exist.

Existence of Creator God   *Summa of Theology* I, q. 44, a. 2, c

The ancient philosophers slowly and by degrees advanced toward knowledge of truth. Not at first intellectually refined, they failed to recognize anything existing except sensible bodies. And those who noticed movement considered it only in relation to certain accidents, rarefaction and condensation by union and separation. Having presupposed material substance to be uncreated, they merely accounted for accidental changes through such causes as affinity, discord, intellect, or something like these. They progressed by understanding that substantial form was distinguished from matter, which they imagined as uncreated. And when they recognized corporeal things to change in their essential forms, they attributed these changes to certain universal causes: the oblique circle with Aristotle (*On Generation* 2) or ideas with Plato. But we should realize that matter is limited by its form to a certain determined species, just as a substance of any one species is limited by an incoming accident to a determined kind of being: for example, man by whiteness. In each of these opinions, therefore, *being* was regarded under a special aspect, either as *this* or as *such,* and so they designated special efficient causes for things. But others raised their thinking to focus on *being* as being, and these designated a cause for things not as *these* nor as *such,* but as *beings.*

Therefore, whatever is the cause of things considered as beings has to be the cause of things not only insofar as they are *such* by accidental forms nor insofar as they are *these* by substantial forms, but also in regard to everything belonging to them in any way at all. And so we must conclude that prime matter is also created by the universal cause of things.

2. CREATION

Summa of Theology I, q. 45, a. 1

We must reflect upon not only the coming forth of a particular being from a particular agent but also the coming forth of all being from the universal cause, which is God; and this coming forth we call creation. Now, when from one particular thing there arises another, this was once nonexistent; as when a man is born, he did not previously exist, but man arises from nonman and white from nonwhite. And so with regard to the coming forth of universal being from the First Cause, it is likewise impossible that any being should be presupposed. Hence just as the birth of a man is from the nonbeing that is nonman, so creation, which is the coming forth of all being, is from nonbeing, which is *nothing.*

Exemplarism in Creation   *Summa of Theology* I, q. 44, a. 3

God is the first exemplary cause of everything. We are assured of this by realizing that an exemplar is needed for producing anything that is to have a definite form. An artist produces a definite form in matter because of the exemplar that he beholds externally or conceives internally. But it is obvious that natural things have definite forms. But the first principle of the determining forms must be the divine wisdom that planned the order of the universe, one of great variety. And we must therefore assert that the exemplars or types of all things are in the divine wisdom, and these types we have called ideas, i.e., exemplar-forms existing in the divine mind (q. 15, a. 1). And although there are many such ideas because they are related to things, they are not really anything else than the divine essence as reflected in the various things diversely sharing a likeness to it. And so it is in this way that God himself is the first exemplar of everything.

Creation as Communication   *Summa of Theology* I, q. 44, a. 4

Every agent acts for an end; otherwise, only by chance would definite results come from an agent's action. Now, the end of the agent and of the recipient differ in respect to each, but the end as such is the same; for what the agent intends to produce and the recipient intends to receive is the one same thing. Yet some things are both agent and recipient simultaneously; these are imperfect agents, and it is characteristic of these even when acting to intend to acquire something. But it is not characteristic of the First Agent, who is agent only, to act to gain some end; he intends only to communicate his perfection, i.e., his goodness. Every creature, however, intends to gain its own perfection, i.e., the likeness of the divine perfection and goodness. Therefore, the end of all things is the divine goodness.

Creation a Relation, Not a   *Summa of Theology* I, q. 45,
Change   a. 3

Because whatever is created is not already something that is moved or changed, creation is accomplished by a relation within the thing created, for anything made through changing or moving must have pre-existed. This certainly occurs when particular things are produced, but this is impossible in the production of being by the universal cause of all being, which is God. So God without change produces things when he creates them. Now, only relation remains when movement is deprived of action and reception. . . . Therefore, in the creature, creation consists in a certain relation to the Creator as to the principle of its being; just as in reception, which implies change, a relation to the principle of this change is implied.

Creation by Will   *On the Power of God*, q. 3, a. 15 and ad. 1, ad. 2

According to the philosopher (*Metaph.* 9: 16) action is of two kinds: one remaining within the agent whose action and perfection it is, such as to know, to will, etc.; the other going from the agent into an external recipient that it activates and perfects, such as to heat, to move, etc. But God's action is not of this latter kind because his essence is his very action, which therefore does not go forth from him. And so it must be understood to be that former kind of action present in anyone having intellect and will, or even a sense faculty which, nevertheless, is not found with God because sensation, while not going forth to an external object, is caused by its action. Hence, whatever is accomplished by God is accomplished by knowing and willing. Nor does this argument take from the natural character of the Son's begetting, for the term of the begetting was not anything external to the divine essence. It must therefore be maintained that every creature came from God by his will and not from any natural necessity.

ad. 1. The analogy of Dionysius [goodness diffusing itself like the sun] should be considered as referring to the universality of diffusion. Just as the sun illuminates all bodies without favoritism, so is it also with God's goodness. But this does not imply the absence of will.

ad. 2. The likeness of the divine nature is communicated to creatures because of its perfection. Yet this communication was made voluntarily, not from natural necessity.

Creation a Continuous Action   *On the Power of God*, q. 5, a. 1

We must certainly admit that things are kept in existence by God, and without God they would instantly become nothing. We may prove this as follows. An effect necessarily depends upon its cause. This belongs to the very nature of cause and effect; this is obvious in regard to formal and material causes, since whenever any material or formal principle is withdrawn, a thing immediately stops existing because these principles comprise its essence. But this applies also to efficient causes as well as to formal and material causes, inasmuch as the efficient cause makes a thing by disposing the matter or inducing a form. And so a thing depends equally upon its efficient cause as upon its matter and form because it depends upon one through the other. We can say the same of final causes, since the end is a cause insofar as it moves the efficient cause to act, for it is first in intention, although not in existence. Therefore, where there is no final cause, there is no action. And so insofar as the existence of anything made depends upon its form, it depends upon its efficient cause. But the form of a made thing can depend upon an efficient cause only indirectly instead of directly as a form; so the form of an enkindled fire does not directly depend upon the enkindling fire specifically inasmuch as it exists to the same degree in reality, the same form of fire in both, distinguished only materially by occupying other matter. Thus because the enkindled fire has its form from a cause, this very form must depend upon a higher principle, which is directly the cause of that form as a species. And since, strictly speaking, the existence of a form in matter requires only accidental movement or change, and because only moved bodies act, as the philosopher proves, it necessarily follows that the principle upon which the form directly depends has to be an incorporeal reality, for the effect depends upon its active cause through the action of a principle. And if any corporeal principle is cause of a form in any way, it is this in virtue of an incorporeal principle, as its instrument. This is indeed necessary for the form to begin existing, which it does not do except in matter, since matter cannot receive form without a special disposition, inasmuch as there is an appropriate matter for every actuality. And so when matter is unsuitably disposed to a special form, it cannot directly receive the form from an incorporeal principle upon which the form directly depends, and so there must be something to change the matter: this will be a corporeal agent, whose activity is to change another. This corporeal agent acts through the power of the incorporeal principle, its action terminating in this or that form insofar as this or that form is within the corporeal agent either actually (as with universal agents) or virtually (as in equivocal agents). And so these inferior corporeal agents are not the cause of the forms in made things except as causing material change, since they only act by disposing matter, as previously explained (q. 3, a. 7, 8), and this is done by modifying matter and educing form from the potentiality of matter. So the form of anything generated naturally depends upon the generator to the extent that it is educed from the potentiality of matter, but not as to its absolute existence. Consequently, when the generating action stops, the eduction of the form from potential into actual being, i.e., the *becoming* of what is generated, stops, whereas the form itself, whereby what is generated gets its existence, does not cease. And so the existence of what is generated but not its becoming remains after the generating action stops. Yet forms that do not exist in matter (such as intellectual substances) or that exist in matter always disposed to the form without any contrary dispositions (such as the heavenly bodies) must come from a principle that is an incorporeal agent not acting by movement; nor are these dependent upon anything for their *becoming* without also depending upon it for their *being*. And so when the action of an incorporeal agent ends, the very existence of things created by it ends, just as when the action by movement of an efficient cause ends, the becoming of the thing generated instantly ends. But this incorporeal agent by whom all things, corporeal as well as incorporeal, are created, is God, as was previously shown (q. 3, a. 5, 6, 8), from whom everything receives not only its form but also its matter. And in regard to this question it is inconsequential whether God made everything immediately, or in a certain order, as maintained by some philosophers. It follows therefore that if the divine action should cease, all things would drop into nothingness instantly. . . .

Continual Creation   *Summa of Theology* I, q. 104,
                                a. 1 and ad. 1, ad. 2

We are bound to say both by reason and by faith that
creatures are kept existing by God. By way of clarification
it should be pointed out that there are two ways for one
thing to preserve another. First, indirectly and accidentally,
as when a person who removes the cause of anything's corruption is said to preserve it, as a man preventing a child
from falling into a fire is spoken of as preserving the child.
God does in this way keep some things in existence, but not
all, inasmuch as it is unnecessary to keep naturally incorruptible things from corrupting. Second, one thing is said to
preserve another independently (per se) and directly, namely,
when what is preserved so depends upon another that it
cannot exist without it. In this way all creatures must be
preserved by God. For every creature's existence so depends
upon God that it could not subsist for a moment but would
cease to be anything if God by his divine action did not preserve it in existence, as Gregory says (*Moral.* xvi).

This is made evident by the following: Every effect depends upon its cause insofar as the latter is its cause. But we
should be aware that an agent may cause the *becoming* of
its effect and not directly cause its *being*. Artificial and natural things reveal this (for example, a builder causes the
becoming of a house but is not the direct cause of its *being*).
Evidently the being of a house results from its form or the
assembling and arranging of materials as well as from the
natural qualities of these materials. A cook prepares food by
using fire's natural activity; a builder makes a house by using
cement, stones, and wood, which can be ordered for the
house's preservation. Therefore the *being* of a house depends
upon the nature of these materials just as its *becoming* depends upon the builder's action. This same principle holds
for things of nature; for if no agent causes the form itself,
it will not be the cause of the *being* resulting from that form,
but the agent will be the cause of only the *becoming* of the
effect.

It is evident, however, that when there are two things of

the same species, it is not possible for one to cause directly the very form of the other, inasmuch as it would then be the cause of its own form, which is identical essentially to the form of the other; but it is possible for it to cause the form insofar as it is in matter, i.e., it may cause *this matter* to receive *this form*. To do this is to cause the *becoming*, as when man generates man, and fire causes fire. And so whenever a natural effect can aptly receive from its acting cause an impression specifically identical with that in the acting cause, then the *becoming* of the effect, not its *being*, depends upon the agent.

Yet often the effect does not possess any aptitude to receive from its cause the impression as it exists in the agent, as is evident in all agents not producing any effect of the same species as themselves: The heavenly bodies cause the generation of other bodies specifically different from themselves. An agent of this kind can cause the form itself and not merely cause it to exist in matter, and so it is also the cause of *being*, not merely the cause of *becoming*.

When therefore the action of the agent causing an effect's *becoming* ceases, the becoming of the thing cannot continue; so neither can the *being* of anything continue when there ceases the agent's action that causes the effect in its *being*, not merely in its *becoming*. Hence hot water remains hot when the fire's action ceases, whereas air does not remain illuminated even momentarily when the sun ceases to shine on it; for water is a matter receptive of fire's heat just as heat exists in fire. And so if it were brought back to the perfect form of fire, it always would keep that form; but when having the form of fire imperfectly and inchoately, the heat will remain only for a time because of the imperfect participation in the principle of heat. But air has not the nature that would allow it to receive light just as it exists in the sun, the principle of light. And thus when the sun's action ceases, so does the light, because it has no root in the air.

Every creature may be related to God as is the air to the sun illuminating it. For as the sun by its nature has light while the air is illuminated by participating in the sun's nature, so only God is being by the power of his own essence, inasmuch as his essence is his existence.

But every creature has being by participation, and so its essence is not its existence. Thus, as Augustine says (*Literal Commentary on Genesis* IV, 12): "If the ruling power of God were removed from his creatures, their nature would cease immediately, and all nature would collapse." In the same work (VIII, 12) he says: "As the air becomes light by the presence of the sun, so is man illuminated by the presence of God, and in his absence returns immediately to darkness."

ad. 1. Being is caused naturally from the form of a creature, granted the influence of the divine action, just as light is caused by the air's diaphanous nature, granted the sun's action. Hence in spiritual creatures and heavenly bodies the potentiality to nonexistence is rather referred to God, who is able to remove his influence, than to something within the form or matter of those creatures.

ad. 2. God cannot allow a creature to be preserved in existence after the divine influence ceases, just as he cannot allow it not to have received existence from himself. Inasmuch as the being of an effect depends upon the cause of its being, the creature needs to be preserved in existence by God. This is not the case with an agent, which causes only the becoming and not the being of the effect.

3. OUR KNOWLEDGE OF GOD

On Speaking of God   *Summa of Christian Teaching*
                                           I, 32

It is obvious from what has been said that we cannot predicate any quality of God and other things univocally; for when an effect does not receive the same specific form as its causing agent, it cannot be called in any univocal sense the name referring to that form (for example, the sun and the heat given off by the sun are not in any univocal sense called hot). Now, the forms of things whose cause is God never arrive at being divine species because they receive in a divided way and particularly what is in God absolutely and universally.

It is therefore clear that nothing can be said univocally of God and of other things.

Moreover, whatever is predicated univocally of many things belongs to each of these things by participation; thus the species is said to participate in the genus, and the individual in the species. But of God nothing is predicated by participation, because whatever is participated is restricted to the kind of participated thing, and so it is possessed partially and not as a universal perfection. The result is that nothing is univocally predicated of God and other things.

How Creatures Are Like God   *Summa of Christian Teaching*
I, 29

Effects that are not as great as their causes have not the same name and reality, and yet between them there must be some likeness, for the nature of action requires that any action produced should be like the agent, inasmuch as everything acts according to its own actuality. Although the form of the effect is somehow present in its transcendent cause, because it is there very differently, the cause is called *equivocal*. Thus the sun causes heat in lesser bodies by acting according to its actuality; and so the heat sent forth by the sun necessarily resembles the sun's active power to cause heat in lesser bodies and by reason of which the sun is called hot, although very differently. And so it is said to resemble somewhat everything that it effectively influences, but nevertheless it is unlike them all, inasmuch as its effects have not heat, etc. in the same way that the sun has heat. God likewise gives all perfections to things and he, therefore, is both like them and unlike them.

And so it is that Holy Scripture often recalls this likeness between God and his creatures, as when it is said (Gen. 1: 26): "Let us make man to our image and likeness"; while at other times this likeness is denied, according to the words of Is. 40: 18: "To whom then have you likened God; or what image will you make for him?" and in Ps. 82: 1: "O God, who shall be like to Thee?"

Dionysius agrees with this argument, for he states (*Divine Names* IX): "The same things are like and unlike to God;

like, according as they imitate him, as far as they can, who is not perfectly imitable; unlike, according as effects are not as great as their causes."

In regard to this likeness, however, it is more appropriate to say that the creature is like God than vice versa. For one thing is like another when it has the same quality or form. But since what is in God perfectly is present in other things by way of an imperfect participation, whatever they are alike in belongs to God absolutely, but not so to the creature. And so the creature possesses what belongs to God and is rightly said, therefore, to be like God. But we cannot also say that God has what belongs to his creature, and so neither is it appropriate to say that God is like his creature; as we do not say that a man is like his portrait, even though we state that his portrait is like him. . . .

What Can Be Attributed to God
Summa of Christian Teaching I, 30

As a follow-up we should treat what is possible and impossible to be predicated of God; also, what is predicated only of God, and of him along with other beings.

Because every creaturely perfection is present in God although in another, superexcellent way, whatever terms denote absolute perfection without any defect are predicated of God and of other things—such terms as goodness, wisdom, etc. But any term that denotes perfections modified by a creaturely limitation cannot be predicated of God except in the manner of simile and metaphor, as when anything belonging to one thing is applied to another—for example, when a man is called a stone because he is intellectually dense. Such are the terms used to denote the species of any creature, such as *man* and *stone;* for there is an appropriate kind of perfection and being belonging to each species, and it is the same with terms signifying the properties that are caused by the principles proper to the species; therefore, these can only be predicated of God metaphorically. But terms expressing these perfections in the superexcellent way they belong to God are predicated only of God, for example, the *sovereign good,* the *First Being,* etc.

I say, however, that some of these terms denote perfection without defect in regard to what the term is used to signify, but every term is defective as to its manner of signifying. For our terms express things as conceived by our intellect; and our intellect, whose knowledge originates in the senses, conceives things after the manner of sensible objects whose form is distinct from the subject of the form because they are composed of matter and form. There is certainly a simple form in these things but an imperfect one since it is not self-subsistent, while, although the subject of the form is subsistent, it is not simple, but rather a concrete sensible. And so whatever our intellect signifies as subsistent is signified concretely, whereas whatever it signifies as simple is signified not as subsisting but as qualifying. And so all the terms we use are imperfect in their manner of signifying, and this imperfection is unsuitable to God, although what is signified is appropriate to God in a superexcellent way, as apparent in the term "goodness" or "the good"; for "goodness" signifies in the manner of nonsubsistence, and "the good" signifies concretely. Accordingly, no term is suitably applied to God but only according to what the term is used to signify. And so, as Dionysius teaches (*On the Heavenly Hierarchy* II, 3), such terms may be either affirmed or denied of God: affirmed because of what the term signifies, denied because of its manner of signifying. Now, the way of superexcellence in which the previous perfections are present in God cannot be expressed in terms of our ordinary usage except either by negation, as when we say that God is *infinite* or *eternal,* or by relating him to other things, as when we say that he is the *First Cause* or the *sovereign good.* For we can apprehend not what God is, but what he is not, and the relations of other things to him, as previously explained.

Divine Attributes Not Syno-   *On the Power of God,* q. 7,
nyms   a. 6

All those who have reflected upon the question have decided that these terms are not synonymous. There is no difficulty here for those holding that these expressions do not signify God's essence, but are only certain notions added to his essence or ways the divine action is present in its effects

or the negation of what they signify in creatures. But granted
that they signify the divine essence as proven (a. 5), there
is great difficulty in this question; for then we have all these
terms with one simple signification, namely, the divine essence. But we should note that a term's signification refers
not to the thing immediately but through the medium of the
mind, because words are the signs of the soul's impressions,
and the mind's conceptions are representations of things, according to the philosopher (*On Interpretation* I).

Now, terms may be prevented from being synonymous
either on account of what is signified or on account of what
the term is used to signify and what is conveyed by the term.
And so the terms applied to God cannot be prevented from
being synonymous on account of signifying various things
. . . but only by the various aspects resulting from the mind's
conception. Therefore the commentator (*Metaph.* XI) says
that in God multiplicity comes from the distinctions in our
intellect and not from being, and we express this same situation when we state that God is one in reality and many things
logically. But it is impossible that these various aspects be in
our mind with nothing corresponding to them in the thing,
for the things regarded under these points of view are attributed to God by the mind. . . .

We should say then that all these numerous, diverse notions are likenesses of God and correspond to something in
God; for it is evident that one form can have only one specific likeness equal to it, whereas it can have many imperfect
likenesses, with each one falling short of a perfect representation of the form. Because, therefore, the ideas we conceive
of the perfections noted in creatures are imperfect likenesses
out of all proportion to the divine essence, there is nothing
hindering the one same essence from corresponding to all
these ideas that imperfectly represent it. And so the variety
or multiplicity in these expressions is caused by the intellect,
which is unable to attain to the vision of the divine essence
in itself, but envisions it through many inadequate likenesses
reflected by creatures as by a mirror. If, however, it saw that
very essence, it would neither need to use many terms nor
many conceptions.

Divine Attributes Signify Es-   *On the Power of God,* q. 7,
sence   a. 5

On the contrary, Augustine says (*Trinity* VII, 7) that
God "to be" is to be mighty or wise; such is his simplicity
that whatsoever you may say of him is his essence.

Moreover, Boethius says (*Trinity*) that in whatever category, except relation, we predicate things of God, all these
things refer to his essence; this also applies to *great,* etc.

Moreover, whatever is attributed to another by way of
participation presupposes one to whom they are attributed
per se and essentially. But these expressions are applied to
creatures by way of participation. Since then they are traceable to God as to their first cause, they are therefore predicated of God essentially and, consequently, they signify his
essence. . . .

The Negative Knowledge of   *Summa of Christian Teaching*
God   I, 14

The chief way to consider the divine essence is the way
of negation, for by its immensity the divine essence transcends every form attained by our intellect; and so in apprehending it we do not know what it is. But by *knowing what
it is not* we get some knowledge of it, and the more things we
are able to deny of it, the nearer we come to knowing it. For
we know anything so much the more perfectly the more completely we recognize it as different from others, because everything has in itself its own distinct being. And so when we
understand a thing's definition, we classify it first in a genus,
thus knowing in general what it is, and then we add its differences in order to distinguish it from other things; and so
we get a complete knowledge of a thing's essence.

But because in considering the divine essence we cannot
get any *what*-genus nor express by affirmative differences its
distinction from others, we have to express its distinction by
negative differences. Now, just as with affirmative differences
one is restricted by another so that as the thing is distinguished from more things we come closer to its complete
description, so when one negative difference restricts another,

a thing is more clearly distinguished from others. Hence, when we say that God is not an accident, we are in this way distinguishing him from all accidents; if we add then that he is not a body, we shall be distinguishing him from some substances, and by such negations he will be gradually distinguished from everything except himself; and at last when he is recognized as distinct from everything else, we shall come to consider him appropriately. Our knowledge will not, however, be perfect, inasmuch as we shall not know *what* he is in himself.

Therefore, to advance in knowing God by negation, let us take as a principle what has been already made evident by the previous remarks, namely, that God is altogether unchangeable. This is also confirmed by the authority of Holy Writ. For it is said (Mal. 3: 6): "I am God [Vulg., the Lord] and I change not"; (Ja. 1: 17): "With whom there is no change"; and (Num. 23: 19): "God is not as a man . . . that he should be changed."

No Time with God   *Summa of Christian Teaching*
I, 15

Time is the measure of only those things that are moved; for *time is the measure of motion*, as stated in *Physics*, IV. But God is absolutely unmoved, as already proven. And so we cannot note *before* and *after* in him. In him, therefore, being does not succeed to nonbeing; neither is it possible for him to have nonbeing after being nor any succession in his being, for apart from time such things are meaningless. Therefore he is without beginning and without end, having all his being simultaneously; such is the notion of eternity.

No Passive Potentiality with   *Summa of Christian Teaching*
God   I, 16

From the fact that God is eternal it necessarily follows that he is not in potentiality; for anything whose substance has any potentiality is able by reason of this potentiality not to exist, since a possibility for being is also a possibility for nonbeing. But it is not possible for God in himself not to be, since he is eternal. Therefore there is no potentiality for being in God.

No Matter with God
Summa of Christian Teaching
I, 17

It follows from the above that there is no matter in God, for matter as such is in potentiality.

Moreover, matter is no principle of activity; hence, as the philosopher says, efficient and material causes do not coincide. But it is proper to God to be the First Efficient Cause of things; and so he is not matter.

No Composition with God
Summa of Christian Teaching
I, 18

We can conclude from the above that in God there is no composition. For any composed thing must have potentiality and act, for without the presence of these, several things cannot become a simple unity. For whenever things are united as an assembly or group they become actually one from things that are not one simply. Here the very parts are related as potentiality to the union: for from being potentially unifiable, they become actually united. But there is no potentiality in God. And so in him there is no composition.

No Finitude with God
Summa of Christian Teaching
I, 43

Now inasmuch as infinity follows upon quantity, as philosophers teach (*Physics* 1: 2), infinity as magnitude cannot be attributed to God, since it was proven that there is but one God (ch. 42), and that in him is no composition either of parts or accidents. Since we have shown that he is not a body, we may not say that he is infinite in the manner of continuous quantity. The only thing left is to see whether infinity as spiritual magnitude is appropriate to him.

Spiritual magnitude can refer to two things: to power and to the goodness or perfection of a thing's very nature. For anything is called more or less white in accordance with the degree of perfection in its whiteness. And magnitude of power is measured by magnitude in what is done or made. But here magnitude of power and action are interrelated, for activity springs from something in act, and hence its degree of perfection in activity registers the degree of magnitude in its power. And so spiritual realities are called great in proportion to their degree of perfection; for Augustine states, "in things that are great not by quantity, to be great is to be good" (*Trinity* VI, 8).

And so we must prove that in regard to this kind of magnitude, God is infinite. But in regard to God infinite is not to be understood as a privation, as in quantitative numbers and dimensions, for such a quantity is naturally finite, and calling it infinite would mean a subtraction of what it has by nature, and hence in these quantities infinity denotes imperfection. But with regard to God infinite is used negatively, because his perfection is not bounded or limited, and he is the supremely perfect being; and God is described as infinite in this way.

For whatever is naturally finite is restricted to some generic notion. But God is not in any genus, and his perfection has the perfections of all genera. . . . Therefore, he is infinite.

Moreover, every act inhering in something else is limited by its recipient, since whatever is in another is in it according to the manner of the recipient. And so an act not existing in any subject has no limitations; for example, if *whiteness* were existing in itself, it would not be limited from having anything belonging to the perfection of whiteness. Now, God is an act existing in no way within another, because he is neither form in matter, nor does his being inhere in any form or nature because he is his own being. It follows therefore that he is infinite.

Moreover, being itself, as absolute, is infinite; for it can be participated by an infinite number of things in an infinite variety of ways. And so anything having finite being must be limited by another thing in some way the cause of its being. But because God is necessary in himself, there can be no cause of his being. Hence he has infinite being and he himself is infinite.

Again: Anything having a particular perfection is more perfect insofar as it more fully participates in that perfection.

Now, there can be no real or imagined way for a perfection to be more fully possessed than by whatever is perfect by its essence and whose being is its good—and such is God. And so nothing more perfect than God can be imagined. Therefore he is perfect in goodness.

Omnipotence of God *Compendium of Theology, c. 19*

We can further infer that God is infinite in power, for power follows from a thing's essence; everything possesses a power of activity appropriate to its way of being. If God is, therefore, infinite in his essence, his power must be infinite.

This is evident to all who inspect the gradation of things. Whatever is in potentiality has receptive and passive power, and anything in actuality possesses active power. And so what is only potentiality, namely, prime matter, has an unlimited power of receptivity, but has no active power. And following the scale of being above matter, the more a thing has of form, the more it has the power of acting. And therefore fire is the most active of all the elements. Hence God, who is pure actuality unmixed with potentiality, has active power infinitely beyond all things.

The Divine Perfection *Summa of Christian Teaching I, 28*

. . . According as anything has being, so is its manner of excellence. And so if there is a thing having the full possibility of being, no excellence found in anything is lacking to it. Now, the fullness of being is found in anything that is its own being; so if there were any separate whiteness, no possibility of whiteness would be absent, for something of whiteness is lacking to a particular white thing by a defect in the recipient of whiteness receiving it according to its mode and perhaps not according to the whole possibility of whiteness. God, therefore, who is his own being, as shown previously (I, q. 4, a. 2), possesses being according to the fullness of being itself; and so he is unable to lack any excellence belonging to anything. . . .

But those things having only existence are imperfect, not

because of any imperfection in absolute being itself, for being according to its totality is not theirs, but because they participate in being in a particular and most imperfect way. . . .

Existence Is Perfection
Summa of Theology I, q. 4, a. 1, ad. 3

To exist is the most perfect thing of all, for compared to existence, everything else is potential. Unless it exists, nothing reaches actuality, and so the act of existing is the ultimate actuality of all things, even of every form. Thus things get existence; existence does not acquire things. For in the very expressions "the existence of man" or "the existence of a horse" or of some other thing, it is existence that is considered to be acquired like a form, not that thing to which existence belongs.

God Is Infinite Perfection
Summa of Theology I, q. 4, a. 2

In God exists the perfections of all things. On account of this, we call his perfection "all-encompassing," for, as Averroes states, no kind of excellence is lacking in him. This is shown in two ways.

First, inasmuch as any perfection present in an effect has to be also present in the effect's cause; and this either in the same way when cause and effect are the same kind of thing (as when man begets man), or in a more perfect way when cause and effect are not of the same kind (as when the sun's power produces things having some likeness to the sun). This is because in their causes effects evidently pre-exist potentially. Now, to pre-exist potentially in a cause is to pre-exist in a more perfect, not a less perfect way, although to pre-exist in matter potentially is to pre-exist less perfectly; for even if matter itself is imperfect, agents in themselves are perfect. Since, therefore, God is the primary active cause of all things, all perfections have to pre-exist in him in a superexcellent way. And Dionysius is saying just this by saying that God "does not exist in any qualified manner," but possesses primordially in himself all being, unqualifiedly and unrestrictedly. And he later adds that God is the being of all that subsists.

Perfections in God Are God   *Compendium of Theology, c. 22*

If we synthesize the various topics considered so far, we see that all perfections in God are really one. It has been previously shown that God is simple (ch. 9). But where simplicity is present, the perfections present are undifferentiated. And so if the perfections of all things are in God, they cannot be differentiated in him. And so in him they are all one. . . .

God Is Goodness   *Summa of Theology* I, q. 6, a. 1, c, and ad. 2, 3

Goodness is found above all with God, for goodness follows upon desirability. Now, beings desire their perfection; and the perfection and form of an effect are imagings of its cause, since whatever anything does expresses what it is. So the cause itself is desirable and can be called "good," a share in imaging it being desired. Evidently, therefore, since God is the First Active Cause of all things, goodness and desirability appropriately belong to him. And thus Dionysius attributes goodness to God as the First Active Cause, stating that God is called good as the "source of all subsistence."

In desiring its own perfection everything desires God himself, since, as we noted, the perfections of all things somehow image the divine existence. And thus among beings desirous of God, some know him in himself—such is the prerogative of reasoning creatures; others know his goodness as participated somewhere or other, and this is open even to sense-knowledge; while other beings, without any knowledge, desire by nature, guided to their goal by some higher being with knowledge.

Only God is by nature good.

For anything must be perfect to be called "good." Now, things are good in three ways: first, they are put into existence; in addition, they have some accidents needed to achieve their activity; and a third perfection arises by reaching an extrinsic goal. And so fire's primary perfection consists in existing by its own substantial form; its secondary perfection comes from heat, light, dryness, etc.; and a third perfection is arrival at its appropriate place of repose.

. But this threefold perfection belongs by nature only to God, not to anything caused; for he alone exists by nature, accidents not being added to him (power, wisdom, and so forth belonging to him by nature, whereas in other things they are accidental). He, moreover, is not directed toward any extrinsic goal, but is himself the ultimate goal of all other things. It is, therefore, evident that only God by nature possesses all kinds of perfection. He alone, consequently, is good by nature.

ad. 2. Although all things are good insofar as they exist, yet existence is not the nature of anything created, and so it does not follow that created things are by nature good.

ad. 3. The goodness of any created thing is not its nature, but something additional: either its existence, or some perfection added to it, or some relatedness to a goal. This added goodness, however, is said to be good exactly as it is said to exist. Now, it is said to exist in a certain way, not as something that is existence. And so it is said to be good because what it possesses is good.

God's Ways of Being Present   *Summa of Theology* I, q. 8, a. 3

God is said to have a twofold way of existing in things. First, as an active cause, and in all things he creates he thus exists. Second, as an object exists within the subject-agent whose action attains it (this refers only to mental actions where the known exists in the knower, and the desired in the one desiring). In this way God exists in a privileged manner in those reasoning creatures actually knowing or loving him or disposed to do so. And since we shall see that this comes from a grace conferred upon a reasoning creature, in this special way God is said to exist in holy persons by grace.

But to learn how he exists in other created things we must go to human affairs for our analogy. And so a king, although not present everywhere in his kingdom, is said to exist throughout his kingdom by his power. Moreover, a thing by its presence is said to be present to everything within its field of vision, so that even to a person who does not exist substantially in every part of the house, everything in the house is said to be present. Finally, wherever anything is substantially, it exists in substance.

4. DIVINE ACTIVITY

God as Knowing *Summa of Theology* I, q. 14, a. 1

God knows most perfectly. This becomes clear when we consider that by having only their own form, nonknowing subjects differ from knowing subjects, whose nature it is to have other forms in addition to their own; for in the knower is the likeness of the thing known. Evidently, then, when compared with knowing subjects, the nonknowing subject's nature is more confined and limited. The former have a greater scope and extension, and so Aristotle says that the soul is in some way all things. But form is limited by matter, and that is why we previously said that insofar as forms are free from matter they more and more approach a sort of infinity. It is obvious then that anything's freedom from matter is the reason it can know, and the capacity to know is in proportion to its freedom from matter. Plants, therefore, are called nonknowing by reason of their materiality. But the senses, inasmuch as they can receive the likenesses of things without matter, can know; and the intellect, since it is even freer from matter and simple, is still more capable of knowing, as we read in Aristotle. And so because God is immaterial in the highest degree . . . it follows that he has knowledge in the highest degree.

Divine Knowledge Is God *Summa of Theology* I, q. 14, a. 2

God knows himself through himself. This is obvious if we consider that although with activities productive of an ex-

ternal effect, the objective or aim or end of the activity is
something outside the agent, with activities taking place within
the agent the object or end of the activity is within the agent
itself: The object within the agent is the activity in process.
And so we read in Aristotle that the sensible in act or actualized is the sense in action, and the intelligible in act or
actualized is the intellect in action. We have actual sensation
or actual knowledge because our intellect or senses are informed by the species or likeness of the sensible or intelligible object. Sense or intellect is other than the sensible or
the intelligible only insofar as they are wholly in a condition of potentiality.

Consequently, since God possesses no potentiality but is
pure actuality, intellect in him and what is known must be
utterly identical; hence he never lacks the knowledge-
likeness that our intellect does when only knowing potentially,
and the knowledge-likeness in him does not differ from the
substance of the divine intellect, as the knowledge-likeness in
us differs from the substance of our intellect when we actually
know; but in him the knowledge-likeness itself is the divine
intellect itself. And so he knows himself through himself.

God Knows Us   *Summa of Theology* I, q. 14,
                         a. 5

God must know beings other than himself, for it is evident
that he knows himself perfectly or else his being would not
be perfect because his being *is* his act of knowing. But if
anything is perfectly known, so is its power. But to know
perfectly the power of a thing is to know the objects to which
the power extends. And so as the First Cause producing all
things the divine power extends to other things, so that God
must know beings other than himself. And this is all the more
obvious when we add that the very being of God, the First
Efficient Cause, is his action of knowing. And so any effects
pre-existing in God as in the First Cause have to be in his
action of knowing. And all there must be in the state of intelligibility; for whatever is in another is in it according to
that subject's state.

To understand the way in which God knows beings other

than himself we must consider the twofold way of knowing
something: in itself or in another. Anything is known in
itself when known through a likeness proper to that thing,
co-extensive with the thing known, as when our eye sees a
man through a man-likeness. Anything is seen in another
when seen through the likeness of its subject, as when a part
is seen in a whole through the knowledge-likeness of the
whole, or when a man is seen in a mirror through the mirror-
likeness, and so forth. . . .

We must therefore say that God sees himself in himself
because he sees himself through his essence. He sees beings
other than himself not in themselves but in himself, since
his essence has the likeness of all other things.

God's Knowledge   *On Truth*, q. 3, a. 3, c

As is stated in *De Anima*: "Practical knowledge differs
from speculative knowledge in its end." Truth, simply, is the
end of speculative knowledge, whereas the end of practical
knowledge, as is said in the *Metaphysics*, is action. Now,
knowledge is sometimes called practical when directed to a
work. This takes place in two ways. In one way, it is directed
in act—that is, actually directed to a particular work, as is the
form preconceived by the artist with the intention of bringing
it into matter. This is called practical knowledge and is the
form whereby knowledge occurs. Often, however, there is a
sort of knowledge able to exist but not actually so ordered.
In this way, an artist conceives a form for his work and is
aware that it can be made without having any intention of
making it. This is not actual practical knowledge but habitual
or virtual knowledge. There are times, however, when
knowledge can in no way be directed toward making. This
knowledge is purely speculative, and this also takes place in
two ways. In one way there is knowledge about things, as
when we reflect upon natural things, whose natures do not
allow us to produce them through knowledge. In another
way there is knowledge about things that are producible but
not in respect to the aspects reflected upon; for a thing receives existence through a productive action, and yet there
are some realities that are separable in our knowledge but

that are unable to exist separately. So even when we think
about something that is producible through knowledge, if we
are considering realities within it that cannot exist separately,
this knowledge is not practical—actual or habitual—but merely
speculative. A builder has this kind of knowledge when in
thinking of a house he reflects upon its genus, differences,
properties, and such things having no separate existence
within the thing. But when we consider all that is simultaneously required for a thing's existence, we are considering
something able to be made.

God has four ways of knowing things. His knowledge being the cause of things, there are some things he knows
through deciding by his will that they should exist at some
particular time. He has actual practical knowledge of such
things.

He also knows other things without any intention of making them. . . . He actually knows these things by merely
virtually practical knowledge, not actually practical knowledge.

Moreover, because he knows what he makes or can make
not only as such things exist with their own act of existence
but likewise according to all the notes known by human intellectual analysis, he knows things he can make even under
aspects that are unproducible.

Finally, he knows some things that his knowledge cannot
cause: evils, for instance.

And so it is true to say that God has both practical and
speculative knowledge.

We should examine which of the previous ways is proper
to the ideas attributed necessarily to God's knowledge. As
Augustine tells us, if we look to the strict meaning of the word
itself, an idea is an *intelligible character* or *likeness* of a
thing. Certain forms have, moreover, a double relation: one,
as related to what is informed by them, such as the relation
that knowledge has to the knower; another to what is extrinsic,
such as the relation of knowledge to what is known. The
latter relationship does not characterize all forms as the first
does. Hence, the word *form* entails only the first relation. For
this reason, a form always has the nature of a cause inasmuch
as a form is somehow the cause of what it informs—whether

this informing occurs through inherence, as with intrinsic forms, or by imitation, as with exemplary forms. Now, an intelligible character and a likeness also have the second relationship, but this does not confer upon them the nature of a cause.

So if we speak of an idea and consider only its proper reference, an idea would include only that sort of knowledge in accordance with which something can be made. This is actually practical or merely virtually practical knowledge, which is speculative in a way. But if, broadly speaking, we mean by "idea" an intelligible character or likeness, then an idea may be purely speculative knowledge.

But if we wish to be precise, we should say that an idea pertains to practical knowledge—actually or virtually practical; whereas an intelligible character or likeness pertains to both practical and speculative knowledge.

God Knows Individuals   *Summa of Theology* I, q. 14, a. 6

. . . Some writers, trying to show that God knows many things through one thing, utilize certain analogies: e.g., if a center had self-knowledge, it would know all the radii, or if light had self-knowledge, it would know all colors. Although these analogies suit part of the situation, namely, they indicate God's universal causality, nevertheless they do not show how multiplicity and diversity are caused by the single universal principle understood as the principle of uniqueness in things, not merely of what they have in common. For color differences are caused not solely by light but also by differences in the transparent medium receiving the light; likewise lines are differentiated by different positions. And so in these cases no knowledge of their source gives specific knowledge of the diversity and multiplicity of things, but only a general knowledge.

In God such is not the case. We have previously seen that everything contributing to any creature's perfection is present primarily in God and in a superexcellent way. But the perfection of creatures does not merely consist in what they commonly share, namely, existence, but also in what distinguishes one from another, e.g., life, knowledge, and other like qualities that differentiate the living from the nonliving, as well as beings with intellect from those lacking it. Indeed, any form that gives anything its own specific characteristics is a perfection. And so all things are present primarily in God, not only in respect to their common features but also their distinct ones. Consequently, because God has all perfections, God's essence is to all essences not as a common feature is to a special feature in the way that the unit is to numbers or the center to lines, but as the complete actuality is to incomplete actualities; . . . as man is to animal, or as the number six, a perfect number, is to the imperfect numbers it contains. Now, it is apparent that through the complete actuality we can know incomplete actualities, not only generally but also specifically. Hence to know man is to know what is proper to animal; and to know the number six is to know what is proper to the number three.

Consequently, because God's essence has all that makes the essence of every other thing perfect, God can know all things in himself and know what is proper to each thing. For each thing's proper nature consists in its participation to some degree in the divine perfection. But unless God knew all the ways in which his perfection can be participated by other beings, he would not know himself perfectly; nor would the nature of existence be perfectly known by God if he did not know all the degrees of existence. Thus it is obvious that God knows all things—what is proper to each, thereby differentiating them from one another.

Summa of Theology I, q. 14, a. 11

God knows individuals, for all perfections present in creatures are present primarily in God in a superexcellent way, as was made evident. Now, our perfection includes the knowing of individuals. And so God must know them. . . .

Divine Ideas   *Summa of Theology* I, q. 15, a. 1

We must maintain that the divine mind has ideas. For *idea*

in Greek is the equivalent of *forma* in Latin, i.e., form; and so by ideas we mean the forms of other things that are separated from the things themselves. Now, anything's form that is separate from that thing can have two uses: either to be the exemplar or type of that whose form it is said to be, or to be the principle whereby that thing is known, just as the forms of sensible things are said to be in the knower. For these two reasons we must argue that there are divine ideas.

This is obvious when we realize that except for what occurs through chance the form must be the intended aim in all generation. Moreover, the likeness of the form must be in the agent if he is to act for the sake of the form. This can take place in two ways. The likeness of what is to be made already exists naturally in those things that act by nature; hence man makes a man, and fire makes fire. The form of what is to be made already exists intelligibly in other agents, those acting through intellect; in this way the form of the house already exists in the architect's mind. This form can be called the idea of the house, because the architect intends to make the house after the structure of the form that he has conceptualized. Now, because the world has not come about by chance but is created by God, who acts intellectually, there must exist in the divine mind a form that the world is made like; and this is what we understand as an idea.

Plurality of Ideas   *Summa of Theology* I, q. 15, a. 2

We must argue that there are many ideas. To grasp the reason for this we should consider that the ultimate end of anything done is what the principal agent aims at, as when an army commander aims at order. Now, that good that is equivalent to the order of the entire universe is that which is best in nature, as Aristotle shows. Therefore, God specially intends the order of the entire universe, and it is not, as some claim, merely intended incidentally through a succession of agents: God, they said, only created the first creature, which in its turn created the second, and so on until the great multitude of things were made; in this opinion God would only have an idea of the first creature. But if the order of the entire universe is intended by him as the direct aim of his creation, he must have an idea of this order. But any plan of direction for the whole must include knowledge of what is particular to each of its parts; just as an architect cannot plan any house without knowing what is special to every part. And so what is proper to the natures of all things must be in the divine mind. Augustine says, therefore, that each and every thing is created by God after its own idea. Consequently, there are many ideas in the divine mind.

That this is not out of harmony with the divine simplicity is easily seen by reminding ourselves that the idea of any work is in the agent's mind as *that which* is known, not as the knowledge-likeness *by which* knowledge exists. This knowledge-likeness is the form that makes the intellect to know actually. Thus in an architect's mind the form of a house is something known by him according to whose likeness he makes the form of a house to exist in matter. Knowing many things does not contradict the simplicity of the divine intellect, but the divine intellect's being informed by many knowledge-likenesses would contradict the divine simplicity. And so the divine mind has many ideas as objects of God's knowledge.

The explanation is this. God perfectly knows his essence; he therefore knows it in every possible way. Now, the divine essence is knowable not only as it is in itself but as it can be participated in to some degree of likeness by creatures. But every creature possesses its own nature inasmuch as it somehow participates in the likeness of the divine essence. In this way, therefore, God, by knowing his essence as imitable in this particular way by this particular creature, knows his essence as the idea or nature proper to that creature; and likewise in other things. It is therefore obvious that God knows the many natures that are proper to many things, and these natures are equivalent to many ideas.

Plato presupposed the ideas as principles of the knowledge of things as well as of their coming into existence; and an idea declared to be in the divine mind has these two uses. As a principle of the making of things, it can be called an *exemplar*, and involves practical knowledge; as a principle of knowing, it is correctly called an *intelligible nature*, belonging also to speculative knowledge. As exemplar it is related to everything known by God, even to that which never exists as well as to all the beings he knows, speculatively, in their own intelligible natures.

Divine Willing   *On Truth*, q. 23, a. 4, c

The principal object of the divine will is that which it naturally wills as a quasi-end of its willing, God's own goodness, and on this account he wills whatever he wills that is distinct from himself. So he creates on account of his own goodness, as Augustine asserts (*Confessions* XIII, 2), i.e., this he does so that his goodness, unable in its essence to be multiplied, may at least through likeness by a kind of participation be diffused upon many recipients. Thus whatever refers to creatures is willed by him as a sort of secondary object of his will. These are willed on account of his goodness. Hence, just as his essence is the reason for his knowing all things, so the divine goodness acts as the reason for willing all things.

In respect to that principal object, God's goodness, the divine will is under necessity, not of force but of natural inclination which, says Augustine (*City of God* V, 10), is not irreconcilable with freedom. God cannot will himself not to be good, nor, therefore, not to be intelligent or powerful or anything at all included within the nature of his goodness.

The divine will is not, however, under necessity with reference to any other object. . . .

On Truth, q. 23, a. 5, c

. . . Some of the divine effects are contingent not merely because of the contingency of secondary causes but rather because of the decision of the divine will, which appointed such an order for things.

Role of Will in God   *Summa of Theology* I, q. 19, a. 1, and ad. 2

Just as there is intellect in God so is there will; for will follows upon intellect. Just as by their form natural things have actual existence, so by its intelligible form is the intellect actually intelligent. But everything is so inclined toward its natural form that when this is absent it tends toward it, and when present it rests in it. This is also the case with every natural perfection that is a natural good. In things without knowledge this inclination toward good is spoken of as natural tendency. But intellectual natures have also inclinations following upon forms intelligibly apprehended in order to repose in their possession or to seek their possession, both of which involve the will. Therefore will is present in every intellectual being just as animal tendency is present in every sensible being. And so since there is intellect in God, there must be will in him. And just as his intellect is his very being, so is his will.

ad. 2. In us will is found in the tending part whose name is derived from tendency, and yet its action is not only to seek what it does not possess but also to love and delight in what it does possess. In this way will is attributed to God whose object, the good, is always his, for, as was said, the will is not distinct from his essence.

God's Free Choice　　　*On Truth*, q. 24, a. 3, c and ad. 2

God has free choice but not in the same way as angels and men have it. That God has free choice is evident from this: The end of his will, his own goodness, is naturally willed, and he wills all other things as ordered to this end; but the latter, strictly speaking, are not necessarily willed . . . because his goodness is without any need for the things ordered to it, and he can manifest his goodness appropriately in a variety of ways. So, just as with us, he decides freely to do this or that. . . .

ad. 2. The capacity to choose evil is not essential to free choice. It is the result of free choice being present in a nature that is created and capable of falling.

God's Antecedent and Consequent Will　　　*On Truth*, q. 23, a. 2, c

We appropriately distinguish the divine will as antecedent or consequent. This distinction is clarified by the words of the one who first made it, Damascene, who says: "Antecedent will is God's acceptance of something on his own account," whereas "consequent will is a concession on our account" (*On Orthodox Faith* II, 29).

To clarify this we may consider that every action involves something of both agent and recipient. The agent is both prior to and more important than the action. So what belongs to the maker naturally precedes what belongs to the thing made. Obviously in the work of nature, the making of a perfect animal depends upon the formative power present in the seed, yet sometimes because of an indisposed matter receiving it, a perfect animal is not made. Thus occurs the birth of monsters. Therefore we state that a perfect animal is made through nature's primary intention, but an imperfect animal occurs through the secondary intention of nature, which determines what the matter can receive, since by reason of matter's indisposition, nature cannot give to it the form of the perfect animal.

There are similar factors involved in God's work with creatures. Although he needs no matter in his operation so that with no pre-existing matter did he create things, yet he now operates in these originally created things, directing them according to their nature previously given. And although he could withdraw from his creatures every impediment making them incapable of perfection, yet through his wisdom he disposes of things according to their state, giving to each one according to its own capacity.

Whatever God himself has ordained for the creature is said to be willed by him with a primary intention or antecedent will. But when the creature by its own failing is restrained from this end, nevertheless God fulfills within it whatever goodness it has capacity for, and this is done according to his secondary intention, being called his consequent will.

God is therefore said to will the salvation of all by his antecedent will because he created all men for happiness. But inasmuch as some men act contrary to their own salvation, the order of his wisdom denies their salvation by reason of their failing so that their damnation through justice is the fulfillment in them in another way of the requirements of his goodness. Therefore, they are found within the secondary order of his will, having fallen from the first, so that his will is still fulfilled in them, although they do not do God's will.

But the failure that is sin, whereby a person becomes worthy of punishment now or in the future, is not itself willed by God either by an antecedent or a consequent will; it is only permitted by him. . . .

Divine Communicative Will   *Summa of Theology* I, q. 19, a. 2

God wills not only himself but things other than himself. This is obvious from the previous comparison. For there is a natural inclination in things of nature to acquire their own good if this is absent and to rest in this good when present; but they also tend to share their own good with others as far as they can. And so we note that every perfect and actual agent produces its like. It therefore belongs to the nature of the will to communicate to others the good it possesses, as far as it can; and this is especially true of the divine will, which shares its perfection in some kind of likeness. And so if natural things when perfect communicate their good to others, much more should it be true of the divine will that it communicates its own good by likeness as far as possible. Consequently, God wills both his own being and the being of others, but he wills himself as the end and others as directed to that end insofar as the divine goodness may allow other things to participate in it.

Divine Essence Is Will   *Compendium of Theology,* c. 33

It is evident that God's will cannot differ from his intellect. For, because any good known by the intellect is intended by the will, it moves the will and is the will's act and perfection. But in God is found no distinction between mover and moved, actuality and potentiality, perfection and perfectible, as is clear from the preceding truths. The will of God, therefore, is distinct neither from the divine intellect nor from God's essence. . . .

God Is Love   *Summa of Theology* I, q. 20,
                                   a. 1, c and ad. 3

It is necessary to affirm that there is love in God since love
is the first motion of the will and of every tending power.
Because actions of the will and of every tending power aim
at good and evil as at their proper objects, and because good
is essentially and especially the object of the will and of tendency, while evil is the object only secondarily and indirectly,
as opposed to good, it follows that the actions of the will and
tendency referring to good must naturally precede those referring to evil; so, for example, joy precedes sorrow, and
love precedes hate, for whatever exists independently is always prior to what exists relatively. Also, the more universal
is naturally prior to what is less universal. Thus the intellect
is directed first of all to universal truth and then to particular
and special truths. Some acts of will and of tendency relate
to good as specially conditioned, such as joy and delight,
which relate to good, present and possessed, while desire
and hope relate to good as not yet possessed. But love relates to good universally, possessed or not. And so love is
naturally the first act of the will and of tendency, and therefore all other tending motions presuppose love as their source
and root. For no one desires or enjoys anything except as a
good loved; nor is anything hated except as opposed to what
is loved. It is likewise evident that sorrow and such things
are related to love as to their first principle. Thus love must
be wherever there is will and tendency, for without love
there will be no willing. But we have shown that there is will
in God (q. 19, a. 1), and so we must ascribe love to him.

ad. 3. An act of love is always directed toward two things:
to the good one wills and to the person for whom one wills
it, inasmuch as to love a person is to will good for the person.
And so when we love ourselves, we will good for ourselves
and union with that good as far as this can be. Love, therefore, is called a uniting force even in God, one that does not,
however, imply composition, since the good that he wills for
himself is none other than himself who is by essence good,
as previously noted (q. 6, a. 1, a. 3). And whenever anyone

loves another he wills good to that other. In this way he is identifying the other with himself and considering the good done to that other as done to himself. Love then is a uniting force, since it joins the other to ourselves and relates his good to our own. And likewise the divine love is a uniting force because God wills good to others; yet this implies no composition in God.

Divine Love Causes Good   *Summa of Theology* I, q. 20, a. 2, c and ad. 1

God loves all existents. For everything existing insofar as it does exist is good because a thing's existence is itself a good as well as whatever perfection it has. But we previously noted (q. 19, a. 4) that God's will is the cause of everything. Nothing has existence or any good, therefore, unless it is willed by God. And so God is willing some good to every existent. It is clear, accordingly, that God loves every existent because loving anything means willing good to it. But God does not love as we do. Because our will is not the cause of anything's goodness but is moved by it as by its object, our love, by which we will good to anything, is not the cause of its goodness; but conversely its real or imagined goodness evokes our love, which is a willing that a thing keep the good it possesses and in addition receive the good it lacks, and we aim at this in our actions; whereas the love of God gives and creates goodness.

ad. 1. A lover goes out of himself and enters into the beloved insofar as he wills good to him, and by his providence he works for that good just as he works for his own good. And so Dionysius says: "On behalf of the truth we dare to say even this, that he himself, the cause of everything, by his abundant love and goodness, goes outside himself through his providence for all existents."

God Loves Some More Than   *Summa of Christian Teaching*
Others   I, 92

We should note that only love seems directed to a twofold object, while other actions of the soul are directed merely to one object. For when we know or enjoy anything, this must be somehow one object, but love is a willing of something to someone, for we are considered to love that for whom we will some good, as previously discussed. So that when we want anything, we are spoken of as simply and properly *desiring* it, not loving it but rather loving ourselves, for whom we desire it; and therefore we are said to love it accidentally and improperly. But actions according to their energy are considered more or less intense. But since the divine action is always of the same force, and the energy of an action is measured by the force from which it proceeds, this measurement cannot apply to God. But there are two ways for love to be more or less intense. One way has to do with the good we will to someone so that we are said to love more that person for whom we will a greater good. Another way has to do with the energy of the action, so that we are said to love more that person for whom, although not willing a greater good, we yet will an equal good with greater zeal and effectiveness. And so nothing prevents our saying that in the first way God loves one being more than another insofar as he wills for it a greater good. . . .

God Is Provident   *Summa of Theology* I, q. 22, a. 2

Some people, such as Democritus and the Epicureans, completely denied that there is any providence, and they held that the world came about by chance. Others taught that only incorruptible beings were subject to providence and that corruptible beings were subject to it only in their species and not in their individualities; for in their species they are incorruptible. They are supposed to have said (Job 22: 14): "The clouds are his covert"; and "he does not consider our things; and he walketh about the poles of heaven." Nevertheless, Rabbi Moses, while agreeing with this opinion concerning those things enduring corruption, excluded men from the generally corruptible things on account of the excellence of their intellect.

It is necessary to state, however, that everything is subject to divine providence, not only in a general way but even as individuals. What follows will clarify this. Because every agent acts for an end, the directing of effects toward that end goes as far as does the causing of the first agent. And so because an effect at times comes from a cause other than and beyond the intention of an agent, among the effects of an agent something occurs that is unrelated to the end. But the causing by God, who is the first agent is concerned with all being, not only with the principles constituting species but also with the individualizing principles, not only with incorruptible but also with corruptible beings. And so anything in any way existent is necessarily directed by God toward some end; as the Apostle says (Rom. 13: 1): "Those things that are of God are well ordered." And so since the providence of God is no less than the exemplar of the ordering of existents toward an end, as was said, we must conclude that all beings insofar as they participate in existence must also be within divine providence. It was also shown that God knows all things (q. 14, a. 6, a. 11), individual as well as universal. And since his knowledge is related to things themselves as art to the works of art, all beings must be subject to his ordering as all things made through art are subject to the ordering of that art.

Evil Not from God

Compendium of Theology, ch. 141

Also eliminated is the doubt as to whether evil deeds are from God. For because we have proven that every agent acts insofar as it acts through God's power, with God being thus the cause of all effects and acts, and since we proved that evil and defects in beings directed by divine providence come from the condition of the secondary causes, which themselves may be defective, it is obvious that evil actions, understood as defective, do not originate from God but from their defective proximate causes; but insofar as they are active and existent they must come from God, just as a limp is from the locomotive power in respect to its movement, but as defective movement, it is from the leg's crookedness.

II. CREATED BEING: NATURE

1. PRINCIPLES OF NATURE

On the Principles of Nature

If anything has the capacity to exist, although it does not exist, then there must be something that does now exist. Since something can be, it is possible for it not to be. Some things can exist, although they do not now exist, and some things are now existing. That which can exist, but does not, is said to be in potentiality. That which now exists is said to be in actuality. Existence, however, is of two kinds: one is essential existence or the substantial existence of anything; e.g., man exists, and this is unqualified existence (*simpliciter*). The other is accidental existence; e.g., man is white, and this is qualified existence (*secundum quid*).

Moreover, something is in potentiality to each kind of existence. There is something such as sperm or menstrual blood potential to being man, and something like man is in potentiality to being white. The name "matter" can be given both to what is in potentiality to substantial existence and to accidental existence; e.g., sperm is the matter of man, and man is the matter of whiteness.

But they differ in this, that whatever is in potentiality to substantial existence is called derivative matter, but whatever is in potentiality to accidental existence is called immanent matter. So in speaking appropriately, that which is potential to substantial *esse* is said to be prime matter; that which is potential to accidental *esse* is said to be a subject. For a subject gives *esse* or existence to an accident, because the accident does not have *esse* except through a subject. Whence it is said that accidents are in the subject, but it is not said that the substantial form is in the subject.

Accordingly, matter differs from subject: not from the fact that something comes to it does any subject exist, but it exists through itself and has (*per se*) complete existence; for man does not have existence through whiteness. Matter, however, is said to have existence because *esse* comes to it, since its own *esse* is incomplete (or, rather, it has no *esse*, as the commentator says in *On the Soul* II). Thus, understood absolutely, the form gives existence to matter; but the accident does not give existence to the subject; rather does the subject give existence to the accident, although we sometimes use one word for the other, namely, matter for subject, and vice versa.

So, just as anything that is potentiality can be named matter, so anything from which a thing derives existence, whether substantial or accidental, can be named form; a man, for example, who is white in potentiality becomes actually white through whiteness, and sperm, which is man in potentiality, becomes actually man through the soul. Because form brings existence into actuality, we state that form is act. Whatever brings substantial existence into actuality is called substantial form, and whatever brings accidental existence into actuality is called accidental form.

In addition, since generation is motion toward form, two kinds of generation correspond to the two kinds of form. To substantial form there corresponds unqualified [absolute] generation, and to accidental form there corresponds a qualified generation. We say that something begins to exist without [absolute] qualification when a substantial form comes, as, for example, when man begins to exist or is generated. But we do not say that something begins to exist without qualification when an accidental form comes, but it begins to exist in this or that way. Thus, when a man becomes white, we do not say that man begins to exist without qualification or is generated, but that he begins to exist as white or is generated as white.

Opposed to these two kinds of generation are two kinds of corruption, namely, unqualified and qualified corruption. Unqualified generation and corruption occur only in the category substance, but qualified generation and corruption occur in all the other categories. Moreover, since generation is a change from nonexistence to existence, corruption must be a change from existence to nonexistence. Yet generation does not come from any nonentity whatsoever, but from nonentity that is an entity in potentiality, as a statue comes from bronze, which is a statue in potentiality and not in actuality.

But three things are required for any generation: *existence in potentiality*, which is matter; *nonexistence in actuality*, which is privation; and that *by which a thing is made to be in actuality*, which is form. For example, a statue made out of bronze, which is in potentiality to the form of statue, is *matter;* its shapeless or unformed state is *privation;* and the shape that allows it to be called a statue is its *form.* But this is not a substantial form, because before the shape is imposed, the bronze already has existence in actuality, and this existence does not depend upon the shape. Rather, this is an accidental form, for all artificial forms are accidental. In other words, art works only upon that which is already established in complete existence by nature.

There are, therefore, three principles of nature: matter, form, and privation. Among these, form does the generating, while from the other two generation takes place. Matter and privation are therefore the same as the subject, but they have different reasons for being the same, just as bronze and what-is-shapeless are, before the arrival of form, the same thing; yet it is called bronze for one reason and it is called shapeless for another. Privation, therefore, is not spoken of as a (*per se*) independent principle but a relative (*per accidens*) principle, since it coincides with matter. Thus, for example, we say that a doctor builds *per accidens* since he does not build because he is a doctor but because he is a builder, the building and doctoring just happening to coincide in the same subject.

There are, however, two kinds of accidents: the necessary, which is inseparable from the thing, such as the ability to laugh in man, and the unnecessary or separable kind, such as white from man. Therefore, although privation is a relative principle (*per accidens*), it does not follow that privation is unnecessary for generation, since matter is never completely without privation, for it has the privation of another form while it has one form, and vice versa, just as in fire there is a privation of air, and in air there is a privation of fire.

It is also noteworthy that although generation is from nonexistence, we say that privation and not negation is the principle, for negation does not determine a subject. Even non-beings can be called sightless, as one might say that a dragon is nonseeing, and we say the same of things unfit by nature for seeing, such as stones. But privation is spoken of only in reference to a determined subject having a certain natural aptitude for a certain condition; for example, blindness is referred only to those things naturally apt to see. Moreover, generation arises not from absolute nonexistence but from the nonbeing that is in a subject, and not just in any subject, but in a determined subject—fire, we may say, does not come from just any nonfire but from that nonfire apt to acquire the form of fire. And hence we say that not negation but privation is the principle.

Privation, however, differs from the other principles insofar as these are principles both of existence and of becoming. For a statue to be made, bronze as well as the statue's shape are required. And when the statue exists, these two must exist. On the other hand, privation is only a principle of becoming, not one of existing. For a statue to be in process, there must not yet be any statue; if it were a statue, it could not become one, because whatever comes to be does not exist except in successive things, like time and motion. As soon as the statue exists, there is no longer the privation of statue, since affirmation and negation cannot be simultaneous, nor can privation and possession. Also privation, as discussed above, is an accidental principle (*per accidens*), but the other two are substantial principles.

From this argument it is also obvious from everything said that matter is innately different from form and from privation. Matter is that in which form and privation are understood, just as form and formlessness are understood to be in bronze. Hence at times matter designates privation; at other times, it does not. When bronze becomes the matter of the statue, it does not imply privation, since in speaking of bronze in this way I do not understand it as shapeless or without form. On the other hand, flour taken as matter in relation to bread implies in itself the privation of the form of bread, which explains why I call it *flour;* its shapelessness or formlessness is understood to be opposed to the form of bread. Now, in generation, there remains the matter or subject but not the privation and not the composite of matter and privation. Therefore, matter that does not imply privation is permanent, but matter that implies privation is transitory.

Notice, moreover, that matter like bronze is already in composition with form. Thus the matter destined for a statue is itself composed of matter and form. Therefore, since bronze possesses a form, it is not called prime matter. Matter, however, without any form or privation but subject to form and privation is called prime matter because there is no matter prior to it. This is called *hyle*, i.e., chaos or confusion in Greek. And since all definition and knowledge take place through form, prime matter can only be defined and known through its relationship to form, not through itself; thus we may say that whatever is related to all forms and privations as bronze is related to statue and shapelessness is prime matter. And this matter is called *primary* without qualification. But anything may be spoken of as prime matter with respect to some category, as water with respect to liquids. This, however, is not primary without qualification, because it is composed of matter and form, and therefore having matter prior to it.

Notice also that prime matter as well as form are neither generated nor corrupted, since all generation is the process of one thing becoming another. Matter is the material of generation, and form is the aim of generation. If, therefore, matter and form should be generated, matter would come from matter and form from form, ad infinitum. Thus, strictly speaking, only the composite is generated.

We should, moreover, observe that prime matter is said to be numerically one in all things. But being numerically one [for prime matter] means two things: namely, that which has a determined form, numerically one, like Socrates. Since in itself prime matter has no form, it is not said to be numerically one when it lacks the qualities that would make it different numerically—prime matter is called numerically one in this way, for it is conceived without any quality that could cause a numerical difference.

Moreover, although prime matter is conceived as without

form or privation—as, for instance, the definition of bronze has neither "shape" nor "shapelessness"—nevertheless, prime matter, I say, never exists as wholly without form and privation. For it is under one form now, under another form then. But never can it exist by itself (per se). Since it contains no form in its definition, it cannot actually exist: actual existence comes only through the form. It only exists potentially. Therefore, nothing actually existing can be called prime matter.

It is evident from all we have said that there are three principles of nature: matter, form, and privation. But generation requires more than these. Whatever exists potentially cannot make itself exist actually. The bronze potentially a statue cannot cause itself to be a statue; an agent is needed to bring the form of the statue from potentiality to actuality. Nor can form extract itself from potentiality to actuality. I am referring to the form of the reality generated that we call the aim of generation. In other words, form exists only when the reality is achieved; but whatever does the achieving is present within the very becoming or while the reality is being achieved. In addition to matter and form, therefore, there must be a principle that acts, and this is called the efficient or the moving or the agent cause, or that which is the principle of motion. And since, as Aristotle comments in *Metaphysics* II (2; 994 b 15), nothing acts without some aim, there has to be a fourth thing, namely, the aim of the agent; and this is called the end.

Although every agent, whether natural or voluntary, has an aim, we cannot conclude that every agent is aware of or deliberates about its aim. It is necessary for those agents whose actions are not determined and who can act for diverse aims to be aware of the aim; such are voluntary agents. Therefore, these must be aware of the aim by which they direct their actions. Actions, however, are directed in natural agents which need not choose the means to the aim. Avicenna gives the example of the harpist who does not need to deliberate about every pluck of the strings because the strokes are already decided for him; otherwise, there would be a pause between each stroke, and so a lack of harmony. We see, however, the fact of deliberation in a voluntary rather than in a natural agent. Thus it is obvious from its higher rank that if the agent works voluntarily, there are occasions when he does not deliberate about what is readily apparent, and no more, therefore, does the natural agent. Hence, a natural agent is sometimes able to aim for an end without any deliberation; this is merely having a natural inclination to something.

From all we have said so far, it is evident that there are four causes: material, efficient, formal, and final. But even though *principle* and *cause* are convertible terms, as we read in *Metaphysics* V (1; 1013), still in *Physics* Aristotle asserts four causes and three principles (*Phys.* I, 6, 7), for the reason that he uses cause there to express what is extrinsic and what is intrinsic. Matter and form are said to be intrinsic to a thing because they are parts constituting the thing. Efficient and final cause, since they are outside the thing, are called extrinsic. On the other hand, he uses principles to denote only the intrinsic causes. As for privation, this is not in the list of causes since it is an accidental principle (*per accidens*), as was said.

When we speak of four causes, we mean substantial causes (*per se*), to which, however, all accidental causes (*per accidens*) are led back, since everything accidental is led back to what is substantial.

Moreover, even though Aristotle in the first book of *Physics* refers to intrinsic causes as "principles," yet "principle," strictly speaking, is applied to extrinsic causes, as apparent in *Metaphysics* V, and "element" is applied to the causes that make up a thing, namely, to the intrinsic causes, but both are called "cause." Nevertheless, one term can sometimes be used in place of the other, for every cause can be called a principle and every principle a cause.

Apparently, however, cause means more than principle, which is usually understood to mean "that from which something proceeds" whether or not what follows really results from it. So, for instance, the craftsman is called the principle of the knife because the existence of the knife comes about by his work. And when anything changes from white to black, white is called the principle of that change; and, on the whole, anything from which motion arises is called a principle. White, however, is not that from which the existence of what follows really results, namely, blackness. On the other hand, cause is predicated only of that principle from which the existence of what follows really results. Therefore we call that from whose existence another results, a cause. That principle, therefore, that is the point of departure for motion cannot strictly be called substantial, although we call it a principle. For this same reason, privation is found among the principles and not among the causes insofar as privation is the point of departure for generation. But it can be called also an accidental cause, insofar as it coincides with matter, as was previously stated.

"Element," strictly speaking, refers only to those causes that constitute a thing, specifically, material causes—nevertheless, not any material cause, but that one of which a thing is primarily composed. Hence, we do not speak of the members of the body as the elements of man, since the members are in their turn made up of other things. But we speak of earth and water as elements, since these are not made up of other bodies, but natural bodies are primarily made up of them.

Therefore, Aristotle in *Metaphysics* V: 3 says, "element is that of which a thing is primarily composed, is in that thing, and is not divided according to form." The meaning of the first phrase, "that of which a thing is primarily composed," is plain from what was previously said. The second phrase, "is in that thing," is said to distinguish "element" from that "matter" that is completely corrupted by generation. Bread, for instance, is the matter of blood, yet blood is not generated save by the corruption of bread; hence bread does not stay in blood. Bread, therefore, may not be called an element of blood. Elements must in some way stay because they are not corrupted at all, as is stated in the book *On Generation and Corruption* I: 10. The third phrase, "and is not divided according to form," is added to distinguish "element" from things having parts that differ in regard to form, i.e., in species, such as the hand whose parts are flesh and bone, which differ in species. An element is not divided into parts that differ in species; it is like water, every part of which is water. For it is not essential to its state that it be individuated in quantity, but it is sufficient if it is individuated according to form. And even when it is not divided in any way, it is called an element, just as letters are the elements of words. Hence, it is evident from what was said that principle somehow is more widely applicable than cause, and cause more so than element. And this is what the commentator [Averroes] says of *Metaphysics* V, 3 and 4.

After seeing that there are four kinds of causes, we should recognize that for the one same thing to have several causes is not impossible—for instance, a statue, whose cause is both craftsman and bronze, the craftsman as efficient cause, bronze as material cause. Nor is it impossible for the same thing to be the cause of contrary things; so the captain is cause both of the safety and the sinking of the ship, of the latter by his absence, of the former by his presence, as the philosopher says in *Physics* II. Notice also that the one same thing can be both cause and caused even with respect to the same object, but from distinctive points of view; walking, for instance, is often the cause of health as its efficient cause, yet health, as aim, is cause of the walking. In other words, at times walking is for the sake of health, and at other times because of health. Likewise, body is the soul's matter, but the soul is the body's form.

The efficient cause is called a cause in relation to the aim, since this aim is made actual only through the agent's operation. Conversely, the aim is called cause of the efficient cause, since the efficient cause functions only by aiming at something. Therefore, the efficient cause is the cause of that which is the aim, as walking in order to be healthy. But the efficient cause does not cause the aim to be an aim; thus it is not the cause of the aim's causality, i.e., it does not cause the aim to be a final cause. A doctor, it is said, causes health to exist actually, but he does not cause health to be the aim.

The aim, on its side, is not the cause of what the efficient cause is, but it does cause the efficient cause to become operative in action; health, for instance, does not cause the doctor to be a doctor—I refer to the health brought about through the doctor's action—but it does cause the doctor to take action. The aim, therefore, is the cause of the efficient cause's causality, since it causes the efficient cause to take action.

Likewise, the aim causes the matter to be the matter and the form to be the form, since it is only for the sake of the aim that matter receives form and only through the aim does form perfect the matter. The aim, therefore, is called the cause of causes, since it causes the causality of all the causes.

Insofar as form exists only in matter, matter is likewise spoken of as the cause of form. In fact, matter and form are defined through their relationship to each other as stated in *Physics* II, 2. They are also defined in relationship to the composite, as the part in relation to the whole, and the simple to the composed.

Since every cause as cause is, moreover, naturally prior to what it causes, we must notice the two ways of being prior, as Aristotle comments in *On the Soul,* II. Because of this variety something can be called both prior and posterior with reference to the same thing, both the cause and what is caused. In regard to generation and time a thing is called prior to another, and also in regard to substance and completeness. Since, therefore, nature's action proceeds from the imperfect to the perfect and from the incomplete to the complete, the imperfect is prior to the perfect, at least in temporal generation, but from the standpoint of substance, the perfect is prior to the imperfect. Thus, for instance, we may say that the man precedes the boy from the standpoint of substance and completeness, but the boy comes before the man from the standpoint of temporal generation. Yet although in things able to be generated, the imperfect is prior to the perfect and potentiality to actuality—since in the one same thing the imperfect is prior to the perfect and potentiality to actuality—nevertheless, absolutely speaking, the perfect and actuality must be prior, because that which brings potentiality into actuality is itself actual, and that which perfects the imperfect is the perfect.

In respect to temporal generation, matter is prior to form, since what receives something is prior to whatever comes to it. But in respect to substance and completeness, form is prior to matter, since only through form does matter have complete existence. In like manner, in respect to temporal generation, the efficient cause is prior to the aim, since from the efficient cause comes the action toward the aim. But in re-

spect to substance and completeness, the aim is prior to the
efficient cause as efficient cause, since the action of the efficient cause is not accomplished except through the aim.
The material and efficient causes are therefore prior in the
process of generation, but the form and aim are prior in the
process of perfection.

There are two kinds of necessity: absolute and conditional.
Absolute necessity comes from the causes prior in the process
of generation, that is, the material and efficient cause. For
instance, the necessity of death comes from matter and from
the combination of contrary components. This necessity is
called "absolute" because nothing can impede it. It is also
called the necessity of matter. On the other hand, conditional
necessity comes from causes posterior in generation, namely
from the form and aim. Thus we say that conception is necessary for a man to be generated. Such necessity is called conditional, because it is not absolutely necessary for this woman
to conceive, but only conditionally, i.e., if a man is to be
generated. This is spoken of as the necessity of the aim.

Three of the causes, moreover, can coincide in one thing,
namely, the form, the aim, and the efficient cause, as is evident in the generation of fire. Fire generates fire; thus insofar
as it generates, fire is the efficient cause. Also, insofar as it
gives actual existence to what was previously in potentiality,
fire is the formal cause. Moreover, fire is the aim insofar as
the agent's action ends in fire and aims at fire.

The aim, however, is of two kinds: the aim of the generating and the aim of what is generated, as evident in the generation of a knife. The form of "knife" is the aim of the
generating; but cutting, the operation of the knife, is the aim
of what is generated, namely, the knife. Often, also, the aim
of the generating coincides with the two previously discussed
causes, for example, when generation occurs from a like
species, as when man generates man, and the olive an olive.
But we cannot say the same of the aim of what is generated.

Notice, also, that the aim coincides with the form in respect to numerical identity, because the form of what is generated and the aim of the generating are numerically identical. But the aim is not numerically identical to but specifically
identical to the efficient cause, since it is impossible that the

maker and what is made should be the same numerically, although they can be the same specifically. Hence, when man begets man, the begetting man and the begotten man differ numerically but are the same specifically. Matter, however, does not coincide with the other causes. This is because matter, since it is being in potentiality, has the nature of the imperfect, whereas the other causes, since they are in actuality, have the nature of the perfect. The perfect and the imperfect do not coincide.

There are, as we have learned, four causes: efficient, formal, material, and final. Each of these causes, however, can be spoken of in several ways. Cause can be spoken of as prior or as posterior. Medical skill and the doctor are, for instance, the cause of health, but medical skill is the prior cause, while the doctor is the posterior cause. It is the same with formal cause and the other causes. Notice also that we always have to return to the first cause. If it is asked, for instance, "Why is this man healed?" the answer should be, "Because the doctor healed him." But to the further question, "How did the doctor heal him?" the answer must be, "Because of the medical skill that the doctor possesses."

We must also notice that the proximate cause is identical with the posterior cause, while the remote cause is identical with the prior one. Thus, these two divisions of causes, namely, prior and posterior, remote and proximate, signify the same thing. Notice, however, that the more universal is always called the remote cause, while the more particular is called the proximate cause. So we say that the proximate form of man is his definition, i.e., "rational animal"; but "animal" is more remote, and "substance" even remoter. All superiors are forms of the inferiors. Likewise, bronze is the proximate matter of a statue, but the remote matter is "metal," and the even remoter matter is "body."

In addition, some causes are substantial and others are accidental. A substantial cause is a cause of anything insofar as it is of this type, just as the builder is cause of the house and wood is the matter of the bench. An accidental cause is one that happens to be united with a substantial cause, as when we say that a teacher builds. The teacher is the accidental cause of the building, that is, not exactly as teacher, but because the builder happens to be a teacher. And it is the same with the other causes.

Again, there are simple causes and complex causes. A cause is simple when either as a substantial cause or an accidental cause, it alone is spoken of as the cause, as when we say that the builder is the cause of the house or that the doctor is the cause of the house. A cause is complex when both are spoken of as the cause, as when we say that the "builder-doctor" is the cause of the house.

A cause is also spoken of as simple when, as Avicenna explains (*Sufficientia* I, 12), something is, without anything added to it, a cause, as bronze, without any other matter added to it, is the cause of the statue—in other words, a statue is made of bronze. Likewise, a doctor is said to cause health, and fire to cause heat. On the other hand, a cause is complex when many things have to happen to that of which it is the cause. Hence, for example, the cause of the ship's movement is not one man but many, and the cause of a house is not one stone but many stones.

Moreover, some causes are in actuality, others in potentiality. A cause in actuality is one that is actually causing something, like the builder as long as he is building, or the bronze when a statue is being formed out of it. A cause in potentiality is one which, although not actually causing something, yet can cause it, such as a builder when not building, and bronze when not yet a statue.

With regard to causes in actuality, however, the cause and what is caused must exist simultaneously, so that if one is present, the other also is. If there is a builder in actuality, he must be building; and if building actually exists, there must be a builder in actuality. But there is not the same necessity with causes only in potentiality.

Notice also that a universal cause causes a universal thing, and a singular cause causes a singular thing. Hence a builder, it is said, is a cause of a house, but this builder is the cause of this house.

Let us call attention when considering the intrinsic principles, namely, matter and form, to the accord and unlikeness among things resulting from these principles as well as to the identity and diversity of the principles.

Therefore, we find that some things are numerically identical, as are Socrates and this man, when Socrates is intended. Others are numerically diverse but specifically identical, like Socrates and Plato, who differ numerically and yet are identical by their human species. Others still are unlike specifically but generically identical, as man and ass are of the same animal category. Others, again, are diverse generically and identical only analogically, such as substance and quantity, which have no common category and are identical only analogically; i.e., they are identical only insofar as they are beings. Being, however, is not a genus, because it is not predicated univocally, only analogically.

For this last statement to be understood, it should be explained that one thing can be predicated of others in three different ways: univocally, equivocally, and analogically. A thing is predicated univocally when predicated with the same name and the same nature, i.e., definition. Thus, "animal" is predicated of man and ass, since each is called animal and each is a sensible, animate substance, which is the definition of animal nature. On the other hand, a thing is predicated equivocally when it is attributed to several with the same name but with an entirely different meaning. Thus "dog" is predicated of a thing that barks and of a heavenly constellation; these two agree in name but not in definition, or in meaning, considering that the definition is precisely what the name signifies, as declared in *Metaphysics* IV (7; 1012 a 23). Finally, a thing is said to be predicated analogically when it is attributed to several whose natures and definitions differ and yet are referred to one identical thing, as "healthy" is said of the animal body, of urine, and of medicine; but in all three its meaning is not entirely identical. "Healthy" is said of urine as a sign of health, of the body as of the subject of health, and of medicine, as of the cause. Yet all these meanings refer to one aim, health.

Often, things that are analogically the same, that is, by proportion, comparison, or association, are referred to one aim, as was plain in the previous example of health. Often, also, they are referred to one agent, as "doctor" is predicated of the person who practices the medical skill, and of the person who without medical skill practices, like the midwife, and even of the instruments; but it is predicated of all as to the one agent, medicine. At other times such things are referred to one subject, as "being" is predicated of substance, of quantity and quality and the other categories. Yet substance and quantity and the others are not all called "being" for exactly the same reason; rather, all are called "being" insofar as it is predicated of substance, which is the subject of the others.

Being, therefore, is said primarily of substance and subsequently of the other categories. Thus, being is not the genus of substance and quantity, since no genus is predicated of its species on the basis of priority and posteriority. Being, in fact, is predicated analogically, and for that reason we say that substance and quantity differ generically but are the same by analogy.

Therefore in things that are numerically identical, the form and the matter are also numerically identical, for example, Tullius and Cicero. In things that are identical in species but numerically different, the matter and form are not the same numerically, but specifically, for example, Socrates and Plato. Likewise, when things are generically the same their principles are generically the same, just as the soul and body of an ass and a horse differ in species but are generically the same. So also when things are alike by analogy or proportion, their principles are identical only analogically or proportionately. Hence, matter and form and privation, or potentiality and act, are the principles of substance and of the other kinds of being. Yet the form and matter of substance and of quantity, as also the privation, differ generically, but they agree only proportionately; in other words, in the order of matter, the matter of quantity is to quantify what the matter of substance is to substance, etc., but just as substance is the cause of all other things, so the principles of substance are the principles of all others.

2. DURATION OF THE WORLD

On the Eternity of the World
against the Grumblers

If in agreement with Catholic belief we suppose that the world did not exist eternally as certain erring philosophers have affirmed, but began in time, as Holy Scripture, which cannot be in error, proclaims, the question arises as to whether it could have existed eternally. To remove this uncertainty we should begin by separating the points of accord with our adversaries from the points of discord.

If the question is put in such a way as to wonder whether anything other than God could have existed eternally, i.e., whether something not made by God could exist, we are confronted with an atrocious error, at least from the standpoint of faith, but also from the standpoint of the philosophers who hold and prove that there cannot exist anything that is not caused by him who supremely and uniquely has existence in the true sense.

Yet if we ask whether there is anything that has always existed although caused by God according to the totality that is in him, we must examine whether this position is tenable. If we should conclude that this is impossible, this will be because God was not able to make a thing with eternal existence, or because such a thing could not be made, although God was able to make it. With regard to the first alternative, all sides agree that God is able to make something with eternal existence by reason of the fact of his infinite power.

And so our assignment is to search out whether anything created could have existed eternally. If we answer that this is impossible, our answer is only understandable in two senses, i.e., there are two reasons for it to be true: either because of the removal of passive potentiality, or because of the conflict in the concepts concerned.

The first sense is clarified in the following way. Before an angel is created, an angel cannot be created, because there is no passive potentiality prior to the angel's existence, because the angel is not created from pre-existing matter. Nevertheless, God was able to make the angel and was able also to cause the angel to be created, since he has in fact created angels and they are created. Taking the question in this way, we should simply concede, in agreement with the faith, that anything caused by God cannot have existed eternally, because this affirmation would imply that a passive potentiality existed eternally, which is heretical. This does not necessitate, however, our concluding that God cannot make it happen that some being should exist eternally.

Considered in the second sense, it is argued that a thing cannot be so created because the concepts are in conflict, just as affirmation and negation cannot be true at the same time; yet some people declare that even this is within God's power. Others argue that not even God could create something like that because it is nothing. It is evident that he cannot accomplish this, because the power used to achieve it would be self-destructive. Yet if it is maintained that God can do such things, this position is not heretical, although I consider it a false one, just as the statement that the past did not occur involves in itself a contradiction. Thus Augustine, in his book against Faustus, writes the following: "Whoever says, 'If God is omnipotent, let him bring it about that what was created was not created' does not grasp that what he really is saying is this: 'If God is omnipotent, let him bring it about that what is true is false because it is true.'" (*Against Faustus* XXVI, 5). Yet, some great teachers have piously said that God can cause a past even not to have occurred in the past; and this was not considered to be heretical.

We must discover, hence, whether these two concepts are logically in conflict, namely, that anything was created by God and yet existed eternally. Whatever turns out to be true, there is no heresy in the position that God can bring it about that something created by him should exist eternally. In my opinion, this position would be false if the concepts are irreconcilable. If these concepts can be reconciled, however, not only is it not false, but it is also not impossible for this to be so; to think otherwise would be an error. Inasmuch as God's omnipotence is beyond all comprehension and power,

anyone stating that something that is intelligible for creatures cannot be done by God openly repudiates God's omnipotence. Any raising of the question of sin would be ir-
relevant here because, considered in this way, sin is nonexistent.

The whole problem amounts to this, whether or not the
ideas—creation of a thing's entire substance by God and the
absence of any origin of duration—are mutually exclusive
or not. That this involves no contradiction is shown in this
way. A contradiction could come either from only one of the
two ideas or from both of them; and in the latter alternative, either because an efficient cause must pre-exist in time
its effect or because nonexistence has to precede existence in
time; indeed, this is the reason for stating that what is created by God is made from nothing.

Therefore, we must first prove that the efficient cause,
namely, God, does not have to precede his effect in time if
he himself wills this.

First of all, no cause that produces its effect instantaneously has to precede its effect in time. Now, God is a cause
that produces his effect, not through movement, but instantaneously. Hence he does not have to precede his effect in
time. From empirical evidence based upon all instantaneous
changes such as illumination and so forth, the major premise
is evident. This can also be proven by reason. In whatever
instant a thing is said to be, the principle of its action can be
affirmed, as is obvious in all things generable. And so at the
same time that fire occurs, there begins also to be heat. In
instantaneous action as in all indivisible things, the beginning
and end of the action are simultaneous, or identical. Hence,
the end of an action can be instantaneously achieved the
moment an agent produces its effect. But the end of an action is simultaneous with the produced effect. Therefore no
intellectual absurdity is involved if we suppose that a cause
producing its effect instantaneously does not precede its effect in time. Because a movement's beginning must precede
its end, there would be contradiction in respect to causes
producing their effects through movement; because it follows that the principle of motion precedes its end. Since people usually think of productions accomplished through move-

ment, therefore they do not easily realize that an efficient cause need not precede its effect in time. And for that reason many who have a limited experience are attentive to only a few features and are too quick to express their opinions.

Nor is this reasoning upset by the consideration that as cause, God acts by his will since neither does the will have to precede its effect in time. This is also true of the person acting by will, except when he acts after deliberation. Heaven forbid that we should attribute such deliberation to God!

Moreover, the cause producing a thing's entire substance is no less able to do so when it produces the whole substance than is a cause in producing a form; it is, in fact, far more powerful, since it does not produce its effect by drawing it from the potentiality of matter, as does the agent producing a form. But an agent that produces only a form can see to it that the form it produces exists as soon as the agent itself exists, as shown by the shining sun. With far more reason, God, who produces the thing's entire substance, can cause his proper effect to exist as soon as he himself exists.

What is more, if there is ever a cause whose proceeding effect cannot co-exist at the same instant, the only reason would be the absence of some element needed for complete causing; for a complete cause and its caused effect exist simultaneously. But God has never been incomplete. Therefore an effect caused by him can exist eternally, as long as he exists, and hence he need not precede it in time.

In addition, by being exercised a person's will loses no power. But all who try to answer Aristotle's arguments to show that things have eternally come from God by contending that the same cause always produces the same effect, state that this would result except that he is an agent who acts by will. Hence, although God is recognized as an agent acting voluntarily, yet it follows that he can see to it that what he causes should never be nonexistent.

And thus it is evident that no logical contradiction is implied in the statement that an agent does not precede its effect in time. God cannot, however, bring into being anything that implies logical contradiction.

We now take up the question of whether logical contradiction is implied in holding that something created was never lacking existence. The reason for hesitation is that when something is spoken of as having been created from nothing, apparently nonexistence must precede its existence in the order of time. The lack of any contradiction is revealed by Anselm in the eighth chapter of his *Monologium*, where he discusses how a creature is said to be made from nothing. "The third interpretation," he states, "by which a thing is spoken of as having been made from nothing, is reasonable if we understand that the thing was, in fact, created, but that there is nothing out of which it was created. In like manner, we may say that when a man for no cause is sad, his sadness arises from nothing. Hence, if we keep in mind the above conclusion, namely, that except for the supreme essence everything that exists was made by it out of nothing, that is, not out of something, there is no absurdity here." From this explanation, therefore, it is evident that there is no order of procedure between what was made and nothing, so that what was made first had to be nothing and afterward be something.

To go on, let us suppose that the above-mentioned order, namely, relationship to nothing, is preserved with this meaning: The creature is made from nothing (*ex nihilo*), that is, it is made after nothing. The word "after" undeniably connotes order. But order is of various kinds; there is an order of time and an order of nature. If the common and the universal do not precede the proper and the particular, neither will it be necessary for the creature, just because it is said to exist after nothing, to have been first nothing in the order of time so that it may later be something. It is sufficient that it is nothing in the order of nature before it is a being; for what is appropriate to a thing is naturally present in it before what it receives exclusively from another. But a creature does not have its existence except from another; moreover, left to itself and considered by itself, it is nothing: Hence, nothing is in it naturally before *esse*. Nor does it follow that because nothing does not precede existence in time, that something must be nothing and being at the same time. For we do not hold that if the creature existed always, it was at any time nothing. We claim that its nature is such that if left to itself, it would be nothing; just as when we say that the air was always illumined by the sun, we should hold that the air was made luminous by the sun. And because all that comes into existence arises from the noncontingent, i.e., from that which does not happen to be as well as from that which is said to become, so we should say that the air was made luminous from being nonluminous or from being dark; not so that it was ever nonluminous or dark but so that it would be such if left only to itself. And this is more clearly seen in the case of stars and planets constantly illuminated by the sun.

It is therefore evident that there is no logical contradiction implied in the statement that something was created by God and was yet never lacking existence. If any contradiction did exist, it is strange that Augustine was unaware of it, for this would have been a most effective way to disprove the eternity of the world; and, indeed, in the eleventh and twelfth books of the *City of God* he lines up many arguments against the world's eternity. Why is it then that he completely omits any reference to this? Nay, rather, he seems to imply, in fact, that there is no apparent logical contradiction here. Hence, in the *City of God* (X: 31) he says of the Platonists: "They found a way of taking care of this by making clear that it was not a beginning of time but a principle of subordination. They explain that if from eternity a foot had always been placed in the dust, always there would be a footprint underneath, and no one would doubt that the footprint came from someone stepping there; and yet the foot would not be prior to the footprint, although the print was made by the foot. In like manner, they go on, the world and the gods created in it have existed always, because their Maker has always existed, and nevertheless they were made." Augustine never challenges this as unintelligible, but argues against his adversaries in another way. He also remarks, in Book XI, c. 4: "They who admit that the world was created by God and yet wish it to have only a principle of its creation, not a beginning in time, so that in some scarcely intelligible sense it was always created, are making an intelligible point, and so they seem to themselves to be defending God by a bold piece of luck." How and why this is scarcely intelligible was discussed in the first argument.

Another strange thing is that the best philosophers of nature failed to perceive this contradiction. Augustine, writing in opposition to those mentioned in the previous reference, says: "Our present discussion is with those who are in accord with us that God is immaterial and the Creator of all natures except his own." And about these philosophers he adds later on: "They surpassed all other philosophers in prestige and authority" (XI, 5). If we carefully reflect on the position of those holding that the world always existed, we see the same situation; for they teach, despite this fact, that it was created by God, and discern in this doctrine no logical inconsistency. Thus only they who so cleverly detected this inconsistency are men with whom wisdom is born!

Yet, since they have some authorities on their side, we must show the fragile foundation offered by these authorities. Damascene, for instance, observes: "Whatever comes to existence from nonexistence is not of such a nature that it can be co-eternal with that which is without beginning and exists eternally" (*On Orthodox Faith* I, 8). Likewise, Hugh of St. Victor, in the first part of his book, *On the Sacraments* I, 1, says: "The ineffable power of omnipotence could have nothing co-eternal with it to assist it in creating."

What these authorities and others like them intended is clarified by what Boethius says: "Some people, upon hearing Plato's view that this world had no beginning in time and would have no end, erroneously conclude the created world is thereupon made co-eternal with its Creator. But it is one thing to endure through an endless life, which is what Plato attributed to the world, and quite another to include the whole presence of endless life simultaneously, which is clearly proper to the divine spirit" (*On the Consolation of Philosophy* V, 6).

Thus it is evident that the difficulty feared by some people is not inevitable, that is, that the creature would be equal with God in duration. Rather we should say that there can be nothing co-eternal with God because there can be nothing immutable except God alone. Augustine's statement in the *City of God* XII, 15 is relevant: "Since the passing of time implies change, it cannot be co-eternal with changeless eternity. Therefore, although the immortality of the angels does not run through time, not being past as if it were no longer present, nor future as if it had not yet arrived, yet their movements proceeding through successive times change from future into past. And thus they cannot be co-eternal with the Creator, in whom we cannot say that there has been any movement that no longer lasts or that there will be any movement that has not yet occurred." In a similar way in his commentary on Genesis (VIII: 23), he said: "The Trinity, because its nature is absolutely changeless, is so eternal that nothing can be co-eternal with it." And he says something similar in the *Confessions* XI, 30.

They also present arguments proposed by philosophers and try to answer them. One of them is quite difficult; it deals with the infinite number of souls: If the world always has existed, the number of souls would now be infinite. But this argument is pointless, since God could have created the world without men and souls; or he could have created men the day he did create them even if he had created all the rest of the world from eternity. Hence the souls that survived their bodies would not be infinite in number. Also, it has not yet been proved that it is impossible for God to create an actually infinite multitude.

There are other arguments that I shall restrain myself from answering at this moment. They have been answered in other writings (*On the Power of God, Summa of Christian Teaching,* and *Summa of Theology*).

Moreover, some of these arguments are so weak that their very feebleness tends to increase the probability of the argument made by the opposing side.

3. AQUINAS ON ARISTOTELIAN NATURE

Physics   *Commentary on Physics* I, lect. 1

1. Since the book of the *Physics,* which we intend to expound is the first book of natural science, in its beginning,

one must designate what the matter and subject of natural science is.

It should be understood, therefore, that every science is in the intellect, and things become actually intelligible through their being in some way abstracted from matter. Hence, accordingly as things are variously related to matter, so do they pertain to various sciences.

Again, since all science is obtained through demonstration, and the medium of demonstration is a definition, necessarily the different sciences are differentiated through the different manners of definition.

2. Accordingly, one should understand that there are some things whose existence depends on matter and that cannot be defined without matter. At the same time there are other things, which, although they cannot exist except in sensible matter, nevertheless, sensible matter does not fall in their definition. These two differ from one another as does "curved" from "snub-nosed." For a snub nose exists in sensible matter, which must be mentioned in its definition, since a snub nose is a "nose that is curved"—and so too are all natural things, e.g., man, stone. A curve, however, although it cannot exist except in sensible matter, nevertheless does not include sensible matter in its definition—and the same is true for all mathematical things, such as numbers, magnitudes, and shapes.

But there are yet other things, which do not depend on matter either as to existence or as to definition. This is either because they never exist in matter, as is the case with God and separated substances, or else because they are not wholly in matter, as is the case with substance, potency, and act, and being itself.

3. With such things is metaphysics concerned, while mathematics deals with those things that depend on sensible matter as to existence but not as to notion. Those things, however, that depend on matter not only as to existence, but also as to notion, are the concern of natural science, called "physics."

Now, because everything that has matter is mobile, the consequence is that *mobile being* is the subject of natural philosophy. For natural philosophy is about natural things, and natural things are those whose principle is nature. Nature is a principle of motion and of rest in that in which it is. It is of those things, therefore, that have within themselves a principle of motion that natural science is concerned.

4. But because those things that follow on something common should be determined first and separately, to avoid, because of their being treated frequently, having to repeat all of that which is common, it was necessary in natural science to put first one book in which would be treated those things that follow on mobile being in common. In a similar manner first philosophy is put before all the sciences, in which are determined those things common to being *as* being.

And this book is the book of the *Physics,* also called the book *Of Physical or Natural Hearing,* because it was taught to listeners—whose subject is mobile being absolutely. I do not say that it is mobile *body,* because in this book it is proved that every mobile being is a body—and no science proves its subject. That is why the book *On the Heavens,* which follows this one, begins with the making known of body.

After this book come the other books of natural science, which treat of the species of mobile beings: in *On the Heavens,* for example, of the being mobile with respect to local motion, which is the first species of motion; in *On Generation,* of the motion to form and of the first mobile beings, namely, the elements, in regard to their changes in common, while their specific changes are treated in the *Meteorology;* of compound mobile beings that are nonliving in the book *On Minerals,* but of those that are living in the book *On the Soul* and subsequent books.

5. The philosopher has set at the beginning of the present book a preface in which he shows the order to be followed in natural science. Hence he does two things:

First, he shows that we must begin by considering principles;

Second, that we must begin with the more universal principles, at 6.

First, then, he gives the following reason. In all sciences that have principles or causes or elements, understanding and science start from a knowledge of the principles, causes, and elements. But the science concerned with nature has principles, elements, and causes. Therefore, in it one must begin by determining the principles.

When he says "understanding," he is referring to definitions; but when he says "science," he refers to demonstrations. For just as demonstrations are from causes, so also definitions, since a complete definition is a demonstration differing only as to position, as is said in *Posterior Analytics* I.

When he says "principles" or "causes" or "elements," he does not mean the same thing in each case. For "cause" applies to more things than "elements," an element being that out of which a thing is primarily composed and that is in it, as is plain in *Metaphysics* V. For example, letters are the "elements" of a word, but not the syllables. But those things are called "causes" upon which things depend for their existence or coming-to-be. Hence even things outside the thing, or which are in the thing but out of which the thing is not primarily composed, can be called "causes" but not "elements." "Principle," however, implies a certain origin in some process. Hence something can be a principle without being a cause. For example, that whence a motion starts is the principle [beginning] of the motion but not the cause; and a point is a principle [beginning] of a line but not the cause.

Consequently, by "principles" he is seen to understand moving and agent [efficient] causes, in which especially there is found a certain process with order; by "causes" he is seen to understand formal and final causes, on which things depend especially for their being and coming-to-be; by "elements," however, strictly the first material cause.

He uses these terms disjunctively rather than combined to designate that not every science demonstrates through all the causes. For mathematics demonstrates through the formal cause only, while metaphysics demonstrates mainly through formal and final causes, and even through the agent cause. Natural philosophy, however, demonstrates through all the causes.

The first proposition of the argument adduced he proves by appealing to what is commonly believed, as in *Posterior Analytics* I; for it is when a person considers that he knows all the causes of a thing, from the first down to the last, that he considers that he knows it. And there is no reason to interpret "causes" and "elements" and "principles" here in a sense different from the above, as the commentator [Averroes] wishes, but in the same way. And he says "down to the elements," because the last thing known is the matter. For matter is for the sake of form, but the form is from the agent for the sake of the end—unless, of course, it itself is the end. Thus we say that it is for the sake of cutting that a saw has teeth, and that they must needs be of iron to be suitable for cutting.

6. Then when he says, "The natural way of doing this . . ." he shows that among principles one must determine first concerning the more universal ones.

First, he shows this through an argument;

Second, by certain signs, at 9.

As to the first he gives this reason. The natural procedure in learning for us is to proceed from the things better known to us to what is better known by nature. But the things that are better known to us are confused, as are universal things. Therefore, we must proceed from universals to singulars.

7. To explain the first proposition he points out that things better known to us and things better known by nature are not the same; rather, things better known according to nature are less known with respect to us. And since the natural way or order of learning is to pass from what is known to us to what is unknown to us, we must therefore proceed from things better known to us to things better known by nature.

But notice that he says that the better known by nature, and the better known absolutely, are the same. The absolutely better known are those things better known in themselves. Now, those things are better known in themselves that possess a greater measure of being, because a thing is knowable insofar as it is being. But it is things that are more in act that are fuller in being. Hence such are the most knowable by nature.

Now, just the opposite happens with respect to us, since we pass from potency to act in knowing; moreover, our knowledge begins from sensible things, which are material, and intelligible in potency. Hence such things are prior known to us rather than separated substances, which are better known according to nature, as is plain in *Metaphysics* II.

He does not say that some things are better known "by nature" as though nature knows them, but because they are better known according to themselves and according to their own nature. Again, he says "better known and more certain," since not just any kind of knowledge is sought in the sciences, but certitude of knowledge.

To understand the second proposition, it must be known that "confused," as used here, refers to things that contain within themselves certain things in potency and indistinctly. Now, since to know something indistinctly is midway between pure potency and perfect act, therefore when our intellect proceeds from potency to act, there first occurs to it that which is confused before that which is distinct. But scientific knowledge is then complete in act when one has arrived by resolution to a distinct knowledge of the principles and elements. This is the reason why things are first known to us in a confused rather than in a distinct way.

That universals are confused is plain, since they contain their species within themselves in potency; and whoever knows something universally knows it indistinctly. But this knowledge becomes distinct when each of the things contained potentially in the universal becomes known in act—for one who knows "animal" knows "rational" only potentially. But one knows something in potency prior to knowing it in act. Therefore, according to this order of learning, by which we pass from potency to act, "animal" is known by us prior to our knowing "man."

8. But this seems contrary to what the philosopher says in *Posterior Analytics* I, namely, that singulars are better known to us, and universals better known by nature and absolutely.

But we should understand that there he takes "singulars" to mean the sensible individuals, which are indeed better known to us, because sense knowledge, which is of singulars, in us precedes intellectual knowledge, which is of universals. But because intellectual knowledge is more perfect, universals being intelligible in act and singulars not—since these are material—universals are better known absolutely and according to nature.

But here [in the *Physics*] Aristotle is using the word "singulars" not in reference to individuals, but to species, which [in comparison to genera] are better known according to nature, as being more perfect and affording distinct knowledge, whereas genera are better known to us as affording knowledge that is in potency and confused.

One must know, however, that the commentator gives a different explanation. For he says that when he says, "The natural way of doing this . . ." the philosopher wants to point out this science's manner of demonstrating, namely, that it demonstrates through effects and through what is posterior according to nature. Hence what is said here should be understood of the sequence in demonstrating, and not of that in determining. And when he says, "Now what is to us plain and obvious . . ." he intends to point out, according to him, just which things are better known to us and less known according to nature, namely, composite more than simple things, understanding "confused" to mean "composite." Then he concludes that the procedure should be from the more universal to the less universal, as a certain corollary.

Hence his explanation is patently defective, for it fails to combine the whole under one intention. Moreover, the philosopher has no intention here of pointing out this science's mode of demonstration, because he will do that in Book II according to the order of determining. Again, "confused" should not be taken to mean "composed," but "indistinct"— for nothing could be concluded from universals, since genera are not composed of species.

9. Then when he says, "For it is a whole that is best known . . ." he shows his proposition by three signs. The first is taken from an integral sensible whole. He says that such a sensible whole is better known according to sense; therefore, an intelligible whole is better known according to intellect. Now, the universal is a certain intelligible whole, because it comprehends many things as parts, namely, its inferiors. Therefore the universal is better known to us according to intellect.

But this proof seems to be ineffectual, because he uses "whole," "part," and "comprehension" equivocally. One should answer, however, that an integral whole and a universal whole agree in that both are confused and indistinct. For just as one who apprehends the genus does not apprehend the species distinctly but in potency only, so one who apprehends a house does not immediately distinguish the parts. Accordingly, since by reason of its confusedness, the whole is better known to us, the same holds good for both wholes. But to be composite is not common to both. Hence it is plain that above he deliberately said "confused" and not "composed."

10. Then when he says, "Much the same thing happens . . ." he gives another example, namely, that of an integral intelligible whole. For the defined is related to its defining elements after the fashion of an integral whole, inasmuch as the elements of the definition are in act in the defined. But he who apprehends the word, e.g., "man" or "circle," does not immediately distinguish the defining principles. Thus the word is like a certain indistinct whole, but the definition "divides into singulars," i.e., distinctly places the principles of the defined.

But this seems to be contrary to what he previously said. For the defining elements seem to be more universal, and such he said to be better known to us. Again, if the defined were better known than the defining elements, they would not make the defined known to us by definition—for nothing is made known to us except from things better known to us.

In reply to this, it should be observed that the defining elements are indeed in themselves better known to us than the defined, but we know the defined before we know that such and such are its defining elements. For example, we know animal and rational before we know man, but we know man confusedly before we know that "animal" and "rational" are its defining elements.

11. Then when he says, "Similarly a child begins . . ." he gives a third example taken from the more universal sensible thing. For just as the more universal intelligible thing is prior known to us according to intellect, e.g., animal prior to man, so the more common sensible is prior known to us according to sense, e.g., this animal prior to this man.

And I say that it is prior known according to sense both according to place and according to time. In regard to place, because when someone is seen a long way off, we perceive him first as being a body before we perceive him as an animal, and then as animal before as man, and then as man before as Socrates. Likewise, in the order of time, a child first apprehends a given person as *a* man before apprehending him as *this* man who is Plato, who is his father. That is why he says: "Children at first call all men 'father' and all women 'mother,' but later on distinguish," i.e., distinctly know, "each."

This plainly shows that we first know something confusedly before we know it distinctly.*

| On Generation and Corrup-
tion | *Commentary on Generation
and Corruption,* Prologue |

1. As the philosopher says in *On the Soul* III, the sciences are divided off in the same manner as things are—for all habits are distinguished by their objects, from which they are specified. Now, the things considered by natural science are motion and mobile being. Thus the philosopher says in *Physics* II that whatever things move, they themselves being moved, these belong to physical speculation. Consequently, it is according to the differences between motions and mobiles that the parts of natural science must be distinguished and ordered.

Now, the first motion is local motion, which is more perfect than the other kinds, and common to all natural bodies, as is proved in *Physics* VII. Therefore, after the study of motions and mobiles in common in the book *Physics,* it was first necessary to treat of bodies as they are moved with local motion. This was in the book *On the Heavens,* which is the second book of natural science. What remains, therefore, is to consider the other subsequent motions that are not common to all bodies but that are found only in lower bodies.

Among these motions, generation and corruption obtain the primacy. For alteration is directed to generation as to its end, and the end is by nature more perfect than what leads to it. Growth, likewise, is subsequent to generation, for growth does not take place without a certain particular generation, namely, that by which food is converted into the thing fed. Thus the philosopher says in *On the Soul* II that

* Translated by P. H. Conway, O.P., and R. F. Larcher, O.P.

food nourishes insofar as it is potentially flesh, but it produces increase inasmuch as potentially it is quantified flesh. Therefore, since these motions are in a certain way consequent upon generation, they must be studied along with generation and corruption.

2. Now, it should be noted that whatever is found in a number of things should first be considered in common before coming to the specific cases. Otherwise the same thing will be frequently repeated, in that what is common will be repeated in each individual case, as the philosopher proves in *On the Parts of Animals* I. Consequently, generation and corruption should be considered in common before coming to the parts [i.e., species] thereof.

Likewise, it should be noted that if in any genus there be found some first thing that is the cause of the other things in that genus, the study of the common genus and of that which is first in that genus will belong to the same study. For that first thing is the cause of the entire genus, and anyone who studies some genus must consider the causes of the entire genus. That is why the philosopher in *Metaphysics* at once studies being in general and first being, which is separated from matter. Now, in the genus of generable and corruptible things there are found certain first principles, namely, the elements, which are the cause of generation and corruption and alteration in all other bodies. Hence Aristotle in this book, which is the third part of natural science, discusses not only generation and corruption in general and other consequent motions, but also generation and corruption of the elements.

With these prefatory remarks to show Aristotle's intention in this book, we now arrive at its exposition.*

* Translated by P. H. Conway, O.P., and R. F. Larcher, O.P.

4. ON BECOMING

Change   *Commentary on Metaphysics*
                                     XII, lect. 2, 2429–38

Since all change takes place from one contrary to another, there must be some grounding subject able to endure change from contrary to contrary. And the philosopher shows this in two ways: first, by noting that one contrary does not become its opposite, as blackness does not itself become whiteness. So if any change takes place between black and white, there has to be something other than blackness becoming white. Second, he also indicates this from the fact that throughout any change, there is something in the end product that has remained. So, in the becoming white of something black, the very body remains but the other contrary, namely, the black, does not remain. Clearly then the matter or grounding subject is a third element over and above the two contraries.

. . . Hence, because there is a third factor called matter in every change, that which is changed or the subject of change must itself be in potentiality to each of the contraries. Otherwise, both could not be received, nor could it become one from being another. Hence any body changed from black to white is as a body in potentiality to both colors, and also matter that is the grounding subject of generation and corruption is in the generation of any substance in potentiality to form and to the privation of this form, itself possessing neither one in actuality, but only in potentiality.

. . . The philosopher then solves the problem of the ancient natural philosophers who denied all generation simply because they did not think that anything could be made out of nonbeing, inasmuch as *ex nihilo fit nihil;* nor could anything come from being, because it would thus be existing before it existed.

He eliminated this difficulty by indicating how a thing is made from being and nonbeing, distinguishing two manners of being: being in actuality and being in potentiality, as when something is changed from being potentially white to being actually white. . . . Likewise is everything made from nonbeing and being in the genus of substance. It comes from nonbeing accidentally inasmuch as it comes from matter modified by the privation of the new form, and for this reason it is called nonbeing. But it comes per se from being, certainly not from being in act but from being in potentiality, i.e., from matter that as previously noted is being in potentiality.

(Matter can also be referred to as nonbeing, not so as to mean that it exists in no way at all, but in the sense that it does not exist as being in actuality.)

Although generation takes place in nonbeing as a potentiality, this is not to say that any manner of thing can come from anything at all; rather, various things come from various matters. For every being that can be generated comes from some determined matter inasmuch as form must always be proportioned to its matter. For even prime matter, which is in potentiality to all forms, receives them in a given order. It is primarily in potentiality to the elementary forms, and through their mediation, in accord with various combined proportions, it is in potentiality to various higher forms; so that it is not the case that anything at all can be made immediately from any kind of matter—except by some possible reduction to prime matter.

Time   *Commentary on Sentences* I,
                                 d. 19, q. 2, a. 1

I say that it must be said, because some want to know the difference between eternity, time, and *aevum,* that time has a beginning and end; *aevum* has a beginning and no end; eternity has neither beginning nor end. But this does not give us their essential difference, even if it were supposed that time would never begin and never end, even then time would not be eternity, as Boethius says (*Consolations of Philosophy* V). Even supposing that always there have been angels, *aevum* would still differ from eternity. What truth there is in this will be clarified from the following points. Hence it should be known that the three aforementioned names signify a certain duration. Every duration occurs, however, because there is something in actuality, for a thing is said to endure as long as it actually exists, not insofar as it is potential. Moreover, there are two ways of being in actuality: either as an incomplete actuality, one mixed with potentiality, whose essence goes into act, and such an act is motion, for there is a motion of existing in potentiality, as the philosopher says (*Physics* III: 6); or according to an actuality unmixed with potentiality, not receiving any addition of perfection, and such is a permanent and lasting actuality. *Esse* is such an actuality in two ways: either so that a thing has its *esse* in act as acquired from another, and then the thing having such *esse* is potential with respect to that act and wholly receives it; or *esse* in act is in the thing from itself so that it is of the essence of its quiddity, and such *esse* is divine *esse*, in which there is no potentiality with respect to its act. Hence it becomes evident that act is present in three ways.

There is the kind without any underlying potentiality; such is the divine *esse* and its operation, and to this the measurement of eternity corresponds. There is another actuality with a certain underlying potentiality; yet a complete act is acquired in that potentiality; and to this *aevum* corresponds. There is, however, another actuality with an underlying potentiality, and for it the act is completed by receiving the addition of perfection according to succession; and to this, *time* corresponds. When therefore anything has a proper measure, the essential difference of that measure comes from the condition of the act that is measured. Moreover, where act is in motion, we find a succession of before and after.

And these two, namely, before and after, which are named through the soul, mean measurement by numbering, which time is. Whence the philosopher says (*Physics* IV: 10), that time is the number of motion according to before and after. And this is number numbered and not simply number. For we say that two dogs are number numbered, and two is simply number—the number of before and after, which time is. Hence it is clear that what time is materially is founded on motion, namely, before and after; but what time formally is, is achieved in the operation of the enumerating soul, on account of which the philosopher says (*Physics* IV: 131), that if there were not a soul, there would not be time. So therefore, there are two reasons for time: either two "nows" between which is time, or two times continued through one "now"; and they are successive. Even continuity approaches time by reason of the motion it measures. Whence, if there should be any noncontinuous motion not being coordinated with relation to the continuous motion of the leaving, the time measuring that motion would not be continuous. From which it is evident that nothing is measured by time unless it is within time by a beginning and end. For even supposing that there always was a motion of the heavens, according to the philosopher (*Physics* VIII: 7), yet each revolution or part of it that is measured by time according to before and after has in itself a beginning and an end; for there is no measuring without a beginning and end. However, in that act that is complete act, we know of no before and after, nor is there any plurality and so no succession; whence the measure corresponding to this is not the number kind but the unity kind. Therefore just as time's before and after known according to number fulfill the definition of time, so the permanence of act as known by the reason, which has the sense of measurement, fulfills the definition of *aevum* and of eternity. But because the *esse* of the aeviternal things is acquired from another, *aevum* measures an *esse* having a beginning; not so eternity, however, which measures *esse* not acquired from another. And so when "beginning" is not uniformly understood, various statements can be made; for eternity is found with that *esse* without any efficient beginning; *aevum*, however, has such a beginning; while time belongs to the actuality that has a beginning and end of duration as measured by time.

MAN

Whatever we most cherish in what is "human" is to be found within the "existence" that St. Thomas considered to be the source of value in man. For in man "existence" is both a creation and a conversion—the basis of a relationship from God and toward God. Creatureship is in no sense a state of separation from God but a mode of relationship to God. All cosmic forces are there to sustain this human existence, and even evil is understood most profoundly when seen as a threat to the plenitude and the possibilities of human existence. Moral evil or sin is the most destructive of all forces precisely because it is the most dehumanizing of all the dangers encountered by man. In fact, to be aware of the depths and heights of human dignity on account of its divine origin and destiny is required for any full appreciation of the horror of dehumanization, that is, the ruin of God's great icon—man. But with St. Thomas the image doctrine or the consideration of man as God's image and nonhuman things as vestiges of God, the emphasis on exemplarism or the looking beyond the imperfect things of experience to their perfect ideas in the divine mind, the view of the universe as sacramental or symbolic, may not be allowed to detract from man's integrity, autonomy, robust reality. In the Thomistic universe all true zeal for God is translated into the promotion of human values. Whatever counts for the humanization and liberation of men is an essential part of the sacred service of God. For Aquinas, created nature is a realm of reality with immanent ends, and man is intended to pass through the accomplishment of immanent ends to reach ultimate ends. To be a Christian, one has to be a man. There is an enthusiastic humanism here precisely because there is true theology. In recognizing distinctions between man and God, Aquinas aims, as we saw, at their union, which makes human destiny in many senses sacred.

There is in fact an excellent philosophical reason why the image doctrine in Thomistic thought does not make of man and his world an unreal or shadowy one, for in a metaphysic where God is infinite existence (*ipsum esse subsistens*) man would never image God without being robustly real!

The truth theory of Thomas is, as one would expect, saturated with existence. From an original contact with a sensible existent, man as intelligent sees what is knowable within it, judging that it exists. An accurate description of a thing's manner of existing is then called "true." Awareness includes self-consciousness, and through intentionality there is a consciousness of "others." The act of existing is as beyond our knowing as God is, so that existence must be refracted to us by way of essences without ever transferring our interest from the existence to the essence simply because of the ease of dealing with concepts. Any loss of interest in existence would bring about, according to Thomas, the capitulation of metaphysics, an event not unheard of in the history of philosophy! By retaining interest in existence Aquinas thereby retained room for mystery in the knowing process. It is not only in theology that mystery has its place. Theology, of course, is a participation in the knowledge of those who see God, but God is never totally known. And because man and his world are made by God, they somehow share in his incomprehensibility. So that a philosopher who recognizes the mystery of created existence will never claim to encapsulate existence, never pretend to arrive at an exhaustive knowledge of reality such as rationalists are famed for claiming. A rationalist metaphysic should never be confused with existential metaphysics, which never boasts of giving final or conclusive answers but offers some valid affirmations supported by experience.

A consideration at this point of the Thomistic analysis of knowledge is instructive as to Aquinas's manner of arriving at conclusions. In the *Summa of Theology* I, q. 84, a. 6, Thomas develops his theory of knowledge in relation to previous theories. He is choosing to follow Aristotle, but finds a contradiction between the philosopher's teaching that "the beginning of our knowledge lies in the senses" and the assumption that "intellectual knowledge transcends the things of sense." In meeting this difficulty he traces the progress in epistemology from Democritus through Plato to Aristotle, concluding that the last thinker had come closest to the truth.

Although the view of the early Greek atomists concerning matter and the soul was totally different from his, he recognized the need to grasp their thought before disagreeing with it. Although matter is not the whole of man, it does belong to human nature, and so Plato's excessive dependence on the ideas as cause and content of human nature appears unreal to Aquinas. If Aristotle is right in declaring man to be made up of matter and form, human knowledge is quite probably achieved through the conjunction of the material and formal principles. But since neither matter alone nor spirit alone can account for human nature, there must be a mediating principle at work in human activity. Aristotle called this the active intellect, which transformed the sensible species of the mind into the impressed intelligible species capable of being received by the possible intellect. This process is abstraction—the elimination of all individuating notes from an intentional form so that it can be assimilated by a totally immaterial faculty. Aquinas is utilizing here the Aristotelian act/potentiality formulation when he explains knowledge as the taking in of an actually intelligible form or, in other words, the bringing of the possible intellect from potentiality to actuality. The active intellect performing this function is not separated from man as the passage of Aristotle's *On the Soul* (III, 5) suggests to some, but the soul in act animates the very formation of the sensible image. Thomas favors his own "theory of abstraction" only because it leaves the intellect totally transcendent while it does not try to explain away its extrinsic dependence upon the body for the images used in the abstractive process.

The proper object of the human intellect is then the essence of sensible realities, their quiddity, not as separated from sensible things, as Plato thought, but as distinguished by mind. By this intellectual abstraction man uses the data presented by the senses and by reflection realizes from whence the data was obtained. Now, Aquinas's adoption of the balanced Aristotelian view of the form/matter content of the human essence is a bulwark against certain subsequent extremes. Although the theories of Democritus are no longer held in their original form, since science has progressed too far for this, some still hold that knowledge can be reduced to physical phenomena. Those who explain the rational powers of man as simply a matter of synapses and the chemical rearrangement of proteins are missing the all-important point. No matter how well they can explain the workings of man's brain, they will not be able to reach man's immaterial power, by which *meaning* is grasped. The difference is qualitative and essential. There is also a contemporary trend to make a sort of "common intellect" out of society and forbid man his own independent access to truth. All is culture-clouded, and society as the climate of thought is the cause of our thoughts. But in Thomas's theory a man can transcend his environment just as he can transcend the material conditions surrounding any essence; material conditions will be his point of departure, and yet arrival at the truth or being of whatever he is studying is not ruled out. As an unlimited power, man's intellect opens man to the infinite, although only love reaches it. The relation of each man to transcendent existence in his knowing and living experience—this is the ground of objectivity.

Existence is likewise the ground for any right understanding of love. As self-communicative, generous, ecstatic, existence within God is the paradigm for all true love and for the vast possibilities of human nobility. Contrary to what some Thomist manuals of the past publicized about St. Thomas's preference for knowledge over love, the texts show that here as elsewhere—in the question of body as related to soul, speculative knowledge as related to practical, nature as related to grace—St. Thomas warred against dichotomy and argued in favor of continuity and convergence. He refers to the important truths—moral and religious ones—as being open to those who love. And he grounds the possibility for a pure love, that is, a love of dedication rather than a love of desire, upon a certain appreciative awareness of the intrinsic value of persons.

As to the other aspects of man, while it is possible to make Thomistic psychology consist in an analysis of each faculty of man separately considered—intellect and the external and internal senses, will and the powers of tendency—such a procedure gives only a truncated view of man. Of course, these various powers are discussed by Aquinas, as indeed they were by Aristotle, but in the Thomistic theory of man, the power is not itself except in relation to other human powers, which are all related to actions animated by a principle of spiritual existence (*esse*), in which all actions more or less participate according to their degree of independence from matter. If any student considers each power individually, he must be careful to restore it to its place in the totality of the human existent—the living, knowing, loving man who acts freely in response to real appeals. In this setup the overall tendency in man is toward the good, the will's end, which is always an existent, something real. Because every knowing subject is orientated toward the good as real—we call this its "finality" or *telos*—every and any action of man participates in this tendency toward the real, and even intellectual knowing becomes thereby related to a real object. Through the will's mediation, the object of knowledge becomes immanent as end to the knowing subject.

Any natural tendency is usually determined by the form of the tending subject, but a knowing or immaterial subject experiences the attraction toward things not by its own form alone, nor in any indetermined way, but as specified by the forms of the things it knows. And because it is the privilege of immaterial being to know itself—and immaterial being, for all its invisibility, is real being—the form that determines its knowledge of itself and of things united to it will be essentially relative to the real. Intentional being therefore has whatever form it has under the influence of our tendency toward the real thing under the attraction of the will's end. We call this real thing an object because it cannot be identified with the subject, but this does not mean that it is "out there." Indeed, through the form of the inclination it determines, it is immanent, and in Scholastic terminology it is known as the intelligible species, that is to say, the intentional being of the object, which specifies self-consciousness.

Self-consciousness for Aquinas is the nexus of metaphysical and psychological conditions of knowledge rather than logical ones. This represents a conjunction at a profound level of the vision of Augustine and the method of Kant. Absolute being or truth imposes itself as the ultimate determining a priori or transcendental condition of all human knowledge.

Therefore, what is signified by our judgments is more than is represented in the concepts we affirm. For because the formal object of the intellect is absolute being—although not on the conscious level—objective thought is made possible. By this self-consciousness or reflection upon one's intellectual activity we find two elements not entirely provided by sense experience: the self or ego, which is the concrete element common to all judgments, and being, the basis of cognitive objectivity, *being,* attainable only by a *spiritual activity* such as intellectual knowing. By applying the principle *actio sequitur esse* (the kind of action denotes the kind of existence) we may argue to the soul's spiritual existence, which is the reason offered by Aquinas for its immortality. But since the Final Cause or absolute being is the first of all causes and really, if only implicitly, attracts me to the perfect good or perfect truth, then every act of the will is a tendency toward this perfect good, and all finite things are desirable through participating in the good. And because every judgment is therefore an *experience* toward the infinite, we may conclude that there is present implicitly in every judgment an affirmation of God.

It likewise follows that since man's ultimate future initiates all human desires toward finite goals, all that man desires, he desires implicitly in process toward his final fulfillment—his Omega. But if man's dynamic orientation toward "being," which insures objectivity in his thinking, stems from his spiritual soul dimension, a major contribution to human knowledge is made by man's body. For it is only by "conversion to the phantasm" (bringing together the universal concept and the concrete image) that man is enabled to judge concrete individuals; so that adequate self-consciousness would mean awareness of the activity of human knowing, which is, after all, rooted in the substantial unity of matter and spirit in the knowing subject. All this is behind the dissatisfaction of existential realists of the Thomist tradition with the so-called radical empiricists. In view of the fact that the Thomist finds the self-experience to be the point of departure for a metaphysics of man and God, he also sees "radical empiricism" to be not radical enough.

So in an integral Thomistic theory of man we study the

human person who knows in the knowing experience the human person who wills in the will experience.

One last word about the important contemporary theme of freedom. Freedom is seen by Aquinas not as independence from an absolute but as independence from the relative. The relative is, after all, the only place where man will meet resistance to his free action. For if God, who is the absolute, is the Maker of man as free, human freedom, by dependence upon the absolute, will only be reinforced. Now, the only way man has of uniting with the absolute, who infinitely surpasses man's intellectual power, is by the surrender of love, and everyone knows that no love that is not freely offered deserves the name of love. And so if man is related to others so that to be man is to be in communion with others, living for them, then indeed love never diminishes man's freedom, since only through love does man become himself. And to be himself is to be free.

All of this shows that Aquinas accepted Augustine's concrete Christian man even while he quite heavily utilized the Aristotelian theoretical analysis of human nature.

Man

1. HUMAN NATURE AND PERSON

Existence, Source of Like-   *Summa of Christian Teaching*
ness to God   I, 19

Things make it clear that *they naturally desire to be;* so that
if some of them are corruptible, they naturally resist corrupting influences, tending toward where they are secure, as fire
tends upward and earth downward. Now, all things have
being insofar as they are like God, who is self-subsistent being; for only by participation are they beings. Consequently,
all things desire to be like God as their last end.

Moreover, all creatures are images of the first agent,
namely, God, because *the agent produces its like* (*On Generation and Corruption* I, 7, 6). Now, an image's perfection is
found in reproducing the original through resemblance; this
is why an image is made. And so all things are made in order
to acquire as their last end a divine likeness.

Each thing tends by its motion or action to some good as
its end, as proven. But anything participates in the good to
the degree that it is like the sovereign goodness, i.e., God.
And so all things by their motions and actions tend to a divine
likeness as to their last end.

Human Vocation: To Become   *Summa of Christian Teaching*
like God   II, 20

From the previous statements it is evident that to become
like God is the last end of all things. Now, if something is
an end, it is good. And so, strictly speaking, it is because he
is good that things tend toward likeness with God.

Yet the goodness gained by creatures is not the goodness found in God; but everything images the divine goodness in its way—for the divine goodness, all in one, is simple inasmuch as the divine being, as proven in the First Book, comprises the totality of perfection. And so since a being is good insofar as it is perfect, God's being is his perfect goodness; for in God to exist, to live, to be wise, to be happy, and anything else obviously belonging to perfection and goodness, are one and the same in God, as if everything adding up to his goodness were God's very being. Moreover, God's being is the substance of the existing God. But this is not the case with other beings, for it was shown in the Second Book that no created substance is its own being. And so, if a thing is good insofar as it exists and there is not anything that is its own being nor its own goodness, then each thing is good by participating in good, just as by participating in being, it is a being. . . .

From the previous statements it is clear that God by his simple being has his perfect and entire goodness, yet creatures do not become perfectly good solely through their being, but through many things. Thus, although each one insofar as it exists is good, it cannot be said to be absolutely good as long as it is deprived of things that its goodness requires; so any unvirtuous man who is enslaved to vice is spoken of as good with restriction, namely, as a being and as a man, but not absolutely; he should in fact rather be called evil. And so to be and to be good are not identical in any creature, but each one is good, however, insofar as it exists; but with God to be and to be good are simply identical.

If, therefore, everything aims at likeness to God's goodness as its end, and likeness to God's goodness is based upon whatever belongs to a thing's goodness, which consists not merely in a thing's being but in all things required for its perfection, as indicated, it is obvious that when we say that things are directed to God as their end we mean this not only in regard to their substantial being but also with regard to anything accidentally belonging to their perfection, which also includes their proper activity.

Procedure in Studying the   *Commentary on Soul* I, lect. 1
Soul

As the philosopher teaches in *On Animals* (XI), when we
consider any genus of things we must first reflect upon what
is common and then upon what is proper to each class of
that genus taken separately. Such a method is followed by
Aristotle in *First Philosophy,* for in *Metaphysics* I he discusses
and reflects upon what is common to being solely as being, and
then he considers what is proper to any particular class of
being. Without this method, there would be constant repeti-
tion. All living beings have one genus, so that when we study
living beings we should consider first what is common to
them all. We should then reflect upon what is proper to a
particular one. A soul is that which all living things have in
common; in this all are alike. And so to deal with the science
of living things we must begin with the science of the soul as
common to them. Consequently, Aristotle begins with the
science of the soul. Later in future books he uncovers what is
proper to individual living things.

Aristotle on the Soul   *Commentary on Soul* II,
lect. 1

After recording in the first book others' opinions on the
soul, Aristotle in the second book begins studying the soul
from his own viewpoint, which is a right one. . . .

Since the three kinds of substance are the composite, the
matter, and the form, and since the soul is neither the composite, the living body, nor the matter, the body, which is the
subject of life, the only remaining alternative is for the soul
to be a substance as *form* or *species* of a certain kind of body,
a physical body having life in potentiality.

He says "having life in potentiality," not merely "having
life," for a composite living substance is understood as *a
living body,* but the definition of a form does not include the
composite. In a living body matter is related to life as potentiality to act. The soul is the act by which the body
lives. . . .

Lest anyone think the soul to be an act like an accidental

form, he adds that the soul is act as substance is act, i.e., as a form; and since every form is in a determined matter, it is consequently the form of a body of a particular kind, as was said.

The difference between substantial and accidental form should be noted. Accidental form does not merely make a thing *exist,* but makes it exist in some way, i.e., as large or as white, etc. But substantial form merely makes a thing exist, so that accidental form is added to an already existing subject. A substantial form is not added to an actually existing subject but to a potentially existing subject, namely, prime matter. It is clear, therefore, that one thing may not have many substantial forms. The first form would make a thing merely exist; all others would be added to an already actually existing subject. So they would be added accidentally to an already actually existing subject, and would not make it merely to exist but to exist in a particular way.

This contradicts Avicebron's position in his book, *Fountain of Life.* He maintains that in any one thing there are as many substantial forms as there are genera and species. In any individual man, for instance, there is one form making him a substance, another making him a body, a third making him a living body, etc. But through our previous discussion we saw that one same substantial form makes an individual a special thing or substance as well as a body and a living body, etc.; for a more perfect form not only contributes to matter whatever is given by a less perfect one, but gives more. So the soul not only makes a thing to be a substance and a body (a stone's form does that), but makes it to be also a living body. We should not imagine that the soul is the act of a body in such a way that the body is its matter and subject as though it were already established as body by one form making it to be body, and the soul then comes as something added to it to make it a living body; for the soul causes the body both to exist and to live. Bodily being as the more imperfect is the material principle related to life.

Thus when the soul departs from the body, the same specific body no longer remains. A dead man's eye and flesh are spoken of as "eye" and "flesh" only equivocally, as the philosopher points out in *Metaphysics* VII. As the soul de-

parts, another substantial form takes its place to establish a
new species, since nothing ever corrupts without another
thing being generated.

When he then says, "There are two kinds of act, etc.," he
studies the second part of the definition. He states that there
are two kinds of *act*, one like knowledge, the other like actual
knowing. . . . It is evident that the soul is an act like knowledge because the soul is an animal whether asleep or awake.
Wakefulness is like actual knowing, which is a use of knowledge, whereas sleep is like habitual knowledge not being
used, since an animal's powers are at rest in sleep.

Science is the first of these two acts in the order of generation within one same being, since actual knowing is related
to habitual knowledge as act to potentiality. As stated in
Metaphysics IX, act is in nature prior to potentiality insofar
as it is the end and perfection of potentiality. And in the order of temporal generation, absolutely speaking, act is prior
to potentiality, since whatever is potential is brought into
act by something already in act. But within one same thing
potentiality is prior to act, for a thing is primarily in potentiality before it is in act. And so he states that science (habitual
knowledge) is prior to actual knowing in the order of generation within one same being.

He then concludes that inasmuch as the soul is an act like
science (habitual knowledge), it is the first act of a physical
body having life in potentiality. He says *first act* not only to
distinguish the soul from act as operation, but also from the
forms of the bodily elements that have their own actions unless controlled.

When he then says, "The body we spoke of, etc.," he begins to consider the definition as it relates to subject. He had
stated that the soul is the act of a physical body having life
in potentiality; he now adds that this applies to every organic
body. An organic body is one having various organs, needed
in a living body for the soul's various operations. The soul
as the most perfect form among forms of corporeal things is
the principle of varied operations. For its fulfillment it
therefore requires a variety of organs. Because of their imperfection the forms of inanimate things are principles of

relatively few operations, and so for their fulfillment they do not require a variety of organs.

The least perfect of all souls is the plant soul; so there is less variety among organs in plants than in animals. In showing every body receptive to life as organic, he uses as his example plants, which have less variety among organs. He says that the plant parts are distinct organs, but that such parts are very simple, that is, homogeneous. There is less diversity in them than in animals. An animal's foot, for instance, has diverse parts: flesh, nerve, bone, etc. But a plant's organic parts are not made up of such diverse parts.

He proves that plant parts are organic in showing them to have diverse operations. The leaf covers the part bearing the fruit, i.e., the part wherein fruit is produced. In its turn, the fruit-bearing part protects the fruit. Plant roots are comparable to the animal mouth, since both take in nourishment.

When he then says, "And so, if there is a common, etc.," he assembles the definition of soul from everything said. He states that if we must have a common definition to predicate of every type of soul it is this: *The soul is the first act of a physical organic body*. We need not add "having life in potentiality," since the word *organic* replaces this.

. . . He says that it is unnecessary for us to inquire whether the soul and body become one, for wax and its shape are doubtless one just as matter and its form are one. In *Metaphysics* VIII it was shown that form is directly joined to matter as its act. Matter joined to form is the same as matter actually existing. He refers to this also when saying that one and being are spoken of in various ways, for example, as being in potentiality and being in act. For just as being in potentiality is not being absolutely [without qualification] but only relatively [qualifiedly], neither is it unity absolutely but only relatively; so that unity is predicated of a thing insofar as the thing has being. Because the body exists through the soul, its form, it follows that it is joined to the soul without any medium; but as the mover of the body, the soul is not necessarily without an intermediary, because the soul moves one part by means of another.

Meaning of Life   *Summa of Theology* I, q. 18,
                                          a. 2, c

On the other hand, we have Aristotle's statement, "for living things, to live is to be."

As is apparent from what was said, our intellect, whose proper object is the essences of things, gets information from the senses, whose proper objects are external accidental qualities. So through its external appearance we get to know the essence of anything; and inasmuch as we name a thing from what we know of it . . . names signifying the essences of things are usually taken from the thing's external qualities. Thus such names are often used strictly to indicate the essences, or they are sometimes understood to mean the qualities prompting the name, but this is a less strict use. So it is apparent that the word "body" intends to designate a certain class of substances insofar as they have three dimensions; and thus the name "body" is often used to indicate three dimensions, by which body is classified as a kind of quantity.

Now, the same is true of life. The word is used of things on account of something that appears externally, namely, self-movement; yet it is not used to designate precisely that but rather the substance whose nature is empowered to move itself or give itself any impulse to action. In this latter sense, "to live" simply means to be such a nature, and life signifies this same thing abstractly, just as "running" signifies abstractly the act of running. So "living" is not an accidental predicate but a substantial one. Yet often "life" is used in the less strict sense to designate the activities of life by which we understand things to have life; so Aristotle says that to live is primarily "to have sensation and understanding."

What Is Soul?   *Summa of Theology* I, q. 77,
                                          a. 1

We cannot agree that the soul's essence is its power, although some have held this. We shall indicate this in two ways. First, because being and every kind of being is divided into potentiality and act, a potentiality or power and its act must be found in the same genus; so that if the act is not in the genus of substance, the potentiality or power directed to that act cannot be in the genus of substance. Whence the divine power, which is the principle of his action, is the divine essence itself. This cannot be the case with the soul or with any creature, as we stated when discussing the angels (q. 54, a. 3). Second, this may also be shown as impossible in the soul. By its very essence the soul is in act, so that if the very essence of the soul were the immediate principle of action, whatever has a soul would always be actually vitally acting, just as that which has a soul is always actually living. The soul as a form is the ultimate end of generation and not an act ordered to a further act; so not by its essence as form is it in potentiality to another act but by its power. Thus the soul itself as subject of its power is called first act having a further relation to second act. Now, it is noticeable that whatever has a soul is not always actual in the sense of vitally acting; so in the soul's definition it is said that it is *the act of a body having life potentially;* but this potentiality does not exclude the soul. Consequently, the soul's essence is not its power, for nothing is in potentiality by reason of an act as act.

Various Souls   *Commentary on Soul* II, lect. 5

Lower living beings whose act is soul have a dual type of being: one, material, whereby they resemble other material things; another, immaterial, whereby they share something in common with higher substances.

These two kinds of being differ from each other. By its material being, which is limited by matter, each thing is only what it is; for example, this stone is a stone and nothing else but a stone. By its immaterial being, which is broader and somehow infinite, inasmuch as it is not limited by matter, a thing is not only what it is but also, somehow or other, other things. All things are therefore in some way present in higher immaterial substances, as in universal causes.

There are two grades of this immateriality in lower beings. There is complete immateriality, as in intelligible being, for in the intellect things exist without matter and without individuating material conditions, and apart even from a bodily organ. Then there is an incomplete or middle state of immateriality in sensory beings. Sensible being is a mean between both, for in sensation something exists without matter, yet not apart from its individuating material conditions nor independent of a bodily organ. The sense deals with individuals, but the intellect deals with universals. In regard to this twofold being, then, the philosopher says in Book III that the soul is in some way all things.

The actions of a living thing by its material existence are those attributed to the vegetative soul. They are destined to the same end to which actions of inanimate things are destined, i.e., to attain and preserve existence, although this is accomplished in living things in a higher and nobler way. Nonliving bodies begin to exist and remain in existence through an extrinsic principle of motion. But living things begin to exist through an intrinsic principle in the semen and remain in existence through an intrinsic principle of nutrition. Evidently it is appropriate for living things to have their activity originate from within. The completely immaterial activities attributed to living things belong to the intellectual part of the soul, but those of a middle kind of being belong to the sensitive part of the soul. In relation to this threefold kind of existence, three kinds of souls are usually distinguished: the vegetative, the sensitive, and the rational.

Since every existence takes place through some form, sensitive being must exist through sensible form and intelligible being through intelligible form. Every form brings with it a certain tendency, and action comes through this tendency. The natural form of fire, for example, brings with it a tendency toward a higher place, giving lightness to fire, and from this tendency comes its action of upward motion. The tendencies that come with sensible and intelligible forms are called sensible striving and intellectual striving respectively, just as the tendency coming with natural form is called natural striving. From this tendency comes such action as locomotion. This is why there are five kinds of powers of the soul—which was the first question raised.

Kinds of Life   *Summa of Christian Teaching*
                                     IV, 11

Wherever there is variety in nature there are various kinds of generation, and, moreover, the higher the nature, the more interior is generation. The lowest of all are the inanimate things, and among these generation occurs only by the action of one upon another, as when fire is generated from fire when a foreign body is transformed by fire, receiving the quality and form of fire.

Plants are next to inanimate bodies, and generation comes from within plants insofar as the plant's intrinsic humor is changed into seed which, entering the soil, grows into a plant. So here are the first traces of life inasmuch as living things are those things that move themselves to act whereas wholly lifeless things are those that can only move extrinsic things. Plants show that they are alive because something within them is the cause of a form. But plant life is imperfect insofar as, although generation comes from within, what is generated little by little emerges, finally becoming completely extrinsic; thus the humor of a tree gradually emerges from the tree, eventually becoming a blossom and then being formed as fruit distinct from the branch, although still united to it; and when the fruit is perfect, it is completely separated from the tree, falling to the ground, and by its seminal power it produces another plant. In fact, if we investigate carefully, we shall find that the first principle of this generation is something extrinsic because the intrinsic humor of the tree is drawn through the roots from the soil when the plant is nourished.

Above the plants is a higher form of life, that of the sensitive soul, whose proper generation ends within although it begins without. Moreover, the farther the generation goes, the more interior is its penetration; for the sensible object impresses a form on the external senses and then goes to the imagination and on to the treasury of the memory. Yet in all this generating process the beginning and the end are in diverse subjects inasmuch as no sensitive power reflects on itself. And so this degree of life transcends plant life because it is more intimate; this, however, is not yet perfect life, in-asmuch as the generation is constantly from one thing to another.

Consequently the highest degree of life is life according to intellect, since the intellect reflects upon itself and can un-derstand itself. But there are several degrees of intellectual life: for the human mind, although itself capable of knowing, takes its first steps toward knowledge from without, since apart from images, it cannot understand, as we have shown (II, 50). So intellectual life is more perfect in the angels whose intellect does not begin from something extrinsic to obtain self-knowledge, but through itself knows itself. Never-theless, the highest degree of perfection is not found in an-gelic life inasmuch as, although the intelligible species is completely within them, it is not their very substance, since to know and to be are in them not the same thing, as already explained (II, 52). The highest perfection of life belongs, therefore, to God, whose knowing is not distinct from his being, as was proven (I, 45). So in God the intelligible species must be the divine essence itself.

Intellectual Principle as Form   *Summa of Theology* I, q. 76, a. 1

. . . For the soul is the first principle of our nutrition, sensation, and locomotion, as it is also of our understanding. So, whether we call this principle by which we primarily understand, the intellect or the intellectual soul, it is the form of the body. . . .

But anyone holding that the intellectual soul is not the form of the body must first explain how it happens that this action of understanding is the action of this particular man, since each one is aware that he himself is understanding. . . . This particular man understands because his form is the intellectual principle.

Only One Soul in Man   *Summa of Theology* I, q. 76, a. 3

. . . Granted that the soul is united to the body as its form, then there cannot be several essentially different souls within one body. There are three reasons for this. First of all, any animal in which several souls exist would not be absolutely one. For only through one form by which a thing has existence is anything absolutely one, inasmuch as a thing receives its existence and unity from the same source; and so things said to have various forms are not absolutely one. . . .

Second, this is shown to be impossible through the way one thing is predicated of another. . . . If a thing is an animal by one form and a man by another form, it follows that only accidentally could one of these two be predicated of the other, if these two forms are not ordered to each other—or if one soul is presupposed to the other, one would be predicated of the other according to the second manner of essential predication.

But both consequences are eliminated, inasmuch as animal is predicated of man essentially, not accidentally; nor is man part of the definition of animal, but vice versa. Consequently, a thing is animal and man necessarily by the same form, or else man would not really be that thing that is an animal so that animal may be essentially predicated of man.

Third, the impossibility of this is seen in the fact that any one action of the soul, when intense, impedes another; this would not be the case without the principle of action being essentially one.

Hence we must conclude that in man the sensitive soul, the intellectual soul, and the vegetative soul are one soul, numerically. This is easily clarified by considering the differences of species and forms. We notice that the species and the forms of things differ from each other as the perfect from the imperfect, as in the real order, things living are more perfect than the nonliving, animals more perfect than plants, man more than brute animals, and in each of these genera are various degrees.

This is why Aristotle (*Metaphysics* VIII) compares the species of things to numbers, which by adding or subtracting units differ in species. And (in *On the Soul* II, 3) he compares the various souls to the species of figures with one containing another, as a pentagon contains and exceeds a

tetragon. In this sense the intellectual soul contains virtually
whatever pertains to the sensitive soul of brute animals and
to the vegetative soul of plants. So, just as a surface of pentagonal shape is not tetragonal by one shape and pentagonal
by another (inasmuch as a tetragonal shape since it is contained in the pentagonal, is itself superfluous), likewise
neither is Socrates a man by one soul and animal by another;
rather, he is both animal and man by the one same soul.

Human Unity   *Summa of Theology* I, q. 76,
                                   a. 4, c

Were the intellectual soul not united as form to the body
but merely as mover, as the Platonists hold, the necessary
consequence would be another substantial form in man in
order to establish the body in its being as movable by the
soul. But if the intellectual soul is united as substantial form
to the body, as previously explained, no other substantial
form in addition to the intellectual soul can be found in man.

To make this clear, we should realize that the substantial
form differs from the accidental form in making a thing to
be absolutely [to be a thing], whereas the accidental form
makes it to be such [to be something], as heat does not
make a thing to be absolutely but only to-be-hot. And so
when the accidental form is received, the thing is not said to
be made or generated absolutely, but to be made such or
disposed in some way; and also when the accidental form
withdraws, a thing is said to be corrupted only relatively, not
absolutely. But a substantial form confers being absolutely,
so that when it comes, a thing is said to be generated absolutely, and when it withdraws, to be corrupted absolutely.
This is why the ancient natural philosophers who considered
prime matter to be actual being (fire or air, or so forth) held
that a thing is never generated absolutely or corrupted absolutely, but all becoming is only alteration, as it says in
Physics I.

If there pre-existed in matter another substantial form besides the intellectual soul and that form made the subject of
the soul an actual being, the soul would consequently not
confer being absolutely; and thus there would be no abso-

lute generation with the coming of the soul and no absolute
corruption at its withdrawal—and this is clearly untrue.

We must then conclude that there is no other substantial
form in man besides the intellectual soul. And just as the soul
virtually contains the sensitive and vegetative souls, so does it
virtually contain all lower forms, and whatever the imperfect
forms do in other things it alone does in man. We may say
the same of the sensitive soul in brute animals and of the
vegetative soul in plants, and universally of all the more perfect forms in relation to the imperfect.

Principle of Unity   *Summa of Christian Teaching*
                                 II, 58

The principle of anything's unity is the very principle of
its being inasmuch as "one" flows from "being." And so because each and every being gets being from its form, it will
likewise get unity from its form, so that if several souls as
various distinct forms are attributed to man, he will not be
one being, but several. Nor can unity be derived from an
order among forms, for to be one with reference to order is
not to be one in an unqualified way, because the least of all
unities is the unity of order.

Man as Person   *Summa of Theology* I, q. 29,
                                 a. 1, c and ad. 2

Although the universal and the particular are present in
all categories in a special way, the individual belongs to the
category of substance. For a substance is by itself an individual, whereas only through their subject, which is a substance, are accidents individual; for we speak of this whiteness insofar as it is within this subject. So we correctly speak
of substances as individuals and more so than other things;
they are called by the special name of "hypostases" or "first
substances."

Now, particularity and individuality are more specially and
perfectly present in rational substances who control their actions—they are not merely acted upon as others are, but act
autonomously. For it is proper to individuals or singular substances to act. So a special name is given among all other

substances to individual beings having a rational nature, and
this name is "person." Thus in this definition of person, the
term "individual substance" is used to refer to a singular
being in the category of substance, and "rational nature" is
added to signify the singular being among rational substances.

ad. 2. In the opinion of some theologians, "substance" as
found in the definition of person refers to "first substance,"
namely "hypostasis." Yet the addition of "individual" is not
unnecessary. For what we eliminate by the word "hypostasis"
or "first substance" is being universal or partial (for we do
not speak of humanity or men in general as an "hypostasis,"
nor do we call a hand an "hypostasis" since it is a part), but
by adding "individual" we eliminate the notion of a reality
that can be assumed by another. Thus the human nature in
Christ is not a person because it is assumed by a greater being, namely, the Word of God.

But it is preferable to say that "substance" is understood
in a general sense as denoting both first and second substance; and by adding "individual" we restrict its range of
reference to first substance.

Other Terms for Person   *Summa of Theology* I, q. 29,
                                  a. 2, c and ad. 1–3

According to Aristotle, we can understand "substance" in
two ways. In one sense "substance" signifies the *whatness*
of a thing; the definition is referring to this when we say
that we are defining a thing's substance. In fact, the Greek
term for this is *ousia*, which may be translated as "essence." Another sense of "substance" is that of subject or
that which underlies whatever subsists in the category of
substance. Substance in general may be spoken of by the
logical term "subject."

Considering substance in this last sense, there are three
names that signify the reality corresponding to three ways
of looking at such substance: these are "a thing of nature,"
"subsistence," and "hypostasis." Insofar as it exists in itself
and not in another we speak of substance as "subsistence,"
since we say that those beings subsist that do not exist in
something else but exist in themselves. Insofar as it underlies

a common nature we speak of substance as a "thing of nature," as, for instance, this man is a being of human nature. Insofar as it supports accidental qualities we speak of substance as "hypostasis" or "substantia." "Person" means in the class of rational substances what these three terms mean in general throughout the entire range of substances.

ad. 1. As used by the Greeks, the strict meaning of "hypostasis" refers to any individual substance, but custom has associated with it a certain dignity, so that it refers to an individual being of rational nature.

ad. 2. Just as we refer in the plural to three "persons" and three "subsistences" in God, so the Greeks refer to three hypostases. But the word "substance," which, strictly speaking, is equivalent in meaning to "hypostasis," is equivocal in our usage, inasmuch as it refers at times to "essence" and at other times to "hypostasis"; in order to avoid misunderstanding, they chose to translate "hypostasis" by "subsistence" rather than by "substance."

ad. 3. Strictly speaking, the definition expresses the essence. A definition includes specific but not individual principles. It follows that essence in things composed of matter and form refers neither to the form alone nor to the matter alone but to what is composed of both matter and form in general, as principles of the species. But what is composed of this matter and this form is characterized as an hypostasis or a person; for whereas soul, flesh, and bones belong to the meaning of "man," *this* soul, *this* flesh, and *these* bones belong to the meaning of *this* man. So "hypostasis" and "person" add individual principles to the notion of the essence, and in things composed of matter and form these are not identical with the essence, as we noted when speaking of the divine simplicity.

Value of Person　　　　　*Summa of Theology* I, q. 29, a. 3, c and ad. 1–4

"Person" refers to that which is most perfect in the whole of nature, namely, to that which subsists in rational nature. Now, because God's nature has all perfection and thus every kind of perfection should be attributed to him, it is fitting to use the word "person" to speak of God; yet when used of God it is not used exactly as it is of creatures but in a higher sense, just as is the case with other words naming creatures, as was clarified when we treated of the names of God.

ad. 1. So the word "person" is not discovered in the text of the Old or New Testament as referring to God. Yet what this word means is often present in Holy Scripture, namely, that he is the peak of self-existence and most perfect in wisdom. If we were restricted to speak of God only in the words used in Holy Scripture, it would follow that no one could speak of God in any other language than the one used in the Old and the New Testaments. Because we must dialogue with nonbelievers, it is necessary for us to discover new words about God expressing the ancient belief. Nor should we avoid such innovation as profane, i.e., as out of harmony with the Scriptural meaning; what St. Paul teaches us to avoid are *profane verbal innovations*.

ad. 2. Although we may not use "person" in its original meaning of God, we may extend this acceptably for our present purpose. Since famous men were represented in comedies and tragedies, the word "person" (*persona:* mask) came to be used to refer to men of high rank. In the ecclesiastical world there grew up the custom of referring to personages of rank. For this reason some theologians define person as "an hypostasis distinguished by dignity." To subsist in rational nature is characterized by dignity and so, as we said, every individual with rational nature is spoken of as "person." Certainly the dignity of divine nature surpasses every nature, and thus it is entirely suitable to speak of God as "person."

ad. 3. "Hypostasis" is suitably used of God not in its primitive meaning, since he does not support accidental qualities, but in its current meaning as referring to something subsistent. Jerome states that the word is poisonous because prior to the awareness in the West of its implications, heretics were forcing the uneducated into admitting that there were several essences as well as hypostases, and this was because "substance," which is equivalent to "hypostasis" in Greek, is usually understood by us to refer to "essence."

ad. 4. We can speak of God as having a rational nature if reason is understood as denoting, not a thinking process, but an intellectual nature in general. God may not be called an "individual" insofar as this implies matter, which is the principle of individuation, but only insofar as this implies incommunicability. Finally, "substance" is applicable to God insofar as it refers to self-grounded existence.

Yet some theologians say that Boethius's definition does not define "person" as we mean it when speaking of person in God. So Richard of St. Victor, desirous of improving it, said that "person" used of God meant the "incommunicable existence of the divine nature."

2. HUMAN KNOWLEDGE

On Truth, q. 8, a. 6, c

Action is twofold. One kind of action comes from the agent and goes out to something external, changing it. Illumination does this and can properly be called an action. A second kind of action does not proceed outside but remains within to perfect the agent. Strictly speaking, this is called "operation." Shining is such an action.

Now, both actions agree in this: Both proceed from an actually existing thing and only insofar as it is in act. Hence, no body shines unless it actually has light, and this is also the case with its illuminating action.

The action of tendency, sense, and intellect is not like the action proceeding into external matter, however; it is like the action remaining within to perfect the agent, so that a knower must be in act to know. Yet in knowing, the knower need not become an efficient cause, nor the known something passive. For insofar as one thing, namely, an intellect in act, results from the knower and the known, these two are but one principle of this act, which is knowing.

I state that one thing results from them insofar as what is known is joined to the intellect either through its essence or through a likeness. So a knower is not related as active or as passive except in another respect, i.e., for the intelligible to be united to the intellect, activity or passivity is required to some extent. Efficient causality is needed since the active intellect must make species actually intelligible; change is needed insofar as the possible intellect receives intelligible species while the senses receive sensible species. Just as an effect follows upon a cause, so knowledge comes with this change or efficient causality. Therefore, the intellect knows all within it that is actually intelligible, just as a luminous body shines whenever light actually exists within it. . . .

Sensation   *Commentary on Sensation* I, lect. 1

1. As the philosopher says in *On the Soul* III (429b 20), ". . . Insofar as the realities it knows are capable of being separated from their matter, so it is also with the powers of mind." For a thing is intelligible in the proportion that it is separable from matter. Hence, those things that are by nature separated from matter, are by nature intelligible in act; those things that we abstract from material conditions become intelligible in act through the light of our agent intellect. Now, since the habits of any potency are specifically distinguished according to the [specific] difference of that which is the per se object of the potency, there is need that the habits of the sciences, by which the intellect is perfected, be distinguished according to the difference that is separation from matter. Therefore, the philosopher in *Metaphysics* VI (1025b 25) distinguishes the genera of the sciences on the basis of their diverse manner of separation from matter. For things separated from matter according to being and notion pertain to *metaphysics;* things separated according to notion and not according to being pertain to *mathematics;* last, things that in their notion refer to sensible matter pertain to *natural science.*

2. And as the diverse genera of the sciences are distinguished accordingly as things are diversely separable from matter, so also, in the individual sciences, and especially in natural science, the *parts* of the science are distinguished according to their diverse manner of separation and concretion. Since universals are more separated from matter, we proceed, therefore, in natural science, from universals to the

less universal, as the philosopher teaches in *Physics* I.
Whence he begins to teach natural science from those things
that are most common to all natural things, namely, *motion*
and the *principles of motion,* and then proceeds by way of
concretion, or of applying common principles, to certain determined movable things, some of which are living bodies.
With respect to these latter, he likewise proceeded in a similar way, dividing this consideration into three parts. For
first he considered the soul in itself, as though in abstraction.
Second, he considered the things pertaining to the soul according to a certain concretion or application to the body,
but in general. Third, he considered the application of all
these things to the individual species of animals and plants,
determining what is proper to each and every species. The
first of these considerations is contained in the treatise, *On
the Soul.* The third consideration is contained in the treatises
he wrote entitled *On Animals and Plants* [i.e., as to "Animals," the works, *On the History of Animals, On the Parts
of Animals, On the Generation of Animals;* as to "Plants,"
the works appear to be pseudo-Aristotelian]. The intermediate consideration is contained in the treatises he wrote of
certain things commonly pertaining either to all animals, or
to several of the genera thereof, or even to all living things—
and such is the present intention of *this* treatise.

3. Hence we must consider that in *On the Soul* II (413b
10) he [Aristotle] established four levels of living things.
The first are those that have merely the nutritive part of the
soul by which they live, such as, e.g., plants. Others, besides
this, also have sensation, but without progressive motion, as
is true of the imperfect animals, e.g., shellfish. Still others
also possess progressive locomotion, as do the perfect animals, e.g., the horse and the cow. Yet others still have intellect also, as, e.g., men. Though the appetitive power is laid
down as a fifth genus among the powers of the soul, it nevertheless does not constitute a fifth level of living things, because it always follows upon the sensitive level of life.

4. Of these degrees, however, the intellect, indeed, is not
an act of any part of the body, as is proved in *On the Soul* III
(429b). Wherefore it cannot be considered by concretion or
application to the body, or to any corporeal organ. Its great-

est concretion is in the soul, while its greatest abstraction is in separated substances. And therefore, besides the treatise *On the Soul*, Aristotle did not write a treatise on the intellect and the intelligible thing; or if he had, it would not pertain to natural science, but more to metaphysics, within whose scope is the consideration of separated substances. But all the others are acts of some certain part of the body. And therefore they can be specifically considered in terms of their application to the body or to corporeal organs, beyond the consideration given them in the treatise *On the Soul*.

5. Now, this mediate consideration must be divided into three parts. One of these contains those things that pertain to the living insofar as it is living. And such are found in the treatise he wrote entitled *On Death and Life*, in which he also determines concerning *Breathing and Exhaling*, through which life is preserved in certain forms, and *On Youth and Old Age*, through which one's stage in life is diversified. Likewise, in the treatises he wrote *On the Causes of Length and Shortness of Life*, and in that he composed *On Health and Sickness*, which also pertain to the disposition of life, and in the treatise that he is said to have written, *On Nourishment and the Nourishable*, which last two books we do not as yet have. Other things pertain to the motive power. These, indeed, are contained in two works: namely, in the treatise, *On the Cause of the Motion of Animals*, and in the treatise, *On the Progressing of Animals*, in which determination is made concerning the parts of animals suitable for movement. The third part, however, pertains to the sensitive power. Regarding this, one may consider that which pertains to the act of the interior, or exterior, sense faculty, and as to this the consideration of the sensitive power is contained in this treatise, entitled *De Sensu et Sensato*, i.e., "On the Sensitive Power and the Sensible Thing," under which is also contained the tract *On Memory and Reminiscence*. Further, in a consideration of the sensitive power, there also pertains that which makes a difference in the sense power in sensing, which difference, with respect to sleep and wakefulness, he established in the treatise entitled *On Sleeping and Wakefulness*.

6. Now, since one must pass from things more alike to

things unalike, the reasonable order of this treatise appears
to be that, after the work *On the Soul*, in which the soul in
itself is treated, there immediately follows this treatise, *De
Sensu et Sensato*—sensing pertaining to the soul rather than
to the body. After this there should be ordered the treatise on
sleeping and wakefulness, which two imply the binding and
loosing of the sensitive power. Thereupon follow the treatises
that pertain to the motive power, which is more closely allied
to the sensitive power. Last, there are ordered the treatises
pertaining to the common consideration of the living, because that consideration concerns the disposition of the body
most of all.*

Nature of Sensation   *Commentary on Soul* II, lect.
                                 24

With the words, "Everything is acted upon, etc.," he
proves from the foregoing the impossibility of the opinion of
the ancient philosophers that like is sensed by like. He states
that everything in potentiality is acted upon or put into movement by an agent, a being in act. While making them to be in
act, the being in act makes them like itself. Therefore, something in one way is acted upon by what is like it, and in another way by what is unlike it. At first, when the thing is being changed and acted upon, it is unlike; but at last when
change and action are completed, it is like. And thus after the
sense has been actualized by the object of sensation, it resembles it, but not previously. The absence of this distinction
caused the error of the ancient philosophers.

. . . First, then, he says that we should accept as universally and generally true of all senses that they receive forms
without matter, as wax receives the impression of a ring
without the iron or gold. But this is apparently the case in all
receptivity, since all recipients accept something from the
agent as agent. But an agent acts through its form, not its matter. So every recipient accepts a form without matter. And
this is indeed sensibly apparent, inasmuch as air does not
receive matter from the fire that affects it, but receives its
form. So that the receiving of forms without matter is evidently not proper to the senses.

* Translated by P. H. Conway, O.P., and R. F. Larcher, O.P.

Allowing that all recipients accept a form from an agent, we must assert nevertheless that there are differences in the way of receiving. For the form accepted into the recipient from the agent sometimes keeps the same way of existing in the recipient as it had in the agent. This occurs when the recipient is disposed to the form just as the agent is, for whatever is received into another is received after the manner of the recipient. So that if the recipient is disposed just as the agent is, the form is received in the same way it is in the agent; and thereupon form is not received without matter. . . . In this way air is modified by fire and likewise anything else acted upon by the active or passive qualities of natural elements.

But at times the recipient accepts the form under a different way of existing than the form has in the agent because the recipient's material disposition to receive is unlike the material disposition in the agent. And in such cases the recipient becomes like the agent in relation to form but not to matter. And thus a sense receives a form without matter, since a form has a different kind of existence in the sense than it has in the sensible object, for in the sensible thing a form has a natural existence, but it has an intentional and spiritual existence in the sense. . . .

Then when he says, "The primary area of sensation, etc." he deals with the sense organs. Because he said already that a sense receives forms without matter—and this is also true of intellect—some may suppose that a sense is an incorporeal power because the intellect is an incorporeal power. To avoid this, he states that sensation has an organ. He also says that the primary area of sensation, i.e., its basic organ, is one having such a power, namely, one that receives forms without matter. Thus a sense organ with this power—an eye, for example—is identical in subject but exists differently since, by nature, a power differs from a body. The power is like the form of the organ. . . . And he adds that "an extended magnitude," the physical organ, for instance, "is what receives sensation"—that which receives sensation is as matter related to form. . . .

How Sense Powers Are Dis-   *Summa of Theology* I, q. 78,
tinguished   a. 3

. . . Powers are not for the sake of organs, but organs for
the sake of powers. So different powers do not exist because
there are different organs, but a difference in organs has been
established by nature to correspond to the difference in powers. There are also different media for different senses whose
acts require suitable media. The intellect, not sense, knows
the natures of sensible qualities.

To distinguish and enumerate the external senses we must
use a criterion pertaining properly and primarily to the
senses. A sense is a passive power capable of being changed
by external sensible objects. The external object causing the
change in the sense is what is directly (per se) perceived by
sense. The powers are diversified according to the diversity
of these external sensible objects.

Two kinds of change occur in the sense; one is natural, the
other immaterial. The natural change comes from the form
being received into the subject. In this case the form is received according to its own natural way of existing, as when
heat is received into something it heats. A spiritual change
comes about when the form causing the change in the subject is received according to an immaterial kind of being, as
when the form of color is received by the pupil, which does
not itself become colored. An immaterial impression is necessary for the sense operation wherein an intentional form of
the sensible object is present in the sense organ. Moreover, if
sensation only required a natural impression, whenever a
natural body underwent change, it would sense.

In some senses only an immaterial change occurs, as in
sight. In other senses a natural change takes place along with
the immaterial one, a change of the object only or even of the
organ. In sound, which is the object of hearing, a natural
change in the object occurs in regard to place, since sound is
caused by percussion and air movement. Natural changes of
alteration occur in odor, the object of smell, because in some
way a body must be altered by heat before producing an
odor. A natural change in the organ occurs in touch and taste

inasmuch as the hand is made hot in touching something hot and the tongue is moistened by the moisture of flavors. In the act of sensing, the olfactory and auditory organs are not affected by any natural change except accidentally.

Since sight is without natural change in organ or object, it is the most immaterial, the most perfect, and the most universal of all the senses. Next come hearing and smelling, whose objects are naturally changed. Local motion is more perfect and naturally prior to the motion of alteration, as proven in *Physics* VIII. Touch and taste are the most material senses . . . so the first three senses (sight, hearing, and smell) do not function through any medium connected with them. . . .

Internal Senses   *Summa of Theology* I, q. 78, a. 4

Avicenna in his book *On the Soul* proposes five internal sense powers: the central sense, fantasy, imagination, memory, and the estimative power.

Inasmuch as there can be no defect in nature pertaining to necessary things, the sensitive soul must have as many actions as a perfect animal needs in order to live. If these actions cannot all be derived from one principle, they demand different powers, since a power of the soul is the proximate principle of the soul's activity. We should consider that the life of a perfect animal requires the apprehension of a thing not only when the sensible object is present but also when it is absent. Otherwise, inasmuch as an animal's motion and action follow apprehension, an animal would never be moved to seek something absent. In perfect animals we see the opposite easily when they are moved by progressive motion, because they are moved by something absent yet known. So through its sensitive soul an animal must receive not only the species of sensible things (which when present change the soul) but must also retain and preserve them. In corporeal bodies, *receiving* and *retaining* come from different principles, for humid things receive well but retain poorly, while the opposite is true of dry things. And so because the sensitive power is the act of a corporeal organ, the power to retain the species must be distinct from the power to receive it.

We should also reflect that were an animal moved only by things pleasant or unpleasant to sense, the animal would only need to apprehend likable or unlikable sense-perceived forms. But an animal must seek some things and avoid others not merely as suitable or unsuitable to the senses but on account of other benefits and advantages or disadvantages. For example, a lamb takes flight when it sees a wolf coming, not on account of its unsightly color or shape but because it is a natural enemy; likewise, birds collect straw not because this pleases their senses but because it is useful for building a nest. So the animal has to perceive such forms that are not perceived by the external senses. Now, for this kind of perception there must be some other principle, because these forms, unlike the sensible forms, do not come from an impression by a sensible object.

So there is a "proper sense" and a "central sense" ordered to receive sensible forms. The "fantasy" or "imagination," which are the same, is ordered to retain or preserve forms; it is a kind of storehouse for forms received through the senses. The "estimative" power is ordered to apprehend forms not received through the senses, whereas the "memory" is the storehouse to preserve these forms. A sign of this is that in animals remembering comes from some form of this kind; for example, that something is harmful or desirable. Memory is ordered to something characterized as past, and this includes intentions of this kind.

We should reflect that there is no distinction between man and the animals in respect to sensible forms, for in similar ways men and animals are altered by sensible objects. But in regard to the previously mentioned forms there is this difference: They are perceived by other animals through a kind of natural instinct, whereas man perceives them through a certain comparison. So what in other animals is called the natural estimative power is called in man cogitative power. This latter power reaches these forms through a comparison. That is why it is called the particular reason; and doctors designate for it a particular organ in the middle section of the head. It compares individual intentions as the intellectual reason compares universal intentions.

As to remembering, man not only like other animals has a memory, which spontaneously recalls past events, but a power of recall, which is the recollection of past events through a kind of syllogistic inquiry regarding individual intentions. . . .

Intellectual Knowledge   *Summa of Theology* I, q. 84, a. 1, c

It is a fact that there is knowledge in the intellect. But if the intellect does not know bodies, it follows that there can be no science of bodies. Then all natural science treating of moving bodies would be eliminated.

The first philosophers who studied the natures of things thought that only bodies were in the world. And since they saw all bodies moving, they considered them to be in constant process, and so concluded that no true or certain knowledge about things was attainable. Whatever is in ceaseless process cannot be apprehended with any certitude, since it disappears before the mind can judge of it. So Heraclitus said, "It is not possible to touch twice the water of a flowing river," as the philosopher relates in *Metaphysics* IV.

Subsequently there arrived Plato who, wishing to retain man's ability to achieve certain and true knowledge with his intellect, proposed in addition to corporeal things another kind of beings separated from matter and motion, and these he called forms or ideas. By participation in these, every individual thing of the sense world was said to be either a man or horse or some such thing. He therefore maintained that sciences, definitions, and whatever pertains to the act of intellect are to be referred not to sensible bodies but to the immaterial and separated forms. The soul does not then actually understand corporeal things, but understands the separated forms of these corporeal things.

For two reasons this view appears incorrect. First, inasmuch as these forms are immaterial and motionless, the knowledge of motion and matter (proper to natural science) and demonstrations through the moving cause and the material cause would be eliminated from sciences. Second, it seems strange indeed that we should have to bring in other beings as intermediaries when seeking to know things that are apparent to us when these other beings cannot be the substances of those things insofar as they differ from them in existence. So the knowledge of these separated substances would not enable us to judge about sensible objects.

In this instance Plato seems to have forsaken the truth, since he thought that all knowledge is by way of some likeness and believed that the form of the thing known must be in the known object in the same way as it is in the knower. He knew that the form of the thing understood is within the intellect as a universal, immaterial, and immobile form. This is evident from the act of the intellect, which understands things as universal and as having a certain necessity, inasmuch as the way of acting is determined by the way of the agent's form. He therefore concluded that things understood immaterially and without motion must subsist in themselves without matter and without motion. But this is not necessary, since in sensible beings we recognize a form to be present differently in one sensible object than in another, as when whiteness is brighter in one thing than in another, or when whiteness is found along with sweetness in one thing and without it in another. Thus also the sensible form is within a real being existing outside the soul in a way different from the way it is in the sense power receiving sensible forms of things without matter, as when a sense receives the color gold, without receiving gold. So also the intellect receives the forms of bodies that are material and moving without matter and without movement in accordance with its own mode of being, since whatever is received is within the recipient in accord with the recipient's mode of being. We must therefore maintain that the soul through intellect knows bodies by means of an immaterial, universal, and necessary knowledge.

Opinions about Knowledge   *Summa of Theology* I, q. 84, a. 6

The philosopher proves (*Metaphysics* I, 1; *Posterior Analytics* II, 15) that the principle of our knowledge is in the senses. The philosophers held three positions about this.

Democritus maintained that nothing except the images coming from those bodies we are thinking about and entering our souls cause our knowledge, as he is quoted by Augustine in his letter to Dioscorus. And Aristotle says (*On Sleep and Wakefulness*, c. 2) that Democritus held knowledge to be caused by a flowing off of images. This is because Democritus and the other natural philosophers did not differentiate intellect from the sense, as Aristotle says (*On the Soul* III, 3). And because the sense is affected by the sensible, they concluded that all our knowledge comes from only the impression made by sensible things. This impression was made, according to Democritus, by the flowing off of images.

Plato opposed this view in holding that the intellect differs from the senses as an immaterial power not using a corporeal organ to act. And since the incorporeal cannot be affected by the corporeal, he argued that intellectual knowledge is not attained through any alteration in the intellect by sensible things but through a participation of the intellect in separate intelligible forms, as we noted (*Summa of Theology* I, 84, 4, 5). He also viewed the sense as in itself an acting power so that as a kind of immaterial power, not even the sense is affected by sensible things. But the sense organs are affected by sensible things, and through this change the soul is somehow stimulated to form within itself the species of sensible things. Augustine seems to take this opinion (*Commentary on Genesis*, 24) when he says that the body does not sense but the soul senses through the body, using it as a kind of messenger to form within itself what is declared without. Thus, in Plato's opinion, intellectual knowledge does not come from sensible things, and not even sensible knowledge comes wholly from sensible things; rather do they stimulate the sensible soul to sense, and likewise the senses stimulate the intellectual soul to understand.

Aristotle preferred a middle path. With Plato he agreed that the intellect differs from the senses. But he maintained that the sense has no operation of its own, only as a part of the body, so that to sense is not the act of the soul alone but of the composite. And he retained this same position in reference to all activities of the sensitive part. But since it is not foolish to hold that sensible things outside the soul produce some effect on the composite, Aristotle agreed with Democritus that the activities of the sensitive part are caused by sensible things impressing the sense, not by an outflow of something from the object, as Democritus said, but by a kind of activity. Democritus held that all activity was done by something flowing from an object, as we find in his book *On Generation*, 8. Aristotle considered the intellect to have an action apart from the body, since nothing corporeal can impress the incorporeal. In Aristotle's mind, therefore, no mere impression of sensible bodies suffices to cause an intellectual action, but something more excellent is required, because the agent is more excellent than the recipient, as he states in *On the Soul* III. By this he does not mean that intellectual activity is caused merely by an impression from some superior things, as Plato viewed it, but that a superior, nobler agent which he calls the agent intellect (which we have discussed, *Summa of Theology* I, 79, 3, 4) causes the phantasms received from the senses to be actually intelligible by abstraction.

Proper Function of Intellect   *Summa of Theology* I, q. 85, a. 1

The philosopher says (*On the Soul* III, 4) that only as separable from matter are things intelligible. So to be understood, material things must be abstracted from matter and from material images, i.e., phantasms.

The knowable object is appropriate to the power of knowing. . . . Now, there are three grades of knowing powers. One knowing power, the sense, acts from within a corporeal organ, and so the object of any sense power is a form existing within corporeal matter. And since such matter is the principle of individuation, every power of the sensitive part can know only individuals. Another knowing power acts neither within a corporeal organ nor in any way connected with matter. This is the angelic intellect, and the object of its knowing power is therefore matterless subsistent form. Although angels do know material things, they only know them in something immaterial, in themselves or God. The human intellect is between the two. It is not the act of a bodily organ, and yet it is a power of the soul that is the form of a body, as we said

(*Summa of Theology* I, 76, 1). So its proper function is to know a form existing individually within corporeal matter but not as in such matter. Now, to know whatever is in individual matter but not as in such matter is to abstract form from individual matter represented by the phantasms. So we must say that our intellect understands material things through abstracting from phantasms; and through material things we thus attain some knowledge of immaterial things, as contrariwise, angels know material things through the immaterial. But Plato, viewing only the human intellect's immateriality and ignoring its union with the body, considered the objects of the intellect to be separated ideas, and that we know not by abstracting but by participating in abstracted things, as was said (*Summa of Theology* I, 84, 1).

Knowledge of Singulars   *On Truth*, q. 10, a. 5, c

. . . Human and angelic intellects know material things in diverse ways. Human intellectual knowledge is directed, first, to material things according to their form, and second, to matter as correlative to form. Because every form is itself universal, our knowledge of matter as correlative to form is universal knowledge. Thus considered, matter is not the principle of individuation. Because form receives its individuation from "quantified matter," existing under definite dimensions as singular, this kind of matter is the principle. Hence the philosopher states: "The parts of man are matter and form understood in general, but this form and this matter are the parts of Socrates."

And so evidently we cannot know singulars directly through our intellect, inasmuch as singulars are directly known through our sense powers' receiving forms from things using a bodily organ. Our senses thus receive them under definite dimensions and from them originate our knowledge of the material singular. For just as we derive our knowledge of matter in general through a universal form, so we derive our knowledge of quantified matter—the principle of individuation—through individual form.

Yet insofar as the intellect has continuity with the sense power having singulars as objects, the intellect has a certain contact with singulars. There is a twofold conjunction here. First, sense motion ends in the intellect, as when motion proceeds from things to the soul. In this way the intellect knows singulars by a certain reflection, as when the intellect, through knowing its object, some universal nature, reflects upon its own act, then upon the species that originates the act, and finally upon the image from which it has derived the species. Thus does it reach some knowledge of singulars.

Against Monopsychism   *On a Common Intellect,* ch. 5

After having proven from the statements of Aristotle and his followers that the intellect is a power of that soul that is the form of the body—although this power called intellect is not the act of any bodily organ, inasmuch as its action does not involve any bodily action, as Aristotle says—we now intend to inquire by reason what one should understand about this. And because, as Aristotle taught, we must begin to investigate the principle of acts by studying actions, we should begin with that action that is, strictly, the intellect's own action—to understand. The most certain definition we can have in reference to this is the one proposed by Aristotle: The soul is the principle by which we live and understand. It is, therefore, the specific form of a particular body as well.

He leans so heavily on this reasoning that he refers to it as a proof. At the outset of the chapter he says: "To clarify what anything is, we should not only give a comprehensive definition as many do when defining terms, but we should show what a thing's intrinsic cause is and prove it." He then gives an example: "just as by establishing the appropriate diagonal one proves what a tetragon or a square is."

The force of this proof and its incontrovertibility is obvious, because whoever wishes to swerve from this point must speak absurdly.

Now, it is clear that the individual man does understand. Unless we had intelligence we would scarcely be asking about the intellect; and while we are inquiring about the intellect we are inquiring about that very principle by which we understand. And thus Aristotle says: "I mean by intellect that by which the soul understands." And so Aristotle concludes:

"But if there is any first principle by which we understand, this must be the form of the body."

He says this because previously he had clarified the point that the primary source of anything's action is its form. This is made evident by the study of action, because everything acts insofar as it is in actuality. But everything is in actuality by its form; so it follows that the primary source of its action must be the form.

Yet if anyone takes the position that the principle of this act of understanding, a principle we have spoken of as intellect, is not the form, he is required to explain in what way action from this principle is the action of this man.

Some philosophers have tried to give diverse solutions to this problem. One of these, Averroes, suggests that the principle of understanding, named possible intellect by him, is neither the soul nor a power of the soul, unless these terms are synonymous; but that it is rather a certain separated substance, as he stated: The understanding belonging to the separated substance is mine or yours insofar as that possible intellect is united to me or to you by the phantasms present in me or in you.

In this way, according to him, the process of understanding takes place. For two things underlie the intelligible species, which as form and act of the possible intellect becomes one with it: These are the phantasm and the possible intellect. And so, he says, the possible intellect through its form establishes a continuity with us, the phantasms acting as intermediaries; and so whenever the possible intellect understands, this man understands.

Three reasons clearly indicate, however, that this is not a true doctrine.

First, because if such were the case, the intellect would not be united with man from the first moment of his birth, as Theophrastus says it is, and as Aristotle implies in *Physics* II, where he states: "The natural term of generation is the form, just as man is generated by man and the sun."

It is clear, moreover, that the natural term of generation is the intellect; but according to Averroes's teaching, the intellect is not united to man from his birth but by the action of his senses when he is in act as a sentient being: "For the phantasm is activated by the senses in act," as asserted in *On the Soul* III.

Second, because the union would be not with one thing but with various things. But clearly the intelligible species as present in phantasms is potentially intelligible; moreover, in the possible intellect, it is according to that which is understood in the act drawn from the phantasms. But if the intelligible species is not the form of the possible intellect unless it is abstracted from phantasms, it follows that the intellect is not united but separated from these images through the intelligible species, unless we claim that the possible intellect has continuity with the phantasm, as reflection in a mirror is connected with the man whose reflection it is. But this is obviously not a sufficient union to account for unity of action, for clearly the action of the mirror or reflecting cannot be attributed to the man reflected; and thus neither can the action of the possible intellect in this type of union be attributed to this man—for example, to Socrates—so that this man is understanding.

Third, because even were we to allow that the numerically one same species is the form of the possible intellect while simultaneously existing in the phantasm, there is not thus a sufficient bond to originate understanding in a man.

The intelligible species is evidently that through which something is understood, whereas man understands this thing through intellectual potentiality; just as through the sensible species something is perceived, but through the sense power one experiences sensation. Similarly, a wall having color—with the sensible species of color being in act in vision—is seen but does not itself see; but an animal with a visual power possessing this sensible species, does see.

Now, the suggested conjunction of the possible intellect with the man having phantasms in his imagination while the intelligible species are present in the possible intellect would be similar to the union of the wall having color with the eye in which the species of its color would be present. Just as the wall does not see—although its color is seen—so it would follow that man would not understand, although the phantasm he possesses would be understood by the possible intellect.

From the position of Averroes, therefore, it is impossible to explain how any man would understand.

But indeed some philosophers, recognizing that Averroes's way does not allow us to conclude how this individual man thinks, raise another point. They propose that the intellect is united as a mover to the body; and so the intellect is a part of this man insofar as unity is achieved by the conjunction of body and intellect, as thing moved is united to its mover. And so the intellect's action is attributed to man just as the eye's action, to see, is attributed to him.

Anyone holding this theory should be asked first, what kind of individual thing is the one we call Socrates. Is Socrates only his intellect—i.e., the mover? Or is he that which is moved by it, i.e., body, and yet animated by a vegetative and sensitive soul? Or is he a composite of both?

From their position, it seems as if the third opinion should be held: namely, that Socrates is a being composed of both. Let us then argue against them with the help of Aristotle's statement in *Metaphysics* VIII, where he states: "Now, when anything has parts, not as an aggregate but as a unified whole, in addition to the parts there is an innate wholeness and there is external cause, since in these bodies, indeed, in others the cause of touch, such as contact, or in others, the humors, is one aspect of being or some other affection of being."

Indeed, such a definition is one reason for the existence of one not by conjunction, as it would be for the existence of that man, but for a unique existence. What is it, therefore, that makes a man one so that he is unified and not many—i.e., with one part of him being "animal" and the other "biped" (although some do say that this is the situation: that he is truly an animal as well as truly a biped so that there are two)?

According to this view, man is not both these things, but they will be men by participation—not of one man but not of two: that is, of animal, and not of biped. And will not the totality make up man, who is both one and many—animal and biped? And certainly (just because some are used to defining man this way and teaching their hearers) this teaching does not solve the problem. But if, as we have said, this one thing is matter, and that other, form—the one in potentiality and the other in act—then the problem seems no longer to exist.

But if you say that Socrates is not an absolutely unified being but some kind of unity resulting from the conjunction of mover and moved, many difficulties follow.

First of all, since anything gets its unity from the fact and the manner of its being, it would follow that Socrates is not a being, that he would not be in any species or genus, and that he would have no action, since only a being has action. For this reason we do not claim that the sailor's ability to understand is to be attributed to the totality that is sailor and ship but only to the sailor; and similarly (if we accept the previous supposition) to understand will not be the action of Socrates but only of the intellect, which uses the body of Socrates; for only in that totality that is a unity is the action of a part the action of the whole; and if anyone says otherwise, he speaks incorrectly.

And if you say that this is the way a heavenly body understands, namely, through a mover, this assumption merely increases the difficulty, for whatever we can learn of the human intellect should lead us to knowledge about higher intellects, and not vice versa.

But when it is said that this individual, namely, Socrates, is a body animated by a vegetative and sensitive soul (which is a consequence of holding that this man is not specifically determined by his intellect but by a sensitive soul, which is somehow dignified by the influence of the possible intellect), then the intellect is unrelated to Socrates except as a mover to what is moved.

By this theory, however, the act of the intellect—to understand—can be attributed to Socrates in no way, as is obvious for many reasons.

First, by reason of what the philosopher says in *Metaphysics* II: "Whenever there is diversity between some effect and the action producing it, the action is in that which is produced. In this way the act of building is in what is built, and the act of weaving is in the cloth; and likewise in other things of the same order, the movement is entirely within the thing moved. But when there is no product apart from the action, the action is in those producing the action, as illusion is in the one seeing and as reflection is in the thing reflecting.

And so even if we allow an intellect to be united as a mover to Socrates, this does not prove that understanding is in Socrates or that he understands; for understanding is an action within the intellect alone. It is also patently false when they say that the intellect is not an act of the being but is the understanding itself; for there cannot be any understanding in any act that does not have the act of understanding; because intellection can only be in an intellect as vision in an eye, and there can be no vision in anyone except in one whose act is seeing.

Second, because the action of a mover is not properly attributed to any instrument of moving or to the thing moved; on the contrary, the action of any instrument is attributed to the principal efficient cause. For we cannot say that a saw uses or guides the artisan, but we can say that the artisan saws, although the work is done by the saw.

Now, the proper action of the intellect is to understand. And so even allowing for the fact that the act of understanding may be transitive in its effect on another—that is, to move —it would not follow that understanding befits Socrates if understanding is united to him only as a mover.

Third, because in reference to those things whose actions are transitive, these actions are attributed in opposite ways to the causes of motion and to the things moved. Accordingly, a builder is spoken of as constructing an edifice, but the edifice is said to be constructed. And so if understanding, like motion, should be transitive action, passing into another, it still could not be said that Socrates understands insofar as intellect is joined to him as a mover; but it must rather be said that intellect understands and that Socrates is understood; or perhaps that intellect, by understanding, moves Socrates, and Socrates is moved.

Yet it often happens that the action of an efficient cause passes over into what is moved, for instance, when what is moved in virtue of its mover initiates movement in another— just as anything in which heat has been generated, generates heat. And so it might be said that man when moved by intellect initiates motion in the act of understanding, so that man understands from the very fact that he is moved.

But Aristotle argues against this in *On the Soul* II, from which we have learned the principle of his argument. For after saying that we know and are healthy primarily through a form, namely, the form of science and the form of health, he adds: "Actions in fact are apparent in the patient and the subject of change," as Themistocles says in his explanation. "For although in one way science and health come from others—for instance, from a teacher and from a doctor—yet within the patient and his disposition for change there are acts that we have shown to be prior because they are in them by nature."

Hence it is the meaning of Aristotle—and apparently true—that when anything moved moves, it must have some act from a mover that has this kind of act; and by this principle, which is both its act and form, it moves (just as when anything is heated it generates heat through the heat that is in it from the heater).

If we grant that the intellect may move the soul of Socrates by illuminating it or by any other way, whatever happens in Socrates through the intellect's influence is that by which he primarily understands. Moreover, Aristotle proves that that by which Socrates primarily understands (just as he experiences sensations by his senses) is in potentiality to all things and has, therefore, no natural determination except this: to be "possible," not mixed therefore with anything bodily, but separate.

If we concede that any separate intellect moves Socrates, we must still hold that what Aristotle calls the possible intellect is in the soul of Socrates just as also the sense that is in potentiality to all sensible things by which Socrates senses.

If it is said, however, that this individual thing that is Socrates is not a being composed of intellect and animal body and that he is not merely an animate body but that he is intellect alone, then this will be a statement of the opinion of Plato who, we are told by Gregory of Nyssa, because of this very difficulty did not want to understand man as consisting of body and soul, but of a soul using a body, wearing the body, so to speak, as a garment.

Plotinus, likewise, as Macrobius points out, maintained that man was this kind of being when he stated: "The true man is not the one apparent to our eyes but he who controls that which is seen." Hence when animal life leaves the body at death, the latter, bereft of its ruler, suffers corruption; this is that which is seen in man to be mortal. But the soul, which is the converted man, is a stranger to all mortal conditions."

Now, this very Plotinus, one of the great commentators, is listed among the commentators of Aristotle, as we learn from Simplicius in his commentary, *On the Categories*.

Nor is this opinion apparently contrary to Aristotle's words, for in *Ethics* IX, he states: "It is the work of a good man to work at what is good even by his own grace. For every individual is seen to be a man by the grace of intellect." But he is not saying here that man is intellect alone but that intellect holds the chief place in man. And so he subsequently states: "Just as any city-state or other organized society seems to be the principal one, so does man." And he adds here: "Every man is either this—intellect—or he is mainly this." And I believe that the previously quoted words of Themistius and of Plotinus were spoken in this latter sense when they said: Man is a soul or intellect.

We may show in many ways that man is not intellect alone, or soul alone:

First, by Gregory of Nyssa himself, who after quoting Plato's opinion, adds: This statement implies a difficult or almost insoluble problem. For what kind of unity can there be in a soul "clothed in a body"? For the tunic and the wearer are not one.

Second, because Aristotle in *Metaphysics* VII demonstrates that "man" and "a horse" and such things are not merely forms but a kind of whole made up of form and matter: a unified, individual being is comprised of prime matter and form, like Socrates. Now, it is similarly the case with other things. And this Aristotle proved by the fact that no part of the body can be defined without some part or power of the soul; and when the soul leaves, one never speaks of an eye or of flesh, except metaphorically. But such would not be the case if man or Socrates were only intellect or only soul.

Third, it would follow that inasmuch as the intellect acts only by an act of the will (as proven in *On the Soul* III), it would also be in the will's power that a man should keep his body when he wished and leave it when he wished, which is obviously false.

And so it is evident that the intellect is not united as a mover to Socrates, and if it were so united, it could not account for the fact that Socrates understands. Therefore, all those desirous of backing this opinion should either admit that they themselves do not understand anything and are thus not qualified to argue about anything, or they should admit the truth of Aristotle's conclusion: We understand primarily by means of species and form.

The same conclusion is reached from the fact that this individual man is classified in some species, since a thing is never allotted to a species except by its form; and so a man's species is determined by his form.

But every species is distinguishable by the principal action proper to it. However, the proper action of man as man is to understand. It is in this that he differs from other animals; and thus Aristotle says that man's ultimate happiness is found in this action. The intellect is the principle by which we understand, as Aristotle says. Therefore it must be united to the body as its form, certainly not in such a way that the possible intellect is itself the act of any bodily organ, but as a power of the soul, which is the act of the physically organized body.

Moreover, the principles of moral philosophy are destroyed in the perspective of this false position. Whatever is our own is here withdrawn. For there we have nothing of our own except our will; and so whatever is in our power is called "voluntary." The will, however, is within intellect, as is evident from Aristotle's statement in *On the Soul* III. This is also evident from the fact that separated substances have intellect and will; and likewise because it is within the will's power to love and hate something general, as one hates as a group all thieves, so Aristotle states in his *Rhetoric*.

Consequently if the intellect is not something that belongs to this man or is truly united with him, but joined to him only through phantasms or joined as a mover, there will be present in man no will of his own, but it will be present in the separate intellect. And so this man will not be master of his own acts, nor will any of his acts be praiseworthy or blameworthy.

The acceptance of such a view is, however, the destruction of the principles of moral philosophy. But since such a position would be both absurd and opposed to human life (for then holding councils and legislating would be useless), it follows that the intellect is so united to us that between it and the self there is formed a unity. But this can only occur in the way stated: namely, that the intellect is also one of the powers of the soul, which is united to us as our form.

And so the conclusion is that this opinion should be adhered to without any doubt not only because of what faith reveals, as they say, but also because to oppose this is clearly to contradict obvious philosophical evidence.

It is easy to dispute the reasons with which some oppose this doctrine. Some hold that it would follow from this position that the intellect would be a material form with sensible characteristics, and so whatever is received in the intellect is received not universally but individually, as in matter. They also claim that as a material form it is not actually intelligible, so that the intellect cannot know itself, although this is clearly false; but no material form is actually intelligible.

The solution of this difficulty is evident from previous statements. We are not saying that the form of the body is the human soul in respect to the possible intellect which, in Aristotle's teaching, is not the act of any bodily organ. It therefore remains true that the soul, in respect to its intellectual power, is immaterial, is receptive of immaterial objects, and knows itself. Therefore, likewise, Aristotle spoke these notable words about the soul: It is the abode of species —not the whole soul, but the intellect.

But if anyone should object that a power of the soul may not be more immaterial or more simple than its essence, it may be answered that the objection is well taken if the human soul's essence were a material form that has no existence of its own but only the existence of the composite—as is true of those other forms below the human form that of themselves have neither existence nor action apart from their conjunction with matter; and on this account they are said to be immersed in matter. But because the human soul is by its essence a form so united to matter that matter does not entirely submerge it—since the dignity of the form transcends the capacity of matter—the soul is not prevented from having an action or a power in which matter is not involved.

Those holding this should also realize that were the intellective principle by which we understand to be essentially separate and distinct from that soul, which is the form of our body, it would be essentially intelligent and intelligible, with no possibility of sometimes understanding and sometimes not understanding. Nor would there be any necessity of its knowing through intelligible objects or acts, but like other separated substances, it would have knowledge through its own essence.

Nor would it be appropriate for it to need our phantasms for understanding. For in the natural order of things it is not usual for higher substances to depend upon lower substances to attain their principal perfection; thus heavenly bodies, for instance, are not formed or disposed toward their action by lower bodies. Serious error is therefore involved in the opinion of anyone saying that the intellect is that kind of principle that is substantially separated, while it is at the same time perfected and made intelligent in act through species received from phantasms.

Knowledge as Existence in Mind   *Debated Questions* VIII, q. 1, a. 1

. . . According to Avicenna in his *Metaphysics* there is a threefold view of nature. The first way to view nature is in respect to the *esse,* which it has in singular things, as a stone's nature in this or that stone. The second way to view nature is in respect to its intelligible being (*esse intelligibile*), as the stone's nature is viewed within the intellect. The third is the viewing of nature as absolute, insofar as it prescinds from both kinds of being (*esse*). Whenever the nature of stone or of anything at all is viewed only in respect to what this nature has in itself (per se), it is viewed in this third way.

Among these three ways to view nature, two are always ordered to each other in the same way: the absolute view of nature precedes the viewing of it according to the *esse* it has in singular things. But the other way of viewing nature, i.e., in respect to the being (*esse*) which a nature has in mind is not always ordered in the same way to the other two. The viewing of nature in respect to the *esse* it has in an intellect receiving its knowledge from things always comes after the other two ways of viewing nature. By this order the thing to be known precedes any knowledge of it, and the sensible thing precedes the sensation of it just as the mover precedes the moved and the cause the caused.

But the viewing of a nature, in respect to the *esse* it has in an intellect that causes the thing, precedes the other two views of nature; for when some form of an artifact arises within the artist's intellect, the artifact's nature or form viewed in itself is subsequent to the artist's intellect, as is the sensible artifact itself possessing this form or nature.

Now, just as the artist's intellect is related to his artifacts, so likewise is the divine intellect related to all creatures.

And so the first view of any nature is in respect to the way it exists in the divine intellect; the second is of the nature itself taken absolutely; the third is in respect to the being (*esse*) it has in things themselves or in the angelic mind; and the fourth is in respect to the being (*esse*), which it has in our human intellect.

In every case, then, the prior is always the explanation of the subsequent, and if this latter is withdrawn, the prior endures, but not vice versa. For Socrates is rational because man is rational, and not vice versa. So, even should Socrates and Plato not exist, rationality would yet belong to human nature. Likewise, the divine intellect is the explanation for the nature viewed absolutely and in singular things, and the nature itself viewed absolutely as well as in singular things is the explanation for our human understanding, and in a certain sense its measure.

Role of Species in Knowledge   *Summa of Theology* I, q. 85, a. 2

Intelligible species are related to the intellect as sensible species to the senses. But the sensible species is not *that which* is sensed but that *by which* sensation takes place. So the intelligible species is not that which is actually understood but that by which the intellect understands. Some maintained that our knowing powers only know their own impressions, i.e., that the sense power senses only the action upon the organ. In this view, the intellect knows only what actually affects it, i.e., the intelligible species received within it. So, the species is *that which* is understood. Two reasons make this opinion obviously false. First, inasmuch as what we understand is what we have scientific knowledge about. If we understood only the species within the soul, there would be no science of things existing outside the soul but only of intelligible species within the soul. Adopting this view, the Platonists maintained that all science treats of ideas which, they stated, are what we actually understand. Second, this opinion follows the error of the early philosophers who declared that everything that appears true is true. So they taught that contradictories could be simultaneously true. It is a fact that any power knowing only its own impressions can judge only of them. So a thing would appear just as the power of knowing was affected. So every judgment of a knowing power would deal merely with its own impression, and thus every judgment would be true. If, for example, the sense of taste knows only its own impression, when anyone with a healthy sense of taste judges honey as sweet, he will judge it truly, and when anyone with a defective sense of taste judges honey as bitter, this also will be a true judgment, since each is judging in the way that his sense of taste is affected. Consequently, every opinion will be equally true following every impression.

We must maintain, then, that the intelligible species is related to the intellect as that by which it understands.

Error or Misjudgment   *Summa of Theology* I, q. 85, a. 6, c

In *On the Soul* III, the philosopher compares the intellect to the senses, for the sense is not deceived in respect to its proper object, i.e., sight in apprehending color—except, perhaps, accidentally, by reason of some organic impediment. So a person with fever judges as bitter something sweet since his tongue is full of bad humors. In respect to common sensibles such as judging size and shape, the sense can be deceived, as when it judges the sun to be only one foot in diameter although it is larger than the earth. It is even more deceived in respect to accidental objects as when it judges gall to be honey by reason of sameness in color. It is clear why it is not deceived about its proper object. Every power as a power is essentially disposed to its proper object, and so it never fails in judging its proper object, because as long as the power remains, the relationship will remain.

The intellect's proper object is a thing's essence, and so, strictly speaking, the intellect cannot err in respect to the essence of anything. But the intellect can err with respect to whatever is found with the essence or quiddity, as when it refers one thing to another in composing or dividing or even in reasoning. Hence it cannot be in error with respect to those statements that are known as soon as the meaning of the terms is known, as with first principles, from which we proceed to conclusions whose scientific certitude has the infallibility of truth.

Accidentally, with respect to the essence of composite things, the intellect may be deceived, not by reason of the organ that the intellectual power does not use, but by reason of the composition that enters into a definition: either when falsity occurs by applying the definition of one thing to another (e.g., that of circle applied to triangle), or when the definition itself is false (e.g., involving an impossible composition, such as defining anything as "a rational animal with wings"). Thus we cannot be deceived with respect to simple things whose definition includes no composition; but when we err we are apprehending nothing with respect to them, as it says in *Metaphysics* IX.

Mental Word   *On the Power of God,* q. 8, a. 1, c

In knowing, the agent may be related to four things: namely, to what is understood, to the intelligible species whereby his intellect is made actual, to his act of knowing, and to his intellectual concept.

This concept is distinguished from the three others. It differs from what is known insofar as the latter is often outside the intellect, whereas the intellectual concept is only within the intellect. Also, the intellectual concept is ordained to what is known as to its end, since the intellect forms the concept of it so that it may understand what is known. It differs from the intelligible species insofar as the latter, which makes the intellect actual, is recognized as the principle of the intellect's act, because only as actual does any agent act; and it is form as principle of action, which makes it actual. And it differs from the act of the intellect because it is recognized as the end of the action and achieved by it. For by its action the intellect forms a definition of a thing or even an affirmative or negative proposition.

In us this intellectual concept is properly called a word, because this is what the spoken word signifies. For the external utterance does not signify the intellect itself nor the intelligible species nor the act of intellect but the intellectual concept by means of which it relates to the thing.

Consequently this concept or word by which our intellect knows something distinct from itself originates from another and represents another. It originates from the intellect through an act of intellect, and it is the likeness of what is known. Now, when the intellect knows itself this same word or concept is its offspring and likeness, i.e., of the intellect knowing itself. And this occurs inasmuch as the effect is like its cause in its form, and the form of the intellect is what is known. So the word originating from the intellect is the likeness of what is known, whether this be the intellect itself or something else. And this word of our intellect is extrinsic to the intellect's essence (for it is not the essence but a kind of passion of it), and yet it is not extrinsic to the intellect's act of knowing, since without it this act cannot be complete.

3. EMOTIONS AND LOVE

Affectivity in Man   *Summa of Theology*, q. 80,
                                          a. 1, c and ad. 3

There has to be some tending power in soul. This is recognized by considering that any form brings with it some incli-

nation; fire, for instance, by its form tends to ascend and to
reproduce itself. Now, form is present in a higher way in
things having knowledge than in those not having it. In those
without knowledge, form is only present to determine the
thing to its appropriate and natural state of being. This natural inclination occurring with natural form is called "natural tendency." In those having knowledge the individual is
determined to its appropriate natural state of being through
a natural form that is receptive, nevertheless, to the species
of other things. Thus the senses receive the species of all
sensible things, and the intellect the species of all intelligible
things, so that man's soul somehow becomes all things by his
senses and intellect. By this knowledge those having knowledge somehow come closer to the image of God, "in whom,"
as Dionysius says, "all things pre-exist."

Consequently, because forms exist in those having knowledge in a way higher than that of natural forms, they must
have an inclination superior to that natural inclination, which
is called "natural tendency." This superior inclination is
present in the tending power by which an animal can desire
not only whatever it is inclined toward by its natural form but
also whatever it apprehends. So we must admit some tending power in the soul.

ad. 3. Every power of the soul is a kind of form or nature
having a natural tendency toward something. Hence every
power desires the object suited to its natural tendency. Superior to the natural tendency is the animal tendency that
comes with apprehension. It does not desire something as
suitable for a particular power (e.g., sight to see or hearing to
hear) but because it is suitable absolutely for the animal.

Human Emotions   *On Truth*, q. 25, a. 3, ad. 6

It is not with regard to their essence that we speak of the
concupiscible and irascible powers as human or rational as
though pertaining to the soul's superior aspect, but by participation insofar as they serve reason, thereby participating
in its government, as Damascene also says.

Emotions as Reasonable   *Summa of Theology* I–II, q. 17, a. 7, c

Any act is under our rule if it lies within our power, as stated (*Summa of Theology* I–II, 17, 6). Therefore, we must reflect upon how the sensitive tendency is within our power in order that we may understand how it comes under the rule of reason. We must observe that the sensitive tendency differs from the intellectual tendency called the will in being a power of a corporeal organ, whereas the will is not. But every act of a power using a corporeal organ, such as an eye, is dependent upon both the power to see and the eye's condition, which helps or impedes vision. So the act of the sensitive tendency is dependent not only upon the tending power but also upon the body's disposition. But whatever concerns a power of the soul is based upon apprehension. The imagination's apprehension (which is of a particular thing) is governed by the apprehension of reason (which is universal) as a particular, active power is governed by a universal active power. So in this way the act of the sensitive tendency is subject to reason's rule. But the quality and disposition of the body is not subject to reason's rule, and thus the movements of the sensitive tendency are prevented from being entirely subject to reason.

It often happens that our sensitive tendency is suddenly put into motion by an apprehension of our imagination or senses and that this motion is beyond our reason's control, although foresight could have prevented this.

Thus the philosopher declares in *Politics* I, "reason rules over the irascible and concupiscible not despotically, as does a master over a slave, but politically or royally, as one rules over free men who are not wholly subject to the ruler."

Kinds of Emotions   *On Truth*, q. 26, a. 4, c

. . . There is first of all a psychic union of a pleasurable object with the man who tends to it when it is apprehended as similar or suitable to him. Out of this arises the emotion of love, i.e., a specifying [qualifying] of the sense tendency by the form of the desirable object. That is why we speak of love as a kind of union of the lover with the beloved.

But there is a further striving after what was united psychically in order that it might be really united, to enable the lover to enjoy the possession of the beloved. In this way there arises the emotion of desire, which generates joy as soon as the object is really possessed.

The first motion of the concupiscible power is therefore love, desire is the second, and joy is the last.

And through their contraries the emotions concerned with evil things are differentiated so that hate is the contrary of love; aversion is the contrary of desire; and sadness, of joy. . . .

Good as Object of Tendency   *On Truth*, q. 22, a. 1, c

Everything—whether it has knowledge or not—tends to good. To clarify this we should remember that certain ancient philosophers taught that suitable natural effects occur from the necessity of their prior causes, although these very natural causes have not been directed in any special way toward the suitability of these effects.

Whatever is orientated or inclined to something by another is inclined to whatever is intended by the one inclining or orientating it. The arrow, for instance, is directed to the very target at which the archer aims. Therefore, since all natural things have been directed by a certain natural inclination toward their ends by the first mover, God, whatever is willed or intended by God is that to which everything is naturally inclined. But inasmuch as God's will can have no other end than himself, and he is essentially goodness, everything must be naturally inclined to good. To desire or to have tendency (*appetere*) is only to yearn for something, tending as it were toward whatever is suitable for oneself.

Hence because all things are destined and orientated by God toward good, and this is done so that in each one there is a principle whereby it tends toward good as though seeking good itself, we must admit that all things naturally tend to good. If everything tended toward good while lacking within itself any principle of inclination, they might be spoken of as being led to good but not as tending toward it. But through an innate principle everything is said to tend to good as self-inclining. Hence we read in *Wisdom* (8, 1) that divine wisdom "ordereth all things sweetly" because each by its own action tends toward that to which it has been divinely directed.

Will in Relation to Intellect   *On Truth*, q. 22, a. 11, c

One thing can be called more excellent than another essentially or in one respect. To show that one thing is essentially better than another, we should compare the two with respect to their essences, not their accidents. A comparison by accidents would show one thing to be better than another in one respect. A man compared to a lion through essence is shown to be essentially nobler because the man is rational, the lion irrational. But when a lion is compared to man in respect to physical strength, he surpasses man. This is excelling only in one respect.

To learn which one of these two powers, will or intellect, is unqualifiedly better, we should look to their essential differences.

The intellect's perfection and dignity consist in having whatever is understood within the intellect itself, because thus does it actually know, which is the basis of its dignity.

The will's and the will-act's nobility consists in directing the soul to some noble thing in its existent state.

Now, if we speak in general, it is more perfect to possess the nobility of something else than to be related to a noble thing outside oneself. So that if the intellect and will are considered in the abstract, without reference to this or that concrete thing, they are so ordered that the intellect is essentially more excellent than the will.

But it may be that to be somehow related to a certain noble thing is more excellent than having its nobility within oneself. This occurs whenever the manner of possession is inferior to the manner of being. But if the value of a thing is in another without any loss of that value present in the thing itself, then the possessor is better than that which is merely related to the value. Now, the intellect receives the forms of those things that are superior to the soul in a manner inferior to that which they have within the things themselves; for we read in the *Causes* that the intellect receives things in its own way. And it is for this reason that the forms of things inferior to the soul, like bodily things, are more valuable in the soul than within the things themselves.

So we may compare the intellect to the will in three ways: 1. Essentially and in general, without any reference to this or that concrete thing. The intellect is in this way more excellent than the will, since it is better to possess what is valuable in anything than to be merely related to the value. 2. In respect to material and sensible things. The intellect is again in this way essentially better than the will. Thus knowing a stone intellectually is better than willing it, because the form of the stone as known by intellect is within intellect better than it is in itself as desired by will. 3. In respect to divine things, superior to the soul. In this way to will is more excellent than to know, for to will or love God is more excellent than to know him. For when God is desired by the will, the divine goodness itself is in a more perfect state in God himself than the participated goodness known by our intellect is in us.

Love According to Aristotle   *Commentary on Nicomachean Ethics* VIII, 1

He says first that of those who love one another for the sake of utility, one does not love the other for the sake of the other but inasmuch as he receives from the other some good for himself. The same is true of those who love each other on account of pleasantness, for the one does not love the other precisely as witty or virtuous in merriment but merely as pleasant to himself. So it is obvious that those who love for the sake of utility love for the good they get, and those who love for the sake of pleasantness love for the pleasure they enjoy. Thus they do not love their friend for what he is in himself but for what is incidental to him, his utility or pleasantness. Therefore, friendships of this sort plainly are not friendships essentially but incidentally, because a person is not loved for what he is but for utility or pleasure.

Then . . . he shows that friendships of this kind are easily dissolved. They are for the sake of something that is incidental to the persons loved, and in this men do not always remain the same. The same man, for instance, is not always pleasant or useful. Therefore, when those who are loved cease to be pleasant or useful, their friends stop loving them. This is very obvious in friendship based on utility, for the same thing is not always useful to a man. It is one thing now, and then another in different times and places. So a doctor is useful for sickness, a sailor for navigation, and so on. Since then friendship was cultivated not for the man himself but for the utility he afforded, when the cause of the friendship vanishes, the friendship too is consequently dissolved.

. . . He says that the friendship between good men and those alike in virtue is perfect friendship. Then . . . he proves his statement by explaining the qualities of this friendship. First, he shows that the friendship just referred to is friendship essentially and not incidentally. Those who are alike in virtue wish one another good inasmuch as they are virtuous. But they are good in themselves, for virtue is a kind of perfection making man good and his work good. It is clear then that such men wish good to one another in themselves. Therefore they have friendship essentially. Second . . . he shows that it lacks nothing. Third . . . he shows that it is rare. . . .

Love in General   *Commentary on Sentences* I,
                              d. 27, q. 1, a. 1–4

Love:
1. What is it?
2. Where is it found?
3. How does it compare with other affections of the soul?
4. How does it compare with knowledge?

Whether Dionysius's definition of love is adequate.

. . . Love pertains to tendency; tendency, however, is a passive power, whence in *On the Soul* III, 54, the philosopher says that the desirable moves as a mover. Moreover, anything passive is completed insofar as it is informed through the term of its action, and toward this its action is directed and stops; just as the intellect, before it is formed through the form of the intelligible, inquires and doubts, although when it has been informed, the inquiry ceases, and the intellect is fixed in that, so that it is said to be firmly immersed in that thing. Likewise, when the affection or tendency is wholly inspired by the form of the good that is its object, it takes pleasure in it and adheres to it as though fixed on it, and it is thus said to love it. Whence love is nothing but a certain change of affection toward the beloved. And because everything that is achieved by the form of anything becomes one with it, so through love the one loving is made one with the beloved because this becomes the form of the one loving; likewise the philosopher says in *Ethics* IX, 4, that a friend is another self (*alter ipse*), and in I Cor. 6: 17 it is said, "whoever adheres to God is one spirit." Moreover, everything acts according to the exigency of its form, which is the principle of acting and the regulator of the operation. Moreover, the good is loved as an end; but the end is the beginning in practical matters as first principles are in knowing. Whence just as the intellect formed through the quiddities of thing is directed by this in its awareness of principles that are apprehended by known definitions and, further, in the apprehension of conclusions that are made known from principles, so the one loving whose affection is informed by the good itself (which has the function of end, although not always of the ultimate end) is inclined through love to act according to the exigency of the beloved, and such an action is especially delightful for it as suitable to its form; whence whatever the lover does or suffers for the beloved is wholly delightful for himself, and he becomes constantly more ardent toward the beloved insofar as a greater delight is experienced in the beloved in regard to those things that he does and suffers on account of him. And just as fire cannot be restrained from the motion that befits it according to the exigency of its form except through violence, so neither can the lover do anything apart from love; and on account of this, Gregory says (*Homily* 30, Gospel) that love cannot be idle, nay, rather that if it exists at all, it achieves great things. And because everything violent is painful as though repugnant to the will, as is said in *Metaphysics* V, 6, likewise also it is painful to act against the inclination of love or even beyond it; to act, however, according to it, is to do whatever is befitting the beloved. For since the lover will accept the beloved as one with himself, it follows that the lover wears the mask (*persona*), as it were, of the beloved in all matters relating to the beloved, and thus somehow the lover serves the beloved insofar as he is guided by the aims of the beloved.

So therefore Dionysius places most adequately the meaning of love in the aforesaid exchange. For he establishes the very union of the lover with the beloved, which is accomplished by the change of the lover's affection into the beloved when he says that love is a joining and uniting force; and he establishes the inclination of that love to do those things related to the beloved, whether this be a superior, an inferior, or an equal. . . .

Whether love is in the concupiscible tendency.

. . . Everything that pursues some end must in some way be determined to that end: otherwise it would no more attain that end than any other.

However, we need a definition coming from the intention of the end, not only from the nature tending to the end (because in this way all things would come about by chance, as some philosophers have proposed). Moreover, to intend the end is impossible unless the end is known as an end as well as the relationship of the means to the end itself. However, knowing the end and the means toward the end constitute not only self-direction to the end but also the direction of other things, as an archer directs an arrow to a target. So therefore in two ways something tends to the end. In one way it is directed to the end by itself, which is the case in one knowing the end and the means to the end. In another way it is directed by another; and in this way all things tend toward their own natural ends according to their nature, directed by the wisdom of the one instituting nature. And according to this we find two tendencies: namely, the natural tendency, which is nothing but an inclination of the thing to its natural end, which is from the direction of the one instituting nature, and again the voluntary tendency, which is the inclination of one knowing the end. And between these two tendencies there is a middle one, which proceeds from the knowledge of the end without the end being known as end and without the relationship between the means and the end itself being known: and this is the sensitive tendency. And thus two tendencies are found in a nature that is alive and aware. But all that is appropriate to a living nature must be traced back to some power of soul in things having soul, and so there must be one power of the soul whose function is to desire as distinguished from that power whose function is to know, just as in separated substances we distinguish intellect and will, as the philosophers say.

So then it is evident that natural tendency differs from voluntary tendency because the natural inclination of tendency is from an extrinsic principle; and therefore it has no liberty, because the free is that which is its own cause: however, the inclination of the voluntary tendency is caused by the will itself, and therefore the will has freedom. But the inclination of the sensitive tendency is caused in part by the one desiring, insofar as it pursues what is apprehended as desirable (whence Augustine says that animals are moved by what they see); and in part by the object, insofar as knowledge of the means to the end is lacking. Therefore it follows that from another who knows the end, the things that profit them are foreseen. And on account of that they do not have entire freedom, but they participate somewhat in freedom. Everything, however, that is from God receives some nature by which it is destined to its ultimate end. Whence it is fitting that in all creatures having some end there should also be found a natural tendency in the will itself with respect to the ultimate end. Whence by natural tendency a man desires happiness, and he wants those things that lead toward the fulfillment of his wish. So, therefore, it should be said that natural tendency is in all powers of the soul and parts of the body with respect to their appropriate good; but the animal tendency, which is for a special good, to which the inclination of nature does not suffice, is from some special power, either the will or the concupiscible power.

And thence it is that all other powers of the soul are forced by their own objects involuntarily, because all the others have a natural tendency only with respect to their own object. However, the will has, apart from a natural inclination, another of which it is itself a willing cause. And likewise it should be said of love, which ends the motion of desire, that natural love is in all powers and in all things; but animal love, so to speak, is in some special power or will in accord with what he calls the end of the intellectual tendency, or in the concupiscible power in accord with what he calls the end of the sensitive tendency.

Whether love is the first and the more principal affection of the soul.

. . . Love is prior to other affections of the soul, for love means the fulfillment of the affection through being informed by its object. In all things, however, it is found that motion proceeds from the first immobile at rest: this is evident among natural things, because the first mover in any genus is not moved by its own kind of movement, just as the first changing one is not changed. This is likewise evident with regard to intellectual things, because the motion of discursive reason proceeds from the principles and quiddities of things by which the informed intellect is perfected. When therefore affection is informed and perfected by love, just as the intellect by principles and quiddities, as previously said, it follows that every motion of the affection proceeds from the repose and perfection of love. And because anything that is first in any genus is more perfect (as the understanding of principles in demonstrable things and the motion of the heavens in natural things), likewise it follows that love is yet more vehement than the other affections, as will become evident through individual examples.

Whether knowledge is higher than love.

. . . In all things there is a twofold perfection: one by which the thing subsists in itself, the other by which it is related to other things. And in material things each one is limited and bounded insofar as it has one determined form through which it is merely one species; and also through a power directed to those things proportionate to it, it has an inclination and order as has a heavy thing toward its center. In both ways, however, immaterial things have a certain infinity because they are somehow all things insofar as the essence of the immaterial thing is the exemplar and likeness of all things either by act or by potentiality, as happens in angels and souls; in this way they have knowledge. Likewise they also have an inclination and order to all things, and in this way they have will, by which all things are pleasing or displeasing either by act or potentiality. And by this they participate in some immateriality, which allows for knowledge and will. Whence animals know insofar as they receive the species of sensible things immaterially in the organs of the senses, and they are inclined to different things through the sensible tendency according to the intentions spiritually perceived from things. It is therefore evident that knowledge pertains to the perfection of the knower by which in himself he is perfected; however, the will pertains to a thing's perfection by its relation to other things. And likewise the object of the knowing power is the true, which is in the soul, as the philosopher says (*Metaphysics* VI, 8): "The object of the tending power, however, is the good, which is in things, as already said."

Therefore the knowing power can be compared to the tendency in three ways. First, in respect to order, and in this way the cognitive power is naturally prior because the perfection of anything in itself is prior to its perfection as related to another. Second, as to capacity, and by this they are equal, because the knowing power is related to all things, and so too is the tendency, whence they also are mutually inclusive insofar as the intellect knows the will and the will seeks and loves those things pertaining to intellect. Third, they can be compared according to excellence and rank; and so they are to each other as transcending and transcended, because if the intellect and the will are considered as well as those things pertaining to them as certain properties and accidents of that in which they are, then the intellect is more excellent and so are those things related to it. If, however, they are considered as capacities, i.e., as ordered to acts and to objects, then the will is more excellent, and so are those things related to it.

But if it is asked which of these is absolutely of higher rank, it must be answered that some things are superior to the soul and some are inferior, whence although through will and love a man is somehow drawn into the very things willed and loved, through knowledge, however, conversely, things known are through their likenesses made into the knower. In respect to those things that are above the soul, love is nobler and higher than knowledge, whereas in respect to those things that are beneath the soul, knowledge is more important. Whence also it is good to know many things that it would be evil to love.

Charity or Love for God

Commentary on Sentences I, d. 27, q. 2, a. 1-4

Whether charity is the same as concupiscence or what charity is.

. . . Love is a certain quieting, as was said above in the preceding question (q. 1, a. 1); whence just as tendency is found in the sensitive and intellective part, so too is love. Moreover, those things that pertain to the sensitive tendency are transferred to the intellective, like the names of the emotions. What, however, is proper to the intellective tendency is not suitable to the sensitive tendency, like the name of will. And likewise love is present in both tendencies. Because it is found in the sensitive tendency, love (*amor*) is appropriately called sensible by the fact that it introduces emotion; and because it is found in the intellective part, love (*dilectio*) is called spiritual, and it includes choice that pertains to the intellective tendency. Nevertheless, love (*amor*) as called sensible is also transferred to the superior part; however, love (*dilectio*) as called spiritual is never transferred to the inferior part. Moreover, all other names that seem to pertain to sensible love are either included by them or include them as adding something more than spiritual and sensible love, for because sensible love in some way unites the lover to the beloved, likewise the lover is related to the beloved as to himself or as to his own perfection.

His attitude toward himself, however, and toward the things that are for his sake is such that his first desire is to have for himself anything that is for his perfection, and therefore sensible love includes the desire for the beloved by which the presence of the beloved is desired. Second, a man through affection directs other things toward himself and seeks for himself whatever is suitable for him; when this process is applied to the beloved, the love includes benevolence, by which he desires certain goods for the beloved. Third, a man acquires for himself those things that he desires for himself by his own efforts; and insofar as this is exercised with regard to the other, well-doing is included in love. Fourth, a man consents to do those things that seem good to him, and when this is done for a friend, the love includes harmony, by which a man agrees to those things that seem good to his friend— but not, however, in speculative matters, because harmony in these things, according to the philosopher (*Ethics* IX, 6), does not pertain to friendship, and there can be disagreement in these matters without prejudice to friendship, because in such things to agree or to disagree is not subject to the will inasmuch as the intellect is coerced by reason. Nevertheless, love adds something to the four previous statements, namely, a repose of the tendency in the beloved without which any one of these four can be. For there are certain things that add something to spiritual or sensible love. For love in the sense of affection adds to love a certain intensity of love, a certain fervor. Indeed, friendship adds two things: one is a certain association of the lover and the beloved in love, as, for example, an awareness that love is mutual; the other is achieved through choice, not only by passion. Whence the philosopher says that friendship is like possession, but affection is like emotion. So therefore it is evident that friendship is most perfect among those things pertaining to love, including all the aforesaid, and so in such a class we should place charity as a certain friendship of man for God, by which man loves God and God man; and thus is achieved a certain association of man with God, as (I John 1: 7): "If we walk in the light, just as he is in the light, we shall have mutual association."

Whether charity is a virtue.

. . . The end of human life is happiness, and so different lives have different kinds of happiness. For whoever is not engaged in public life cannot attain the happiness of a public career, which provides the best in civic life. It likewise follows that whoever arrives at contemplative happiness must become a participator in contemplative life. Whence the happiness that man can attain naturally is in accord with human life, and of this the philosophers have spoken, so it is said (*Ethics* I, 16): "happy, moreover, as men are happy." But because there is promised to us a certain happiness in which we shall be equal to the angels, as is clear in Matt. 22, and this not only exceeds the powers of man but even of the angels who are brought to this by grace just as we are, and because this is natural only to God, it is therefore likewise fitting that man should arrive at that divine happiness because he has become a participant in divine life. But it is especially friendship that makes one man associate with another, for as the philosopher says (*Ethics* IX, 14): "each one converses with his friend of those things in which he takes particular delight, and he considers his life to be friendship, the wish to enjoy his friend's company." And so some men hunt together, some drink together, and some philosophize together, etc. And therefore it was natural to believe in a kind of friendship with God by which we might enjoy his company, and this is charity, as was said above.

This communication of divine life, however, exceeds the power of nature, just as does the happiness to which it is ordained. And so it is fitting that nature should be fulfilled through some superadded good, and this is the function of virtue. We can thus appropriately say that charity is a theological virtue diffused into our hearts through the Holy Spirit, who is given to us (Rom. 5).

Whether reason is the subject of charity.

. . . To know in what power any virtue is present, we should consider to what power its activity corresponds. But charity's principal action is to love God; this action belongs to the function of the leader, but tendency to that of the follower. So it must be traced back to tendency. However, the sensitive tendency cannot accomplish this act because its object cannot be God. Therefore it follows that it belongs to the intellective tendency not insofar as it is elective of those things that are for the end but insofar as it orientates itself toward that very ultimate end; and this is a matter of will, whence the proper subject of charity is the will.

Some, however, say that charity is in the concupiscible part, but this cannot be so, because the concupiscible part belongs to the sensitive tendency. And if it is called a human concupiscible power, this is only through participation in reason, unless when they use the word "will" they mean the irascible and concupiscible.

Whether charity is one virtue or many.

But on the contrary, there is only one mover in any genus. But charity moves all other virtues to its end through their own acts. Therefore charity is one virtue. Besides, the object of charity is God, inasmuch as this is a theological virtue. But God is supremely one. Therefore charity is only one virtue.

Whether God can be loved by us through his essence while we are progressing on the way.

. . . Among ordered powers, where the operation of the first power ends, the operation of the next begins, just as it is evident that the sense ends at the imagination, which is put into operation by sense action; and the intellect begins where the imagination ends because it gets its objects from phantasms, as was said in *On the Soul* II. And so there can be no knowledge of things without phantasms, except of things signified by phantasms. And so when a man is progressing on the way and receiving knowledge from phantasms, he cannot immediately see God. But it is suitable that from the visible things from which he receives phantasms, he arrives at his knowledge. Moreover, although he may not see the essence itself immediately, nevertheless, intellectual knowledge ends at God himself, inasmuch as man apprehends being itself from its effects.

And so since affection follows the intellect, where intellect's operation ends, the operation of affection or of will begins.

Moreover, it was said that the intellect's operation, namely, its knowledge, ends at God himself, whose *esse* (being) it apprehends from effects. And so the will's operation toward God himself can be immediate, with no intervening medium pertaining to the will. But for the intellect to arrive at knowing God, there must be many preceding media.

Whether God can be loved wholly.

. . . For love to be, three things must concur: the lover, the beloved, and love, and each has its own way of existing. For the way of the beloved is that by which it is lovable; and the lover has a way of existing by which he is a lover, that is, born to love. But the kind of love depends upon the relation of the lover to the beloved, because love is the mean between the two (this is also the case with sight). If, therefore, "wholly" refers to the loved and seen thing's way of being, then the saints who are in the fatherland love God totally and see him totally; for just as there is nothing that they do not essentially see and love (for which reason they are said to see and love everything), so also nothing in regard to God remains unseen and unloved by them. Hence they see and love God wholly, because they see and love the whole God.

Likewise is this the case if "wholly" refers to the lover's way of being; because according to their total way of being, that is, according to their whole possibility, they will see and love, with none of their powers deprived of the divine vision and love; and thus is God understood to be loved with the whole heart (*ex toto corde*). But if "wholly" refers to love's way of being, then no one will love wholly nor see wholly; for love's and vision's way of being, as was said, is measured by the visible to be seen and the lovable to be loved. But God's way of being visible and lovable surpasses any way that man can see and love, because infinite is his light and goodness; and therefore he is not totally seen and loved by others, since only by himself is he seen as clearly as he is visible, and loved as fervently and intensely as he is lovable; and so only he himself comprehends himself by perceiving and loving.

Whether the love by which we love God has a mode.

. . . A mode brings with it a certain measurement. But an action is measured by the reason for acting; so mercy receives its measure in the alleviating of misery from the quantity of misery, which moves to mercy. But the cause for loving God is his divine goodness, which is infinite. The act of the creature, however, which proceeds from a finite potentiality, is finite; and so it cannot be commensurate with the reason for loving. Therefore in the love of God no measurement is proposed beyond which it is not fitting to proceed; but no matter how much anyone loves, he will always love further, and for this reason it is said that there is no prefixed measure beyond which it is not fitting to progress.

Whether the mode of loving, which is of precept, can be observed during life.

. . . The "whole" is the same as the "perfect," as the philosopher says. But the nature of the perfect consists in having nothing lacking to it. This occurs, however, in two ways: either so that nothing is lacking of those things that it has by nature, or that nothing is lacking of those things that it ought to have (just as something has a perfect quantity when its quantity is as human nature requires, although it has not a giant's quantity, which is possible in human nature).

Therefore there is a primary perfection of human nature in the state of glory when man will have all that is possible for human nature to have; but there is a secondary perfection in created nature, when, for example, a man has all that he ought to have according to that time.

And in accordance with this, there can be a twofold wholeness in the love of God. One by which man expends his all for the love of God, burying himself in love; this kind of perfection or wholeness is not commanded as something to be done, but this is rather shown by understanding what is received, as Augustine says (*On the Perfection of Justice*, 17), and this perfection or wholeness excludes any interruption of the act of love, even for a time.

There is another kind of wholeness by which man lacks nothing of anything he ought to possess in his time with respect to the love of God; and this perfection or wholeness is commanded in the precept and may be fulfilled now as, for example, when nothing of what should belong to the love of God is omitted; and this wholeness excludes all that is contrary and repugnant to the divine love, but not, however, that which interrupts the act of love for a time; because only those in the state of beatitude can be acting always according to the act of a power, for the perfection of the happy one is in action; but the perfection of a power is in the habit [or permanent disposition].

God Is Loved in All Things
Commentary on Sentences II, d. 38, q. 1, a. 2, c

. . . There is one ultimate end of all things, just as there is one first principle; nevertheless, each thing must have its own proper end, just as it has its proper principle, just as those things that are of one kind communicate in one end, which is common to all in that kind but not to all things.

Nor can there be any proper relation of anything to the ultimate end except through the mediation of its own kind of
end.

But the proper end of each thing through which it is ordered to the ultimate end is its proper operation. Hence the
end of rational nature, through which it is ordered to its
proper end, is perfect action proper to its nature. But an action's perfection is threefold: specifically in reference to object, disposition, and delight. For insofar as the object is
higher, so the action tending toward it is more beautiful and
more perfect; whence in respect to the object an action is
not perfect except from a habit [or disposition]. Hence insofar as the disposition is the more perfect, the action will be
more perfect; and the most perfect action will be from the
noblest habit. Likewise, as the philosopher says in *Ethics* X,
6, "delight perfects action as beauty does youth; for delight
itself is a certain grace of action; and therefore it is fitting
that some of these should be the common end of the will of
those declared righteous."

But perfect action itself is happiness. The highest object,
however, is God. But the most perfect permanent disposition
is charity, as proven in *Ethics* X, 7; and therefore it is written that God is the end of the righteous will as is charity and
good delight, and happiness; yet so that God is the ultimate
end with happiness completing charity, and delight as a subordinate end joined to the ultimate end.

When an action tends toward an object there is no right
relation of the will to God except through the mediation of
these three.

Human Love Compared with Divine Love

Summa of Christian Teaching
I, 91

It also follows that with God love is an act of his will.

It is proper to love's nature that the lover wills the good of
the beloved. Now, God wills his own and others' good, as
stated above. Accordingly, then, God loves both himself and
other things.

. . . True love requires one to will another's good as one's
own. For a good willed merely as conducive to another's

good, is loved accidentally; thus he who wills wine to be preserved that he may drink it, or who loves a man that he may be useful or pleasing to him, loves the wine or the man accidentally, but, strictly speaking, himself. Now, God loves each thing's good as its own, since he wills each thing to be inasmuch as it is good in itself, although he directs one to the profit of another. God therefore truly loves both himself and other things.

. . . Since everything naturally wills or desires its own good in its own way, if the love's nature is that the lover wills or desires the good of the beloved, it follows that the lover is referred to the beloved as to a thing that is in a way one with him. Wherefore it appears that the proper notion of love consists in the affection of one tending to another as one with himself in some way; for which reason Dionysius describes love as a *unitive force.* Hence the greater the thing that makes the lover one with the beloved, the more intense is the love; for we love those more who are united to us by the origin of birth, or by frequent companionship, than those who are merely united to us by the bond of human nature. Again, the more the cause of union is deeply seated in the lover, the stronger the love; wherefore sometimes a love that is caused by a passion becomes more intense than a love arising from natural origin or from some habit, although it is more liable to be transitory. Now, the cause of all things being united to God, namely, his goodness, which all things reflect, is exceedingly great and deeply seated in God, since he himself is his own goodness. Wherefore in God not only is there true love, but also most perfect and most abiding love.

. . . On the part of its object, love does not denote anything inconsistent with God, since that object is a good; nor, again, as regards the way in which it is referred to its object, since a thing when possessed is loved not less, but more, because a good is more closely united to us when possessed. Wherefore in natural things movement toward an end is more intense if the end be near (although the contrary happens accidentally sometimes, for instance, when we discover something repugnant to love in the beloved, for then possession diminishes love). Accordingly, love is not inconsistent with the divine perfection, as regards its specific nature. Therefore it is in God.

It belongs to love to seek union, as Dionysius says. For since, on account of likeness or compatibility between lover and beloved, the affection of the lover is somehow united to the beloved, the tendency inclines to the completion of the union, namely, that the union that was begun in the affections be completed in actions. Wherefore it belongs to friends to rejoice in mutual companionship, living together, and in common pursuits. Now, God moves all other things to union, for inasmuch as he gives them being and other perfections, he unites them to himself as far as possible. Therefore God loves both himself and other things.

Love is the source of all the emotions. For joy and desire only concern a good that is loved; fear and sorrow concern only an evil that is contrary to the beloved good; and from these all the other emotions arise. Now, joy and delight are in God, as we have shown above. Therefore in God there is love.

Someone, however, might think that God loves not one thing more than another. For if intenseness and remissness are proper to a changeable nature, they cannot apply to God, from whom all change is far removed.

None of the other things that are said of God by way of operation are applied to him more or less, since he knows not one thing more than another, nor rejoices more in this than in that.

Accordingly it must be observed that while other operations of the soul are about one object only, love alone appears to be directed to a twofold object. For if we understand or rejoice, it follows that we are referred somehow to some object; whereas love wills something to someone, since we are said to love that to which we will some good, in the way described. Hence when we want a thing, we are said simply and properly to *desire* it, and not to love it, but rather to love ourselves, for whom we want it; and in consequence we are said to love it accidentally and improperly. Accordingly other operations are intense or remiss in proportion to the action's energy alone. But this cannot apply to God, because energy of action is measured by the force from which it proceeds, and every divine action is of one and the same force. On the other hand, love may be intense or remiss in two ways. In one way as regards the good that we will someone, according to which we are said to love that person more for whom we will a greater good. In another way, as regards the energy of the action, according to which we are said to love that person more, for whom, although we will not a greater good, nevertheless we will an equal good with greater fervor and efficacy. In the first way, accordingly, nothing forbids us to say that God loves one thing more than another, according as he wills for it a greater good. But in the second way this cannot be said, for the very reason stated in the case of other operations.

It is therefore clear from what has been said, that none of our emotions strictly speaking can be in God except joy and love, and yet even these are not in him as they are in us, as passion.

That joy or delight is in God is confirmed by the authority of Scripture. For it is said in the Psalm, "At thy right hand are delights even to the end," divine wisdom, which is God, as we have proved, says (Prov. 9): "I was delighted every day, playing before him," and (Luke 15: 10): "There is joy in heaven upon one sinner doing penance." Also the philosopher says (*Ethics* VII) that God rejoices with one simple delight.

Scripture also makes mention of God's love (Deut. 33: 3): "He hath loved the people"; (Jer. 31: 3): "I have loved thee with an everlasting love"; (I John 16: 27): "For the Father himself loveth you." Certain philosophers also taught that God's love is the principle of things, in agreement with which is the saying of Dionysius (*On Divine Names* IV) that God's love did not allow him to be unproductive.

It must, however, be observed that even other emotions, which, by their specific nature, are inapplicable to God, are applied to God in Holy Writ, not indeed properly, as we have shown, but metaphorically, on account of a likeness either to effects or to some preceding emotion.

I say of effects because sometimes his will, by the ordering of his wisdom, tends to an effect to which a person is inclined through a defective passion; thus a judge punishes out of justice, as an angry man out of anger. Accordingly, sometimes

God is said to be angry, inasmuch as by the ordering of his wisdom, he wills to punish someone, according to the saying of the Psalm: "When his wrath shall be kindled in a short time" (Ps. 2: 13). He is said to be merciful, inasmuch as out of his goodwill he removes man's unhappiness, even as we do the same through the passion of mercy. Hence the Psalm says: "The Lord is compassionate and merciful, long-suffering and plenteous in mercy" (Ps. 102: 8). Sometimes also he is said to repent, inasmuch as in accordance with the eternal and unchangeable decree of his providence, he makes what he previously destroyed, or destroys what previously he made, even as those who are moved by repentance are wont to do. Hence (Gen. 6: 7): "It repenteth me that I have made man." That this cannot be taken in the proper sense is clear from the words of I Ki. 15: 29: "The Triumpher in Israel will not spare and will not be moved to repentance."

I also say on account of a likeness to some preceding emotion. For love and joy, which are properly in God, are the principles of all the emotions: love by way of moving principle, joy by way of end; wherefore even an angry man rejoices while punishing, as having obtained his end. Hence God is said to grieve, inasmuch as certain things occur contrary to those he loves and approves of, just as we grieve for what has happened against our will. As we see (Is. 59: 15–16): "And he saw that there is not a man, and he stood amazed, because there is none to oppose himself."

By what has been said we can reject the error of certain Jews who ascribed to God anger, sorrow, repentance, and all such passions in their proper sense, failing to discriminate between the proper and the metaphorical expressions of Scripture.

Love for God Is Friendship　　　*Summa of Theology* II–II, q. 26, a. 3, ad. 3

Man's desire to enjoy God belongs to that love of God falling under love of concupiscence. But because the divine good is in itself greater than our share of good in enjoying him, we love God with the love of friendship rather than with that of concupiscence.

Summary of Theology II–II, q.
26, a. 13, ad. 3

Since God is man's total good, God will be for everyone the total reason for his love. But were we to adopt the impossible position that God is not man's good, God would not be man's reason for loving. So in the order of love, after God man should love himself more than all others.

Love Stimulated by Reflection on God's Works   *Summa of Christian Teaching* II, 2

This meditation on the divine works is indeed necessary in order to build up man's faith in God.

First, because through meditating on his works we are able somewhat to admire and consider the divine wisdom; for things made by art are indications of the art itself, since they are made in likeness to the art. Now, God brought things into being by his wisdom, and for this reason it is said in the Psalm: "Thou hast made all things in wisdom" (Ps. 103: 24). Hence we are able to gather the wisdom of God from the consideration of his works, since by a kind of communication of his likeness it is spread abroad in the things he has made. For it is said (Eccles. 1: 10): "He poured her out" (namely, wisdom) "upon all his works." Wherefore the Psalmist, after saying: "Thy knowledge is become wonderful to me; it is high, and I cannot reach to it" (Ps. 138: 6), and after referring to the aid of the divine enlightening, when he says: "Night shall be my light" (Ps. 138: 11), etc., confesses himself to have been helped to know the divine wisdom by the consideration of the divine works, saying: "Wonderful are thy works, and my soul knoweth right well" (Ps. 138: 14).

Second, this consideration leads us to admire the sublime power of God, and consequently begets in men's hearts a reverence for God; for we must needs conclude that the power of the maker transcends the things made. Wherefore it is said (Wis. 13: 4): "If they" (the philosophers, to wit) "admired their power and their effects" (namely of the heavens, stars, and elements of the world), "let them under-

stand . . . that he that made them is mightier than they." Also
it is written (Rom. 1: 20): "The invisible things of God . . .
are clearly seen, being understood by the things that are
made": his eternal power also and divinity. And this admira-
tion makes us fear and reverence God. Hence it is said (Jer.
10: 6–7): "Great is thy name in might. Who shall not fear
thee, O King of nations?"

Third, this consideration inflames the souls of men to the
love of the divine goodness; for whatever goodness and perfection is generally apportioned among various creatures is
all united together in him universally, as in the source of all
goodness, as we proved in the First Book. Wherefore if the
goodness, beauty, and sweetness of creatures are so alluring
to the minds of men, the fountainhead of the goodness of
God himself, in comparison with the rivulets of goodness
that we find in creatures, will draw the entranced minds of
men wholly to itself. Hence it is said in the Psalm (91: 5),
"Thou hast given me, O Lord, a delight in thy doings, and
in the works of thy hands I shall rejoice"; and elsewhere it
is said of the children of men (Ps. 35: 9): "They shall be
inebriated with the plenty of thy house" (that is, of all creatures), and (Ps. 35: 10): "Thou shalt make them drink of the
torrent of thy pleasure. For with thee is the fountain of life."
Again it is said (Wis. 13: 1) against certain men: "By these
good things, that are seen" (namely, creatures that are good
by participation), "they could not understand him that is,"
good to wit, nay more, that is, goodness itself, as we have
shown in the First Book.

Fourth, this consideration bestows on man a certain likeness to the divine perfection; for it was shown in the First
Book that God, by knowing himself, beholds all other things
in himself. Since then the Christian faith teaches man chiefly
about God, and makes him to know creatures by the light of
divine revelation, there results in man a certain likeness to
the divine wisdom. Hence it is said (II Cor. 3: 18): "But
we all beholding the glory of the Lord with open face, are
transformed into the same image."

Accordingly, it is evident that the consideration of creatures
helps to build up the Christian faith. Wherefore it is said
(Eccles. 42: 15): "I will . . . remember the works of the

Lord, and I will declare the things I have seen; by the words of the Lord are his works."

Love among Men

*Commentary on Epistle to
Galatians* IV, 5

. . . [the Apostle Paul] shows that he has reason to love them, when he says: You know how, through infirmity of the flesh, I preached the gospel to you heretofore. Here he touches on three things that usually cause men to love one another. The first is the mutual help of fellowship, and this is also the cause of love being consolidated among men (Luke 22: 28). . . .

The second thing that strengthens love among men is mutual love and affection toward one another (Prov. 8: 17): "I love them that love me." . . .

The third thing that strengthens love is doing good to one another. As to this he says: For I bear you witness that, if it could be done, i.e., had been just to do so . . . or had been to the advantage of the Church, you would have plucked out your own eyes and would have given them to me. As if to say: You loved me so much that you would have given me not only your external goods but your very eyes.*

Perfect Love of Neighbor Required for Salvation

*On the Perfection of Religious
Life,* ch. 13, 14

Now that we have considered the perfection of charity insofar as it pertains to the love of God, there remains for us to consider the perfection of charity insofar as it pertains to the love of neighbor.

Just as there are a number of degrees of perfection with regard to the love of God, so too with regard to love of neighbor. For there is a perfection that is required for salvation such that it falls under the necessity of precept, and there is a further and superabundant perfection that falls under counsel. The perfection of love of neighbor necessary for salvation has to be considered from the standpoint of the manner in which our neighbor must be loved. This manner of lov-

---

* Translated by R. F. Larcher, O.P.

ing one's neighbor is described in the precept: "Thou shalt love thy neighbor as thyself" (Matt. 22: 39).

The reason why perfect love of God requires that the whole heart of a man be somehow converted to God is that God is the supreme and universal good. Hence the way in which we must love God is fittingly expressed by the command, "Thou shalt love the Lord thy God with thy whole heart." But our neighbor is neither the universal good nor the supreme good; rather he is a particular good existing among us. Hence the manner in which he must be loved is not that we love him with our whole heart but that he be loved as oneself.

From the fact that one must love his neighbor as oneself, this love must possess four qualities. First, it must be a genuine love, for since it is the very nature of loving that one will good to the beloved, it is evident that the affection of love strikes two targets: first, the one to whom we will the good, and second, the good we will unto him. And although both of these are said to be loved, yet what is truly loved is the one to whom we will the good. Accordingly, the good that one wishes to another is incidentally loved, inasmuch as it ricochets from the main target of the act of love. For it would be silly to assert that one truly and simply loved an object whose destruction is sought. Yet there are many good things that we love, but when they are used to fulfill our love, they are consumed (such as wine when it is imbibed, and a horse when it is exposed to battle). Hence, it is clear that when we desire to make certain things serve our needs, we are really loving ourselves; whereas the things themselves are loved only incidentally, nay, even loved unto their extinction.

It is hardly necessary to point out that everyone by nature truly loves himself so as to want good things for himself, for example, happiness, virtue, knowledge, and all the things required to sustain life. Whatever a person turns to his own use, he does not love truly; he loves rather the use to which it is put; yea, more, he loves himself. Now, it is a fact that just as we can employ certain things for our use, it is possible to do the same even with men. Hence if we love our neighbor only to the extent that he can be of use to us, then surely we are not genuinely loving him, much less loving him as we

love ourselves. This comes to light in friendships called useful, i.e., friendships founded on pleasure. For when you love
someone because he is a source of advantage or of pleasure,
you are really loving not the friend but yourself; because you
are seeking from him a good that serves your purpose or
serves your pleasure. To love your neighbor in that manner
is to love him as you love wine or a horse. Such things we do
not love as ourselves, as though wishing them well; rather we
are turning whatever good is in them to our own advantage.
Thus the commandment to love our neighbor as ourselves
requires that our charity toward him be genuine. For charity
proceeds "from a pure heart and a good conscience and an
unfeigned faith," as St. Paul writes (I Tim. 1: 5). Consequently, "charity does not seek its own" (I Cor. 13: 5) but
wills good to those whom it loves. Of this St. Paul gives himself as an example to the Corinthians: "Not seeking that
which is profitable to myself but to many, that they may be
saved" (I Cor. 10: 33).

The second consequence of the command to love our
neighbor as ourselves is that it must be just and orderly.
Love is orderly and just, when the greater good is preferred
to the lesser good. Need we be reminded that among all good
things that affect man, the good of the soul is paramount,
and after that comes the good of the body, with the lowest
place being occupied by the good that consists in external
things? Do we not see, moreover, that every man naturally
follows this arrangement in loving himself? For no one would
prefer to lose his reason as against losing his sight. Again, a
person will sacrifice all his external possession to safeguard
and preserve his bodily life: "Skin for skin and all that a man
hath he will give for his life" (Job 2: 4). Now there are very,
very few who fail to observe this natural order of love of
self, when it comes to natural goods.

But when it comes to higher things, there are some who
pervert the natural order of love; for many persons sacrifice
the good of virtue or of knowledge for the sake of health or
for bodily pleasures. We even see cases where persons expose
their body to great dangers and prodigious labors in quest
of external goods. Such persons do not have a well-ordered
love; indeed, we can safely say that they do not love them-

selves genuinely, for the simple reason that they do not love the chief part of themselves as they should. For a thing seems to be what is paramount in it. Thus when the chiefs of a city do something, we say that the city has done it. Now, it is evident that the chief part of man is his soul, and that among the powers of the soul the chief is the reason or intellect. Hence anyone who bypasses the good of his soul for the goods of the body or for the pleasures of the senses clearly does not love himself truly; hence the Psalmist says: "He that loves sin, hates his own soul" (Ps. 10: 6). From these premises it follows that right order in our relations toward our neighbor is what God aims at when he commands us to love our neighbor as ourselves, i.e., that we desire the good for him in that order in which we should desire it for ourselves: first, spiritual goods, and then bodily goods including external goods. But if someone wishes for his neighbor external goods to the extent of hurting his body or wishes him bodily goods to the extent of hurting his soul, such a one does not love his neighbor as himself.

The third consequence that follows from the command to love our neighbor as ourselves is that love of neighbor be holy. A thing is called holy because it is ordered to God; thus an altar is called holy because it is dedicated to God, and in general whatever is set aside for divine worship is called holy. Now, the reason why one should love his neighbor as himself is that both share something in common, and whenever two things are related in that way, they are in that sense one, so that either of them regards the other as he regards himself. For some are alike by a natural likeness based on common parentage, others are alike by a national likeness in that they are citizens of the same country, are under the same ruler, and are governed by the same laws. In daily affairs and in business we find some who have it in common that they are partners in business or are fellow soldiers or are skilled in the same trade. Among all such, there can exist an honorable and well-ordered love. Yet no mutual interest can make that love holy; only its being ordered to God can do that. For just as the citizens of one state have in common the fact that they are subject to one ruler by whose laws they are ruled, so all men by the very fact that they naturally tend toward happi-

ness have a bond of unity under God based on his being the
supreme ruler of all and the foundation of happiness and the
lawgiver of all justice.

Consider now the fact that right reason points out that the
common good must be preferred to private advantage and
that each part of a whole is by nature dedicated to the good
of the whole. A sign of this is that a person will instinctively
expose his hand to receive a blow directed to the head or
heart, on which the whole life of man depends. But in the
previously mentioned community in which all men are fellow citizens on account of their common end, which is happiness, each man is a part; but the common good of the entire
community is God, in whom the happiness of all consists.
Thus both right reason and the very tendencies of nature lead
each person to ordain himself to God, as the part is ordained
to the whole. This ordination is made perfect through charity,
by which each one loves himself for the sake of God. When,
therefore, someone loves even his neighbor for the sake of
God, he loves his neighbor as himself. This is what makes
such a love holy. St. John indicates this when he writes: "This
commandment we have from God that he who loves God love
also his brother" (I John 4: 21).

Fourth, the way in which we are commanded to love our
neighbor requires that this love be efficacious and dynamic.
It is only too clear that everyone loves himself in such a way
that he not only would like benefits to accrue to him and disadvantages repelled, but he takes positive measures and exerts
himself to procure what is good and repel what is evil. Therefore, it is then that a person loves his neighbor as himself,
when he not only has goodwill toward him but also strives
effectively in act and in work to see that good comes to him
and that evils be turned away or relieved. So it is that St. John
says: "My little children, let us not love in word nor in tongue,
but in deed and in truth" (I John 3: 18).

Of the Perfection of Love of   *On the Perfection of Reli-*
Neighbor that Falls under   *gious Life,* ch. 14
Counsel

Now that we have finished with our consideration of the
perfection required for salvation, we turn to that type of

perfection of love of neighbor that is more excellent than
ordinary perfection and falls under counsel. This perfection
can be looked at from three different viewpoints: first, its
extent; second, the intensity; and third, the works it produces.

Love of neighbor is more or less perfect according to the
number of persons it includes. Three degrees of perfection
are possible from this viewpoint, for there are some persons
who love other men either on account of the favors they bestow or on account of some bond, either natural or social.
Such a degree of love is essentially limited to one's circle of
social or business friends. Of this Our Lord says: "If you love
them that love you, what reward shall you have? Do not even
the publicans this? And if you salute your brethren only,
what do you more? Do not also the heathens this?" (Matt.
5: 46, 47).

There are others who go beyond this and extend their love
even to strangers, but only to the point of not holding any
bad will toward them. This degree of love is essentially limited
by our natural inclinations, for every man is by nature
friendly to every other man. This comes to light when a man
gives directions to a stranger who is lost or gives him a helping hand if he has fallen.

But because every man naturally loves himself more than
his neighbor and because whatever prompts us to love something also prompts us to hate its opposite, it follows that love
of one's enemy lies beyond the limits of natural love. So it
is that the third degree of love of neighbor is that which includes even one's enemies. This is the degree of love that Our
Lord speaks of in St. Matthew: "Love your enemies,
do good to those who hate you" (Matt. 5: 44). It is by this
that the children of the heavenly Father are recognized and
in this that the perfection of love consists. Then Our Lord
concludes: "Be ye therefore perfect, as also your heavenly
Father is perfect" (Matt. 5: 48). That this love is beyond the
general run of perfection is made clear by St. Augustine, who
says that such love is peculiar to the perfect children of God,
but that all the faithful should strive for it. By praying to God
and by fighting against our natural inclinations this love can
both be obtained and become operative in us. Yet this excellent love is not too great to be obtained through the Lord's

Prayer, when we ask: "Forgive us our trespasses, as we forgive those who trespass against us."

At this point we may be able to forestall a possible misunderstanding. Since the word "neighbor" means every man, and since the commandment to love our neighbor as ourselves admits of no exception, it might seem that it is by a necessity of precept that one's enemies be loved. This misunderstanding can be cleared up, if we recall what was previously said about the perfection of the love of God. It was said that in regard to the command "Thou shalt love the Lord thy God with thy whole heart" we can distinguish between what is of necessity of precept and what is of counsel. Further, we pointed out what pertains to the perfection of love as it is found in the blessed. For if the command "Thou shalt love the Lord thy God with thy whole heart" is understood to mean that one's heart be always actually borne toward God, that pertains to the perfection of the blessed. If it is taken to mean that one's heart never accept anything contrary to the love of God, that pertains to the necessity of precept. But that a man even give up things that are lawful in order the more freely to give himself to God is of the perfection of counsel. In like manner here, in regard to the love of one's enemies, it must be understood that what is of necessity of precept is that one neither exclude his enemy from the generality of the love by which he is bound to love his neighbor nor accept in his heart anything contrary to this love. But actually to love one's enemy outside cases of necessity pertains to the perfection of counsel. For in certain cases of necessity we are bound by necessity of precept to love our enemy and do good to him by a special act, for example, if he were dying of starvation or were in some situation of this kind. But outside these cases of need, we are not bound by necessity of precept to bestow any special affection or do a special good work on behalf of an enemy, any more than we are bound to do so for anyone else.

Only the love of God in the soul can produce genuine love of one's enemies. In every other instance of love, some good moves us, e.g., some benefit bestowed, common parentage, common race, common nationality, common citizenship, or something of this type. But to love one's enemies, nothing can be a motive, except God alone. For they are loved inasmuch as they are creatures of God, made to his image and capable of enjoying him. Moreover, because charity prefers God to all other goods, it does not permit the evils or the losses it endures from its enemies to be a reason for hating them; rather it considers the divine good in order to love them. Consequently, the stronger the love of God becomes in a man, the easier it is for his soul to bend, so as to love his enemies.

Second, the perfection of love of neighbor can be considered from the viewpoint of its intensity; for it is evident that the more intensely someone is loved, the easier other things are spurned for his sake. It is possible, accordingly, to judge how perfect is one's love of neighbor by considering what a man gives up for the love of his neighbor. From this standpoint three degrees of perfection are found.

First of all, there are some who despise external goods for the love of their neighbor either by administering them in individual cases to his neighbor or by entirely dedicating all to the needs of his neighbor. This is what St. Paul touches upon when he says: "If I should distribute all my goods to feed the poor" (I Cor. 13: 3). The same is expressed in the Canticle of Canticles: "If a man should give all the substance of his house for love, he shall despise it as nothing." Our Lord imparted the same doctrine, when in giving someone the counsel to follow perfection he said: "If thou wilt be perfect, go sell what thou hast and give to the poor and thou shalt have treasure in heaven: and come follow me" (Matt. 19: 21). In this counsel Our Lord seems to ordain the surrender of all external goods to two objectives: to love of neighbor when he says "and give to the poor," and to the love of God when he says "and come follow me." It comes to the same thing when anyone does not refuse to endure a loss in his external goods for the love of God or of neighbor. Hence the Apostle commends those who "took with joy the being stripped of their own goods" (Heb. 10: 34); likewise, it is said in the Book of Proverbs: "He that neglecteth a loss for the sake of a friend is just" (Prov. 12: 26). Far from this degree of love are those who, having the goods, do not care to help their neighbor in his needs. Of such St. John says: "He

that hath the substance of this world and shall see his brother
in need and shall shut up his bowels from him: How doth the
charity of God abide in him?" (I John 3: 17).

The second degree of love considered from the standpoint
of its intensity is that one expose his body to labors for the
love of his neighbor. St. Paul cites himself as an example of
this: "Now whether we be in tribulation, it is for your exhortation and salvation" (II Cor. 1: 6) and "I labor even unto
bands, as an evildoer; but the word of God is not bound.
Therefore, I endure all things for the sake of the elect that
they also may obtain the salvation" (II Tim. 2: 9, 10). But
they are far from this degree of love who omit no pleasures
or endure no inconvenience for the love of others. Against
such the Prophet Amos inveighs: "You that sleep upon beds
of ivory and are wanton on your couches; that eat the lambs
out of the flock, and the calves out of the midst of the herd;
you that sing to the sound of the psaltery: they have thought
themselves to have instruments of music like David; that
drink wine in bowls, and anoint themselves with the best
ointments: and they are not concerned for the affliction of
Joseph" (Amos 6: 4, 5, 6). Ezechiel, too, says: "You have
not gone up to face the enemy, nor have you set up a wall
for the house of Israel, to stand in battle in the day of the
Lord" (Ezech. 13: 5).

The third degree of intensity of love is that one lay down
his life for his brethren. Hence it is said: "In this we have
known the charity of God, because he hath laid down his
life for us: and we ought to lay down our lives for the
brethren" (I John 3: 16). Beyond this degree love cannot
go, for the Lord says: "Greater love than this no man hath
that he lay down his soul for his friends" (John 15: 13). Accordingly, it is in this that the perfection of brotherly love
consists. But there are two things that pertain to the soul.
First, that it receive a special life from God; in regard to this
special life, one ought not lay down his soul for his friends.
For everyone must love this life of the soul as he loves God,
and, of course, he must love God more than he loves his
neighbor. No one, therefore, may by sinning despise this life
of the soul even to save his neighbor. Second, the soul can be
considered from the viewpoint that it gives life to the body

and is the principle of human life. In this regard we ought to lay down our soul for the brethren, for we ought to love our neighbor more than our body. Hence it is meet to lay down one's bodily life for the salvation of his neighbor. Indeed, this falls under the necessity of precept in certain cases of need; for example, when one sees his neighbor being led astray by unbelievers, he ought to expose himself even to the danger of death to free him from such seduction. But for anyone to do this outside these cases of special need belongs to the perfection of justice or to the perfection that falls under counsel. In St. Paul we have an example of this: "But I most gladly will spend and be spent myself for your souls" (II Cor. 12: 15). A commentary on this passage says that it is perfect charity to be prepared to die for the brethren. In addition, since slavery is so opposed to true life that it is akin to death, if anyone permits himself to be enslaved for the love of his neighbor, this love would be on the same level as one who exposes himself to the danger of death for the love of his neighbor. Still, the latter seems to be more perfect, for men more naturally flee death than slavery.

The perfection of brotherly love can be considered in the third place from the effects it produces; for the greater the goods we bestow on our neighbor, the more perfect seems the love. But in this matter there are three degrees to be considered. First, there are some who serve their neighbor's bodily needs by clothing the naked, by feeding the hungry, by taking care of the sick, and by other works of this type. Such works Our Lord regards as being done to himself, as is said in the Gospel: "Amen, I say to you, as long as you did it to one of these, my least brethren, you did it to me" (Matt. 25: 40).

Second, there are others who dispense spiritual benefits, which, however, do not go beyond helping them on a natural plane, such as teaching the ignorant, counseling the doubtful, and calling back those who are straying. These are commended in the Book of Job: "Behold thou hast taught many and thou hast strengthened the weary hands: Thy words have confirmed them that were staggering, and thou hast strengthened the trembling knees" (Job 4: 3, 4).

Third, there are others who bestow spiritual and super-

natural gifts upon their neighbor, such as teaching them
about God and the things of God or leading others to God by
dispensing the sacraments. Of these St. Paul makes mention
to the Galatians: "He therefore who gives you the spirit and
works miracles among you" (Gal. 3: 5) and to the Thessalonians: "When you had received of us the word of the
hearing of God you received it not as the word of men but
(as it is indeed) the word of God" (I Thess. 2: 13). Again,
to the Corinthians he wrote: "For if he that cometh preaching
another Christ, whom we have not preached; or if you receive another Spirit, whom you have not received; or another
gospel, which you have not received, you might well bear
with him" (II Cor. 11: 4). Conferring these kinds of benefits
implies a special perfection of brotherly charity, because
through them a man is united to his ultimate end, in which
the height of human perfection consists. Hence, in order to
pinpoint this perfection, it is asked in the Book of Job:
"Knowest thou the great paths of the clouds and the perfect
knowledge?" (Job 37: 16). According to St. Gregory these
clouds signify holy preachers. These clouds pursue the subtlest
of pathways, i.e., the roads of holy preaching and the perfect
sciences, while in respect of their merits, they deem themselves to be nothing, because they are so far below the things
that they impart to their neighbor. It is needless to say that it
is an additional quality of this perfection to impart these
spiritual goods not to just one or two persons but to a whole
multitude, for even the philosophers admit that the good of
the race is more perfect and more divine than the good of
one or two. That is why the Apostle says: "And he gave some
to be pastors and teachers for the perfecting of the saints,
for the work of the ministry; for the building up of the body
of Christ, that is, the entire Church" (Eph. 4: 11, 12), and
again: "So you also, forasmuch as you are zealous of spirits,
seek to abound unto the edifying of the Church" (I Cor.
14: 12).*

* Translated by R. F. Larcher, O.P.

4. HUMAN FREEDOM

Freedom's Root   *Summa of Theology*, q. 82, a.
                            4, c and ad. 1

There is a twofold way of moving another: first, as an end,
as when we assert that the end moves the agent. In this way
the intellect moves the will, since the good as known is will's
object, moving the will as an end. A second way of moving
another is as an agent, as that which changes moves what is
changed, and that which pushes moves what is pushed. In this
way the will moves the intellect as well as all the soul's powers, as Anselm declares (*On Spiritual Topics* II). This is because whenever several active powers are ordered, the power
directed to the universal end moves the powers directed to
particular ends. This is observable in nature as in government, for the heavens striving to preserve all generable and
corruptible things move all lower bodies. Each inferior body
tries to preserve its proper species or the individual. Likewise
one to whom the common good of the entire realm is confided
moves by his directives the individual rulers of their own
cities. But the will's objective is the good and the end in
general. Now, each power is directed toward an appropriate
good fitting for it, as sight to the sensing of color and the intellect to the knowing of truth. Thus the will as an agent
moves all the soul's powers to their appropriate acts, with the
exception of the natural vegetative powers not subjected to
free choice.

ad. 1. There are two ways of considering the intellect.
First, as apprehending universal being and truth. Second, as
a definite thing and a particular power having a definite act.
The will can also be considered in two ways. First, in respect
to the common nature of its object, that is, inasmuch as it wills
the common good. Second, as a particular power of the soul
having a definite act. So that if we compare the intellect and
will in regard to the universality of their objects, as stated
(*Summa of Theology* I, 82, 3), then the intellect is, speaking

absolutely, higher and more excellent than the will. And if we consider the intellect according to the universal nature of its object, and the will as a particular kind of power, again the intellect is higher and prior to the will because the will itself, its act, and its object are included within the notion of *being* and *truth*, which the intellect perceives. So the intellect knows the will, its act, and its object just as it knows other things, such as wood or stone falling under the universal idea of *being* and *truth*. But when we consider the will in respect to the universal nature of its object or goodness, and consider the intellect as a particular thing and special power, then the intellect, its act, and its object, that is, truth, are included under the common notion of good, since each of these is a particular kind of good. In this way the will is higher than the intellect and can move it. We recognize why then these powers when they act include one another, inasmuch as the intellect knows that the will is willing, and the will is willing the intellect to know. The good is also included in the true insofar as it is a sort of truth known, and truth is included under the notion of good insofar as it is a desired good.

Freedom   *Summary of Theology* I, q. 82,
                                                        a. 1, c

There is more than one kind of necessity. Generally speaking, necessity is defined as what must be. Now, a thing may have necessity from one of its intrinsic principles, either from the material principle (as when it is said that whatever is composed of contraries must necessarily be corruptible) or from the formal principle (as when it is said that a triangle must have its three angles equal to two right angles). This is said to be a *natural* and *absolute necessity*. Second, necessity may be attributed to something from an extrinsic principle, either by reason of the end or the agent. Necessity comes from the end when something cannot be accomplished without what is needed or cannot be fittingly accomplished, as food is needed for life, and a horse for a journey. We speak of this as a "necessity imposed by an end" and often refer to it as "utility." Necessity comes from the agent when the latter so coerces someone that he cannot do the contrary. We refer to this as "necessity by coercion."

Such necessity by coercion is contrary to the will. For we consider violent whatever is contrary to a thing's inclination. But the will's own motion is an inclination toward something, so that something is voluntary when it follows the will's inclination just as something is natural when it follows the inclination of nature. Just as something cannot possibly be violent and natural simultaneously, so something cannot be absolutely coerced or violent and simultaneously voluntary.

Yet necessity of the end is not contrary to the will, even when the end is attainable only in one way; for example, the desire to cross the ocean makes it necessary to desire a ship. Nor is natural necessity contrary to the will. So just as the intellect by necessity adheres to first principles, the will by necessity adheres to its final end or happiness, for in practical matters the end is comparable to the principle in speculative matters, as asserted in *Physics* II. For whatever is found naturally and unchangeably in anything must be the ground and principle of all else, inasmuch as a thing's nature is that which is primary in everything, and every motion arises from something immobile.

Willing Freely   *Summa of Theology* I–II, q. 10, a. 2, c

The will is moved in two ways: first, as exercising its act, and second, in the specification of its act by the object. In the first way, there is no object that necessarily moves the will, since a person can refuse to consider an object and thereby avoid willing it.

In respect to the specification, there is one kind of object that moves the will necessarily, whereas others do not. When any power moves in response to its object, there is a formal reason why the object moves the power. The visible object stimulates the power of sight under the formality of color as actually visible, so that whenever color comes before the power of sight, it necessarily moves sight unless the person looks elsewhere. But this has to do with the exercise of the act. Should something not entirely colored, i.e., in one part

colored, in another not, come before our vision, our power
of sight would not necessarily see this object because it might
turn toward the part not colored and thus not see color. Just
as the actually colored thing is the object of sight, so is goodness the will's object. So that if any universally good object
in every respect faces the will, it tends to this by necessity
if it wills at all, since it cannot will the contrary. But whenever any object that is not good in every respect faces the
will, it does not necessarily tend toward this. When something
good lacks something, it has the character of "not good,"
and so only the perfect good with nothing lacking to it is
beyond rejection by the will. Happiness is such a thing. Every
particular good as lacking some element of goodness can be
considered as "not good." Therefore, a good like this can
be either rejected or accepted by the will, since the will can
tend toward an object in respect to its various aspects.

Intellectual Source of Choice   *Summa of Theology* I–II, q.
                                         13, a. 6

Since whatever can possibly not be does not necessarily
exist, man chooses without necessity. A twofold power of
man accounts for his being able to choose or not to choose.
Man can will or not will, act or not act; he can will this or
that and do this or that. The very power of reason accounts
for this. The will can tend toward anything apprehended by
reason as good. But the reason can consider to be good not
only willing and acting, but not willing and not acting as well.
Moreover, the mind can see in every particular good its goodness as well as its lack of goodness, suggesting the notion of
evil. Hence the mind can apprehend any one of these goods
as worth or not worth choosing. Only the perfect good or
happiness cannot in any way be perceived as evil or defective.
Thus of necessity man wills happiness, and it is impossible
for him to will not to be happy or to be unhappy. But since
choice does not deal with the end but with the means to the
end, as previously discussed (*Summa of Theology* I–II, 13,
3), it does not deal with the perfect good or happiness but
with other particular goods. Consequently man does not
choose necessarily but freely.

How the Will Moves *Summa of Theology* I, q. 105, a. 4, c

Just as the intellect is moved by the object and by the Creator of intellectual power, so the will is moved by its object or the good and by the one who creates the power of willing. Although the will can be moved by good as its object, only God can move it completely and efficaciously. For nothing can move a movable thing completely unless the active power of the mover goes beyond or at least equals the potentiality of the movable thing. But the will's potentiality includes the universal good, since the latter is its object, as the intellect's object is universal being. Now, every created good is a particular good, whereas only God is the universal good. Therefore God alone fulfills the will's capacity and moves it completely as object. Likewise, only God causes the power of willing. Merely to will is to be inclined toward the object of the will or universal good. But to incline toward the universal good belongs to the first mover, to whom the final end is proportionate; as in human affairs the directing of subjects to the common good belongs to the ruler of the community. Consequently, God rightfully moves the will in both ways, but in the second way especially through an interior inclination of the will.

Analysis of Free Choice *On Evil*, ch. 6

Some have proposed that man's will is moved necessarily to making some choice, although they do not hold that the will is coerced. For not every necessity from an external principle (violent motion) is coercive, but only that which originates from without where both certain natural movements are discovered to be necessary but not coercive. For the coercive is opposed to the natural just as it is also opposed to voluntary motion, because the latter comes from an internal principle, while violent motion comes from an external one. This opinion [of the Latin Averroists] is therefore heretical because it destroys merit and demerit in human actions. For why should there be any merit or demerit for actions one cannot avoid doing? It is, moreover, to be included among

the excluded opinions of philosophers: for if there is no freedom in us but we are moved of necessity to will, then deliberate choice, encouragement, precept, punishment, praise,
and blame are removed, and these are the very problems
that moral philosophy considers. Not only is this contrary
to the faith, but it undermines all the principles of moral
philosophy. If one said: "There is no motion," the principles
of natural science would be destroyed; positions that destroy
in such a way the principles of a science are called *positiones
extraneae*.

Now, some take this position to provoke people; others
because of sophistical problems they cannot solve, as is expressed in *Metaphysics* IV. Principles to be considered so
that this problem may be solved: As there is a principle of
proper activity in everything, so there is one in men. In men
this active or motive principle is properly intellect and will,
as is said in *On the Soul* III, 49. This principle partly agrees
with the active principle in natural things, and partly differs
from it. It agrees inasmuch as in natural things a form is
found as the principle of action and, consequent upon the
form, an inclination called natural tendency, from which
action follows. So in men is found an intellectual form and
an inclination of will consequent upon the proposed form
from which there follows external motion. In this there is a
difference, because the form of a natural thing is a form
individuated through matter; whence the consequent inclination is itself determined to one thing, but the known form is a
universal under which many can be apprehended. Whence,
although acts are in singular things, in which there is nothing
that equals the scope of the universal, there remains an inclination of the will that tends indefinitely toward many
things. For example, an artist conceives the form of a "house"
in the universal, under which are comprehended the diverse
figures of a house; his will can be inclined to a square house
or round house or another shape. However, the active principle in brute animals holds a middle position. For the form
apprehended through the senses is individual, as is the form
of natural things; and from that there also follows an inclination to one action as in natural things, yet the same
form is not always received in the same sense as in natural

things, because fire is always hot, but fire is received now as one form, now as another; now as a delightful form, now as a grim form; whence the animal at one time avoids it and at another time seeks it. In this way, the active principle in brute animals agrees with the active human principle. Second, it must be considered that any power is moved in two ways: in one way on the part of the subject, in the other way on the part of the object. Indeed, on the part of the subject as, for example, when vision, is affected to see, more clearly or less; but on the part of the object, for example, the sight now sees white, now sees black. The first change indeed has to do with the specification of the act, for the act is specified through the object.

It must be considered, however, that in natural things the specification of the act is from the form; the exercise itself is from the agent causing the very motion. An agent, moreover, acts on account of the end. Whence it follows that the first principle of motion with regard to the exercise of the act is from the end. If, however, we should consider the objects of the will and of the intellect, we find that the object of the intellect is the first principle in the genus of formal cause, for its object is being and the true, but the object of the will is the first principle in the genus of final cause, for its object is the good under which are comprised all ends, just as under the true are comprised all apprehended forms. Whence the good itself, inasmuch as it is a certain apprehensible form, is contained under the true as a certain truth; and the true itself, inasmuch as it is the end of the intellectual operation, is contained under the good as a certain particular good. If therefore we should consider the motion of the powers of the soul on the part of the object specifying the act, the first principle of motion is from the intellect, for in this way the good known also moves the will itself. If, however, we should consider the motion of the soul's powers on the part of the exercise of the act, the principle of motion is from the will. For the power concerned with the principal end always moves the power concerned with means to act, as the military power moves the bridlemakers to work, and in this way the will moves itself and all other powers. For I know because I will, and in like manner I use all my powers and habits because I will; whence the commentator defines habit in *On the Soul* III as that which one uses when he wills. So, therefore, to show that the will is not moved from necessity, it is fitting to consider the movement of the will both as to the exercise of acts and as to the determination of acts, a determination that is from the object. Therefore, as to the exercise of the act, first it is manifest that the will is moved by itself; for just as it moves other powers, so it moves itself. Nor on account of this does it follow that the will is accordingly in potentiality and in act in the same respect. For just as a man by his intellect moves himself from knowledge to discovery, inasmuch as he goes from something known only in potentiality to something known in act, so through the fact that man wills anything actually, he moves himself to will something else actually. For example, through man's willing health he moves himself to will to take medicine. For example, since he wills good health, he begins to deliberate on the things that bring good health; at last, determined by counsel, he takes the medicine. So, therefore, deliberation precedes the will to take the medicine that indeed proceeds from the will of the one willing the consideration. When, therefore, the will moves itself to counsel, the counsel is a certain nondemonstrative inquiry; but open to opposites, the will does not move itself from necessity. But since the will not always wills to take counsel, it must be moved to this by another; and if by itself, the will's movement must precede counsel, and counsel should precede the act of the will; and since this cannot proceed to infinity, it is necessary to argue that because the will is not always in the act of willing, anyone's will is moved to its first motion of willing by something exterior, under whose impulse the will begins to will.

Some have argued therefore that this influence comes from the celestial body. But this cannot be. For since the will is in the reason, according to the philosopher (*On the Soul* III, 42), and this is not a corporeal power, it is impossible that the power of a celestial body should directly move the will itself. To argue, moreover, that man's will is moved by the impression from a celestial body as the tendencies of brute animals are moved is, according to the opinion of those claiming this, not to distinguish the intellect from the sense.

For the philosopher refers to them (*On the Soul* II, 150) the saying of some orators that the will in men is so remarkable that it is inspired by the father of men and of gods, that is, heaven or the sun.

It follows, therefore, as Aristotle concludes in the chapter on "Good Fortune" (*Eudemian Ethics* VII, 18) that what first moves the will is something beyond will and intellect, doubtless, God who, since he moves all things in accordance with their condition, lifting light things and lowering heavy things, so he moves the will according to its condition, not necessarily but indefinitely tending toward a variety of things. Hence it is evident that if the will's motion is considered with regard to the exercise of its activity, it is not moved by necessity; if, however, the will's motion is considered on the part of the object determining the act of the will to will this or that, it must be considered that the object moving the will is an apprehended, suitable good; whence if something good is proposed that is apprehended as good but not as suitable, it will not move the will. When, however, in one act consideration and choice are about particular things, it is required that whatever is known as good and suitable is good and suitable in particular and not only in the universal. If then anything be known as in all respects a suitable good, this will necessarily move the will; and for this reason, man necessarily seeks happiness, which according to Boethius (*Consolation of Philosophy* III, 2) is the state of total possession of all good. I say, however, that of necessity with regard to the determining act it is not possible to will the opposite; not, however, with regard to the exercise of the act, because someone can will not to think of happiness; for the act of the intellect and the act of the will are themselves particular. If, however, the good is such that it is not found to be good in all respects, it will not necessarily move even with regard to determining the act, because even when considering it, someone can will its opposite, since perhaps that opposite is good or suitable in some respect, just as what is good for health is not good for pleasure, etc. The fact that the will may be moved to one particular object rather than to another can happen in three ways. Indeed, in one way, inasmuch as one is more important, and thus the will is moved according to the reason; for instance, man chooses what is useful for the will when he chooses what is useful for health. In another way, inasmuch as he thinks of one particular circumstance and not of another; this happens ordinarily through some opportunity revealed from within or without, i.e., as such a thought occurs to one. The third way influences through the character of men; because, according to the philosopher (*Ethics* III, 5): of whatever character a person is, so does his end seem to him. And the will of the angry man and the will of the placid man move in contrary motions to something different in each case, since not the same thing is suitable to both; just as the sick and the well take different food. If, therefore, the character that determines the goodness and suitability of anything to anyone is natural and not subject to the will, as all men desire naturally to be, to live and to know, the will chooses it from natural necessity. If, however, the character is unnatural but subject to the will, as, for instance, when man through a permanent disposition or passion sees something as either good or bad in some respect, the will is not moved necessarily; for he is able to rid himself of the character so that something may not appear desirable to him, as, for example, if anyone should calm his anger so that he may not judge of anything when angered. Nevertheless, it is easier to remove emotion than disposition. So, therefore, in regard to any will being moved necessarily by an object, it is not so moved by all objects; and in regard to the exercise of its act, it is never necessarily moved.

On Spiritual Freedom   *Commentary on Epistle to Galatians* V, 4, 5

After indicating what the spiritual state consists in, namely, charity, the Apostle then deals with the cause of the state, namely, the Holy Spirit, whom he says they must follow. And he mentions three benefits obtained from the Holy Spirit.

First, freedom from the bondage of the flesh; second, freedom from the bondage of the law (v. 18); third, the conferring of life, or security from the damnation of death (v. 25).

. . . "The good which I will I do not; but the evil which
I will not, that I do" (Rom. 7: 19). However, free will is
not taken away; for since free will consists in having choice,
there is freedom of the will with respect to things subject to
choice. But not all that lies in us is fully subject to our choice,
but only in a qualified sense. In specific cases we are able to
avoid this or that movement of lust or anger, but we cannot
avoid all movements of anger or lust in general—and this by
reason of the "fomes" introduced by the first sin. . . .

. . . to be under the law can be taken in two ways: either
as to its obliging force, and then all the faithful are under the
law, because it was given to all—hence it is said: "I have not
come to destroy the law but to fulfill it" (Matt. 5: 17), or as
to its compelling forces, and then the just are not under the
law, because the movements and breathings of the Holy
Spirit in them are their inspiration; for charity inclines to
the very things that the law prescribes. Therefore, because
the just have an inward law, they willingly do what the law
commands and are not constrained by it. But those who
would do evil but are held back by a sense of shame or by
fear of the law are compelled. Accordingly, the just are under the law as obliging but not as compelling, in which sense
the unjust alone are under it: "Where the spirit of the Lord
is, there is liberty" (II Cor. 3: 17); "The law," as compelling,
"is not made for the just man" (I Tim. 1: 9).*

Friendship and Freedom   *Summa of Christian Teaching*
IV, 22

1. Having reflected upon what God does in us through
the Holy Spirit, we should reflect upon how we are urged
toward God through the Holy Spirit.

2. Friendship seems to call for real dialogue between
friends. Now, man converses with God by contemplating
him, as the Apostle was wont to say: "Our conversation is
in heaven" (Phil. 3: 20). Insofar as the Holy Spirit forms us
into lovers of God, he fashions us into contemplators of God.
So the Apostle says: "But we all beholding the glory of the
Lord with open face, are transformed into the same image

* ASC 1, trans. R. Larcher, O.P.

from glory to glory, as by the Spirit of the Lord" (II Cor. 3: 18).

3. In friendship we quite rightly delight in the friend's presence, are happy with what he says and does, and find our security in every worry so that we normally rush to friends for consolation in time of sorrow. Because the Holy Spirit makes us the friends of God, whom he brings to abide in us and us in him, it is therefore through the Holy Spirit that we experience joy in God as well as security amidst earthly troubles and temptations. And so the Psalmist says: "Restore unto me the joy of thy salvation and strengthen me with thy lordly Spirit" (Ps. 50: 14); and (Rom. 14: 17): "The Kingdom of God is not meat and drink; but justice, and peace, and joy in the Holy Spirit"; and (Acts 9: 31): "The Church had peace and was edified, walking in the fear of the Lord, and was filled with the consolation of the Holy Spirit." That is why Our Lord gives the name Paraclete or Comforter to the Holy Spirit as we see in (John 14: 26): "But the Paraclete, the Holy Spirit . . ."

4. Likewise in friendship there is consent between friends concerning what each desires. Now, God's desire is made known to us through his commandments. So our love for God is properly shown by responding to his requests, as the Word through John says: "If you love Me, keep my commandments" (John 14: 15). So inasmuch as through the Holy Spirit we are made into lovers of God, it is likewise through him that we are led to respond to God's requests, as the Apostle's word puts it: "Whosoever are led by the Spirit of God, they are the sons of God" (Rom. 8: 14).

Nevertheless, we should remember that God's sons are moved not as slaves but as free men. Since the free man is one who exists for his own sake (*Metaphysics* I, 2), action that comes from our own selves is free action. And such action is done by our will; whatever we do against our will we do as slaves, not freely, whether the violence is absolute, as whenever the "entire principle is external, without anything coming from the one moved" (*Nicomachean Ethics* III, 1) —for example, a man is pushed into movement; or whether violence is mingled with the voluntary—for example, when we wish to do or to endure what is less contrary to our will in order to avoid what is more contrary to it. But in making us lovers of God, the Holy Spirit so inclines us to act that he makes us act voluntarily. Hence, freely out of love, not slavishly out of fear are the sons of God moved by the Holy Spirit. So the Apostle says: "You have not received the spirit of bondage again in fear; but the spirit of adoption of sons" (Rom. 8: 15).

The will, certainly, is ordained to the truly good. But when a man is diverted from the truly good on account of passion, bad habit, or disposition, he acts slavishly, inasmuch as he is diverted by something extrinsic when one considers the will's natural order. But if we are thinking of the act of the will as tending toward an apparent good, a man acts freely when following passion or bad disposition; but he acts slavishly if his will remaining as it is, he refrains from what he wills, for fear of a law to the contrary.

And so because the Holy Spirit inclines the will by love toward the true good, to which the will is naturally ordained, he destroys that slavery by which the slave of passion coming from sin acts contrary to the will's order, and that slavery by which a man acts according to a law, contrary to the will's inclination; its slave and not its friend, so to speak. This is why the Apostle says: "Where the Spirit of the Lord is, there is liberty" (II Cor. 3: 17); and: "If you are led by the Spirit, you are not under the law" (Gal. 5: 18).

5. MAN'S CREATION

Man's Individual Creation   *On the Power of God,* q. 3, a. 9, c and ad. 7, 9, 11, 20

Again, it is written (Ps. 32: 15): "He maketh the heart of each one of them." So one soul is not generated by another, but all are individually created by God.

In times past this question has been answered in various ways by various persons. Some said that just as its body is from the parent's body, so is the child's soul procreated from the parent's soul. Others said that all souls were created separated from bodies, but they maintained that they were all simultaneously created apart from bodies and later each was united to a body, as this was begotten either by an act of its will, as some thought, or by God's command and action, as others thought. Others held that souls are created at the same time they are infused into bodies. Although formerly all these opinions were held as probable and the one most true was doubtful, as we may learn from Augustine "On the Soul and Its Origin" (*On Genesis* X, 21, 22), yet later the first two were condemned by the Church, which approved the third. So we read in *On Church Doctrine* XIV: "We do not believe in the fiction of Origen that human souls were created at the beginning with other intellectual natures, nor that they are procreated together with their bodies by coition, as the Luciferians with Cyril and certain Latin writers have presumed to maintain. But we affirm that the body alone is begotten by sexual procreation, and that after the formation of the body the soul is created and infused."

That the opinion that the rational soul is transmitted with the semen, which we are now examining, was rightly condemned will become clear by a careful investigation. For this three arguments will suffice.

The first argument. The rational soul is distinguished from other forms insofar as the latter have an existence by which the things they inform subsist so that the form has not subsistence of its own, whereas the rational soul subsists by its own existence, and this is apparent by their respective ways of acting. Inasmuch as only that which exists can act, a thing is related to operation or action as it is related to being; so since the body must necessarily participate in the action of other forms but not in the action of the rational soul, i.e., to know and to will, it necessarily follows that the rational soul has subsistent existence, although other forms do not. On this account only the rational form can exist in separation from the body. It is thus evident that the rational soul is brought into existence not as other forms are, which, strictly speaking, are not made but are spoken of as being made when this or that thing is made. That which is made is made per se, strictly speaking. And it is made either of matter or from nothing. But whatever is made from matter must be made from matter subject to contrariety, inasmuch as generation is from contraries, according to the philosopher (*On the Generation of Animals* I, 18). Hence because a soul has no matter at all, or at least none subject to contrariety, it cannot be made out of something. So consequently it comes into being by creation as made from nothing. But to hold that the soul is made by the generation of the body is to declare that it is not subsistent and thus ceases with the body.

The second argument. The action from a material force cannot rise to produce a wholly spiritual and immaterial force because a thing does not act above its species; in fact, the agent should be more perfect than the patient, according to Augustine's statement (*On Genesis* XII, 16). Now, a man's generation is brought about through the generative power exercised through bodily organs: moreover, the seminal force acts only by means of heat (*On the Generation of Animals* II, 3); and so since the rational soul is a wholly spiritual form neither depending upon the body nor exercising its action in common with the body, it cannot in any way be produced through the procreation of the body, nor be brought into existence through an energy deriving from the seed.

The third argument. Every form coming into existence through generation or the forces of nature is educed from the potentiality of matter (*Metaphysics* VII, 7). But the rational soul cannot be educed from the potentiality of matter: for any form whose action is independent of matter cannot be produced from corporeal matter. Consequently the rational soul is not generated by the generative power. This argument is given by Aristotle (*On the Generation of Animals* II, 3).

ad. 7. The disposition of the rational soul is in harmony with the disposition of the body, both because it receives something from the body and because forms are differentiated according to the difference in their matter. So it is that children are like their parents even in things concerning the soul, and not because one soul is begotten from another.

ad. 9. Several opinions exist concerning the life of the embryo. Some think that in human generation the soul like the human body is subject to stages of advance so that as the human body is virtually in the semen without the human body's perfection of having distinct members but gradually attaining this perfection by the seminal force, so also the soul at the beginning of generation is there with virtually all the perfection that later appears in the perfect human being, although this perfection is not present actually, inasmuch as there is no indication of the soul's action, but the perfection is reached by degrees: so at first we find indications of the vegetative soul's action, next of the sensitive soul, and finally, of the rational soul.

Gregory of Nyssa discusses this opinion (*On Man*), but it cannot be admitted. It signifies either that the soul in its species is within the semen at the beginning (yet through lack of organs without its complete action) or that within the semen at the beginning is some energy or form not yet having the species of soul (just as the semen does not yet appear to be a human body) but that is gradually transformed into a soul at first vegetative, next sensitive, and finally rational by the action of nature. The former alternative is refuted first by the authority of the philosopher. He in fact declares (*On the Soul* II, 1) that when we state that the soul is the act of a physico-organic body having life in potentiality we do not exclude the soul as we exclude it from the semen and the fruit. So we conclude that insofar as the soul is not in the semen, the semen is animated potentially. Second, inasmuch as the semen has no definite likeness to the members of the human body (or its resolution would be a sort of corruption) but is what remains from final digestion (*On the Generation of Animals* I, 19), it was not perfected by the soul while within the begetter's body so that it could not possess a soul at the first moment of its separation. Third, even allowing it to be animated when it was separated, this cannot pertain to the rational soul, for since it is not the act of a particular part of the body, it cannot be separated when the body is separated.

The second alternative is likewise evidently erroneous. For inasmuch as a substantial form is brought into act not gradually or by degrees but instantaneously (or movement would have to be in the genus of substance, just as it is in that of quality), the force within the semen at the beginning cannot advance by degrees to the various kinds of soul. Hence the form of fire is not so produced in the air that it gradually advances from imperfection to perfection, since no substantial form is subject to increase and decrease, but only matter is modified by previous change to be more or less disposed to receive form. And form does not begin to be in matter until the last moment of this change.

Others state that the vegetative soul is first of all within the semen, and this remains when later the sensitive soul is introduced by the generator's power, and finally by creation the rational soul is introduced. So they argue that there are three essentially different souls in man. But against this is the authority of the book *On Church Doctrines* XV: "Nor do we say that there are two souls in one man as James and other Syrians write; one, an animal soul, by which the body is animated and which is mingled with the blood, the other a spiritual soul, which obeys the reason." It is impossible, moreover, for one same thing to have several substantial forms: because, inasmuch as the substantial form makes a thing to exist, not in this or that way, but simply, establishing this or that thing in the genus of substance, if the first form does this, when any second form comes, it will find the subject already established as a substantial being and so will adhere to it accidentally; hence it would follow that the sensitive and rational souls in man would be united accidentally to the body. Nor can we say that the vegetative soul, which in a plant is the substantial form, is not the substantial form in a man but only a disposition to the form, because whatever is in the genus of substance cannot be an accident of anything.

Others say that the vegetative soul is potentially sensitive, and its act is the sensitive soul; thus the vegetative soul at first in the semen is advanced to the perfection of the sensitive soul by the action of nature; and further, the rational soul is the act and perfection of the sensitive soul so that the sensitive soul is advanced to its perfection as rational soul not by the generator's action but by the Creator's action. Thus they maintain that the rational soul is within man partly from within, as in its vegetative and sensitive nature, and partly from without, as in its intellectual nature. But this is completely impossible, since it means either that the intellectual nature is distinct from the vegetative and sensitive souls (and we then return to the second opinion) or that these three natures constitute the soul's substance, so that the intellectual nature is as the form to the matter of the sensitive and vegetative natures. Consequently, the rational soul would not be immortal, inasmuch as the sensitive and vegetative natures are corruptible by being educed from matter. But this opinion involves the same impossibility we have shown, as implied in the first opinion, namely, that a substantial form is brought into act by degrees.

Others state that the embryo's apparent vital function comes from the mother's soul but that it has no soul until perfected by the rational soul. But this cannot be the case, for living things differ from nonliving things by being self-moving in relation to vital functions, so that nutrition and growth, the functions proper to a living being, cannot occur in the embryo from any extrinsic principle, such as the mother's soul. The mother's nutritive power, moreover, would assimilate food to the mother's body and not to the embryo's body, inasmuch as nutrition is directed to the individual just as generation is directed to the species. Moreover, sensation cannot be caused in the embryo by the mother's soul. And so others say that before the infusion of the rational soul, the embryo has no soul, but a formative force within the embryo exercises these vital actions. Again, this is impossible, inasmuch as before the embryo reaches its ultimate completion it reveals variety in its vital actions; and since these cannot be exercised by one power, there must necessarily be a soul having various powers.

We must then differ by saying that as soon as the semen is severed, it contains not a soul but a soul force. And this force is derived from the form contained in the semen, which by nature is spumy and therefore has corporeal form. Now, this form acts by disposing matter and forming it to receive the soul. And we should advert to the difference between the process of generation in respect to men and animals, in air or water. Generation in air is simple, since only two substantial forms are implicated, one that is voided and one that is induced, all in one instant, so that the form of water is present until the induction of the form of air, and there are no previous dispositions to the form of air. But in the generation of an animal several substantial forms appear: first the semen, then blood, and so forth, until we come to the form of an animal or of a man. This kind of generation is therefore not simple, since it consists of a series of generations and corruptions. For as previously proven, the one same substantial form cannot be educed into act by degrees. So that through the formative force first within the semen, the form of the semen is voided and another form induced, and when this is voided, another comes, and thus appears the vegetative form; and when this is corrupted a soul both vegetative and sensitive is induced; and this being voided, a soul simultaneously vegetative, sensitive, and rational is induced not through the previously mentioned force but through the Creator. In this opinion, before having a rational soul the embryo is a living being having a soul, which is voided when a rational soul is introduced. Thus it does not follow that two souls exist in the same body nor that the rational soul is generated along with the body.

ad. 11. Although the soul is not at the outset within the semen, the soul force is there as was stated, and this force is based upon the spirit within the semen, and is called soul force because it comes from the generator's soul.

ad. 20. Man has not two existences simply because when it is said that man's body is from his begetter and his soul from his Creator we are not to infer that the being derived by the body from its begetter is distinct from that which the soul receives from its Creator, but that the Creator gives existence to the soul in the body, while the begetter disposes the body to participate in this existence through the soul united to it.

6. MAN'S IMMORTALITY

Soul as Immortal *On the Soul,* a. 14, c

There is a necessity to admit that the human soul is incorruptible. To prove this we must reflect upon the fact that anything belonging to something through its very nature (per se) cannot be withdrawn from it; for example, animality cannot be withdrawn from man, nor can number ever exist without being even or odd. It is also clear that the very act of existing comes with form, for everything has its act of existing through its proper form, and thus its act of existing can nowise be separated from its form. Things composed of matter and form are therefore corrupted by a loss of the form, giving them their act of existing. Nor can a form itself be corrupted in itself (per se), but only accidentally, by a disintegration of the composite, when the composite existing through its form ceases to exist as a composite. Such is the case if the form is one not possessing its own act of existing but merely that by which a composite exists.

But should there be any form having its own act of existing, then that form is necessarily incorruptible. For nothing having an act of existing (esse) ceases to exist unless its form is withdrawn from it. But it is clear that man's knowing principle is a form with its own act of existing and is not merely that by which something exists. For, as the philosopher demonstrates in On the Soul III, 4, intellectual knowing is not an act accomplished by any bodily organ. The chief reason why there is no bodily organ capable of receiving the sensible forms of all natural things is that the recipient must itself be without the nature of the thing received, just as the eye's pupil has not the color it perceives. But every bodily organ has a sensible nature. Yet the intellect, by which we know, is capable of knowing all sensible natures. So its action, i.e., knowing, cannot be executed through a bodily organ. Thus it is apparent that the intellect has its own action unshared by the body. Now, anything acts in accord with its nature, inasmuch as things existing of themselves have their own action, while things not existing of themselves have no action of their own. Thus heat in itself does not produce warmth, but something hot does. It follows that the intellective principle by which man knows has its own way of existing superior to that of body and independent of it.

It is also obvious that such an intellective principle is not something composed of matter and form, since the species of things are received in it in an absolutely immaterial way, as manifest by the intellect knowing universals, which are considered as abstracted from matter and material conditions. The one conclusion resulting from this is that the intellective principle by which man knows is a form having its own act of existing. This principle must therefore be incorruptible. This certainly agrees with the philosopher's declaration that the intellect is something divine and everlasting (*On the Soul* III, 5). Now, it was demonstrated in previous articles (a. 2, a. 5) that the intellective principle by which man knows is not a substance existing separated from man but is that which formally inheres in him as either a soul or a part of the soul. So from the previous reflections we conclude that the human soul is incorruptible.

Now, all who maintained the human soul to be corruptible neglected some of the points we have just made. Some of these persons, thinking the soul a body, stated that it is not wholly form but something composed of matter and form. Others maintained that the intellect does not differ from the senses, declaring that the intellect only acts through a bodily organ, that it does not have a higher kind of existence than the body's and so that it is not a form having its own act of existing. Others maintained that the intellect by which man knows is a separate substance. But the error of all these opinions has been proven in previous articles. It follows therefore that the human soul is incorruptible.

Let us consider two more arguments pointing to this: first, upon investigating the intellect itself we recognize that even corruptible things are incorruptible insofar as they are known by intellect; for the intellect knows things in and through universal concepts, and things existing in this way are not subject to corruption. Second, the natural tendency also offers an argument for the soul's incorruptibility. Natural tendency cannot be frustrated. But we notice that men desire ceaseless existence. This desire is rooted in reason, for since to exist (*esse*) is in itself desirable, any intelligent being who knows existence as absolute and not merely as relative, must desire existence as absolute and forever. So it is evident that this is not a vain desire but that man, inasmuch as his soul is intellective, is incorruptible.

MAN AS MORAL

Thomas's manner of thinking is different from that with which most of us are familiar today, just as, say, Chaucer's manner of writing poetry is different from T. S. Eliot's. But Chaucer was a pretty shrewd observer of human behavior. And so was Thomas Aquinas. But because he aimed at systematizing and at lucidity of expression, Aquinas did not involve himself in the palpitating problems of human existence the way our novelists do today. In ethics we may look to Aquinas for broad general principles only, since on the speculative level this is the only valid offering.

Although willing to change an opinion when any new evidence or justified criticism is produced, Aquinas would never have favored "the shifting of accent from being to doing, and still more, not doing, an absorption in means to the exclusion of end." And yet he considered the "doing" important because change is a perfection in creatures, insofar as it is all part of a movement toward God. The movement is a movement of love to which intellectual life ministers, a response to the absolute good of God's own love for man. Human beings grow with such responses. And thus the pursuit of happiness is subordinated to the quest of the good—the perfection of human nature with its by-product, happiness. The pattern for man's perfection is discovered by examining human nature's hierarchized tendencies, which spell out God's will for the man trying to be moral. The end of man is to become thoroughly human, to achieve the perfection of the whole man, body and soul together, to achieve a perfect personality according to his own possibilities. Rationally aware, man, unlike the animals, can know his end and is free to determine its achievement if he acts without ignorance, passion, coercion. But morality is not the actualizing of all potentialities without a sense of hierarchy. This calls for a careful weighing of values, the work of gradation. There are intellectual, moral, social, bodily values and, above all, religious ones. All have their claim to our appreciation, but not all may be sacrificed for the sake of others. Yet because the love-worthiness of God is intimately related to man's perfection, Thomist ethics can promote the love of God for his own sake and the love of others for their sake, seeking first the Kingdom of God, and thereby unite the ethics of duty with the ethics of eudaimonism in a response to love.

In other words, in Aquinas's view the moral man is the free man. The free man acts from the motivation of love for what is true and good, and so he has internalized the natural law of his tendencies, the divine law revealed to him, and the civil laws that are promulgated. As Gerald Vann has put it: "St. Thomas' moral doctrine does not aim at the niggardly ordering of the individual's conduct in blind obedience to a code. It is a cosmic scheme; its end is God's glory and the *ordo universi*, the fulfilment of the world." The good and the true to which the moral man responds are not abstractions. Thomist morality is theocentric. God is loved in all that is good, for charity is the soul of all man's virtuous acts. Man finds himself in loving God—doing what he should—and in finding himself, man finds freedom or wholeness.

The primacy given by Aquinas to existence rather than to "spirit" as opposed to "matter" makes for a positive rather than a negative morality. Any Thomist faithful to the value placed by Thomas upon "be-ing" and its transcendental epiphanies as truth, goodness, and beauty will be characterized by an attitude of openness and receptivity to truths expressed by the most divergent philosophers as well as to the social acts of self-declared unreligious people who are working for all forms of human progress in the modern world. The famous *Summa* should not be translated as ending the search for truth but as establishing an attitude of "redeeming the truth," or "spoiling the Egyptians." What is striking in each *Summa* is the number of sources sympathetically interpreted. Thomas's own metaphysical insight into reality as existential is far from arid. Yet its fruitfulness largely depends upon the recognition of its depth and breadth. A principle like "existence" can scarcely be classified as a rationalist's principle of thought, nor may it be deprived without violating its meaning of the power to assimilate future intellectual discoveries. A philosophy of existence is always ready to be relevant if we are there to make it so. Such a philosophy combines the stability of permanent principles with the dynamism of emphasis upon development, for it grounds all human perfection and social progress as well as religious response in being-as-act or the power of love. Hence the critic of Thomism who continually opposes "being" within the Thomist framework to "becoming," as though he were opposing substance to action or Parmenides to Heraclitus, misses the mark. The stability of being as Aquinas sees it is dynamic, just as the dynamism of reality is stable, because it is rooted in the very act of existing, *actus essendi*. Moreover, the face of this being, the face it turns toward man, is "love," the most active of all active things, stronger than death, the secret source of all human happiness and all human tragedy.

When being as love is recognized to be the supreme good, the moral life consists in responding to this love in all human choices. Finite realities are chosen for their own value, which simultaneously mediates God's creative love. Because Thomas relates human happiness to the perfect love for God, human perfection is not man's direct aim in the moral life. Hence Aristotelian teleology is profoundly transformed. The famous Aristotelian discussion of the highest power of man's "nature" is replaced by the conception of a relation to the highest "existence" (*esse*). And so the question of man's last end is no longer a question of which power of man is higher as establishing him in his *specific* nature; it is rather a question of which power of man can go out to the supreme existent even when his superintelligibility, his superexcellence, defies conceptualization. And man's whole religious life or his life of faith is thereby integrated into the ethics of the end, or total fulfillment without defrauding human values of their intrinsic desirability nor subordinating God as a mere utility value to man's powers. God is transcendent and yet remains present by his creative will in all created things. He is very specially in conscious beings in whom the act of faith is made under the dynamism of the will seeking reality or the good. And so whenever God calls man by the gift of faith, the will can reach the supreme existent beyond all knowing. Whenever man's free response to God's call resembles that of God's Son, man becomes the perfect "icon," fully human and morally perfect through participation in divine *agape*, the principle of Christian existence. As St. Paul teaches, love is the new law. And man's ability to respond in love is his greatest responsibility and his greatest opportunity to be truly human.

While Aquinas certainly emphasizes the function of knowledge in morality, he does not underrate action. And although there is a definite doctrinal content to faith as St. Thomas defines it, yet whenever he speaks of living faith, it is always of faith working through love. Although he writes articles concerned with ethics as a science, his insights show that he looked upon the moral as well as the religious life as the "art of loving God" and human persons. Only love can bring the human person into communication with Father, Son, and Holy Spirit, and therefore when man is fulfilling his concrete destiny he is a "god by participation." The Trinity is the norm for a Christian ethic that emphasizes interpersonal relationships rather than moral self-sufficiency, which is the Aristotelian norm.

Some may think that an ethic of human existence dynamically directed toward absolute personal being involves the belittlement or the depreciation of the human or temporal order. On the contrary, man's orientation toward the absolute gives him a concern for all that is related to the absolute. Man's own relationship to God, his religious dimension, allows him to participate in God's direction of the world—human prudence collaborating with divine providence. This confers on man a creative responsibility for progress in the sciences and technology and art in the human city. Never can this city be truly seen except as it is—in relation to God, a situation giving to every temporal fact an ineffable eternal value.

If metaphysics and religion insist on the world's ontological dependence upon God and God's preferential love for people, then metaphysics and religion are not impedimental to the building up of the human city. Moreover, man is rescued from his ambiguity and his ambivalence by his call to imitate God's creative freedom. The infinite good, which grounds human choice, also makes possible man's growth in freedom or wholeness—the fruit of success in the art of loving God and man as they should be loved, for their own sake.

All that man achieves will endure forever because his accomplishments are part of him, and he is immortal as related to the eternal God. The Incarnation was for the sake of the Resurrection. So all man's world will rise again with Christ. To exist with spiritual *esse* or existence is to exist forever, and love is everlasting.

Thomistic ethics may use Aristotelian terminology, but the new wine in the old bottles is the spirit of love. Because the Christ of the Scriptures declared that all the laws of morality could be summed up in the love of God and of neighbor, it is truer to speak of Thomistic ethics as scriptural rather than as Aristotelian. And while much Christian mysticism did follow the Neoplatonic tendency of returning the multiplicity to unity by a detachment often descending to rejection of this world, the mystical life for Thomas was characterized by the contemplation that matures from a Christian moral life. This is the injection of unity into multiplicity. Such oneness is given by charity, the form of all the Christian virtues. Man's multiple life concerns, life problems, and life activities are unified by love. This response to God in and through the concrete events of the everyday is Biblical contemplation, not Greek. The man, moreover, who responds to incarnate values is not a Stoic sage but a very human one whose passions energize the love he offers God and man.

There is a sense in which Aquinas in his moral doctrine followed neither Plato nor Aristotle nor the Stoics but Augustine. For Aristotle the universe was a closed system with no absolute standards provided by Plato's idea, but whereas Platonists accurately noted man's restlessness and yearning, they rooted this in man's relation to the body rather than to the eternal ideas. Aquinas steered his way between Plato's dualism with its disrespect for matter and Aristotle's ethical naturalism. Aquinas was sure that he preferred the complex human situation of admitting the body to be an essential element in human nature to the unreal logic of dualism, but he was not sure that he knew the man to whom he would be willing to confide the establishment of the moral code in terms of an ideal human society. Thomas Aquinas was certain that the free man created by God in dynamic relationship to himself was not himself without both intellectuality and human love, which could transcend self-interest. He agreed with St. Paul that man is body, soul, and spirit, and his existential realism provides for this vision of man developing within the world in a human community open to infinite love. Responding to the divine call that is creation, the universe is an ardent aspiration, an ascension, a return toward "unity" or wholeness.

This means that all social and political successes—achievements for the common good of human persons and for the fostering of the government of free men—are eternal, not ephemeral. Any good done for any man will last forever— and none is excluded from the moral life, which is always measured by the real possibilities at any given historical moment. And because salvation is God's accomplishment, no man is prevented by economic or cultural or historical circumstances from sharing in it. Only consent is required, and the sincere efforts that witness to it. Love of the other for his own sake, which is available to all, is the one universal force capable of uniting men to one another, insofar as it really unites them to God. Love is likewise the greatest force for change in the world, for only love can change the heart of man radically, enlarge it, decentralize man, and prepare him to look out upon the world from another hearth. As man gradually widens and deepens his view of the world, his illusions leave him and he responds more adequately to the exigencies of each situation under the attraction of a love causing the cosmic and personal growth that prepares for the union of "all in all."

Aquinas was as interested in action as any American pragmatist is, but Aquinas never divorced action from being. That is why action always raised the question of source and end. The Thomistic experience of action is wider and deeper than the pragmatist's experience. What Buber calls the "everyday" is what Aquinas called the "contingent" and what Dewey called "process." But Aquinas's analysis of the action experience is within the deeper orientation of the human will toward absolute goodness, man's implicit experience of the transcendent in all his tendencies—an experience that keeps man human. Because Aquinas taught that God's act was one with his being, God may never be viewed as object but always as subject, a creative freedom. This means that God is never restricted by needs. Whenever he acts, God is acting to communicate good. The deep, intuitively known law of human morality is just this: Do good. Now, man does good when he images God in action by incarnating some of that absolute good to which the aspiration of his will opens him. If man is to be human, his "now" brings him the transcendent; his "everyday" has in it the eternal. Just as "a bell is no bell until you ring it, a song is no song until you sing it," a human being is not human unless he humanizes his environment by the communication of goodness. Not all acts of man are human acts. To be human they must be done with knowledge and freedom. Not all human acts have moral value. What determines the success of action is not its cash value but its moral value, which is measured by its power to perfect man as a person in the image of God, the communicator of good.

Space and time and heredity have their share in the making of man, and today we hear much of these. Yet man transcends them. He is ultimately responsible to make himself. And that is what morality is all about.

Man as Moral

1. AQUINAS ON ARISTOTELIAN ETHICS

Aristotle's View of Ethics *Commentary on Nicomachean Ethics* I, 1

1. As the philosopher says in the beginning of the *Metaphysics*, it is the part of the wise man to order. The reason for this is that wisdom is the most powerful perfection of reason, whose property is to know order. For although the sensitive powers know certain things absolutely, nevertheless, to know the order of one thing to another belongs to intellect or reason alone. Now, there is found a twofold order in things. One is of the parts of some whole or of some plurality to one another, as the parts of a house are ordered to one another. The other is the order of things to an end. And this latter order is more primary than the first. For as the philosopher says in *Metaphysics* XI, the order of the parts of an army to one another is because of the order of the whole army to the leader.

Now, order is compared to reason in a fourfold way. For

there is a certain order that reason does not produce but considers only, as is the order of natural things. But there is another order, which reason, by considering, produces in its proper act—for example, when it orders its concepts one to another, and the signs of the concepts, which are significant sounds. Then there is a third order that reason by considering produces in the operations of the will. The fourth order is that which reason by considering produces in external things, of which things it itself is the cause, as in the case of a chest and a house.

2. And, since the consideration of reason is perfected through habit, according to these different orders that reason properly considers one has the different sciences. For it pertains to *natural philosophy* to consider the order of things that human reason considers but does not produce (in such a way that under natural philosophy we include *metaphysics*). But the order that reason by considering produces in its proper act pertains to *rational philosophy,* whose role it is to consider the order of the parts of a statement to one another, and the order of the principles to one another and to the conclusions. The order of voluntary actions pertains to the consideration of *moral philosophy.* But the order that reason by considering produces in external things constituted by human reason pertains to the *mechanical arts.* Thus, therefore, it is proper to moral philosophy, upon which we are at present intent, to consider human operations accordingly as they are ordered to one another and to an end.

3. But I say *human* operations, which proceed from the will of man according to the order of reason. For if there be found any operations in man that are not subject to will and reason, these are not properly called "human," but, rather, "natural"—as is evident of the operations of the vegetative soul. Such operations in no way fall under the consideration of moral philosophy. So, just as the subject of natural philosophy is motion, or the movable thing, so the subject of moral philosophy is human activity ordained to an end, or even man as he is voluntarily acting because of an end.

4. Now, it should be understood that, since man is naturally a social animal, as needing for his life many things that he cannot prepare for himself by himself, consequently he is

naturally a part of some multitude [group], from which he
receives help in living well. And he needs this help for two
things. First of all, for those things that are necessary for life,
without which the present life could not be gone through—
and in this man is aided by the *domestic* group of which he is
a part. For every man has from his parents generation and
nurture and education. And likewise each of those who are
parts of the domestic family help one another in the necessities of life. In another way, man is helped by a group of
which he is a part toward perfect sufficiency of life, namely,
in order that man not only live, but live well, having everything that suffices for living. And in this respect man is helped
by the *civil* group, of which he makes up a part, not only as
to corporeal things, insofar, namely, as there are in the city
many products that one household would not be sufficient to
produce, but also as to moral things, insofar, namely, as,
through the public power, unruly youths are coerced by the
fear of punishment, whom paternal admonition does not succeed in correcting.

5. But it should be understood that this whole, which is
the civil multitude, or the domestic family, has solely a unity
of *order*, according to which it is not something absolutely
one. Therefore a part of this whole may have an operation
that is not the operation of the whole, as a soldier in an army
has an activity that is not that of the whole army. Nevertheless, the whole itself has a certain operation, which is not
proper to any of the parts, but to the whole, e.g., a battle of
the whole army. And the pulling of a ship is the operation
of the multitude pulling the ship. There is also a whole that
has a unity, not only of order, but of composition, or connection, also, or even of continuity (according to which latter unity something is absolutely one); and therefore, in this
case, there is no operation of the part that is not that of the
whole. For in continuous things the motion of the whole and
of the part is the same, and likewise in composite, or connected, things, the operation of the part is principally that of
the whole. And therefore it is necessary that, in such a case,
the consideration, both as to the whole and to its parts, pertain to the same science. But it does not pertain to the same

science to consider the whole that has only a unity of order, and its parts as well.

6. Consequently, *moral philosophy* is divided into *three* parts. The first of these considers the activities of one man ordained to an end and is called "monastics." The second considers the operations of the domestic group and is called "economics." The third considers the activities of the civil multitude and is called "politics."

7. Since, therefore, Aristotle is beginning to set forth moral philosophy from its first part, in this book, called *Ethics*, i.e., of moral things, he first sets out a preface in which he does three things: First, he shows what his intention is; second, the method of treatment, at the words, "We must be content, then, in speaking of such subjects . . . ." (I, 3); third, how the hearer of this science should be, at the same place, "Now each man judges well the things he knows . . . ."

As to the first he does two things. First, he prefaces what he has to say with certain things that are necessary to show what he proposes. Second, he manifests what is proposed, at the words, "If, then, there is some end . . . ." (I, 2). As to the first, he does two things: First, he proposes the necessity of the end; second, the comparison of habits and acts to the end, at the words, "Now, as there are many actions, arts, and sciences . . . ." (I, 15). As to the first, he does three things: First, he proposes that all human things are ordained to an end; second, the diversity of ends, at the words, "But a certain difference is found among ends . . . ." (I, 12); third, he proposes the comparison of ends to one another, at the words, "When there are ends apart from the actions . . . ." (I, 14). As to the first, he does two things: First, he proposes what he intends; second, he manifests that which is proposed, at the words, ". . . And for this reason the good has rightly been declared . . . ." (I, 9).

8. As to the first, it should be considered that there are two principles of human acts, namely, intellect or reason, and appetite, which are the moving principles, as is said in *On the Soul* III. In the intellect or reason, the speculative and the practical are considered. In the rational appetite, elections and execution are considered. Now, all these are

ordered to some good, as to an end, for truth is the end of speculation. As to the end of the speculative intellect, therefore, he sets down "doctrine" through which science is transmitted from the master to the disciple. But as to the practical intellect, he sets down "art," which is the right notion of things to be produced, as is had in Book VI. As to the act of the appetitive intellect, there is set down "election," while as to execution, there is set down "action." But he does not make mention of prudence, which is in the practical reason, as is art, since it is properly through prudence that election is directed. He says, therefore, that each of these manifestly desires some good as the end.

9. Then when he says, ". . . And for this reason the good . . . . ," he manifests what he has proposed, through the effect of the good. Concerning this, it should be considered that the good is numbered among the first things—to such an extent that, among the Platonists, good is prior to being. But according to the truth of things, good is convertible with being. Now, first things cannot be made known through any other prior things, but are made known through subsequent things, as causes are made known through their proper effects. Since, then, the good is properly the mover of the appetite, the good is described through the motion of the appetite, as motive force is accustomed to be manifested by movement. And therefore he says that the philosophers declared well that the good is "that which all things desire."*

2. PROVIDENCE AND HUMAN ACTION

Providence Leaves History   *Summa of Christian Teaching*
Undetermined   III, 94

There is a problem connected with what was asserted, for if all things including the contingent events of the temporal world are under divine providence, it evidently follows that either providence is uncertain or all events are necessary.

* Translated by P. H. Conway, O.P., and R. F. Larcher, O.P.

For the philosopher shows (*Metaphysics* VI) that if we suppose a per se cause for every effect or that any existing per se cause has necessarily an effect, we must admit that all future events occur necessarily; for if every effect has a per se cause, it will be traceable to some past or present cause. So that if we inquire whether a certain man will be killed by robbers, this effect is preceded by a cause, namely, his encounter with robbers; and this effect has its own cause, namely, that he traveled; and this had a cause, namely, that he intended to get water; and this was caused by his thirst; and the thirst was caused by his eating of salt meat, which he is now eating or which he has just finished. So that if given the cause we must of necessity allow the effect, i.e., if he eats the salt meat, of necessity he is thirsty; if he thirsts, he necessarily seeks water, and to seek it he leaves the house; and it is necessary that if he travels, the robbers meet him, and if they meet him, they kill him. So from beginning to end, it is necessary that this salt-meat eater be killed by robbers. The philosopher then concludes that it is untrue that the establishing of a cause makes an effect necessary, inasmuch as some of the causes may be ineffective. Nor is it true, moreover, that every effect has a per se cause, although whatever is accidental, namely, that a man seeking water should encounter some robbers, has no cause.

This argument shows that all effects do happen by necessity when they are traced to a per se cause, past or present, which, when it is given, brings about an effect by necessity. So that we must either say that not all effects are subject to divine providence (and hence providence would not be concerned with everything, contrary to what was previously proven), or we must say that allowing for providence, what it sees is without necessity and thus providence will be uncertain; or else everything happens necessarily, since providence is not only in the present and past but from eternity, since there is nothing not eternal in God. . . .

In order to solve these problems, we should remember some previously made points to clarify the fact that nothing escapes divine providence; that the order of divine providence is entirely unchangeable; and yet we may not con-

clude that whatever occurs under divine providence happens
of necessity.

First, we should reflect that since God causes all existents
by giving them their very existence, the order of his providence has to include everything, since to those things to
which he has given existence, he must give a continued existence as well as perfection through their attaining their last
end.

Now, two things are noteworthy in regard to anyone exercising providence, namely, forethought about the order of
things and the establishment of this order, the former pertaining to the knowing power and the latter to the command-
ing power. And there are differences in providence derived
from the designing of the order, for the more able any order
is to include the smallest things, the more perfect is that
providence. For our defective knowledge, which fails to include all individual things, prevents our arranging all particulars beforehand; and any man is considered more apt for
providing insofar as his foresight extends to more particulars, so that one whose foresight is limited to general considerations has only a small share of prudence. This is also
true of all productive arts. On the other hand, in respect to
the causing of the order foreknown in things, the governor's
providence has a higher order and perfection when it is more
universal, achieving the realization of its forethought through
more ministers; in fact, the mere organizing of these ministers has a great deal to do with the order of providence. Now,
God's providence must be eminently perfect, since he is simply and universally perfect, as proven in the First Book.
Therefore God in his providence orders all things, even the
slightest, through the eternal forethought of his wisdom, and
all things that act do so as instruments moved by him, serv-
ing him obediently in order to bring forth into the world the
order of providence meditated, so to speak, from eternity.
And if everything capable of acting must act as his minister,
no agent can prevent the realization of divine providence by
acting in opposition. Nor can divine providence be impeded
through any agent's defect or any patient's defect, because
God disposes all active and passive powers in things. Nor can
the realization of divine providence be impeded by any

change in the author of providence, because God is completely unchangeable, as shown. Consequently, divine providence can never fail.

Second, we should note that every agent aims at a good, and at a greater good, as far as it can, as proved. Now, in respect to the whole and the parts, the good and the better are not the same, for within the whole the good consists in integrity resulting from the order and composition of parts. So for the whole it is better to have differentiation of parts needed for the ordered perfection of the whole rather than having equal parts, with each one at the same level as the most excellent part. Yet each inferior part would be better, detached from the whole, if it were on the same level as a higher part. For example, consider the human body: The foot would be a more excellent part should it possess the eye's beauty and power; but the whole body would be less perfect if deprived of the foot's service.

Consequently, any particular agent's intention differs from that of a universal agent inasmuch as a particular agent aims at the good of the part absolutely, trying to make it as good as possible, whereas the universal agent aims at the good of the whole. So any defect is outside the intention of the particular agent, whereas it is within the intention of the universal agent. Hence the birth of a female is obviously outside the intention of any particular nature, i.e., of this particular force in this particular seed, which tends to make the most perfect possible embryo. Yet universal nature or the power of the universal cause of generation among inferior things aims to generate a female as a necessary condition for the generation of many animals. Likewise corruption, diminishment, and every defect are not aimed at by any particular nature but by universal nature, since each thing avoids defects and aims at its own perfection. Evidently, then, the particular agent aims within its own species for the greatest perfection of its effect, whereas universal nature aims at special perfection in any particular effect, e.g., the perfection of a male in one effect and that of female in another.

The first observable distinction among the parts of the entire universe is that between the contingent and the necessary, for the higher beings are necessary, incorruptible, and unchangeable; while the lower anything is, the more it differs from this condition, so that the very lowest are in their own being corruptible, changeable in their disposition, and produce their effects contingently and not of necessity. Thus every agent that is a part of the universe tends to remain steadfast in its existence and natural disposition and to realize its effect, whereas God, who rules the universe, intends to realize some of his effects through necessity and others through contingency. Hence he adapts to such effects his various causes, some necessary and others contingent causes. Consequently it is part of the order of divine providence that such an effect not only be produced but be produced necessarily and that another effect be produced contingently so that some things subject to divine providence are necessary and some contingent and not all necessary. Hence it is clear that although divine providence is the per se cause of any particular future effect and is both present and past (though, more accurately, eternal), it does not follow as the first argument claimed that this particular effect will occur necessarily, since divine providence is the per se cause that this particular effect will occur contingently. And this cannot fail.

Creatures Have Their Own Activity
On the Power of God, q. 3, a. 7

We must unreservedly admit that God works in the actions of nature and will. Yet some who failed to understand this correctly made the mistake of attributing to God every action of nature, in the sense that nature through its own power does nothing at all. Various arguments convinced them of this. According to Rabbi Moses, some sages in the Moorish books of law stated that all natural forms are accidents, and inasmuch as no accident can pass from one subject to another, they concluded that it was impossible for any natural agent through its form to produce a similar form in another subject, and so they declared that fire does not heat, but God creates heat in whatever is made hot. And when anyone objected that a thing placed near the fire always becomes hot unless somehow impeded, indicating that fire is the per se cause of heat, they answered that God's established order provides that only when fire is present will he cause heat, and yet the fire itself has no part in the action of heating. This view is clearly contrary to the nature of sensation, inasmuch as the senses do not perceive unless acted upon by the sensible object (evidently the case for touch and for all senses except sight, for some hold that this is done by the visual organ projecting itself upon the object), it would follow that a man does not feel the fire's heat if the fire's action does not effect in the sense organ any likeness of the heat within the fire. As a matter of fact, should this heat likeness be effected in the organ by some other agent, the touch, although sensing heat, would not sense the fire's heat nor perceive that the fire is hot (which, indeed, the sense judges to be the case, and the senses err not in regard to their proper object).

This is also contrary to reason, which tells us that nature does nothing in vain. For if natural things had no action of their own, their forms and forces would be purposeless; e.g., if a knife does not cut, its sharpness is superfluous. It would also be superfluous to set fire to the coal if God ignites coal without fire.

It is also contrary to God's goodness, which is self-communicative to the extent that God made things like himself not only in being but in acting.

The argument they propose is entirely frivolous. When we say that an accident does not pass from one subject to another, we are referring to the same identical accident, and we are not denying that an accident inhering in a natural thing can produce an accident of like species in another subject; for this necessarily happens in any natural action. But they are presupposing that all forms are accidents, which is not true; for then there would be no substantial being in natural things, since its principle can only be a substantial and not an accidental form. Also, this would put an end to generation and corruption and entail many other absurdities. . . .

It is noteworthy that one thing may cause another's action in various ways. First, by giving it the power to act. Thus a generator moves heavy and light bodies, since it gives them the power from which their movement results. By giving natural things the forces whereby they can act, God causes all natural actions, not merely as the generator gives, while not preserving the power of heavy and light bodies, but also as maintaining its very being, insofar as he is the cause of all power, given not as the generator causing its becoming, but by causing the very being. Thus God is called a cause of any action by both giving and maintaining the natural power in its being. For, second, the preserver of a power is spoken of as causing the action as a sight-preservative remedy is said to make a man see. Third, since nothing moves or acts of itself unless it is an unmoved mover, anything is said to cause another's action by moving it to act. And by this we do not mean that it causes or preserves the active power but that it puts the power into action, as a man causes a knife to cut by making the sharpness effective through moving the knife to cut. And since in acting the inferior nature does not act except as moved, because these lower bodies both are subject to and cause change (whereas the heavenly bodies cause it but are not subject to it, and yet this they do not unless they are moved), it necessarily follows that God causes the action of every natural thing by moving it and putting its power into action.

We also discover that the order of effects follows the order of causes on account of the likeness of the effect to its cause. Nor can the second cause by its own power influence the effect of the first cause, even when it is the instrument of the first cause in respect to that effect, inasmuch as an instrument is somehow the cause of the principal cause's effect, not through its own form or power but insofar as it participates somewhat in the principal cause's power by being moved through it (e.g., the ax causes the craftsman's handiwork, not through its own form or power but through the power of the craftsman who moves it, so that it participates in his power).

Fourth, one thing causes the action of another as a principal agent causes the action of its instrument, and again in this manner we must admit that God causes all action in natural things. For the higher the cause the greater is its scope and efficacy; and the more efficacious the cause, the more profoundly it penetrates its effect and the more remote the power bringing the effect into action. Now, every natural thing is a being, a natural thing, of this or that nature; the first is common to all things, the second to all natural things, and the third to all members of a species, while the fourth is proper, if we consider accidents, to this or that individual. So that this or that individual thing by its action cannot cause another individual of the same species except as the instrument of that cause, which contains within its scope the whole species and in addition the entire being of the inferior creature. So that no action from these lower bodies achieves the production of a species except through a heavenly body's power, nor does anything produce being except through God's power. For being is the first and most common effect, more intimate than all other effects; so it is an effect producible only by God through his own power, and for this reason (*On Causes* IX) no intelligence gives being unless it has divine power. God is therefore the cause of every action insofar as every agent is an instrument of the acting divine power.

If we attend to the subsisting agent we find that every particular agent is related immediately to its effect, but if we attend to the power by which the action is done, the power of the higher cause is more immediately related to the effect than the power of the lower cause, insofar as only through the power of the higher cause is the lower cause's power connected with its effect, and thus we find it stated in *On Causes* I that the power of the first cause has a primary place in producing an effect and is present more profoundly within it. So that the divine power has to be present to every acting thing as is the heavenly body's power to every acting bodily element. But there is this difference: God's essence must be wherever his power is, whereas the heavenly body's essence is not where its power is. Accordingly we may assert that God acts in all things insofar as each thing needs his power for it to act, although we may not say that the heavenly body acts always in a bodily element even when the latter acts by its power.

God is therefore the cause of everything's action because he gives to everything its power to act, preserves it in existence, and puts it into action, and because by his power every other power acts. And if we add to this that God is his own power and that he is present in all things not as a part of their essence but to maintain them in existence, we shall conclude that he acts immediately within every agent, while not eliminating the action of the will and of the nature.

Creatures as Causes
Summa of Christian Teaching
III, 70

If God can produce all natural effects through himself, it is yet not superfluous for him to produce them through certain causes, inasmuch as this is not owing to the insufficiency of his power but to the immensity of his goodness, which made him will to communicate his likeness to things not only in respect to their being but also in respect to their being causes of other things; for in these two ways all creatures have in common the divine likeness given to them. . . . Likewise in this way the beauty of order appears in creatures.

It is also evident that the same effect is attributed to a natural cause and to God, not so that one part is caused by God and another part by the natural agent, but the whole effect comes from each, yet differently, just as the whole of the one same effect is attributed to the instrument and likewise attributed to the principal agent.

God, Principal Cause
Summa of Christian Teaching
III, 67

It is obvious that any action when unable to continue when a certain agent's influence is withdrawn is an action of that agent. Thus colors cannot be seen when the sun's action disappears from the air, so that sun is doubtless the cause of color's visibility. The same is true of violent motion, which stops when the violence of the coercive force disappears. Now, because God not only gave existence to things at their origin but causes their existence by preserving it as long as they exist . . . so he not only gave them active forces when he first created them but constantly causes those forces in them. Hence with the withdrawal of the divine influence, all action would cease. So every action of anything is traced to him as its cause.

Anything putting an active power into action is called the

cause of that action: for the craftsman who puts nature's forces into action is called the cause of that action, as the cook is the cause of the cooking done by the fire. But every putting of power into action is done principally and primarily by God; for active forces are put into their proper actions through a bodily or a soul movement. But the first principle of either movement is God, for he is the wholly immutable first mover, as proven (I, 13). Every movement of the will by which some powers are put into action also comes from God as the primary object of tendency as well as the first willer. Every action should therefore be attributed to God as its primary and principal agent.

The order of effects follows the order of causes. Now, being is the first of all effects, since all other effects are determinations of being. So being is the proper effect of the first agent, and only through the power of the first agent is it caused by other agents. And secondary agents which, so to speak, particularize and specify the action of the first agent cause as their proper effects the other perfections that are particular types of being.

Existence Is God's Effect

Summa of Christian Teaching
III, 66

That which is what it is by its essence is the proper cause of everything which is what it is by participation. So fire is the cause of all things that are afire. But only God is by his essence being, whereas all others are beings by participation, because in God alone existence is his essence. So the existence of every existing thing is his proper effect, so that anything bringing something into existence does this insofar as it acts through God's power. Hence it is said (Wis. 1: 14): "God created that all things might be"; and several places in Holy Scripture it is said that God makes all things. In *On Causes* also it is asserted that not even an intelligence gives being except *inasmuch as it is something divine,* i.e., acts by God's power.

Real Causing Requires Intel-   *On Truth*, q. 3, a. 1, c
ligence

We likewise see that anything acts for the sake of an end
in two ways. The agent himself may choose his end—and
this is the case with all intellectual agents—or the agent's
end may be chosen by another principal agent. For example,
an arrow's flight is toward a definite end, but the archer
chooses this end. Likewise, any action of a nature toward a
definite end presupposes an intellect that has pre-established
the end of the nature and directed it toward that end. That
is why every action of nature is said to be the action of intelligence. Therefore, if anything imaging something else
comes into existence through an agent that itself has not
chosen the end, the form imaged will not have the character
of exemplar or idea merely because of what has occurred.
Thus we do not say that the form of the man who generates
is the idea or exemplar of the man who is generated, but we
use these terms only when an agent acting for an end has
himself chosen the end, whether the form imaged be within
him or outside him. For we say that the form of art in the
artist is the exemplar or idea of the artifact, and we also say
that a form outside the artist is an exemplar if he images it
when he makes something. Hence this seems to comprise the
character of an idea: It must be a form imaged because of
the intention of an agent who previously himself chooses the
end.

Therefore it is obvious that all who assert that everything
happens by chance cannot admit the existence of idea. Yet
this view is criticized by philosophers inasmuch as whatever
happens by chance happens not uniformly but only in a few
instances. Yet we recognize that the course of nature constantly or mostly proceeds in a uniform way.

Likewise all who assert that everything comes from God
by necessity of nature and not by a will-decision cannot admit ideas, because those acting through the force of natural
necessity do not themselves choose the end. But this cannot
occur here, since if anything acts for an end without itself
choosing the end, this end is chosen for it by something su-

perior to it, and hence there would have to be a cause superior to God. But this is certainly impossible, because all who speak of God understand him as the First Cause of things.

For such reasons Plato affirmed the existence of ideas, bypassing the Epicurean opinion that all happens by chance, and that of Empedocles and others who asserted that all happens by natural necessity. This reason for affirming ideas, namely, on account of the previous planning of works to be done, is suggested by Dionysius, who says: "We say that exemplars in God are the intelligible characters of things that come to be, the individually pre-existing causes of subsistent beings. These theology calls 'predefinitions.' They predetermine and cause godly and good inclinations in creatures. It is through these that the supersubstance predefines and produces all things." Yet although an exemplary form or idea has in some sense the nature of an end, and the artist receives the form by which he functions, if it is outside of him, we cannot say that the divine ideas are outside of God. They can only be within the divine mind, for it is unreasonable to assert that God acts for the sake of any other end than himself or that from any source other than himself he receives that whereby he acts.

Evidence against Chance   *On Truth*, q. 5, a. 2, c

Moreover, whatever is without a definite cause happens by accident. So that if the previously mentioned opinion were true, all the harmony and utility present in things would have happened by chance. This was precisely what Empedocles maintained. He declared that by accident the parts of animals came together through friendship, and this was his explanation of the animal and of frequent occurrences. Of course, this explanation is absurd, since whatever happens by chance happens only rarely, but experience shows that harmony and utility are present in nature always, or almost so. This cannot be the effect of mere chance; it must exist because some end is intended. But nothing without intellect or knowledge can tend directly toward an end. It can do this only if another's knowledge has settled an end for it and di-

rects it to that end. So that inasmuch as natural things are
without knowledge, there must be some pre-existing intelligence directing them to an end, like an archer giving a definite motion to an arrow to wing its way to that end. Now,
the strike made by the arrow is considered not only the arrow's doing but also that of the person who directed it. Likewise, philosophers call every work of nature the work of
intelligence.

So the world is governed through the providence of that
intellect that gave to nature this order, and we may compare
the providence through which God governs the world to the
domestic foresight through which a man governs his family
or to the political foresight through which a ruler governs a
city or land, directing the actions of others toward a definite
end. With respect to himself, however, there is no providence
in God, since all in him is end, not means.

Godly Action Directed by In-   *Summa of Christian Teaching*
tellect   II, 24

Moreover, according to the philosopher, "it is the office
of a wise man to set things in order." For it is possible to
order things only through knowing their relation and proportion to one another and to something higher, or their end
inasmuch as the ordering of something to another is for the
sake of their direction to an end. But only someone gifted
with intellect can know the mutual relations and proportions
of things, and to judge of things is the prerogative of wisdom
within the highest cause. So all directing is necessarily
achieved through the wisdom of someone gifted with intelligence. Thus in the world of mechanical arts, architects are
called the wise men of their craft. Now, there is a mutual
order in the things produced by God, because this order is
always or nearly always uniform. It is clear then that God
brought things into existence through ordering them.
And so God brought things into existence through his
wisdom. . . .

Providence and Human Acts   *On Truth*, q. 5, a. 5, c

. . . The nearer anything is to its first principle, the higher is its position in the order of providence. Spiritual substances above all are nearest the first principle, and for this reason they are said to be made to God's image. Therefore, through God's providence, they are not only provided for, but they are self-provident. These substances can therefore exercise choice in their actions, whereas other creatures cannot. . . .

Concerned as it is with directing to an end, providence has as its norm the end. Because the first provider is himself the end of his providence, his norm of providence is within him. So the failures in the things for which he provides cannot be due to him but only to those beings within his providence. But creatures to whom his providence is communicated are not the ends of their own providence. They are directed to another end, namely, God. So from God's norm they must derive the rightness of their own providence. Hence, in creaturely providence the failures taking place may be due not only to those things within their providence but to the providers themselves.

Yet the rightness of a creature's own providence will be firmer the more faithful the creature is to the norm of the first provider. So the failures of such creatures are blameworthy—which is not true of the failures of other creatures— for they can both fail in their actions and are the cause of their actions. And since it is as individuals that these creatures are incorruptible, they are provided for as individuals. So their defects will have their reward or punishment as belonging to these individuals themselves, not merely as they are ordered to other things.

Man is to be found among these creatures since his form —i.e., his soul—is a spiritual being, the root of all his human acts and that whereby even his body is related to immortality.

So human acts fall under divine providence insofar as men themselves have providence over their own acts. And the defects in these acts are directed to the men themselves and not to others. Thus when a man sins, God orders the sin to the sinner's good so that after his fall, when arising, he may be a more humble person; or at least it is ordered to a good achieved in him by divine justice when he is punished for his sin. The defects occurring in sensible creatures, however, are ordained to others; for instance, the corruption of some fire is directed to generation of some air. Hence, to point out this special manner of providence exercised by God over human acts, we read in Wisdom 12: 18: "Thou being master of power . . . with great favor disposeth of us."

The Meaning of Human Action   *Summa of Christian Teaching*
                                     I, 74

The known good is the object of the will. . . .

Summa of Christian Teaching
I, 86

The end is the reason for willing the things that are for the sake of the end.

Summa of Christian Teaching
I, 37

. . . Now, the good gets its nature from being something desirable. This is the end that also moves the agent to act. In this sense it is said that the good is diffusive of itself and of being.

Intellect, Principle of Action   *Summa of Christian Teaching*
                                       III, 2

If an agent did not act for any definite result, it would be indifferent to all results. But anything indifferent to many results does not produce this rather than that. Therefore, no result comes from anything indifferent to either of two results unless it is determined by something to one of them. For it would be impossible for it to act. Hence every agent tends to some definite result, which is called its end. . . .

Moreover, the principle of every agent's action is either its nature or its intellect. Now, intellectual agents unquestionably act for the sake of an end, inasmuch as they previously intellectually conceive what they achieve through action, and from such preconception their action arises. This is what is meant by intellect being the principle of action. Just as the whole likeness of the result achieved through the actions of an intelligent agent exists in the intellect that pre-conceives it, so, likewise, does the likeness of a natural result pre-exist in the natural agent, and because of this, the action is determined to a definite result. For fire generates fire, and an olive tree, an olive tree. Hence the agent acting with nature as its principle is just as much directed in its action to a definite end as is the agent that acts through intellect as its principle. Therefore, every agent acts for an end. . . .

End Is Intended by Will   *Summa of Theology* I–II, q. 1, a. 3, ad. 2

The end insofar as it pre-exists in the intention belongs to the will, as previously stated (a. 1, ad. 1). And therefore it makes a human or moral act the kind that it is.

Voluntariness   *Summa of Theology* I–II, q. 6, a. 1, c

For an act to be human it must have voluntariness. To make this evident we should reflect that some acts have a principle within the agent or within that which is moved, but other acts or movements have an extrinsic principle. For when a stone is moved upward, its principle of movement is outside the stone, but when it is moved downward, its principle of movement is within the stone itself. Now, some beings moved by an intrinsic principle move themselves; others do not. For inasmuch as every agent or moved thing acts or is moved in view of an end, as said, those things are perfectly moved by an intrinsic principle in which there is some inner principle by which they are not merely moved but by which they are moved to an end.

But for anything to be done for the sake of an end, some knowledge of the end is required. So any being acting or moved by an inner principle with knowledge of the end, has within itself the principle of its own act not only so that it can act, but act for an end. And in the case of anything lacking knowledge of the end, although within it is a principle of action or movement, the principle of action or motion for the sake of an end is not within it but in some other being, from which the principle of its movement toward the end is received. So things like this are not said to move themselves but to be moved by other things.

Now, those beings possessing a knowledge of the end are said to move themselves, inasmuch as within them is a principle not merely of acting but of acting for the sake of an end. Therefore, since both arise from an inner principle, namely, that they act, and act for the sake of an end, their movements and acts are called voluntary. In fact, voluntary means just this: that movement and act come from a thing's own inclination. So it is that the voluntary is spoken of in the definitions of Aristotle (*Nicomachean Ethics* III, 1) and of Gregory of Nyssa and of Damascene (*On Orthodox Faith* II, 24) to be not only that "whose principle is within," but they add: "with knowledge." Thus when a man knows to the extreme degree the end of his work and moves himself, his acts are marked by the greatest degree of voluntariness.

Ignorance   *Commentary on Sentences* II, d. 22, q. 2, a. 2, c

One kind of ignorance completely excuses from wrongdoing; another kind, however, partially excuses; and yet another kind excuses neither completely nor partially. To clarify this, let us reflect upon the threefold division of ignorance.

First, on the part of the knower himself: the agent can know some things, and ignorance of these is called vincible or affected; and there are other things that he cannot know, and this is called invincible ignorance. Where there is ignorance with respect to what the agent can know there are two possibilities: either, first, it is of something in itself lying within the agent's knowing power, as happens with a man ignorant of any precept immediately knowable; or second, it comes within his power not as itself but through its cause, as is the case with an intoxicated man; for the intoxication causing his ignorance was within his power but not the consequent ignorance because his use of reason is impeded.

Second, ignorance may be classified in relation to the knowable object. For there is a kind of ignorance of what the agent is obliged to know; this is called, according to the philosopher, universal ignorance, and according to legal experts, ignorance of the law. This varies with various people, for one man is obliged to know some things that another man is not obliged to know. Another kind of ignorance is of that which the agent is not obliged to know, and this deals with the knowledge of the particular circumstances of an act. The philosopher calls this particular ignorance, and the lawyers, ignorance of fact.

A third division is classed in relation to the act. For one kind of ignorance is that which is the cause of the act; for if one were not ignorant, one would not do it; and here one is said to do wrong through ignorance, and this is characterized by actual repentance. And another kind of ignorance is that which, although not the act's cause, is accidentally related to the act; and about this, as the philosopher says in *Ethics* III, 2, one is not said to act through ignorance but while ignorant. For such an act, therefore, he is not repentant. Thus a man, thinking he is making love to one woman, actually does so to another, to whom he would still have made love even if he had known who she was. Yet another kind of ignorance is that which often accompanies the affective aspect of sin. Thus on account of the concupiscence associated with sin and unrepressed by the will, there is prevented rational judgment about a particular proposed action. This is what *Ethics* IV, 4 refers to when it states that pleasure corrupts the prudential judgment. This is ignorance of choice, and in this way every evil person is said to be ignorant.

Ignorance as Related to Action — *Summa of Theology* I–II, q. 6, a. 8, c

Inasmuch as ignorance eliminates the knowledge that is a prerequisite to voluntariness, ignorance can cause involuntariness. But not every kind of ignorance eliminates this kind of knowledge. So we should realize that ignorance is related to the will act in three ways: concomitantly, consequently, and antecedently.

Concomitant ignorance is so related to action that even with knowledge the act would nevertheless be done. For ignorance does not here lead to the desire that it be done, but it so happens that while something is being done, something is being ignored. . . . This is the case of a man who, wishing to kill his enemy, does this in ignorance, believing that he is killing a deer. Such ignorance does not cause involuntariness, as Aristotle notes (*Nicomachean Ethics* III, 1), since it does not cause anything repugnant to the will; but it does make the act nonvoluntary, since one cannot actually desire that of which one is ignorant.

Consequent ignorance is related to the will through the ignorance being voluntary. This happens in two ways according to the two kinds of voluntariness explained. In one way, the act of will extends to the ignorance, as with the man wishing to be ignorant either to excuse his sin or so that he may not be prevented from sinning, as is said in Job 21: 14: "We do not desire the knowledge of thy ways." This is called affected ignorance. In a second way, ignorance is called voluntary as related to that which a man can and should know. For in this case not to act and not to desire are called voluntary. . . . Ignorance is found here either when one does not actually think of what he can and should be thinking (and this is ignorance from a bad choice, arising from passion or habit), or when a man is not careful to attain the knowledge he should have (and in this way, ignorance of the universal principles of moral law that one is obliged to know is called voluntary, since it arises from negligence). Since this ignorance is voluntary in one or another of the preceding ways, it cannot, absolutely speaking, cause involuntariness. But relatively speaking, it does cause involuntariness in the sense that it pre-exists the will's movement in performing an act that would be eliminated if the knowledge were present.

Antecedent ignorance is that which is not voluntary and yet causes an act of will that would otherwise not be done. This occurs when a man is ignorant of some circumstance of an act that he was not expected to know, but had he known this, he would not have done what he did; for example, a man having taken all necessary precautions and unaware that someone is passing along the road, shoots an arrow, which kills a traveler. Such ignorance does cause involuntariness, absolutely.

Circumstances of Action   *Summary of Theology* I–II, q.
7, a. 3, c, a. 4, c

Circumstance means something standing around the substance of the act and yet somehow touching it. This may happen in three ways: first, as touching the act itself; second, as touching the cause of the act; third, as touching the effect.

Now, it touches the act either through quantity, of time or place; or through the quality of the act, e.g., the way of acting. From the standpoint of the effect, we refer to what a man did. From the side of the cause of the act, in respect to final cause, the reference is to that for which; in respect to the material cause or object, it is that in which; in respect to the principal, efficient cause, it is who acted; and in respect to the instrumental, efficient cause, it is by what means.

The motive force and object of the will is the end. Therefore, the most important circumstance is that which touches the act from its end aspect, namely that for the sake of which; secondarily, it is that touching the very substance of the act, i.e., what one did. The other circumstances are more or less important insofar as they come more or less close to these.

Evil and Reason   *On Evil*, q. 2, a. 4, c

Acts are human to the extent that they are acts of reason. And thus it is clear that they differ specifically when considered as human acts. So it is apparent that it is characteristic of the very species of human acts for some to be good and some evil. So we should say without qualification that some human acts are in themselves good or evil, and not that all are morally indifferent (except, perhaps, when they are regarded solely in their genus). . . . .

Since an act of man takes its species from the nature of its object and is accordingly good or evil, an act thus specified as good never can be evil; nor can one specified as evil ever be good. Yet it can happen that to an act good in itself may be added another act evil according to some relationship; and because of this kind of evil act, the good is said to produce evil at times, but it is not in itself evil. Thus to give alms to the poor or to love God is an act good in itself, but to use an act of this kind for some inordinate end, i.e., for cupidity or vanity, is quite another act and an evil one. . . .

Individual Acts Never Indif- *On Evil*, q. 2, a. 5, c
ferent

If we refer to the moral act in its species, then not every moral act is good or evil, but some are morally indifferent, since the moral act derives its species from the object through its relation to reason. . . . Now, one kind of object involves agreement with reason, and this makes the moral act good in a general way, e.g., clothing the naked. Another kind involves a clash with reason, e.g., taking what belongs to another, and this makes it evil in a general way. A third kind neither involves agreement nor disagreement with reason, e.g., lifting a straw from the ground, and this is an indifferent act.

But if we speak of the moral act as an individual act, then every particular moral act must be good or evil by reason of some circumstance, for the singular act cannot take place without circumstances making it right or wrong. If anything at all is done when it should, where it should, as it should, etc., then this kind of act is well ordered and good; but if any of these be defective, the act is badly ordered and evil. This may be chiefly examined in regard to the circumstance that is the end, for whatever is done because of a just need or a pious usefulness is done in a praiseworthy way, and is a good act; but whatever has no just need or pious usefulness is an idle act.

Human Action   *Summa of Theology* I–II, q.
                              1, a. 1, c

Among man's acts only those proper to man as man are properly called human actions, for it is as master of his own actions that man differs from other, irrational creatures. So only those actions of which man is master are properly called human. Now, through reason and will man is the master of his acts, and consequently free choice is spoken of as the "power of will and reason." Hence, acts properly called human are those proceeding from a deliberate will act. But other actions belonging to man can certainly be spoken of as actions of man (*hominis actiones*), but not properly human actions, insofar as they do not belong to man as man.

Human Good

Commentary on Nicomachean Ethics I, lect. 9

We must come again to the good that is the objective of our inquiry, namely, to happiness, so that we may discover what it is. And we should first admit that various goods are intended in various works and arts. Thus health is the good intended in the medical art, victory the intended good in the military art, and other goods in other arts.

And if we inquire what is the good intended in any art or any enterprise, it should be known that the good is that for whose sake all else is done. For in medicine, all is done for the sake of health; in the military art, all for the sake of victory; and in building, all for the sake of making a house. Also, in any business at all there is an intended good for whose sake all is done. Now, this intended good in each and every work or act of choice is called the end; for the end is simply *that for the sake of which all else is done*.

Hence, if we immediately discover an end to which all that is done in the human arts and works is directed, then such an end will be the good that is worked for, absolutely; that is, what is intended in all human works. But if in this matter several goods are discovered, reason must transcend this plurality until it comes to the thing itself, that is, some *one* thing. For man's ultimate end as man must be *one* by reason of the unity of human nature, just as there is one end for the medical doctor as a medical doctor because of the unity of the medical art.

And this ultimate end of man is called the *human good*, which is happiness.

Happiness Is Action

Debated Questions VIII, q. 9, a. 19, c

Blessedness or happiness consists in an action and not in a habit, as the philosopher proves in *Ethics* I, 8. So the happiness of man can be related to any potentiality of the soul in two ways: in one way, as the object of the potentiality, and in this way happiness is principally related to the will. For happiness is a word for the ultimate end of man and his highest good. And the end and the good are the will's objective. In another way it is related as act to potentiality; and in this way happiness originally and essentially consists in an intellectual act. Formally and from the point of view of fulfillment, happiness consists not in a will act, for it is impossible for the very act of the will to be the will's ultimate end.

Man's ultimate end is that which he primarily desires. But what is primarily desired cannot be a will act. For first of all, a potentiality must be directed to some object before it can be directed to its own act. The act of any potentiality is not known prior to its reflection upon that act, for the act terminates in the object, and thus a potentiality is directed toward its object before it is directed to its act. For example, sight first sees color rather than itself as seeing color. Likewise the will wants some good before it wants its act of wanting. So the will act cannot be primarily the object of will, and so it cannot be the ultimate end.

Yet whenever any external good is desired as an end, that act of desiring is a kind of interior end for us, inasmuch as we attain it first completely. For example, we say that eating is an end and the happiness of the one who considers food as his end; also, possession is the end of the one who takes money as his end.

Now, the end of our desire is God. So the act by which we are primarily united to him is originally and essentially our happiness. But through the act of the intellect we are primarily united to him, and so the vision of God, which is an intellectual act, is essentially and originally our happiness.

But because this action is most perfect and the object most worthy, the greatest joy follows crowning this action and perfecting it, as beauty does youth, as is asserted in *Ethics* X, 4. So this joy belonging to the will is that which completes happiness formally. Therefore the ultimate source of happiness is in vision, but its completion is in joy.

Man's Ultimate End Is Beyond   *Compendium of Theology,*
His Unaided Powers   104–5

Now, there are two ways for a thing to be in potentiality: in one way, naturally, with respect to whatever can be brought into act by a natural agent; in another way with respect to whatever cannot be brought to act by a natural agent but by another agent, and this is clear in the area of bodily things. For a man coming from a body or an animal from semen—this is natural potentiality. But that a bench be made out of wood or a seeing agent from a blind one is not a matter of natural potentiality, and the same occurs in connection with our intellect.

For our intellect is in natural potentiality in respect to some intelligible objects, namely, those that can be brought into act by the agent intellect which is our innate principle by which we are rendered actually intelligent. Now, we cannot find our ultimate end in our intellect being brought into act this way, for the agent intellect is perfected by making actually intelligible the images that are potentially intelligible. . . . But images are received through the senses, so that our intellect is brought into act by the agent intellect only in respect to those intelligible objects that we can get to know through sensible things. But man's ultimate end cannot consist in this kind of knowledge, for natural desire rests whenever the ultimate end is attained. But no matter how proficient in knowing by way of this sense knowledge, the natural desire to know other things still remains.

For many are the things unreached by the senses and about which we can get only a slight awareness through the senses; so we may perhaps know that such things exist but not what they are, since the essences of immaterial substances are of a different genus from the essences of sensible things, and they transcend them beyond all proportion. Even among the things falling within the range of sensation, there are many whose intelligible essence we cannot know with certitude, some in fact we cannot know at all, and others only slightly. One thing always remains: the natural desire for a more perfect knowledge.

But a natural desire cannot exist in vain. Hence we attain
the ultimate end in this way: Our intellect is actuated by an
agent more sublime than the one connatural to us [the agent
intellect]. And this can satisfy our natural wish for knowledge.
But our wish to know is such that when we know effects we
want to know their cause. In respect to any kind of thing
known in any of its conditions, our wish is not satisfied until
we know its essence, so that our natural wish for knowledge
cannot be satisfied until we know the First Cause not merely
in some way, but in its essence. Now, the First Cause is
God. . . . Hence it is the intellectual creature's ultimate end
to see God through his essence.

We should consider how this may be. It is clear that our
intellect, which knows nothing except through its species,
cannot know the essence of one thing through the species of
another. And the further is the species, by which the intellect
knows, from what is known, the less perfect knowledge does
our intellect possess of the thing's essence. Thus were it to
know an ox through the species of an ass, it would know its
essence imperfectly, i.e., only in terms of its genus; and far
more imperfectly were it to know it through a stone, since it
would know it through a more distant genus. And were it to
know it through the species of anything having nothing generically in common with an ox, it would not know the essence of
the ox at all.

From what was previously said it is clear that no creature
has anything generically in common with God, so that God
cannot be known in his essence through any created species
at all, not only not through a sensible species but not even
through an intelligible one. Hence, for God himself to be
known in his essence God himself must become the form of
the intellect knowing him and unite with it not so as to constitute one nature but as the intelligible species is to the
knower. For just as he is his own existing being, so likewise
is he his own truth, which is the form of the intellect.

Moreover, everything that is true of a form must be true
of any disposition toward that form. Our intellect is not
naturally in ultimate disposition to that form that is truth,
for if it were, it would from the outset seek it. Hence when
it does seek it, it is necessary for it to be elevated by some

newly added disposition, which we call the light of glory. By this our intellect is perfected by God, who alone in his own nature has this form, just as heat's disposition to the form of fire can come only from fire; and it is with respect to this light that Psalm 35 says: "In thy light we shall see the light."

Now, when this is attained, the natural wish necessarily is satisfied, since the divine essence (which in the aforementioned manner may be united to the intellect of the one who sees God) is the adequate principle for knowing all things and is the source of all good, so that there would be nothing left to desire. And here likewise is the most perfect way to seek the divine likeness, namely, to know him in the same way that he knows himself, i.e., through his essence. Of course, we may not comprehend him precisely as he comprehends himself, not that we should be ignorant of any part of him (for he has no part), but insofar as we may not know him as perfectly as he is objectively knowable. For our intellectual power cannot in its knowing act be adequate to his truth whereby he is knowable, because his clarity or truth is infinite, whereas our intellect is finite; and his intellect is infinite, just as his truth is. And thus he knows himself to the fullness of his knowability, just as a man knowing demonstratively comprehends a demonstrable conclusion, but this is not the case of the one knowing it in a more imperfect way, for example, by probable reasoning.

And inasmuch as we say that happiness is man's ultimate end, man's beatitude or happiness consists in this: to see God through God's essence, although a man may be quite remote from God in the perfection of his happiness; for God possesses this happiness through his own nature, but man has it by a participation in the divine light, as was said previously.

3. MORAL DISPOSITIONS

Permanent Human Disposi-   *Summa of Theology* I–II, q.
tions   49, a. 1

. . . the philosopher asserts in *Metaphysics* V that *habit is a disposition* whereby whatever is disposed is disposed well or ill either in regard to itself or in regard to another. And so health is such a habit or durable disposition. Hence we must declare habit to be a quality.

Summa of Theology I–II, q. 49, a. 2, c

The philosopher in *Categories* VI considers disposition and habit as the first kind of quality. And Simplicius in his *Commentary on the Categories* explains how these kinds differ in this way. He states that some qualities are natural, present in any subject naturally, always present. But some come from without and may be lost. Among the latter habits or dispositions are differences according to ease or difficulty in being lost. . . .

And so . . . the philosopher in *Metaphysics* V, 25 states that by *habits* we are directed well or ill with regard to the passions. For whenever anything is appropriate to a thing's nature, it is recognized as a good; but when inappropriate, it seems evil. . . .

Powers Open to Permanent   *Summa of Theology* I–II, q.
Dispositions   50, a. 3, c

In *Ethics* III the philosopher says that some virtues, such as temperance and fortitude, are present in the soul's irrational parts.

Sense powers can be considered in two ways. First, insofar as they act from natural impulse, and second, insofar as they act under reason's rule. Insofar as they act by natural impulse they are ordered, just as nature is, to one thing. So that just as habits are not present in natural powers, so habits are not present in sense powers, insofar as they act from natural impulse. Insofar as they act under reason's rule, they can be ordered to various things. In this way sense powers can have habits by which they are well or badly disposed toward something.

Cause of Permanent Disposi-   *Summa of Theology* I–II, q.
tions   51, a. 3, c

In *Ethics* I the philosopher says that just as one swallow
does not make spring, so neither does one day nor a brief
time make a man blessed or happy. But happiness comes
from action according to a perfect, virtuous disposition, as
stated in *Ethics* I. Hence, one act does not cause a virtuous
habit nor, for the same reason, any other habit.

As already stated (I–II, 51, 2), a disposition is caused
by action when a passive power is moved by an active principle. But to generate any quality in a passive power, the active principle must gain entire control over the passive principle. Thus we see that when a fire is unable immediately to
consume a combustible object, it does not immediately cause
it to burst into flames, but by gradually ridding it of contrary dispositions and thus completely gaining control over
it, it imposes its likeness upon it.

It is likewise clear that the active principle of reason cannot gain entire control of the tending power in one act, for
the tending power is inclined in various ways to a variety of
things, whereas reason in one act judges something to be desirable in its particular conditions and circumstances. So the
tending power is not so entirely controlled that in most cases
it is directed effectively to one same thing, as is the case with
nature. This belongs to a virtuous habit. This is why a virtuous disposition cannot be caused by one act but only by
many.

We should consider two passive principles among the
knowing powers: one, the possible intellect; the other, that
which Aristotle calls passive intellect, i.e., the particular reason or the cogitative power, along with memory and
imagination.

In respect to the first passivity [possible intellect] in one
act an active principle can entirely overcome this passive
principle's potentiality. Hence, one self-evident assertion
forces the intellect to assent firmly to a conclusion. A probable statement does not do this, however, so that even with
respect to the possible intellect, many acts of reason are

needed to cause a habit of opinion. Yet one act of reason can result in a habit of science in respect to this same possible intellect. But in respect to the inferior knowing powers, the same acts must be many times repeated to imprint something firmly upon the memory. This is why in his book *On Memory and Recall* the philosopher states that meditation strengthens the memory. One act may also cause bodily habits if the active principle is great in strength. Thus a strong medicine often restores health immediately.

Strengthening of Permanent	*Summa of Theology* I–II, q.
Dispositions	52, a. 3, c

The one same thing does not cause contrary things. But as stated in *Ethics* II some acts lessen the disposition from which they come, namely, if they are carelessly done. Hence not every act increases disposition.

It is true that similar acts cause similar dispositions, as declared in *Ethics* II. Similarity or dissimilarity proceed not only from sameness or otherness in quality but also from sameness or otherness in the manner of participation, since not only is black different from white but also the less white is different from the more white, inasmuch as there is movement from the less white to the more white as from one opposite to another, as stated in *Physics* V.

But the will controls the use of disposition, as previously shown (I–II, 49, 3). And just as anyone having a durable disposition may not use it or may do an action contrary to it, so he may use the disposition in acting out of proportion to the intensity of the disposition. But if the intensity of an act is in proportion to the intensity of the disposition or else exceeds it, this act either increases the disposition or disposes it toward growth, if we may employ an analogy here by comparing the growth of a disposition to the animal's growth (since not every morsel of food causes the animal actually to grow, nor does every drop of water cause a hole in a stone, but repeated eating finally brings growth). So that when acts are repeated, a disposition grows. But if the intensity of the act is not proportionate to the intensity of the disposition, this act does not promote the disposition toward growth but toward frailty.

Loss of Permanent Disposi-   *Summary of Theology* I–II, q.
tions   53, a. 3, c

The philosopher says (*On the Length and Brevity of Life,* 2) that forgetfulness as well as deception corrupt science. And in *Ethics* VIII he states that lack of communication destroys many friendships. Hence some virtuous dispositions are decreased or destroyed by lack of exercise.

As expressed in *Physics* VIII, there are two ways for anything to cause movement. First, per se, as an agent through its own form causes motion; fire causes heat in this way. Second, *per accidens,* as an agent removes an impediment. In this latter way the failure to act causes the destruction or diminishment of dispositions, since this removes the act that wards off whatever can destroy or weaken a disposition. For we asserted (I–II, 53, 2) that durable dispositions are per se destroyed or weakened by contrary agents. So that when a disposition's contrary is gradually wearing down the disposition, there must be a counteraction coming from the disposition. Failure to act over a lengthy period may diminish or totally destroy such dispositions, as can be seen in respect to both science and virtue. It is clear that a disposition of moral virtue inclines a man to choose promptly the mean in his moral activity and the use of his passions. But when anyone fails to use a virtuous disposition to temper his passions or actions, many acts and passions escape virtue's control because of the impulses of the sensitive tendencies and external causes. Hence failure to exercise a virtue does weaken or destroy it.

This is also true with respect to intellectual dispositions, by which man is inclined to judge correctly and promptly of the forms in his imagination. Thus when one ceases to use intellectual dispositions, extraneous forms arise in the imagination and incline him toward acts opposed to the disposition. Unless a man uses his intellectual dispositions frequently, he will not be able to suppress these extraneous images and will become less able to make right judgments, often becoming totally disposed to the contrary. Hence, failure to act weakens or destroys an intellectual disposition.

4. JUSTICE AND LAW

Obligation toward God's Will   *On Truth*, q. 23, a. 7, c

Everyone is obliged to conform his will to God's. To understand this we should consider that there is one thing within every genus that is primary and the measure of everything else within the genus, since in this one thing the nature of the genus is most perfectly present. . . . In this sense God himself is the measure of all things, as can be taken from the commentator's words (*Metaphysics* X, 2).

Every being has the act of existing in proportion to its approach in likeness to God. But insofar as it is unlike him, it approaches nonbeing. And we can say the same of all attributes present both in God and creatures. Thus is his intellect the measure of all knowledge, his goodness of all goodness, and more precisely, his goodwill of every goodwill. So, every goodwill is good by being conformed to the divine goodwill. Hence, since everyone is obliged to have a goodwill, he is thereby obliged to have a will conformed to the divine will.

But there are many ways of looking at this conformity. Here in speaking of the will we mean the volitional act. When we speak of conformity to God in reference to the power of will, the conformity is natural, as belonging to the image. So it does not come under any commandment. But the act of the divine will is not only the act of will but likewise the cause of all that are acts. So our will act can therefore conform to the divine will either as an effect to its cause or as a will to a will.

Conformity of effect to cause is not found in the same way among natural and voluntary causes. The conformity is, with natural causes, present by a likeness of nature. So man begets a man, fire enkindles fire. But with voluntary causes we say that the effect conforms to the cause when the cause is ful-

filled in the effect. So an artifact images its cause not on
account of having the same nature as the art within the
artist's mind, but because the form of the art is fulfilled in
the artifact. So when whatever the will wants is accomplished,
the effect of the will is conformed to the will. And thus our
will act conforms to the divine will whenever we will what
God wants us to will.

But there are two ways of looking at conformity of one
will to another by act: 1. according to the specific form, as
man is like man; and 2. according to an additional form, as a
wise man is like a wise man.

One will is like another specifically, I state, when the two
share the same object, since the act derives its species from
the object. But there are two notable aspects in any object
of will: one material, so to speak, the thing willed; another
formal, so to speak, the reason for willing or the end. It is
very much like sight's object where color is certainly material
and light is formal, inasmuch as by light the color is made
actually visible. So there are two kinds of conformity possible
with respect to object. For instance, a man wills something
that God wills. Such conformity is, somehow, founded upon
the material cause, inasmuch as the object is, so to speak,
the matter of the act. So it is the least among the kinds of
conformity. The other kind of conformity comes from the
reason for willing or the end. Such conformity takes place
when one wills something for the very same reason for which
God wills it. This conformity is founded upon the final cause.

But when an act emerges from a disposition, it receives
an added form. In this way our will is said to be conformed
to the divine will whenever a person wills something out of
charity just as God does. This conformity is, in a sense,
founded upon the formal cause.

Source of Justice on Earth   *On Truth*, q. 23, a. 6, c

Because justice is a kind of "rightness" as Anselm teaches
(*On Truth*, 12) or "equality," as the philosopher teaches
(*Nicomachean Ethics* V, 1), justice in its essential nature will
depend primarily upon whatever has that measure by which
the equality and rightness of justice are established among

things. Now, the will cannot be characterized as the first rule but as ruled, inasmuch as it is directed by reason and intellect. This is not only true for us but for God as well, although the will in us is really distinct from the intellect. This is why the will and its rightness are not the same thing. But in God the will is really identified with the intellect, so that the rightness of his will is really the same as the will itself. So the primary thing upon which the essential nature of all justice depends is the wisdom of the divine intellect, which establishes things perfectly, in proportion to one another and to their cause. The essential nature of created justice consists in this proportion. In asserting that justice depends only on the will, one is declaring that the divine will does not act according to the order of wisdom, a blasphemous assertion.

Natural Law   *Summa of Theology* I–II, q. 94, a. 2

The order of the precepts of the natural law is the order of our natural inclinations. For there is in man a primary and natural inclination to good, which he has in common with all things, inasmuch as every thing desires the preservation of its own being (*esse*) according to its nature. Through this inclination the natural law pertains to everything that makes for the preservation of human life and all that impedes its death. There is in man a second inclination to more specific ends according to the nature he has in common with other animals. According to this inclination, those things are said to be of natural law "that nature has taught all animals," instincts such as the union of husband and wife, the education of children, and so forth. Third, there is in man a certain inclination to good according to his rational nature, and this is proper to man alone: thus man has a natural inclination to know the truth about God and to live in society. And in respect to this, there come under the natural law all actions pertaining to such inclinations: notably that a man should avoid ignorance, that he must not offend those with whom he deals, and all other actions of this kind.

Universality and/or Particu-   *Summa of Theology* I–II, q.
larity of Natural Law   94, a. 4

As was said above, the actions to which man is naturally
inclined pertain to the natural law; among these it is proper
to man that he should be inclined to act according to reason.
Reason, however, proceeds from general principles to concrete particulars, as made clear in *Physics* I, 1. The speculative reason of man does this in one way, the practical reason
in another way. For the speculative reason is chiefly used
in respect to necessary truths, which are impossible to be
other than they are; so that truth is found just as surely in
the particular conclusions as in the general principles themselves. But practical reason is used in respect to contingent
matters in which human actions are located; hence, although
there is a certain necessity in the general principles, the more
one descends to the particulars, the more is the conclusion
open to exception.

So therefore it is clear that as far as the general principles
of reason are concerned, whether speculative or practical,
there is one standard of truth or uprightness for all, and this
is equally known by all. With regard to the particular conclusions of speculative reason, there is again one standard
of truth for all, but this is not equally known to all; it is universally true, for example, that the three interior angles of a
triangle are equal to two right angles; but this conclusion
is not known by all people.

When we come to the particular conclusions of the practical reason, however, there is neither the same standard of
truth or uprightness for all, nor are these conclusions equally
known to all. All people realize that it is right and true to act
according to reason. And from this principle it follows as a
particular conclusion that debts should be paid. And in most
cases this is true; but it could happen in some special case that
it would be injurious and therefore irrational to repay a debt
(if, for example, the money were to be used for a war against
one's own country). Such exceptions are all the more likely
to occur the more we get down to concrete cases, as when it
is said that debts are to be paid with such a precaution or in

such a way. The more specialized the conditions stated, the greater is the possibility of an exception arising so that it might not be upright to return or not to return the payment.

So it must be said that the natural law, as far as general first principles are concerned, is the same for all, both as a norm of uprightness and as equally knowable. But as to certain concrete cases that are conclusions from the general principles, it is the same for all only in the majority of cases, both as a norm and as knowable. So in special cases it can admit of exceptions, both with regard to uprightness because of certain impediments (just as in nature the generation and change of bodies is subject to accidents caused by some impediment), and with regard to knowability. This can also happen because in some persons reason is depraved by passion or by some evil habit, as Caesar says in *The Gallic War* VI, 23, of the Germans, that once upon a time they did not think robbery to be wrong (although it is obviously against natural law).

Immutability and Development of Natural Law   *Summa of Theology* I–II, q. 94, a. 5, c and ad. 3

Natural law can be understood to change in two ways. One is in that certain additions are made to it. And nothing stops natural law from changing in this way, for much that is useful to human life is added to natural law by divine law as well as by human laws.

In another way, natural law can be understood to change by having something subtracted from it, as though something might cease to be of natural law that formerly was of natural law. And thus as far as the first principles of natural law are concerned, natural law is entirely unchangeable. Moreover, as far as the secondary precepts, which we have said to be certain particular conclusions following upon the first principles, natural law again does not change, in the sense that it remains a general law for the majority of cases that what the natural law prescribes is right. It can nevertheless change in some particular case or a small number of cases on account of some special causes preventing the observance of such precepts, as was said above.

ad. 3. Something is said to be of natural law in two ways. First, if there is a natural inclination to it (as, it is wrong to injure one's neighbor). Second, if nature does not lead us to do the contrary.

> *Summa of Theology* I–II, q. 91, a. 2, ad. 1

This argument would stand if the natural law differed from the eternal law, but it is nothing else but a participation in eternal law. . . .

> *Summa of Theology* I–II, q. 91, a. 3, ad. 2

Of itself human reason is not the rule of things, and yet the principles received in it by nature are general rules and norms of all things having to do with human behavior, which natural reason does rule and measure, although it does not measure natural things.

Political Power, Its Need   *Summa of Theology* I–II, q. 90, a. 3, ad. 2

A private person has no authority to compel right action. He can only advise, but if his advice is not accepted, he has no coercive power. But law must have coercive power if it is to have authority to compel right action, as the philosopher says (*Ethics* X, 9). But the coercive power belongs to the community as a whole as well as to its public authority, who must inflict the punishments, as we shall see later. He alone therefore has the right to make laws.

Law, General Definition   *Summa of Theology* I–II, q. 90, a. 4, c

. . . From the preceding we may gather the definition of law. It is nothing other than a reasonable direction of beings toward the common good, promulgated by the one who is charged with the community.

Types of Law: Eternal Law   *Summa of Theology* I–II, q. 91, a. 1, c

As we said above, law is nothing other than a certain dictate of the practical reason "in the leader" who governs any perfect community. It is evident, however, if we presuppose that the world is ruled by divine providence, as shown in the First Part, that the entire world community is governed by divine reason. And thus the rational guidance of things in God, as in the existing ruler of the universe, has the significance of law. . . . It is fitting to call a law of this kind the eternal law.

Natural Law   *Summa of Theology* I–II, q. 91, a. 2, c

Since all things that are subordinated to divine providence are regulated and measured by the eternal law, as was clearly shown, it is evident that all things participate to some degree in the eternal law, inasmuch as from it they receive certain inclinations to the actions and ends proper to them. But the rational creature above all is subject to divine providence in a more excellent way, insofar as it is made a participator in providence itself, providing for itself and for others. Whence it participates in the eternal reason itself and through this it possesses a natural inclination to right action and right end. And such participation by the rational creature in the eternal law is called natural law. Hence when the Psalmist said (Ps. 4: 6): "Offer up the sacrifice of justice," he added as though being asked the question, what is the sacrifice of justice, "Many say, who sheweth us good things?" and then replied, saying: "The light of Thy countenance, O Lord, is signed upon us," as though the natural light of reason, by which we discern what is good and evil, which pertains to natural law, were nothing other than the impression of the divine light in us. Hence it is evident that the natural law is nothing other than the participation in eternal law by the rational creature.

Human Law *Summa of Theology* I–II, q. 91, a. 3, c

Just as in speculative reason we proceed from indemonstrable principles, known naturally, to the conclusions of the various sciences so that this knowledge is not innate in us but obtained by the work of reason, so also the human reason has to proceed from the precepts of the natural law as though from certain common and indemonstrable principles to other more specialized regulations. And such specialized regulations arrived at by the effort of reason are called human laws, when the other conditions necessary for true law as set forth above are present. Thus Cicero says (*Rhetoric* II, 53): "The beginning of law proceeds from nature; then come certain customs judged useful; finally reverence and religion sanction what proceeds from nature and is established by custom."

Aristotle's View of Politics *Commentary on Ethics* I, lect. 11

. . . He says that since political science uses the other practical sciences, as already noted, and since it legislates what is to be done and what omitted, as previously stated, it follows that the end of this science as architectonic embraces or contains under itself the ends of other practical sciences. Hence, he concludes, the end of political science is the good of man, that is, the supreme end of human things.

Then . . . he shows that political science is the most important science from the very nature of its special end. It is evident that insofar as a cause is prior and more powerful, it extends to more effects. Hence, insofar as the good, which has the nature of a final cause, is more powerful, it extends to more effects. So, even though the good be the same objective for one man and for the whole state, it seems much better and more perfect to attain, that is, to procure and preserve the good of the whole state than the good of any one man. Certainly it is a part of that love that should exist among men that a man preserve the good even of a single human being. But it is much better and more divine that this be done for a whole people and for states. It is even sometimes desirable that this be done for one state only, but it is much more divine that it be done for a whole people that includes many states. This is said to be more divine because it shows greater likeness to God, who is the ultimate cause of all good. But this good common to one or to several states is the object of our inquiry, that is, of the particular skill called political science. Hence to it, as the most important science, belongs in a most special way the consideration of the ultimate end of human life.

But we should note that he says political science is the most important, not simply, but in that division of practical sciences that are concerned with human things, the ultimate end of which political science considers. The ultimate end of the whole universe is considered in theology, which is the most important without qualification. He says that it belongs to political science to treat the ultimate end of human life. This, however, he discusses here, since the matter of this book covers the fundamental notions of political science.

Politics as a Science   *Commentary on Politics,* Prologue

1. As the philosopher teaches in *Physics* II, art imitates nature. The reason for this is that, as principles are related to one another, so proportionately are the operations and effects related. Now, the principle of those things produced according to art is the human intellect, which is derived from the divine intellect according to a certain likeness, which divine intellect is the principle of natural things. Hence it is necessary both that the operations of art imitate the operations of nature, and that the things that are according to art, imitate the things that are in nature. For if an instructor in some art should produce a work of art, it would be necessary for a disciple, who was to receive the art from him, to give heed to his work, so that he himself might operate according to the instructor's likeness. Therefore the human intellect, to which intelligible light derives from the divine intellect, must necessarily, in the things that it makes, be informed through inspecting those things that are produced naturally, so as to operate in a similar way.

2. Hence the philosopher says that if art were to produce the things that are of nature, it would operate in a way similar to that of nature; and conversely, if nature were to produce the things that are of art, it would produce them in a way similar to that in which art produces them. However, nature does not perfect the things that are of art, but only prepares certain principles, and affords in a certain way an exemplar for the artisans. But art is able to inspect those things that are of nature, and use them for the perfecting of its own work; it cannot, however, perfect the works of nature themselves. From this it is evident that human reason, in respect to the things that are according to nature, is knowing only, but in respect to those things that are according to art, it is both knowing and able to produce [factive]. Hence it is necessary that those human sciences that are of natural things, be speculative; while those that are of things made by man, be practical, or operative according to the imitation of nature.

3. Now, nature proceeds in its activity from simple to composite things, in such a way that, in those things that are produced by the operation of nature, that which is most composite is the perfect thing, and the whole and the end of the others, as appears in all wholes in respect to their parts. Hence, human reason, also, proceeds from the simple to the composite, as from the imperfect to the perfect.

4. Since human reason disposes not only of the things that come into man's use, but also of men themselves, who are ruled by reason, in both it proceeds from the simple to the composite. It does so, indeed, in those things that come to man's use, when out of lumber it constitutes a ship, and out of lumber and stones, a house. It does so in men themselves, when, for example, it orders many men into some one community. In these communities, which have different degrees and orders, the ultimate is the community of the state, ordained to the per se sufficiency of human life. Hence, among all human communities, it is the most perfect. And, since the things that come to man's use are ordained to man as to their end, and the end takes precedence over the things that are for the end, it is therefore necessary that this whole, which

is the state, take precedence over all wholes that may be known and constituted by human reason.

5. From what has been stated, therefore, concerning the doctrine of politics, which Aristotle transmits in this book, we may gather four points.

First, the need for this science. For it is necessary that there be, of each of the various things that can be known by reason, some doctrine [i.e., teachable science or art] set forth for the perfection of human wisdom, called "philosophy." Hence, since that whole that is the state is subject to a certain judgment of reason, it was necessary, for the completeness of philosophy, to set forth the doctrine of the state, named "politics," i.e., civil science.

6. Second, we may grasp the genus of this science. Since practical sciences are distinguished from the speculative in the respect that the speculative are ordained to the knowing of truth while the practical are ordained to a product, it is necessary that this science be comprised under practical philosophy—the state being a certain whole, in respect to which human reason is not only knowing, but also operative. Further, since there is a certain notion that has its act in the manner of a making, by an operation passing out into external matter, properly pertaining to the arts called "mechanical" (such as, e.g., carpentry, shipbuilding, and the like), while there is a certain other notion, whose act is in the manner of an action, where the operation remains within the one who operates, as in the case of taking counsel, choosing, willing, and such things, pertaining to moral science, it is plain that political science, which considers the ordering of men, is not contained under the factive sciences, i.e., the mechanical arts, but under the active, i.e., the moral sciences.

7. Third, we may gather the dignity and the order of politics in relation to all the other practical sciences. The state holds the first place among all the things that may be constituted by human reason. For it is to it that all human communities are referred. Further, all the wholes constituted by the mechanical arts out of things that come to the use of men, are ordained to men as their end. If, therefore, the science to take precedence is that which is the more noble and more perfect, then politics must needs, among all the

practical sciences, hold the first and architectonic position in relation to all the others, as concentrating on the ultimate and perfect good in human things. For this reason, the philosopher says at the end of *Ethics* X that it is with politics that the philosophy concerned with human affairs is brought to completion.

8. Fourth, from what has been said we may gather the mode and order of a science of this sort. For just as speculative sciences, which consider some whole, perfect the knowledge of the whole by means of a consideration of the parts and principles, manifesting thus the passions [properties] and operations of the whole, so, too, this science, by considering the principles and parts of the state, transmits knowledge of it, manifesting its parts and passions and operations. And since it is practical, it manifests over and above how things may be brought to completion in particular cases, as is necessary in every practical science.*

Political Life, Natural to Man   *Summa of Theology* I, q. 96, a. 4

Government should be considered in two ways. In one way it is opposed to slavery; so a ruler is he to whom a slave is subject. In a second way it should be considered in opposition to any kind of subjection. According to this way, anyone whose office entitles him to rule and direct free men may also be called a ruler. The first kind of government or slavery or the rule of man by man did not exist in the state of innocence. When government is considered in the second way, however, even in the state of innocence, some men would have ruled others. The reason for this is that a slave differs from a free man insofar as the latter is "a free agent of his own actions," as is stated in *Metaphysics*. A slave, however, is related to another. Therefore someone is governed as a slave when he is controlled simply for the utility of the one governing him. But because everyone desires his own welfare, he cannot without regret yield this to another. Because such government cannot exist without suffering to those sub-

* Translated by P. H. Conway, O.P., and R. F. Larcher, O.P.

ject to it, such domination of man over man could never have been in the state of innocence.

A free man may be ruled by another when the latter directs him to his own good or to the common good. And such government over man by man would have existed, for two reasons, in the state of innocence. First, because man is a naturally social animal; men even in the state of innocence would have lived in society. Social life among many could not exist, however, unless someone took the position of authority to direct them to the common good. For many people are by their very multiplicity interested in a multiplicity of ends, while one person is concerned with one end. So in the beginning of *Politics*, the philosopher says: "Whensoever a plurality is ordered to one end, there is always found one in authority, directing." Second, if one man had a greater degree of knowledge and justice than others, it would be unfitting that these should not be used for the good of the others, as is said in I Pet. 4: "Everyone using the grace he has received for the benefit of his fellow men." So Augustine in *City of God* XIX, 14, says: "The just govern not by desire to dominate, but through the duty of giving counsel"; and in Chapter 15 he states: "This is prescribed by the natural order: for thus did God create man." And from this explanation we have the answer to all the objections concerning the first kind of government.

Political Order   *Summa of Theology* I–II, q. 72, a. 4

There is a threefold order necessary for man. The first comes from comparison with the rule of reason, inasmuch as all our actions and our passions should be measured by the rule of reason. Another order comes from comparison with the rule of the divine law, through which man ought to be directed in all things. If man were naturally a solitary animal, this double order would suffice; but because man is naturally a social and political animal, as is proved in *Politics* I, 2, it is necessary to have a third order, regulating man's conduct with the other men with whom he must live.

Nature of Law   *Summa of Theology* I–II, q.
                                     90, a. 1, a. 2 and ad. 3

Law is a certain rule or measure of action by which someone is led to act or restrained from acting. The word "law"
comes from *ligando* (binding), because by it we are obliged
or bound to act. But reason is the rule and measure of human
action, and reason is the first principle of human action, as is
clear from what we said elsewhere. For it is reason that
directs action to the end that is the first principle of acting,
according to the philosopher.

ad. 3. Reason has its power to move from the will, as was
said above; for from the fact that someone wills the end,
reason commands those things that are for the sake of that
end. But if the will is to have the authority of law in whatever
it commands, it must be regulated by reason. And only in
this way is to be understood the saying, "The will of the
prince has the force of law; in any other way the will of the
prince would be more iniquity than law. . . ."

Since every part is related to the whole as the imperfect
to the perfect, and since one man is a part of the perfect
community, it is necessary that the law be ordered properly
to the common welfare; so the philosopher, in defining law,
mentions both happiness and political communion. For he
says (*Ethics* V, 1): "We call that legal and just that establishes and keeps the welfare of the community through common political action"; for the perfect community is the city,
as was said in *Politics* I, 1.

Purpose of Law   *Summa of Theology* I–II, q.
                                     92, a. 1

It is evident that the purpose of law is to lead those subject
to it to their own virtue. And since virtue is "that which
makes its possessor good," it follows that the proper effect
of law is to make good those to whom it is given, either absolutely or in a certain respect. For if the intention of the
lawmaker is directed toward what is truly good, which is
the common good regulated according to divine justice, it
will follow that through law men will be made absolutely

good. If, however, the intention of the lawgiver is directed, not to what is absolutely good but to what is useful or pleasurable to him or repugnant to divine justice, then law does not make men good absolutely, but only in a certain respect, namely, insofar as it refers to some particular political regime. In this way good is found even in intrinsically evil things, as when someone is called a good thief because he operates expertly to attain his goal.

Eternal Law   *Summa of Theology* I–II, q. 93, a. 1

Just as with every artist there pre-exists the idea of what he will create by his art, so with every ruler there pre-exists an ideal of the order with regard to what should be done by those subject to his rule. And just as the ideal of those things that have yet to be produced by any art is called the art or exemplar of the things to be made, so the ideal of the ruler for the actions of his subjects has the quality of law insofar as the conditions mentioned above with respect to the ideal of law are present. Now, God by his wisdom is the creator of all things and may be compared to them as the artist is compared to the artifact, as was suggested in Part I. He is also the ruler of all actions and motions found in each creature, as was also shown in Part I. Hence just as the ideal of divine wisdom, as source of creation, has the quality of art or exemplar or ideal, so also the ideal of divine wisdom in moving all things to their proper end attains the quality of law. And according to this, the eternal law is nothing else than the ideal of divine wisdom, which is directive of all actions and motions.

All Law Comes from Eternal   *Summa of Theology* I–II, q.
Law   93, a. 3, c and ad. 2

In any ruling we see that the ideal of government flows from the government head to his subordinates, just as the plan of what should be done in a city flows from the king through statutes to the lower administrators; or, also, in artistic construction, the sketch of what is to be fashioned is passed from the architect to the lesser craftsmen. Since there-

fore the eternal law is the plan of government in the supreme
ruler, it is necessary that all plans for government that are
produced by lower officials should flow from the eternal law.
But the plans of lower officials are all other laws besides the
eternal law. Whence all laws insofar as they participate in
right reason flow from the eternal law. And on account of
this Augustine says in *On Free Choice* I, that "in temporal
law nothing is just and legitimate if men have not derived
it from the eternal law."

ad. 2. Human law has the quality of law insofar as it is
according to right reason; and accordingly it is clear that it
flows from the eternal law. Insofar as it deviates from reason,
it is called an unjust law, and thus it has the quality not of
law but more of violence. Nevertheless, even an unjust law,
insofar as it preserves something of likeness to law on account of its relationship to the authority of the lawmaker,
flows in this respect from the eternal law; "For all power is
from the Lord God," as is said in Rom. 13.

Need for Human Law   *Summa of Theology* I–II, q.
                                95, a. 1

It is clear from the foregoing that in man there is a natural
aptitude to virtuous action. But men can achieve the perfection of such virtue only by practicing a certain discipline.
And men who are capable of such discipline without help
from others are indeed rare. It is fitting therefore that we
should help one another to attain that discipline leading to
virtuous living. Some young men are, in fact, readily inclined
to a life of virtue by having a good natural disposition or
upbringing or especially by divine help, and for these the
paternal discipline through advice is sufficient. But because
there are others of evil disposition and prone to vice, who
cannot easily be moved by words, it is necessary to restrain
them from evil by fear. When they are thus kept from doing
evil, a quiet life is assured to others; and they are themselves
led eventually by force of custom to do voluntarily what
once they did only from fear and thus to practice virtue.
This kind of discipline, compelling by fear of punishment,
is the discipline of law. Hence it was necessary for the peace

and virtue of men that laws be enacted. And the philosopher says in *Politics* I, 2: "Man, if perfect in virtue, is the best of animals; but if he becomes separated from law and justice, he is the worst of animals. For man, unlike other animals, has the weapon of reason wherewith to exploit his base desires and cruelty."

Human Laws Subordinated to Natural Law	*Summa of Theology* I–II, q. 95, a. 2

. . . St. Augustine says in *On Free Choice* I, 5: "There is no law unless it be just." Whence in proportion to its justice a law has the force of law. But in human affairs something is called just insofar as it is right or accords with the rule of reason. But the first rule of reason is natural law, as was evident from the above. Hence all humanly enacted laws are in accord with reason to the extent that they flow from natural law. And if a human law disagrees in any particular with natural law, it will not be a law but a corruption of law.

But we should be aware that something may flow from natural law in two ways. First, as a conclusion from more general principles; second, as a determination from certain general principles. The first way is close to the scientific method, by which demonstrative conclusions are derived from first principles. The second way is like that of the arts, in which some common form is determined to a particular instance (as, for instance, when an architect, starting from the general idea of a house, then goes on to design the particular plan of this or that house). So, therefore, some derivations are made from the general principles of the natural law by way of formal conclusions—such as the conclusion, "Murder should not be done," which is derived from the general principle, "Do no evil to anyone." Other conclusions are reached as determinations of special cases. Thus the natural law prescribes that whoever sins shall be punished, but that a specific penalty should be the punishment is a particular determination of the natural law.

Both types of derivation are found in human law. Those reached the first way are sanctioned not only by human law, but by natural law as well; but those reached the second way have the force of human law alone.

Powers of Human Law
Summa of Theology I–II, q. 96, a. 1, c

. . . Whatever exists for the sake of some end must be proportionate to that end. But the end of law is the common good; for, as Isidore says (*Etymologies* II, 10): "Laws must be promulgated not in view of some private interest, but for the general benefit of the citizens." So human laws must be proportionate to the common good. But the common good is composed of many private goods. It is therefore necessary for the law to consider these many particular goods, both with respect to persons and to affairs and with respect to the times. For the political community is composed of many persons; and its good is obtained through many activities; nor is its welfare confined to any one time period but must be constant through successive generations of citizens, as Augustine says in *City of God* XXII, 6.

Limits of Human Law
Summa of Theology I–II, q. 96, a. 2

It is necessary that laws should be imposed on men according to their condition, since, as Isidore says (*Etymologies* II, 10), the law ought to be "possible both with respect to nature and with respect to the custom of the country." But the power or the faculty of acting proceeds from an interior habit or disposition; for not everything that is possible to a virtuous man is likewise possible to anyone without the habit of virtue, just as a child cannot do what a grown man can. And consequently the same law is not imposed upon children and adults; for children are allowed to do many things that are punished by law and even abhorred in adults. Likewise, many things are permitted to men still imperfect in virtue that would not be tolerated in virtuous men.

But a human law is promulgated for the sake of the majority of men, and the greater number of these are not perfect in virtue. And therefore human law does not prohibit every vice from which virtuous men abstain, but only the

graver vices from which the majority of men can abstain;
and especially those vices damaging to others and which unless prohibited would make it impossible for human society
to endure, such as murder, theft, etc., which are prohibited
by human law.

Law Related to the Common Good · Summa of Theology I–II, q. 96, a. 3

The object of the various virtues may be referred either
to the private good of some person, or to the common good
of the community; so, for instance, the virtue of fortitude
may be exercised by someone either for the preservation of
the state or for that of his friend; and likewise with respect
to other virtues. Law, however, as was said, is related to the
common good. And so there is no virtue whose practice may
not be prescribed by law. Nevertheless, the human law does
not prescribe all the acts of all the virtues, but only those
that may be directed toward the common good—either immediately (when some things are done directly for the sake
of the common good) or mediately (as when the legislator
enacts certain provisions relative to good discipline, through
which citizens are educated and accustomed to respect the
common good of justice and of peace).

Obligation of Human Law · Summa of Theology I–II, q. 96, a. 4, c

. . . Laws enacted by men are either just or unjust. If
they are just, they have the power to oblige in conscience
from the eternal law, from which they are derived; according
to Prov. 8: 15: "By me kings rule, and lawmakers decree just
laws." Now, laws are called just either with respect to their
end, as when they are directed to the common good; or with
respect to their author, as when the law enacted does not ex-
ceed the power of the lawmaker; or with respect to their
form, as when the burdens they impose are distributed equitably to promote the common good. For since every man is
part of the community, that which he is and possesses belongs to the community, just as any part as a part belongs
to the whole; whence nature allows harm to the part in order

to save the whole. And according to this principle, laws of such a kind that they distribute the burdens equitably are laws both binding in conscience and legal.

However, laws are unjust for two reasons. In one way they are unjust when they go against the human good, as contrary to what was previously established: either with respect to the end (as when some ruler enacts laws burdensome to his subjects and not directed to the common good, but directed more to his own gain and vanity), or with respect to their author (as when someone without jurisdiction makes laws), or finally with respect to their form (as when the burdens are distributed inequitably throughout the community). Laws like this have more in common with violence than with legality; as Augustine says in *On Free Choice* I, 5: "An unjust law is considered no law." Hence such laws do not oblige in conscience except perhaps to avoid scandal or disorder, for to avoid these a man may be obliged to yield his rights, as Matt. 5: 40–41: "Whoever will force you one mile, go with him another two; and if anyone should take away your coat, give him your cloak also."

Second, laws may be unjust by being contrary to the attainment of the divine good, such as tyrannical laws enforcing idolatry, or enforcing any other action against the divine law. Such laws may under no circumstances be obeyed, for as it is said in Acts 5: 29: "We must obey God rather than man."

Human Laws Coercive

Summa of Theology I–II, q. 96, a. 5, c and ad. 3

Law, as has been previously explained, has two essential characteristics: first, that it is a rule of human action; second, that it has coercive power. There are, therefore, two ways of being subject to law. In one way as one who is ruled is subject to the rule. And in this way all who are subject to a power are subject to the rule made by that power. There are, however, two ways of being not subject to a power. In one way when someone is wholly absolved from such subjection, as when the citizens of one state or kingdom are not subject to the laws of another nor to its ruler. In another way as when persons are subject to a higher law. So, for instance, one who is subject to a proconsul must obey his command except when dispensed by the emperor, for in those matters wherein he is subject to higher commands, he is not bound by the orders of a subordinate. In this case it happens that one subject to a certain law in principle is in some matters exempt from it when in these matters he is subject to a higher law.

The second way in which anyone may be said to be subject to the law is as one coerced by force. And in this way virtuous and just men are not subject to the law but only evil men. For whatever is forced and violent is contrary to the will. But the will of good men agrees with the law, whereas the will of wicked men disagrees with the law. And so in this sense the good men are not under the law, but only the wicked.

ad. 3. A ruler is said to be above the law with respect to its coercive force; for no one can be, strictly, forced by himself, and law has its coercive force only from the power of the ruler. So the prince is said to be above the law because if he should act against the law, no one can bring a condemnatory judgment against him. . . .

So in God's judgment, a ruler is not free from the directive power of law, but should freely and not through force obey the law. A ruler is above the law also insofar as he may, if it be expedient, change the law or dispense from it in respect to time and place.

Changeability of Human Law   *Summa of Theology* I–II, q. 97, a. 1

Human law, as was said above, is a certain dictate of reason by which human actions are directed. And for this reason, there can be two causes for changing human law justly. The first is on the part of reason; the second is on the part of men whose acts are regulated by law. On the part of reason, because it seems to be natural to human reason to proceed gradually from the imperfect to the perfect. So we see in the speculative sciences that those who first philosophized arrived at an inadequate view of things, which their successors later developed into something more perfect. It is the same likewise in practical affairs. For the first who intended to arrive at something useful to the human community, not able to consider everything themselves, established certain regulations, imperfect and deficient in many ways; these regulations were later modified by their successors so that those best adapted to promote the public interest were retained.

On the part of the men whose actions are regulated by law, the law can be rightly changed on account of altered human conditions, for different laws are required for different conditions. So, Augustine proposed this example in *On Free Choice* I, 6: "If a people is well-ordered, serious, and a very vigilant guardian of the public interest . . . . a law allowing them to elect their own magistrates to administer public affairs is justified. . . . But if that people should gradually become dishonest and the elections corrupt, and the government in the hands of dishonorable and criminal men, the power of appointing to office is rightly taken from such people, and the choice should be limited to the few and honest."

Limits of Changeableness   *Summa of Theology* I–II, q. 97, a. 2

As was said, a change in human law is justified only insofar as it benefits the public interest. Now, the very change of law is itself somewhat harmful to the general safety, because in the observance of law custom has great value—so much so that any action that is opposed to general custom, even if it should be itself inconsequential, seems more serious. Hence when law is changed, its coercive power is diminished by the setting aside of custom. Thus human law should never be changed unless the benefits accruing to the public interest are able to compensate for the harm done. This may happen either because some great and obvious aid comes from the new laws or because the customary law either involves clear injustice or its observance is excessively harmful. Hence it is said by a legal expert that "in setting up new constitutions, their usefulness must be very evident in order to renounce a law that has long been considered equitable."

Custom   *Summa of Theology* I–II, q. 97, a. 3, c and ad. 3

. . . all law proceeds from the reason and will of the legislator: divine and natural law from the rational will of God; human law from man's will regulated by reason. Now, man's reason and will are manifested in action both by word and deed; for the way one acts shows what one considers good. It is clear, however, that human law can be changed and explained by means of words insofar as they manifest the interior motives and concepts of human reason. In like manner law can be changed and explained by means of oft-repeated actions that result in custom; and hence new customs can arise having the force of law. For such exterior actions, frequently repeated, effectively declare the interior movement of the will and the concept of reason; for whatever is frequently done would seem to arise from a deliberate judgment of reason. And in this way custom has the force of law, may abolish law, and is the interpreter of law.

ad. 3. The community in which a custom is introduced may be of two conditions. If it is a free community able to make its own laws, the consent of the whole community in observing a certain custom has more power to enact a law than the authority of the ruler whose power to legislate derives from the fact that he represents the community. Whence it is permitted to the entire community, although not to single individuals, to establish a law. If, on the other hand, it is a community having no freedom to legislate for itself or to abrogate a law coming from some higher authority, a custom becoming established in such a community may yet attain the force of law insofar as it is tolerated by those whose duty it is to legislate for the community. For from the fact that it is so tolerated, it follows that the legislator approves what custom has established.

Legal and Moral Obligation   *Summa of Theology* I–II, q. 100, a. 9

. . . as was said above, a precept of law has coercive power: Whatever the law compels falls directly therefore under the precept of law. But the law's compelling power comes from the fear of punishment, as is said in *Ethics* X; for that strictly falls under the precept of law for which a legal penalty is inflicted. But divine law differs from human law in the imposition of its penalties. For a legal penalty is inflicted only for those matters about which the legislator is competent to judge, because the law punishes from a judgment made. Now, man, who is the legislator in human things, has competence for judging only in exterior acts, because "men see those things that appear," as is said in I Kings 16: 7. But only God, who is the divine lawgiver, can judge the interior movements of the will, according to Psalm 7: 10: "God is the searcher of hearts and reins."

Accordingly, we must say that the practice of virtue is in one respect subject both to human and divine law, while in another respect, it is subject to divine but not to human law. Again, there is a third sense, in which it is affected neither by divine nor by human law. Now, the practice of virtue consists in three things, according to the philosopher in *Ethics* II, 4. The first of these is that a person should act consciously. And this is subject to judgment both by divine and human law; for whatever a man does in ignorance, he does accidentally. Whence in judging whether something is punishable or pardonable according to human law as well as according to divine law, the question of ignorance must be considered.

The second point is that a man should act voluntarily, or deliberately, choosing a particular action for its own sake. This requires a twofold interior motion of the will and of intention, and of these we have spoken previously. Not human law but only divine law is the judge of these two. For human law does not punish the person who wills to kill and does not kill, although divine law does punish him (Matt. 5: 22): "Whosoever is angry with his brother shall be in danger of the judgment."

The third point is that a man should act upon a firm and unchangeable principle; and such firmness strictly proceeds from a durable disposition, as when a man acts from a rooted habit. And in this case the practice of virtue does not fall under the precept either of divine or of human law, for no man

is punished either by God or man for transgressing the law
if he duly honors his parents, although he may not have the
durable disposition of piety.

Virtues   *Summa of Theology* I–II, q.
                               55, a. 4, c

We have the authority of Augustine, from whose words
principally (*On Free Choice* II, 19) we have assembled
this definition.

This definition perfectly contains the fully essential notion
of virtue, for from all its causes is assembled the perfect essential notion of anything. Now, the definition given above
includes all of virtue's causes. For the formal cause of virtue
as of all else is taken from its genus and difference when it is
defined as *a good quality*, for *quality* is the genus of virtue,
and the *difference*, *good*. But if we substituted *habit*, the
proximate genus for *quality*, we would have a more appropriate definition.

As with all accidents, there is no *matter* out of which virtue
is formed, but it has matter about which it is concerned and
matter in which it exists, namely, the subject. The object of
virtue is the matter about which it is concerned, and this
could not be contained within the definition, since the object
places the virtue in a given species, and we are here defining
virtue in general. And so the subject acts as material cause
and is expressed when we state that virtue is a good quality
of the mind.

The end or purpose of virtue, an operative habit, is action.
But we should note that some operative habits are always
directed to evil, like vices or vicious habits. Others are sometimes directed to good, sometimes to evil. Thus opinion is
concerned both with the true and the untrue, but virtue is a
habit always directed to the good, and so its differentiation
from those habits always directed to evil is expressed in the
words "by which we live righteously"; and its differentiation
from those habits sometimes directed to the good, sometimes
to evil, is expressed in the words "of which no one makes bad
use."

Finally, God is the efficient cause of infused virtue, to

which this definition applies, and this is expressed in the words "which God works in us without us." With the omission of this phrase the rest of the definition applies to all virtues in general, acquired or infused.

Summary of Theology I–II, q.
61, a. 5, c

Macrobius, in his *Commentary on the Dream of Scipio* I, says: "Plotinus along with Plato, outstanding among teachers of philosophy, says: 'There is a fourfold kind of virtue. First of all, there are social virtues; second, there are perfecting virtues; third, there are perfect virtues; and fourth, there are exemplary virtues.'"

As Augustine declares in *On the Morals of the Catholic Church* VI, the soul in order to be virtuous must follow something. This is God, whom to follow is to live rightly. So that just as in God the types of all things pre-exist, the exemplar of human virtue must pre-exist in God. In this way virtue may be said to exist primordially in God, so that we speak of *exemplary* virtues. Thus in God the divine mind itself may be spoken of as prudence; while temperance is the centering of God's gaze upon himself, just as in us prudence is that whereby the passions are conformed to reason. God's fortitude is his unchangeableness; his justice is the observance of the eternal law in his works, as Plotinus asserts.

Moreover, because man is a social animal by nature, these virtues that are in man according to the human condition are called *social* virtues, since through them man behaves well in human affairs. . . .

Yet since it is fitting for man to do all he can to strive toward the divine reality, as the philosopher himself says in *Ethics* X, 7, and as Scripture often exhorts us—for example: "Be ye . . . perfect, as your heavenly Father is perfect" (Matt. 5: 48), there must be virtues between the exemplary or divine virtues and the social or human virtues. These virtues are differentiated by their motion and goal; some are virtues of men on the way of tending toward divine likeness, and these are called perfecting virtues. So, prudence by contemplating divine realities, does not overestimate things of earth, but directs all to God; fortitude keeps the soul from fearing to neglect the body and rising to divine things; and justice is the soul's wholehearted consent to all this. In addition, there are the virtues of those already enjoying divine likeness; these are the *perfect* virtues.

Unbelief and the Law   *Summa of Theology* II–II, q. 12, a. 2

. . . as was said above, unbelief is not in itself contradictory to public authority, since the latter derives from the law of nations, which is human law. But the distinction between believer and unbeliever is according to divine law, which does not destroy human law.

War and Morality   *Summa of Theology* II–II, q. 40, a. 1

Three conditions are necessary for a just war. First, that the ruler have the authority to declare war. A private individual may not declare war, for he can rely on his superior's judgment to protect his rights; nor has he any right to mobilize the people, which must be done in war. But since responsibility for public action is committed to the rulers, they are charged with the defense of the city, the kingdom, or the province subject to them. And just as in punishing criminals they are justly defending the state with the civil arm against all internal disturbance; as the Apostle says (Rom. 13: 4): "Not without cause does he carry a sword; for he is God's minister, an avenger to execute wrath upon him who doth evil," so also they are responsible to defend the state against external foes with war weapons. Rulers are told in Psalm 81: "Rescue the poor; and deliver the needy out of the hand of the sinner." Hence Augustine says in *Against Faustus* XXIII, 73: "To maintain peace within the natural order of men, rulers require the power and decision to declare war."

Second, a just cause is required, so that those who are attacked for some fault merit such an attack. Hence Augustine says in *Eighty-three Questions:* "Those wars are usually defined as just that avenge injuries, as when a nation or state should be punished for neglecting to amend some injury inflicted or to restore what was taken unjustly."

Third, a right intention on the belligerents' part is required —either to promote some good or to avoid some evil. Hence Augustine says in the book *On the Lord's Words:* "For the true worshipers of God even wars are peaceful, not waged out of greed or cruelty, but from the zeal for peace, to restrain evil or to assist the good. But it can happen that even if war is waged by legitimate authority with just cause, nevertheless the war may be made unjust through evil intention. For Augustine says in *Against Faustus* LXXIV: "The desire to hurt, the cruelty of vendetta, the implacable and severe spirit, arrogance in winning, the thirst for power and such things—all these are rightly condemned in war."

Revolution and Tyranny *Summa of Theology* II–II, q. 42, a. 2, c

. . . Tyrannical government is unjust because it is not directed to the common good but to the private good of the ruler, as is clear from the philosopher in *Politics* III and *Ethics* VIII. Therefore the overthrow of such government is not strictly sedition, unless perhaps when accompanied by such disorder that the community suffers greater harm than from the tyrannical government. A tyrant is himself, moreover, far more seditious when he spreads discord and strife among the people subject to him so that he may dominate them more easily. For tyranny is the directing of affairs to the private benefit of the ruler with harm to the community.

Private Property *Summa of Theology* II–II, q. 66, a. 1

. . . External things may be looked at in two ways. First, as to their nature; and the nature of things is not subject to human power, but only to divine power, whose will all things obey. Second, as to the use of such things; and in this way man has a natural control over external things, because through his reason and will he can use external things for his own advantage, as though they were made for him, for things less perfect exist for the benefit of the more perfect, as was said above. And by this reasoning the philosopher proves in *Politics* I that the possession of external things is natural to man. This natural control over other creatures, which man possesses by his reason, which makes him the image of God, is made evident in the very creation of man, Genesis 1, where it is said: "Let us make man to our own image and likeness, and he shall rule over the fish of the sea. . . ."

Limits of Private Property   *Summa of Theology* II–II, q. 66, a. 2, c and ad. 1

. . . Man should consider two points with respect to external possessions. One of these is the power of acquiring and disposing. Private possession is permissible in this respect, and it is likewise necessary for human life, for three reasons: first, because everyone is more careful to procure something that concerns himself alone than something that is common to all or to many others (for each one, escaping work, leaves for the other man any common task, as happens when there are a great many officials); second, because human affairs are handled in a more orderly fashion when each one goes about his own business, there would be complete confusion if everyone tried to do everything; third, because this leads to a more peaceful condition for man, while everyone is content with what he has. Hence we see that among those possessing something in common, disputes arise more often.

The other point that concerns man with regard to external things is their use. And in respect to this, man should not hold external things for his own use but for the common benefit, so that each one should readily share material things with others in their need. Whence the Apostle says (Tim. 1), "Charge the rich of this world to give easily, to communicate to others."

ad. 1. The possession of things in common is attributed to natural law, not because natural law decrees that all things should be held in common and that there should be no private possession, but because there is no distinction of property according to natural law but rather according to human agreement, which belongs to positive law, as was said above.

Hence private property is not opposed to natural law but is an addition to natural law devised by human reason.

Obligation to Share Property   *Summary of Theology* II–II, q. 66, a. 7, c

. . . What belongs to human law cannot abrogate what is required by natural law or divine law. Now, according to the natural order founded by divine providence, material things are ordered to the alleviation of human needs. Therefore, the division and ownership of things that proceed from human law must not interfere with the alleviation of human needs by those things. Likewise, whatever a man has in superabundance is owed of natural right to the poor for their sustenance. So Ambrose says, and it is also found in Gratian's Decree XLVII: "The bread that you withhold belongs to the hungry; the clothing that you store away to the naked; and the money that you bury in the earth is the redemption and security of the penniless." But because there are many who suffer need, and they cannot all be assisted from the same source, it is entrusted to the will of the individuals to provide from their own wealth assistance to those suffering need. If, however, there is such urgent and obvious need that there is clearly an immediate emergency for sustenance, as when any person is immediately endangered without means of alleviation, then he may legitimately take from another person's goods what he needs, either openly or secretly. Nor is this, strictly speaking, fraud or robbery.

Obedience   *Summary of Theology* II–II, q. 104, a. 1, c and ad. 1, ad. 3

Just as the actions of natural things proceed from natural forces, so also do human actions proceed from the human will. Now, in natural things it is necessary for higher things to move lower ones to their actions by reason of the divinely conferred excellence of the natural power. Hence also in human affairs, it is necessary for superiors to move inferiors through their will in virtue of the authority established by God. But to move through reason and will is to command. And so just as in the natural order instituted by God, inferior natural things must be subordinated to the movement of higher things, so likewise in human affairs, inferiors are obliged to obey their superiors according to the order of natural and divine law.

Limits of Obedience   *Summa of Theology* II–II, q. 104, a. 1, c and ad. 1, ad. 3

As already stated, the obedient man is moved to the command of the ruler by a certain necessity of justice, just as a natural thing is moved by some naturally necessitated motion. . . . Likewise, there can be two reasons why a subject is not obliged to obey his superior in all things. First, on account of a command of a higher power. The Gloss says in reference to the text of St. Paul, Romans 13: ". . . Therefore when the Emperor commands one thing and God another, one should ignore the former and obey the latter." Another way in which the inferior is not obliged to obey his superior occurs when the latter commands something in matters where he is without authority. For, as Seneca says in *On Services* III, 20: "He errs who thinks that slavery includes the whole man: his best part escapes it. The body is enslaved and subjected to a master, but the mind is free." And so in those things depending upon the interior movement of the will, man is not obliged to obey man but only God. Man, however, is obliged to obey man in regard to external bodily actions; but even here in what regards the nature of the body he is not obliged to obey man, but only God, for all men are equal by nature. Such is the case in reference to sustaining the body and the procreation of children. Hence in the contracting of matrimony or making a vow of chastity or such things servants are not obliged to obey their masters, nor children their parents. But in what has to do with the disposition of human actions and dealings, a subject is obliged to obey his superior in the sectors of their superiority, just as a soldier obeys his general in matters of war; a servant, his master in the tasks assigned him; a son, his father in matters included in the discipline and management of family life, etc.

ad. 1. As was said previously, servitude by which one man is subject to another man, belongs to the body; not to the

soul, which remains free. Now, in the state of this life we are
freed from defects of soul by the grace of Christ; not, however, from bodily defects, as is clear through the Apostle
(Rom. 7), who says of himself that "he obeys the law of God
with his mind, but the law of sin with his flesh." And so those
who become sons of God through grace are free from the
spiritual servitude to sin, but not, however, from bodily
servitude, by which they are bound to temporal masters, as
the Gloss says in the commentary upon I Timothy 6: 1: "All
are under the yoke of servitude . . . ."

ad. 3. Man is bound to obey secular rulers to the extent
that the order of justice requires. Therefore if rulers have no
just title to power, but have usurped it; or if they command
unjust things, their subjects are not obliged to obey them, except perhaps in some cases in order to avoid scandal or
danger.

Need for a Divine Law   *Summa of Theology* I–II, q. 91, a. 4, c

Besides natural law and human law it was necessary that
there should be divine law to direct human life, and this for
four reasons. First, because it is by law that man is directed
to proper actions in relation to his final end. And if man were
destined to an end that was not out of all proportion to the
natural power of man, it would not be necessary for him to
have any directive on the part of reason beyond the natural
law and the humanly enacted law derived from it. But because man is ordained to an end of eternal happiness that
is out of proportion to natural human power, as indicated
above, it was necessary that he be directed to this end not
merely by natural and human law but by divinely given law.
Second, on account of the uncertainty in human judgment,
especially in contingent and specific matters, it often happens
that quite diverse judgments are passed by different people
on human actions leading to diverse and contrary laws. So
that man might know without any doubt what he should both
do and avoid, it was necessary for his acts to be directed by a
divinely given law, where error is known to be impossible.
Third, because man can only make a law in regard to things

that he can judge. But the judgment of man cannot penetrate to the interior motives, which are hidden but can only reach the exterior actions, which appear. Nevertheless, the perfection of virtue requires that man should be upright in both kinds of action. And since human law cannot sufficiently regulate and order interior actions, it was necessary that divine law should be given to do this. Fourth, because as Augustine says in *On Free Choice* I, human law can neither punish nor even prohibit all that is evilly done, for while desirous of preventing all that is evil, it would destroy much that is good, and therefore it would impede what is useful for the common good and hence necessary for human development. So that no evil should remain unprohibited and unpunished, it was necessary that there should come a divine law through which all sins are forbidden.

MAN AS RELIGIOUS

Just as the philosophy of Thomas Aquinas is present not only in his commentaries and systematic works but also in his mystical and Biblical ones, so his religious and theological thought appears in the midst of discussions of mundane things and technical academic problems. But this is to be expected of someone who holds, as Thomas Aquinas did, that all views about creatures are relevant to the truth about the Creator. Although Aquinas deeply appreciated the need to formulate whatever is understandable in divine revelation, he never lost sight of the fact that man's happiness lies not in scientific knowledge but in continuous union with God: "Not merely learning about divine things but also experiencing them—which does not come from mere intellectual acquaintance with the terms of scientific theology, but from loving the things of God and clearing to them by affection" (Thomas Aquinas, *Commentary on Divine Names* XI, 4). For the "Word of God the Father breathes love" (*Commentary on St. John's Gospel* VI, 5). That is why Thomas Aquinas meditated and studied and memorized and commented on Scripture; yet the name of Aquinas has been overly identified with the famous *Summas*.

So we see that it would be inaccurate to suppose that St. Thomas equated "faith" with the content of the *Summa of Theology*. The *Summa* was an attempt to formulate Scripture, an ever-flowing river of revelation that can never channel the sea. Aquinas was aware that the Hebrew prophets and the Christian Apostles experienced encounters with Yahweh and with Christ within the events of history. These were privileged events insofar as they were saving events—and the record of these encounters was transmitted to believers through tradition and Scripture. There were signs of the truth of the Christian faith, but such signs are recognizable only by those with faith. Faith therefore remains a gift. It contains knowledge about a transcendent personal being who freely reveals himself to men. As commentator on Scripture, Aquinas never tried to suppress the questions that arose. Yet the discussion of such questions required theological rather than spiritual exegesis. There could but result a Biblical theology that is also a theology of history. As he put it: "Since sacred teaching intends to deal with divine things, since also a thing is understood to be divine inasmuch as it is related to God as its principle or its end . . . this teaching will consider things as coming forth from God as from their principle, and as being brought back to God as to their end." The theologian is really studying history—free actions—considered in relation to God. Revelation is the Word of God in history, in Scripture, in the Church where the Holy Spirit dwells. None of these forms or modes of God's presence may substitute for the God they reveal. All modes point to one Being, a presence who reveals me to myself. He is the uncreated one who is able to be present to himself, to the world, and to man, a person who is with God within history, which is wholly ordered in love toward God. This is the Augustinian "economy," which includes grace, for it is the "order of love" where all nature is related to God by the divine desire we call "grace." Therefore no form or mode of God's presence is the object of our faith. Faith is the contact of created reality with uncreated reality so that we may say that the object of faith, understood this way, is a subject, a presence of the tripersonal God.

Now, it is the role of the Church to witness to revelation as did the Prophets, the Apostles, and Christ, but after many centuries of human history there is needed a wealth of historical knowledge to recognize what was revealed, what belongs to tradition and Scripture. It should be admitted that historical scholarship was lacking at the time of Aquinas, and he did not attempt to establish the supernatural nature of revelation. He took it for granted. But he would have been the last to identify our understanding of revelation with the divine reality that is revealed, as he would have been the last to claim that any finite statement is final. His words in the *Summa of Theology* had only the humble role of trying to explain God's action in the world. The soul turns toward the reality behind the words. The believer or the theologian wants to experience God, not the knowledge of God. Aquinas knew full well that because God is transcendent, God will always be ultimately mysterious to us; yet because men are intelligent beings, they will seek to understand whatever they can of the divine mysteries. Men cannot live without revelation, and therefore rationalists exaggerate when they claim for man a power to know all the truths and values man needs to know.

If one views the *Summa of Theology* in isolation from its aim, it is far too easy to conclude that Aquinas overstressed the conceptual content of revelation. But it is advisable to admit that the *Summa* was written for teachers of "beginners in the faith," to serve that sacred teaching God gave us. Such beginners are led from what they know to what they do not know, from what they believe to a formulation that makes their faith more accessible to them. Naturally, a *Summa of Theology* written in the thirteenth century would be a development or explication of the faith marked by patristic and medieval culture. Or St. Thomas's readers may be semibelievers, accepting some truths and not others, and then St. Thomas will be concerned to show that those truths not accepted are in fact entailed in those the reader does believe. Yet unbelievers who are potential beginners in the faith will find in the *Summa* reasoned arguments concerning God's existence and the soul's immortality, a natural theology that never could usurp the place of faith/revelation, but then what sense would there be in approaching an unbeliever from the standpoint of faith?

Aquinas gives to reason the function of removing obstacles to the leap of faith. We do not find reason here attempting to prove the principles or premises of God's sacred teaching (*sacra doctrina*). Sacred teaching has declared the purpose of human existence and thereby ended its ambiguity. But this *kerygma* or divine message for man has to be made explicit if absurdity is to be banished. But this never means that it therefore is easy to accomplish. If divine revelation was accomplished by deeds that were recorded in words, it is fitting that its theological expression should be a call or challenge to action. This is what the call to salvation is—an end or goal to be freely achieved. This is God's real creation, and man's, too. Since natural creation is a call, and since supernatural revelation is a call, then neither is the theological formulation of revelation simply for the sake of increasing one's knowledge. God's knowledge may not be dichotomized into Aristotle's two types of knowledge—speculative and practical—and so if by faith we participate in God's knowledge, the truths of faith expressed in dogmas or articles are presented as ends to be accomplished, not as essences. Faith is concerned with the future.

Now, if St. Thomas's claim that "sacred teaching" is a science should seem to put him on the side of dogma as merely speculative, we should remind ourselves that for St. Thomas the word "science" above all denoted knowledge with certainty, but the certainty is God's. If God's knowledge is the most certain kind, and if our participation by faith in his knowledge lets us share that certainty about what is supremely worth knowing—God himself—then sacred teaching surpasses in dignity all other sciences. If we regard our own limited intelligence, then nothing is more doubtworthy than revelation, because it utterly escapes verification; but if we keep attentive to God, who reveals himself, then revealed truth provides greater certitude than all human sensations and judgments.

St. Thomas is clearer than his critics about reason's role in regard to the articles of faith or the principles of sacred teaching. Reason cannot prove their truth but can draw conclusions that participate in their truth, and this is a reasonable way for man to use his reason, since it would be highly unlikely that rational man should not use his reason on what means most to him—the God who created and called him both to be and to become perfect, i.e., whole.

Today Catholics are becoming more self-conscious as believers by retracing the paths along which faith has come, exploring the sources of revelation, making an enormous effort to understand revelation by distinguishing between the original data and the development of these data in history. To do this a man must relive Church history, and inasmuch as the Church has moved forward a great deal since the thirteenth century, no one may simply repeat what St. Thomas said as if nothing more remains to be said. Yet it is true that an understanding of how St. Thomas expressed the faith theologically is a necessary step to take before expressing that same faith in new formulations.

Theology would be untrue to itself if it ever ceased to be born of the theologian's communing with the Word of God. It is a sacred science only insofar as it communicates this Word. Hence the *Summa of Theology* was not written apart from Biblical influence. In it Aquinas quotes from all the books of the Old Testament except Abdias and Aggeus as well as from all the New Testament books except the Epistles to Philemon. He recognized that the infallible criteria for all dogma claiming to belong to God's sacred teaching are canonical Scripture and divine tradition. In guiding the Church to remain faithful to this divine revelation, the Holy Spirit renders the Church infallible when she teaches solemnly concerning dogma and morals, just as the men who wrote the Scriptures were infallible because they wrote under the inspiration of the Holy Spirit. Only because God in the Apocalypse declared himself the Alpha and Omega, the beginning and the end, did St. Thomas make use of philosophy to show what this would mean regarding God's being: that God must be self-subsistent and therefore only one. Therefore, all other things are beings by participation, and so made by God. This is what God's being the Efficient and Final Cause of all means. Calling God also the Exemplary Cause is not a mere aping of Platonists, who made much of exemplarism; it is likewise a truth grounded in revelation: "Let us make man to our image and likeness" (Gen. 1: 26). Because God expresses his own perfections in the things we experience, the scholastics were led to identify the Platonic forms or ideas with the divine Essence as Exemplary Cause—certainly a development of Platonism under Biblical influence.

Neoplatonic categories in their "synthetic stretch" as well as Aristotelian categories in their analytic precision have, through the alchemy of Aquinas, become subject to the logic of the Incarnation—a logic of largesse with possibilities as yet unknown to us. And thus the dialectical framework of an Abelard, the psychological framework of a Peter Lombard are not so much superseded as subsumed in the immensity of an ontology of existence, the least inadequate of all schemas for dealing with the historical process of the created universe whose intelligibility is never achieved apart from the personal category of "freedom."

It was likewise from Scripture, not from the Plotinian triad of one, *nous,* world soul that Augustine and Aquinas learned of the tripersonal nature of God. It was scriptural revelation of God as triune that permitted the Augustinian analogy from the human soul to the Trinity. That the Son was Word belonged to revealed data, as did his role as perfect image; that the Holy Spirit was love also belonged to revealed data. This allowed Augustine to see in man's life of knowing and loving a reflection of the intimate life of God. Because of what Christ said concerning his Father and the Holy Spirit, men felt justified in using metaphysical reasoning and psychological analogy to indicate that if one was "from the other," there was process, therefore relation as well as opposition and, consequently, distinction. In such a situation relations, even opposing ones, are identified with substance; and so in the divine reality "being a person" means "being a subsistent relation"; therefore to be God is to be tripersonal. The Trinity remains a strict mystery, but it is intelligible in the sense that it is shown by metaphysical reflection not to be repugnant to reason. If, as we learn from revelation, there are three persons in God, then each must be God, and God must be tripersonal, for only by thinking of what it would mean to be a relation that was wholly substantial and wholly relational can we make any sense of what we are saying when we speak of God as Trinity.

This is why St. Thomas's theology is essentially independent of physical theories—it is based not upon the data of experience but upon divine revelation. As a theologian, Aquinas sees himself as well as the teaching church or *magisterium* as a servant of revelation. No theologian is autonomous, nor is the *magisterium* autonomous. As a servant of revelation in the *Summa of Theology,* St. Thomas illustrates his fidelity by considering what God has said of himself as origin and end of all creatures and as savior of men in Christ. When he proposes objections to the Church's teaching, Aquinas aims to show how faith and reason can assist in answering them. He does not claim to speak with finality or infallibility. He respectfully refers to the authority of the Fathers of the Church and uses philosophical sources to discuss things.

But he follows a strictly theological order: God creates

men, who return to God through good human actions accomplished in Christ, who gives men access to the trinitarian life of divine fellowship. Within this over-all pattern of origin and return, Aquinas considers almost every speculative and moral question. His precision or brevity is not intended to suggest that all is easy to know and easy to do, but in the interest of systematic theology he tries to cover all aspects as neatly as possible. This terseness necessarily eliminates an elaboration that may well be necessary to postmedieval believers whose whole culture cannot be counted on for an understanding of Catholic faith. So it is that some of the significance of Aquinas's statements can be missed in this latter day. Take the much misunderstood question of the sacraments. It is far too usual to encounter those who think that the famous expression *ex opere operato* means that the seven sacraments give grace or participation in divine life mechanically or automatically, almost magically. First of all, this expression only appears in Aquinas's earliest work on the *Sentences*. Moreover, material objects like water and oil are called the "matter" of each sacrament; the spoken formulas are called the "form," giving meaning to the sacrament; but for St. Thomas matter plus form does not simply add up to a divine communication of divinity. No, the "form of the words" is the Word of Faith found in the Church. And so when Aquinas says that the efficacy of the sacrament comes from the form (*ex opere operato*), he is saying that the sacrament is constituted by Christ. It is independent of us but not independent of Christ, who constitutes it, for indeed a sacrament can be made only by God as his gift. And because Christ the Savior constitutes the sacraments, he is present in each with saving power for every human need. But just as Christ's presence with the Apostles did not free them from making personal efforts, so Christ's presence in the sacraments will not save man without man's cooperation. Here is applied that general Thomistic principle that whatever is received is received according to the mode of the recipient. Therefore sacraments do not confer grace upon us as though we were things but as men having free will to respond, men of responsibility. They are part of a larger vision of the world as a re-creation. In the Old Testament the

transcendent personal God dealt with men in the Jewish community; now the world community is destined to become
one man, the new man (Eph. 2: 15), "one person" (Gal.
3: 28), "perfect man" (Eph. 4: 13) in Christ, who through
his Incarnation became head or lord of a new kingdom where
the Church is the privileged but not the only channel of
grace, so that those who are reborn of the Church sacramentally are born of God, whose people are united in love or
grace through the Holy Spirit abiding in the Church, whence
he carries on the divine economy or the religious education
of man, giving men a fuller understanding of the divine
reality that they contact by faith.

So St. Thomas Aquinas would not have agreed that the
definitions of Nicaea and Constantinople represent a "Hel-
lenization of the Christian faith." This position suggests that
original "faith" by contact with Greek philosophy was transformed into metaphysical dogmas found in the great creeds
as if the "original faith," inasmuch as it was "revelation received" and not "revelation expressed," was not itself an
interpretation influenced by the Hebraic culture of those receiving it. The question of whether the faith should be
preached to the generations of classically educated people in
the patristic and medieval periods so as to be understandable
to them in terms of their customary categories of thought
was almost another Peter-Paul controversy, i.e., it was a question of whether Christ's teaching was to be Catholic, universal, or confined to the Jewish people, whether all people were
to be God's chosen people.

But since, as we said at the outset, Aquinas wrote the
Summa of Theology to assist learners toward a better awareness of what they believed, he looked upon philosophical
argument as subservient or ancillary to the understanding of
the sacred teaching of the salvific message, the *kerygma,*
while holding for philosophy's autonomy. And so today if
philosophy does not help some believers to know better what
they believe, then philosophy should not be forced upon
them. Aquinas readily admitted that man had many ways to
obtain knowledge. Besides reason there is intuition, and besides the intellectual approach to reality, there is the affective approach, Pascal's heart reasons. Aquinas spoke of

knowledge by connaturality or inclination, an experienced awareness, the type of knowledge of morality possessed by good men. One may have a feeling for what is right, and there is also liturgical experience to educate men in what they believe. But if dogma is relative to changes in human culture, it is also true that there is development likewise in human feelings with which liturgical experiences must keep pace.

Aquinas never hesitated to change where change was justified. Most of the patristic commentators had discussed the "spiritual" meaning of the Bible. M. L. Lamb, in his preface to the valued translation of the *Commentary on St. Paul's Epistle to the Ephesians*, credits Aquinas with taking a great step forward in Biblical scholarship by distinguishing the "psychological and theological structures operative in the transmission of revelation." Aquinas, recognizing the instrumental nature of prophetic or Biblical communication, saw that the divine choice of Biblical writers included the individual's talents as well as his cultural gifts and literary skills. The inspired author, like any instrumental cause, has, in St. Thomas's view, his own contribution to make, but this must be distinguished from what the instrument is doing or saying under the power of God, the principal cause. Because Thomistic psychology gave to the image an indispensable role in knowledge, the image or sensible action in Scripture provides a literal sense that calls for discovery, inasmuch as it is in and through this literal sense that any idea or spiritual meaning can be grasped.

Like Christ incarnate, Scripture is both human and divine. It is a disservice to Christianity to ignore or eliminate the human meaning; and thus the work of historical restoration is required. Like all historical restoration, that of the Bible demands competent and dedicated scholars. Their task is difficult, but like the original authors of Scripture, they are expressing the meaning of faith.

While we can find in St. Thomas's scriptural attitudes an implicit respect for literary forms used by writers, he himself lacked the scholarly tools since made available to exegetes, and yet his scriptural commentaries reveal the theological questions that concerned medieval men and indicate that Scripture rather than Aristotle was the source of much of the Thomistic theological thinking. Yet as a teacher in a thirteenth-century medieval university there would cling to his expression of Christian truth the mark of his own culture characterized by the intellectual excitement of the rediscovery of Aristotle in Arabian terms. This cultural element in the human environment of this Christian teacher would mark his style just as surely as the speech of Peter showed him to be a Galilean. As M. D. Chenu so well said in his indispensable work *Toward Understanding St. Thomas,* "Let us expel the idea, modern in its origin and still plaguing us today, that there was an opposition between scholastic and positive theology. Controversy against Protestantism, and later, rationalism has brought about, as a result of the demands of polemic, a dislocation of that internal unity of theological knowledge within which St. Thomas and his contemporaries labored—I was going to say, breathed. St. Thomas was a Master of Theology, he commented upon Scripture . . . yet the very pith of his work was Scriptural, and his theology had as its roots the Gospel Movement of his day. . . ."

Hence the communication of truth by older theologians like Augustine and Aquinas to present and future Christians must also follow the slow path of proceeding from the *Sitz im Leben* to the meaning of the passage. A certain familiarity with the culture is required. Once released, the "meaning" like seed can be cast into the soil of new cultural conditions and continue to be fruitful. Yet only through the study of archaeology, paleontology, philology, and many other ancillary sciences having a contribution to make to our understanding of the *Sitz im Leben* is the meaning of Scripture released so that it may capture new relevance.

We are in the spirit of St. Thomas when instead of repeating him, we renew him. To keep young, the world of thought must change.

1. THEOLOGICAL VIRTUES AND REVELATION

Advantage of Faith   *Commentary on Apostles'
                                Creed,* a. 1

None of the philosophers before the coming of Christ could by bending all effort to the task know as much about God and things necessary for eternal life as after the coming of Christ a little old woman knows through her faith.

Faith   *Summa of Theology* II–II, q.
                                1, a. 1, c

The object of every science includes two things: first, what is materially known and is, one might say, the material object, and second, that by which it is known, or the formal aspect of an object. Hence in the science of geometry the conclusions are what is materially known, whereas the medium of demonstration, whereby the conclusions are deduced, is the formal aspect of the science.

So if in faith we are referring to the object's formal aspect, this is nothing other than the first truth. For the faith we mean only assents to what is revealed by God. Thus the medium through which faith comes is the divine truth. But if we are referring to what faith assents to, materially, not only God but many other things are included, and yet they only fall within the assent of faith as related to God, since through some effects of the divine action, man is assisted on his way toward the enjoyment of God. So even from this viewpoint the object of faith is the first truth, since what falls within faith does so insofar as it is related to God, just as the medical art's object is health, since it considers things only in relation to health.

Faith, Both Intellectual and Voluntary *Summa of Theology* II–II, q. 2, a. 2, c

Action from a power or a durable disposition depends upon how the power or disposition is related to its object. But there are three aspects to the object of faith. Because *to believe* is the intellect's act insofar as the will moves it to assent . . . the object of faith can be referred to intellect or to the will, which moves the intellect.

In reference to intellect, two things are notable with regard to faith's object: One of these is the material object of faith, and in this sense an act of faith is *to believe in a God* (since, as explained, only what refers to God is proposed to our faith); the other is the formal aspect of the object—this is the medium whereby we assent to this or that point of faith, and in this way an act of faith is *to believe God* because, as explained, the formal object of faith is the first truth, to which man adheres so that for its sake he assents to whatever he believes.

Third, if we look at the object of faith in respect to the intellect as moved by the will, an act of faith is *to believe in God;* for the first truth is related to the will under its aspect of end.

Good Intended in Faith *Summa of Theology* II–II, q. 4, a. 3, c

. . . The act of faith is directed to the object of the will, i.e., the good, as to its end; and this good that is the end of faith, the divine good, is the proper object of charity, so that insofar as the act of faith is perfected and formed through charity, charity is called the form of faith.

Hope *Summa of Theology* II–II, q. 17, a. 6, c

A theological virtue is one having God as that to which it adheres. This adherence occurs in two ways: first, for its own sake; second, because through it something else is had.

Thus charity makes us cling to God for his own sake, uniting
our minds to God by the emotion of love.

Hope and faith, on the other hand, make man cling to
God as to a principle whereby other things come to us. Now,
from God we get both knowledge of truth and perfect goodness, so that faith makes us cling to God as our source in
knowing the truth since we believe that what God declares
is true, whereas hope makes us cling to God as our source
of perfect goodness, i.e., inasmuch as through hope we trust
the divine assistance to become happy.

Charity   *Summa of Theology* II–II, q.
                                      23, a. 1, c

According to the philosopher (*Ethics* VIII, 2, 3) not all
love can be characterized as friendship, only love expressing
benevolence, i.e., loving someone by wanting his good. But
if we do not want good for the one we love, but for ourselves (as we are said to love wine, or a horse, etc.), it is a
sort of concupiscence rather than love of friendship. For to
speak of having friendship for wine or for a horse is absurd.

Yet friendship does not amount to well-wishing but requires mutual love, inasmuch as friendship is between friend
and friend, and well-wishing itself is based upon a kind of
communication.

Thus, since God communicates his happiness to us, there
must be between man and God a communication upon which
some kind of friendship is based, of which it is written (1 Co.
1: 9): "God is faithful: by whom you are called unto the
fellowship of his Son."

The love that is based upon this communication is charity,
and so it is clear that charity is the friendship of man for God.

Charity Proportioned to Man's   *Summa of Theology* II–II, q.
End   23, a. 2, c

. . . There is no perfect action coming from an active
power unless through some form, as the principle of that
action, it is connatural to that power. So God, who moves all
things to their appropriate ends, gave to each thing its form
whereby it tends to the end he appointed; and thus he

"ordereth all things sweetly" (Wis. 8: 1). But it is clear that the act of charity is beyond the will's nature, so that without a form being superadded to the natural power inclining it toward the act of love, this very act would be less perfect than the natural acts and the acts of the other powers, nor would it be easy and pleasurable to do. But clearly such is not the case, because no virtue has such a strong tendency toward its act as charity does, nor does any virtue operate with as great pleasure. So for us to act with charity there is required some habitual form superadded to the natural power, inclining that power to the act of charity and making it act with ease and pleasure.

Charity Superior to Soul   *Summa of Theology* II–II, q.
                                      23, a. 3, ad. 3

Every accident is inferior in being to substance, because substance has existence through itself, whereas an accident has its existence in another. But under its species aspect, an accident resulting from its subject's principles is inferior to its subject as any effect is inferior to its cause; but an accident resulting from a participation in some higher nature is superior to its subject inasmuch as it is a likeness of that higher nature, just as light is superior to the diaphanous body.

In this sense charity is superior to the soul because it is a participation in the Holy Spirit.

Relation of Revelation and   *Summa of Theology* II–II, q.
Faith to Theology   1, a. 1, c

1. God is the object of faith, which assents to propositions concerning God under the formal aspect of their being revealed by God:

. . . The object of any knowing habit [in this case, that of faith] has two aspects, namely, that which is materially known, which is, as it were, the material object, and that through which it is known, which is the formal notion of the object. Thus, in the science of geometry, what are materially known are the conclusions, while the formal notion under which they are known constitutes the middles of demonstration, through which the conclusions are known. Hence, in the faith, if we consider the formal notion of its object, it is nothing other than the first truth [i.e., God as the guarantor of all truth]. For the faith of which we are speaking does not assent to anything except insofar as it is revealed by God. Hence it is founded upon the divine truth as a middle [of demonstration, whence derives the certitude of the conclusions]. But if we consider materially the things to which faith assents, not only is it God, but also many other things, which, however, do not fall under the assent of faith except insofar as they have some order to God, namely, as through certain effects of the divinity, man is aided in his tending toward divine fruition [e.g., by faith in the sacraments, in the divine foundation of the Church, etc.].

2. This revelation is contained in Scripture (and tradition), and appropriately summarized under certain articles of faith.*

Scripture   *Summa of Theology* II–II, a. 9, ad. 1

. . . The truth of the faith is contained diffusedly in sacred Scripture, and in various manners, and obscurely in some. Hence, in order to bring forth the truth of faith from sacred Scripture there is required long study and training. But all those for whom it is necessary to know the truth of faith cannot arrive at this—a great number, being occupied with other concerns, cannot devote themselves to study. Therefore it was necessary that, from what was set forward in sacred Scripture, a certain clear summary be gathered together, to be proposed for belief by all. This summary is not *added to* sacred Scripture, but is, rather, *drawn from* sacred Scripture.*

Tradition   *Exposition of 1 Corinthians,* 11: 25

[In the Mass, where the words of consecration of the bread and wine are proposed as Christ's words, the words *mysterium fidei* do not appear in sacred Scripture, whereas the remainder do, in the Gospels of Sts. Matthew, Mark, and Luke, and in I Corinthians. The following are the words of St. Thomas on the opinion that solely the scriptural words of consecration suffice for valid consecration.] Some say therefore that whatever forms of these words are written down in canonical Scripture suffice for consecration. But it is seen to be more probable that consecration takes place solely by those words that the Church uses from the tradition of [i.e., as transmitted by] the Apostles. For the Evangelists intended to set down the Lord's words insofar as this pertained to the narrating of events, but not as they were ordained to the consecrating of the sacraments, which consecrations were maintained secret by the early Church because of unbelievers. [Later, while expounding each of the phrases in the consecration of the wine, one has the following statement of St. Thomas on the words *mysterium fidei*.] . . . He [Christ] says, "the mystery of faith," i.e., the hidden object of faith, since, namely, faith in the passion of Christ was hidden in all the sacrifices of the Old Testament as truth is in a sign. This [expression] the Church has from the tradition of the Apostles, since it is not found in canonical Scripture. 3. The defining of the faith in articles is the office of the Roman Pontiff.*

Summa of Theology II–II, q. 1, a. 10, c

. . . To the authority of him, therefore, pertains the issuing of a creed [composed of articles of faith], to whose authority it pertains to settle in a final way those things that are of faith, that they may be held by all with a faith that is unshaken. Now, this pertains to the authority of the Sovereign Pontiff, to whom the more important and more difficult questions of the Church are referred, as stated in the *Decretals*. Hence the Lord said to Peter, "I have prayed for thee, that thy faith fail not; and thou, being once confirmed, confirm thy brethren" [Luke 22: 32].
4. Theology, as the science of which God is the subject, argues from the divine knowledge of God contained in the Scriptures, whose main aspects are summarized under specific articles of faith.*

Summa of Theology I, q. 1, a. 8, ad. 2

. . . [Sacred doctrine, i.e., theology] uses the authority of canonical Scripture as being that proper to it, and reasons from it with necessity. . . . For our faith is based upon the revelation made to the Apostles and Prophets, who wrote the canonical books. . . .*

Summa of Theology I, q. 1, a. 7

. . . God is the subject of this science. For as an object is related to a power or habit [thus God is related to the act and *habit* of faith as its *object*], so is a subject related to a science [thus God is the *subject* of the *science* of faith, whose principles are the articles of faith]. That is assigned as the proper object of any power or habit, under whose notion all things are referred to that power or habit. Thus man and stone are referred to sight insofar as they are both colored. Hence the "colored" is the proper object of sight. But all things are treated in sacred doctrine [i.e., theology] under the notion of God—i.e., either because they are God, or because they have an order to God [e.g., the Blessed Trinity as to the former; the sacraments as to the latter]. Hence it follows that God is truly the subject of this science. This is also clear from the principles of this science, which are the articles of the faith, which is of God. Now, the same thing is the subject of the principles and of the whole science, since the whole science is contained virtually in its principles.*

Articles of Creed   *Summa of Theology* II–II, q. 1, a. 6, c

. . . The things to be believed in the Christian faith are said to be distinguished into articles insofar as they are divided into certain parts, having a certain relationship to one another. Now, the object of faith is something "not seen" concerning the divine. . . . Hence, where there occurs something that has a special notion of "not seen," there is then a special article [e.g., those referring to the Persons of the Blessed Trinity and to the Incarnation], but where many things are known, or not known, according to a same notion, here articles should not be distinguished [e.g., in reference to the belief in the passion, death, and burial of Christ, which together have the same aspect, but which differ, in the notion of what is to be believed, from the article on the resurrection of Christ].*

Relation of Theology to Philosophy   *Commentary on IV Books of Sentences*, Prologue, q. 1, a. 1, c

[This comprises, for St. Thomas, all the remaining arts and sciences acquired by human reason, both speculative and practical.]

. . . All those who have rightly esteemed the matter have placed the end of human life in the contemplation of God. This contemplation of God is twofold: One is by means of creatures, which is imperfect . . . , and in this contemplation the philosopher [i.e., Aristotle] set contemplative happiness [*Ethics* X], which happiness, nevertheless, is the happiness of a wayfarer [on the road to heaven]. It is to this happiness that the whole of philosophical knowledge, deriving from notions of creatures, is ordained. But there is another contemplation of God, by which he is seen immediately through his essence. This contemplation is perfect, and shall be in the fatherland, and is possible to man according to the supposition of faith. Hence the things that are means to the end must be proportioned to the end, and consequently a man, while he is in the state of a wayfarer, is led to that [ultimate] contemplation by knowledge not derived from creatures, but immediately inspired by the divine light. This knowledge is the doctrine of theology.

From this we are able to have two conclusions. One is that this science commands all the other sciences as the ruling science. The other is that this science uses for its service all the other sciences, as though its vassals, as is the case with all arts ordered to one another where the end of one is under the end of another. Thus the end of preparing powders [pharmacy], which is the making of medicines, is ordered to the end of the medical art itself, which is health. Hence the doctor commands the one who prepares the powders [the pharmacist] and uses the powders he prepares for his end. In the same way, since the end of the whole of philosophy is beneath the end of theology, and ordered to this end, theology should command all the other sciences and use those things that are transmitted in them.*

Scriptural Interpretation   *Commentary on Epistle to Galatians IV, 7*

Then he discloses the mystery when he says which things are said by an allegory.

> First, he tells what sort of mystery it is;
> second, he explains it (v. 24).

He says therefore: These things that are written about the two sons are said by an allegory, i.e., the understanding of one thing under the image of another. For an allegory is a figure of speech or a manner of narrating, in which one thing is said and something else is understood. Hence "allegory" is derived from *alos* (alien) and *goge* (a leading), leading, as it were, to a different understanding.

Here it should be noted that "allegory" is sometimes taken for any mystical meaning; sometimes for only one of the four, which are the historical, allegorical, mystical, and anagogical, which are the four senses of sacred Scripture, all of which differ in signification. For signification is twofold: one is through words, the other through the things signified by the words. And this is peculiar to the sacred writings and no others, since their author is God, in whose power it lies not only to employ words to signify (which man can also do), but things as well. Consequently, in the other sciences handed down by men, in which only words can be employed to signify, the words alone signify. But it is peculiar to Scripture that words and the very things signified by them signify something. Consequently this science can have many senses. For that signification by which the *words* signify something

---

* The preceding eight excerpts are translated by P. H. Conway, O.P., and R. F. Larcher, O.P.

pertains to the *literal* or *historical* sense. But the signification whereby the things signified by the words further signify other things pertains to the *mystical* sense.

There are two ways in which something can be signified by the literal sense: according to the usual construction, as when I say, "The man smiles"; or according to a likeness or metaphor, as when I say, "The meadow smiles." Both of these are used in sacred Scripture, as when we say, according to the first, "Jesus ascended," and when we say, according to the second, "Jesus sits at the right hand of God." Therefore, under the literal sense is included the parabolic or metaphorical.

However, the mystical or spiritual sense is divided into three types. First, as when the Apostle says that the Old Law is the figure of the New Law. Hence, insofar as the things of the Old Law signify things of the New Law, it is the *allegorical* sense. Then, according to Dionysius in the book *On The Heavenly Hierarchy*, the New Law is a figure of future glory; accordingly, insofar as things in the New Law and in Christ signify things that are in heaven, it is the *anagogical* sense. Furthermore, in the New Law the things performed by the head are examples of things we ought to do—because "What things soever were written were written for our learning" (Rom. 15: 3); accordingly, insofar as the things that in the New Law were done in Christ and done in things that signify Christ are signs of things we ought to do, it is the *moral* sense. Examples will clarify each of these. When I say, "Let there be light," referring literally to corporeal light, it is the literal sense. But if it be taken to mean "Let Christ be born in the Church," it pertains to the allegorical sense. But if one says, "Let there be light," i.e., "Let us be conducted to glory through Christ," it pertains to the anagogical sense. Finally, if it is said, "Let there be light," i.e., "Let us be illumined in mind and inflamed in heart through Christ," it pertains to the moral sense.*

* Translated by R. F. Larcher, O.P.

Resurrection: Old Testament   *Exposition of Job* XIX, lect. 2

> Who will grant me that my words may be written?
> Who will grant me that they may be marked down
> in a book? With an iron pen and in a plate of
> lead, or else be graven with an instrument in
> flint stone? For I know that my Redeemer liveth,
> and in the last day I shall rise out of the earth.
> And I shall be clothed again with my skin: and
> in my flesh I shall see my God. Whom I myself
> shall see, and my eyes shall behold; and not
> another. This my hope is laid up in my bosom.

Job had said above that his hope had been taken from him "as from a tree that is plucked up"; it was his hope of recovering temporal prosperity that he referred to, a hope that in various ways his friends kept trying to rouse in him. That he should not have this hope he showed in manifold ways above, by arguing to a conclusion of incongruity. Now, however, he reveals his mind manifestly to show that what he said before was spoken not because he despaired of God, but because he cherished a higher hope about him, one relating not to present but to future goods. And because he was about to talk of things great and wonderful and sure, he expressed beforehand his longing that they be perpetuated for the benefit of posterity. . . .

Job indicated the words he wished to be preserved with such great care when he said, "For I know that my redeemer liveth." Clearly, he is designating this as cause: Things we do not know with certainty we do not care to entrust to memory. And therefore he says expressly, "For I know," since he knows, I presume, with the certitude of faith. But this hope concerns the glory of the future resurrection, in relation to which he first denotes a cause in the first place when he says, "My redeemer liveth." Here we must consider that man, who was destined to be immortal by God, incurred the penalty of death through sin, as it says in Rom. 5: 12: "Wherefore as by one man sin entered into this world and by sin death," and that the human race was to be redeemed from this sin by Christ; this is just what Job foresaw through his spirit of faith. Christ redeemed us from sin through his death by dying for us; however, he did not die in such a way that death swallowed him up. For, although he was dead according to his humanity, he could not die according to his divinity. As a result of this divine life, human life, too, is restored to life by rising again, as it says (2 Cor. 13: 4): "For although he was crucified through weakness, yet he liveth by the power of God." Now, the life of Christ, rising again, is poured forth on all men in a common resurrection, whence the Apostle says in the same place: "For we also are weak in him; but we live with him by the power of God toward us"; whence also the Lord says (Jn. 5: 25): "When the dead shall hear the voice of the Son of God, they that hear shall live. For as the Father hath life in himself, so he hath given to the Son also to have life in himself." Therefore the principal cause of human resurrection is the life of the Son of God. This life did not take its beginning from Mary, as the Ebionites said, but always was, as the Apostle says (Heb. 13: 8): "Jesus Christ, yesterday, and today, and the same forever." Therefore he says clearly not that the redeemer "will live" but that he "liveth." And for this reason he declares the resurrection yet to come, determining its very time when he adds, "and in the last day I shall rise out of the earth." . . .

After having spoken concerning the resurrection—its cause, time, and mode, and the glory and identity of the one who is rising again—Job adds, "This my hope is laid up in my bosom" in order to show that he has this hope not only in words but deep in his heart, to show that his hope is not uncertain but most sure, not worthless but priceless. For what is hidden away in the heart is held in secret and is kept firmly and is considered dear.*

Resurrection: New Testament *Catena Aurea*, Matt. 28, Mark 14, Luke 23, Jn. 21

BEDE: When St. Matthew has vindicated the Lord's resurrection as declared by the angel, he relates the vision of the

* Translated by M. Wallingford, R.S.C.J.

Lord that the disciples had, . . . For when coming to his passion the Lord had said to his disciples, "After I am risen I will go before you into Galilee"; and the angel said the same to the women. Therefore the disciples obey the command of their master. Eleven only go, for one had already perished.

JEROME: After his resurrection, Jesus is seen and worshiped in the mountain in Galilee; though some doubt, their doubting confirms our faith.

REMIGIUS: This is more fully told by Luke; how when the Lord after the resurrection appeared to the disciples, in their terror they thought they saw a spirit.

BEDE: The Lord appeared to them in the mountain to signify that his body, which at his birth he had taken of the common dust of the human race, he had by his resurrection exalted above all earthly things; and to teach the faithful that if they desire there to see the height of his resurrection, they must endeavor here to pass from low pleasures to high desires. . . .

AUGUSTINE: . . . We are then obliged to understand that this appearance to the eleven disciples on the mountain in Galilee took place last of all. In the four Evangelists we find, in all, ten distinct appearances of Our Lord after his resurrection. . . .

JEROME: Observe the order of these injunctions. He bids the Apostles first to teach all nations, then to wash them with the sacrament of faith, and after faith and baptism then to teach them what things they ought to observe: "Teaching them to observe all things whatsoever I have commanded you." . . .

JEROME: He then who promises that he will be with his disciples to the end of the world shows both that they shall live forever and that he will never depart from those who believe. . . .

BEDE: When the rites of the old Passover were finished he passed to the new, in order, that is, to substitute the sacra-

ment of his own body and blood for the flesh and blood of
the lamb. Wherefore there follows: "And as they did eat,
Jesus took bread"; that is, in order to show that he himself is
that person to whom the Lord swore, "Thou art a priest
forever after the order of Melchizedech." There follows:
"And blessed, and broke it."

THEOPHYLACTUS: That is, giving thanks, he broke it, which
we also do, with the addition of some prayers.

BEDE: He himself also breaks the bread, which he gives to
his disciples, to show that the breaking of his body was to
take place, not against his will, nor without his intervention;
he also blessed it, because he with the Father and the Holy
Spirit filled his human nature, which he took upon him in
order to suffer, with the grace of divine power. He blessed
bread and broke it, because he deigned to subject to death
his manhood, which he had taken upon him in such a way as
to show that there was within it the power of divine immortality, and to teach them that therefore he would the more
quickly raise it from the dead. There follows: "And gave
to them, and said, Take, eat: this is my body."

THEOPHYLACTUS: That, namely, which I now give and
which ye take. But the bread is not a mere figure of the body
of Christ, but is changed into the very body of Christ. For
the Lord said, "The bread that I give you is my flesh." But
the flesh of Christ is veiled from our eyes on account of our
weakness, for bread and wine are things to which we are
accustomed; if, however, we saw flesh and blood we could
not bear to take them. For this reason the Lord, bending
himself to our weakness, keeps the forms of bread and wine,
but changes the bread and wine into the reality of his body
and blood.

CHRYSOSTOM: Even now also that Christ is close to us; he
who prepared that table, himself also consecrates it. For it is
not man who makes the offerings to be the body and blood
of Christ, but Christ, who was crucified for us. . . .

CYRIL: As soon as the Lord of all had been given up to be
crucified, the whole framework of the world bewailed its

rightful master, and the light was darkened at midday, which was a manifest token that the souls of those who crucified him would suffer darkness.

AUGUSTINE: What is here said of the darkness the other two Evangelists, Matthew and Mark, confirm, but St. Luke adds the cause whence the darkness arose, saying, "And the sun was darkened."

AUGUSTINE: This darkening of the sun it is quite plain did not happen in the regular and fixed course of the heavenly bodies, because it was then the Passover, which is always celebrated at full moon. But a regular eclipse of the sun does not take place except at new moon. . . .

BEDE: By invoking the Father, he declares himself to be the Son of God, but by commending his spirit, he signifies not the weakness of his strength, but his confidence in the same power with the Father. . . .

AMBROSE: He gave up his spirit because he did not lose it as one unwilling; for what a man sends forth is voluntary, what he loses, compulsory.

THEOPHYLACTUS: The dinner being ended, he commits to Peter the superintendence over the sheep of the world, not to the others: "So when they had dined, Jesus saith to Simon Peter, 'Simon, son of John, lovest thou me more than these?'"

AUGUSTINE: Our Lord asked this, knowing it: He knew that Peter not only loved him, but loved him more than all the rest.

ALCUIN: He is called Simon, son of John, John being his natural father. But mystically, Simon is obedience, and John, grace, a name well befitting him who was so obedient to God's grace that he loved Our Lord more ardently than any of the others, such virtue arising from divine gift, not mere human will.

AUGUSTINE: While Our Lord was being condemned to death, he feared and denied him. But by his resurrection Christ implanted love in his heart and drove away fear. . . .

CHRYSOSTOM: That which most of all attracts the divine love is care and love for our neighbor. . . .*

2. THE TRINITY

Procession of the Divine Persons   *Summa of Theology* I, q. 27, Prologue

We have previously studied about the unity of the divine essence; we now study about the trinity of persons in God. And since the divine persons are distinguished by their relations of origin, the order of our exposition is completely outlined; we shall have to consider: 1. the origin or procession; 2. the relations of origin; 3. the persons.

On the topic of procession, five questions come up: 1. Is there any procession in God? 2. Is there in God a procession that can be called begetting? 3. Besides begetting, can there be any other procession in God? 4. Can this procession be called begetting? 5. Are there only these two processions in God?

Two Processions   *Summa of Theology* I, q. 27, a. 3, c

There are two processions in God: that of the Word, and another. To show this, let us realize that in God the only procession is the action remaining in the agent himself rather than toward any external term. And in an intellectual nature, this immanent action is realized in the act of knowing and of willing. The procession of the Word belongs to the act of knowing. As to the will's action, it is within us the case of another procession: the procession of love, which makes the beloved be in the lover just as the procession of the Word makes what is said or known be within the knower. So that besides the procession of the Word there is in God another procession: This is the procession of love.

* Translated by John H. Newman.

Summa of Theology I, q. 27,
a. 3, ad. 3

. . . Although in God will is one with intellect, the procession of love keeps a distinction of order from the procession of the Word, because it is essential to love to proceed from an intellectual knowing.

Summa of Theology I, q. 27,
a. 4, c

. . . Hence that which proceeds in God by way of love does not proceed as a begotten term, nor as a son, but rather as a "spirit": this word evokes a kind of *élan* or vital impulse, insofar as we say that love moves us and urges us to do something.

Divine Relations   *Summa of Theology* I, q. 28,
a. 1

Relations really exist in God. To make this evident, let us consider that the category of relative predicates is the only one that is founded merely on reason and not on reality. This is not the case with other kinds; those like quantity and quality signify formally and properly something inhering in a subject, while relative predicates signify formally and properly only a relationship to another thing. This relationship sometimes exists in the very nature of things, namely, when realities are by nature ordered to each other and tend toward each other. Such relations are necessarily real. So a heavy body tends and is ordered to the center of the earth; consequently there is in the heavy body a relationship to the central place. It is the same in other similar cases. But sometimes also the relationship signified by the relative predicate exists only in reason's apprehension, which establishes a comparison between one thing and another. It is then only a relation of reason, as when the mind, comparing "man" to "animal," considers it the species of a genus.

But when a thing proceeds from a principle of like nature, both—that which proceeds and its principle—belong necessarily to the same order; and therefore real relations exist between them. Since then in God the processions are realized in identity of nature . . . necessarily the relations considered from the fact of these processions are real relations.

Relations Considered   *Summa of Theology* I, q. 28, a. 2, c

To clarify this question let us first note that in each of the nine kinds of accident there are two aspects to consider. There is, first of all, the being (*esse*) appropriate to each of them as an accident; and for all, this consists in existing within the subject; indeed, accidental being is existing in another. The other aspect to be considered in each of these is the formal reason proper to each one of these kinds. But in the kinds other than relation (for example, in quantity and quality), the proper formal reason is found in the relation to the subject: So we say that the quantity is a measure of the substance, and quality of its disposition. On the contrary, the proper formal reason of relation is not found in its relationship to the subject in which it exists; it is found in its relation to something external. If then we consider relations, even in created things, as relations, under this aspect they are found *assistantes* (adjacent) and not fixed from within, i.e., that they signify a relationship closely connected in some way to the thing referred to, since through relationship it tends to the other. While if we consider the relation as accident, it is thus inherent in the subject and has in it an accidental being. Gilbert of Porré considered relation only under the first aspect.

But that which in creature possesses an accidental being, when transferred to God possesses in him substantial being; for nothing in God exists as an accident in a subject; anything existing in God is his essence. Whence if one considers relation under that aspect which in created things gives it accidental being in the subject, in this way the relation that really exists in God gets its being from the divine essence and makes only one with him. But as a relation, it does not signify a relationship to the essence, but indeed to its opposite. Thus it is clear that real relation in God is really identical with the essence, and differs from it only by mental consideration; inasmuch as the relation evokes a relationship to its opposite, it does not evoke the term "essence." It is also apparent that in God there is no distinguishing of relative being and essential being; this is one and the same being.

Relation in God   *Summa of Theology* I, q. 29, a. 2, ad. 2

In God's case as with creatures, relation implies not only reference to another, but also something absolute, yet there is a difference. What is present in the creature over and above what is present in the meaning of relation is something other than the relation; but in God there is no distinction, but both are one and the same; and this is not perfectly clarified by the word "relation," as though understood in the usual meaning of that term. For it was previously shown (q. 13, a. 2), in discussing the divine names, that more is present in the perfection of the divine essence than can be signified by any name. Thus there consequently does not exist in God anything in reality besides relation, but only in the various names given by us.

Relations Really Distinct   *Summa of Theology* I, q. 28, a. 3, c

In God, said Boethius, "substance contains unity, relation multiplies the trinity." If then relations are not really distinguished from one another, there will be no real trinity in God; there will merely be a trinity of reason. But this is Sabellius's error.

To attribute a predicate to a subject is necessarily to attribute to it everything contained in the predicate's definition. For example, if the predicate "man" is attributed to someone, the predicate "reasonable" is also necessarily attributed. But relation, by definition, involves a relationship to another, relationship that relatively opposes the thing to that other. Whence, because there is real relation in God, there must also be real opposition. But relative opposition includes in its very definition a distinction. So there must be real distinction in God, not, certainly, from the viewpoint of the essence wherein the highest unity and simplicity are verified, but according to its relative reality.

Opposite Relationships Require Distinction

Summa of Theology I, q. 28, a. 4, ad. 1

According to the philosopher (*Physics* III), there are limits to this argument, and only if the identity is real and logical is it true that two things identical with the same thing are identical with each other (as, for example, a tunic and a garment); but not if they differ logically. So in the same spot he states that although action is the same as motion, and passion also; yet it does not follow that passion and action are the same; for action implies reference in the thing moved to motion *from which;* whereas passion implies that something is *from another.* So, although fatherhood, like sonship, is really the same as the divine essence, yet these two in their own proper idea and definitions imply opposite relationships. So they are distinguished from each other.

Divine Relations Based on Action

Summa of Theology I, q. 28, a. 4, c

. . . A real relation in God can be based only upon action. These relations are not based upon God's action in reference to any extrinsic procession, inasmuch as God's relations to creatures are not real in him (q. 13, a. 7). Consequently real relations in God are understood only in reference to those actions by which there are intrinsic, not extrinsic processions in God. These are only two: . . . one coming from the intellect's action, the procession of the Word, and the other from the will's action, the procession of love. Two opposite relations arise in reference to each of these processions: One of these is the relation of the person proceeding from the principle, the other is the relation of the principle himself. The procession of the Word is called begetting in the proper sense of the term, and thus it is applied to living things. Now, in perfect living beings, the relation of the principle of begetting is called fatherhood, and the relation of the one proceeding from the principle is called sonship. But the procession of love has not its own proper name, so neither have the relations derived from it. We give the name "spiration" to the relation of the principle of this procession, and that of *procession* to the relation of the proceeding term, although these two names are properly those of procession or of origin, and not of relation.

Word Really Proceeds   *Summa of Theology* I, q. 28, a. 4, ad. 1

Wherever the knowing and the known, the willing and the willed are two, there can be a real relation of intellect to the thing known, of will to the thing willed. But in God knowing and known are absolutely one, for in knowing himself, God knows all things. It is the same with his will and the object of his will. Thus it follows that these kinds of relations are not real in God; neither is the relation of the thing to itself. Yet the relation to the Word is a real relation, inasmuch as the Word is what we understand to proceed from an intelligent action, and is not the thing known. In fact, what we call "word" when we know a stone is what the intellect conceives of the thing known.

Procedure in Study of Persons   *Summa of Theology* I, q. 29, Prologue

We have first of all set forth the notions that seemed prerequisite with regard to processions and relations; we must now begin the study of the persons. It will comprise two parts: the persons considered in themselves and the persons in relation to one another. About the first, we should primarily consider persons in general, then each person in particular. The study of persons in general comprises four questions: 1. the meaning of the term "person"; 2. the number of persons; 3. the attributes that this number implies or excludes, such as those that call for difference, solitude, etc.; 4. our knowledge of the persons.

On the topic of the meaning of the word "person" we shall see: 1. the definition of person; 2. the comparison of this term with those of essence, of subsistence, and of hypostasis; 3. whether the term "person" is appropriate for God; 4. what it signifies in him.

Person and God   *Summa of Theology* I, q. 29,
                                     a. 2, and ad. 1, 2, 3, 4

Essence, hypostasis, subsistence . . . what these three names signify in common with the entire genus of substances, this name *person* signifies in the genus of rational substance.

ad. 1. As used by the Greeks, the strict meaning of "hypostasis" refers to any individual substance, but custom has associated with it a certain dignity, so that it refers to an individual being of rational nature.

ad. 2. Just as we refer in the plural to three "persons" and three "subsistences" in God, so the Greeks refer to three hypostases. But the word "substance" which, strictly speaking, is equivalent in meaning to "hypostasis," is equivocal in our usage, inasmuch as it refers at times to "essence" and at other times to "hypostasis"; in order to avoid misunderstanding they chose to translate "hypostasis" by "subsistence" rather than by "substance."

ad. 3. Strictly speaking, the definition expresses the essence. A definition includes specific but not individual principles. It follows that essence in things composed of matter and form refers neither to the form alone nor to the matter alone but to what is composed of both matter and form in general, as principles of the species. But what is composed of this matter and this form is characterized as an hypostasis or a person; for whereas soul, flesh, and bones belong to the meaning of "man," *this* soul, *this* flesh, and *these* bones belong to the meaning of *this* man. So "hypostasis" and "person" add individual principles to the notion of the essence, and in things composed of matter and form these are not identical with the essence, as we noted when speaking of the divine simplicity.

ad. 4. Boethius says that genera *subsist,* since if it belongs to certain individuals to subsist, they do this as subjects of genera and species comprised in the category, substance; the genera and species do not themselves subsist except in the theory of Plato, who made the essences of things subsist apart from singulars. On the contrary, the function of *substare* belongs to the same individuals with regard to accidents, which make no part of the definition of genera and species.

The individual composed of matter and form has the function of subject for accidents properly from its matter. So Boethius says that the form cannot be a subject (*On the Trinity,* 2). It subsists by itself through its form. This is not an addition to something already subsisting, but gives actual being to matter so that the individual can subsist. This is why Boethius relates *hypostasis* to matter and act-of-being or *subsistentia* to form: This is because the matter is principle of *substare,* and the form principle of *subsistere.*

Summa of Theology I, q. 29,
a. 3, c, and ad. 1, 2, 3, 4

"Person" refers to that which is most perfect in the whole of nature, namely, to that which subsists in rational nature. Now, because God's nature has all perfection, and thus every kind of perfection should be attributed to him, it is fitting to use the word "person" to speak of God; yet when used of God it is not used exactly as it is of creatures, but in a higher sense, just as is the case with other words naming creatures, as was clarified when we treated of the names of God.

ad. 1. So the word "person" is not discovered in the text of the Old or New Testament as referring to God. Yet what this word means is often present in Holy Scripture, namely, that his is the peak of self-existence and most perfect in wisdom. If we were restricted to speaking of God only in the words used in Holy Scripture, it would follow that no one could speak of God in any other language than the one used in the Old and the New Testaments. Because we must dialogue with nonbelievers, it is necessary for us to discover new words about God expressing the ancient belief. Nor should we avoid such innovation as profane, i.e., as out of harmony with the scriptural meaning. What St. Paul tells us to avoid are profane verbal innovations.

ad. 2. Although we may not use "person" in its original meaning of God, we may extend this acceptably for our present purpose. Since famous men were represented in comedies and tragedies, the word "person" (*persona:* mask) came to be used to refer to men of high rank. In the ecclesiastical world there grew up the custom of referring to personages of rank. For this reason some theologians define person as "a hypostasis distinguished by dignity." To subsist in rational nature is characterized by dignity and so, as we said, every individual with rational nature is spoken of as "person." Certainly the dignity of divine nature surpasses every nature, and thus it is entirely suitable to speak of God as "person."

"Person" as Common Noun   *Summa of Theology* I, q. 30, a. 1, ad. 1

. . . This is usually understood of the divine persons: that each of them subsists distinct from the others in the divine nature. Thus the term "person" is common in our understanding of the three divine persons.

Significance of "Trinity"   *Summa of Theology* I, q. 31, a. 1, ad. 1

In its etymological meaning, the word "Trinity" evidently signifies the one essence of the three persons, in that "trinity" means triune unity. But strictly speaking, it rather signifies the number of persons in one essence; and hence we cannot say that the Father is the Trinity, as he is not three persons. Yet it does not mean the relations themselves of the persons, but rather the number of persons related to one another, so that the word is not expressive of relativity.

Careful Use of the Word   *Summa of Theology* I, q. 31,
"Trinity"   a. 2, c

Because as Jerome notes (Ep. 57), words badly used run the risk of heresy, in speaking of the Trinity we must do so carefully and modestly: "Nowhere," says St. Augustine, "is error more dangerous, the search more arduous, the finding more fruitful." But in speaking of the Trinity we should avoid two contrary errors and proceed with care between them—namely Arius' error, a making of the trinity of persons a trinity of substances; and that of Sabellius, who made of the unity of essence a unity of person.

To avoid Arius' error we should avoid speaking of "diversity" or of "difference" in God—this would ruin the unity of essence. We can, however, appeal to the term "distinction" because of the relative opposition; it is in this sense that one should interpret the expressions "diversity" or "difference" of persons when encountered in a reliable text. Moreover, to preserve the simplicity of the divine essence, we should avoid the terms of "separation" and "division" that belong to the parts of a whole; lest equality be lost, we avoid using the word "disparity"; and to preserve likeness we should avoid the terms "alien" and "divergent." For Ambrose says (*On Faith* I), "in the Father and in the Son" there is no divergence, but one Godhead, and according to St. Hilary there is nothing separable in God.

But to avoid Sabellius's error, we should not use the word "singularity" (isolatedness), which would deny the communicability of the divine essence; according to St. Hilary, in fact, it is a sacrilege to call the Father and the Son "a singular God." We should also avoid the term "unique," which would deny the plurality of persons; St. Hilary says in the same place: "We exclude from God the idea of singularity or uniqueness." Yet we do say the "only Son," for there is no plurality of sons in God. But we do not say the "only God," for Godhead is common to several. We avoid the word "confused" to respect the order of nature among the persons. So Ambrose says: "What is one is not confused; and there is no multiplicity where there is no difference." We should also avoid the word "solitary" lest we detract from the society of the three persons; for, as Hilary says (*On the Trinity* IV), "We confess neither a solitary nor a diverse God."

But the masculine meaning of other (*alius*) denotes only a distinction of *suppositum;* and so we can properly say that the Son is other than the Father, because he is another *suppositum* of the divine nature, as he is another person and another hypostasis.

Trinitarian God Transcends   *Summa of Theology* I, q. 32,
Reason   a. 1, c

It is impossible to reach the knowledge of the Trinity by natural reason. For, as previously explained (q. 12, a. 4,

a. 12), man through natural reason cannot reach any knowledge of God except from creatures. But we go from creatures to knowing God as from effects to their cause. So by natural reason we can only know of God what necessarily belongs to him as the principle of all things. . . . Now, the creative power of God is common to the entire Trinity; and so it belongs to the unity of the essence and not to the distinction of the persons. So by natural reason we can know what belongs to the unity of the essence but not what belongs to the distinction of persons. . . .

Need to Know God as Trinity   *Summa of Theology* I, q. 32, a. 1, ad. 3

The knowledge of the divine persons was necessary for two reasons. The first was to give us the right idea of creation. To assert that God made all things through his Word is to reject the error according to which God produced things by natural need; and to place in him the procession of love is to show that if God has produced creatures, this is not because he needed them for himself nor for any other cause extrinsic to him; it is through love of his goodness [the desire to share].

Also Moses, after having written: "In the beginning God created heaven and earth," added, "God said, 'Let there be light,'" to manifest the divine Word; and then said: "God saw the light that it was good," to show the approval of the divine love. And in the same way he describes the production of the other works.

The second reason and the principal one was to give us a true notion of the salvation of the human race, salvation which is accomplished by the incarnation of the Son and by the gift of the Holy Spirit.

Appropriate Terms   *Summa of Theology* I, q. 32, a. 2, c

. . . Since we confess the Father, the Son, and the Holy Spirit to be one God and three persons, to those who ask: "Whereby are they one God?" and "Whereby are they three persons?" we answer that they are one in essence or Godhead; so there must be some abstract terms whereby we may answer that the persons are distinguished; and these are the properties or notions signified by the abstract terms, as fatherhood and sonship. Thus the divine essence is signified as "what"; and the person as "who"; and the property as "whereby." . . .

So-Called "Notions" in God   *Summa of Theology* I, q. 32, a. 3, c, and ad. 2, 3

A notion is the proper idea whereby we know a divine person. But the divine persons are multiplied by reason of their origin, and origin includes the idea of someone *from whom another comes* and of *someone who comes from another*, and by these two ways a person can be known. So the person of the Father cannot be known by the fact that he is from another but by the fact that he is from no one; and so the notion that pertains to him is unbegottenness. As the source of another, he is knowable in two ways, for insofar as the Son is from him, the Father is known by the notion of *fatherhood;* and as the Holy Spirit is from him, he is known by the notion of *common spiration.* The Son is knowable as begotten by another, and so he is known by *sonship* and is also known through another person proceeding from him, the Holy Spirit, so that he is known in the same way the Father is known, by *common spiration.* The Holy Spirit is known from the fact that he is from another or from others; hence he is known by *procession;* but not by the fact that another is from him, as no divine person proceeds from him.

So in God there are five notions: unbegottenness, fatherhood, sonship, common spiration, and procession. Only four of these are relations, for unbegottenness is not a relation, unless by reduction, as is seen later (q. 33, a. 4, ad. 3). Only four are properties. For common spiration is no property, inasmuch as it belongs to two persons. Three are personal notions, i.e., constituting persons: *fatherhood, sonship,* and *procession.* Common spiration and unbegottenness are spoken of as notions of persons, but not personal notions, as we shall see (q. 40, a. 1, ad. 1).

ad. 2. The divine essence is signified as a reality; the persons are also signified as realities; whereas the notions indicate ideas intimating the persons. So, although God is one by unity of essence, and triune by trinity of persons, he is not fivefold by the five notions.

ad. 3. Because real plurality in God is based upon relative opposition, the several properties of one person, since they are not relatively opposed to each other, do not really differ. Nor can we predicate them of each other, since they are mentally distinct. . . .

Discussion of Trinity Still *Summa of Theology* I, q. 32,
Open a. 4, c

. . . Anyone may hold contrary opinions about the notions, if he does not intend to uphold anything at variance with the faith. But if anyone should hold a false opinion about the notions, knowing or believing that what is contrary to the faith would follow, he would fall into heresy.

Person of the Father *Summa of Theology* I, q. 33,
a. 1, c, and ad. 1, 3

The word *principle* signifies only that from which something proceeds: for we call anything from which anything in any way proceeds a principle, and vice versa. Since the Father is the one from which another proceeds, it follows that the Father is a principle.

ad. 1. The Greeks use indifferently the words "cause" and "principle" when referring to God; on the contrary, the Latin doctors avoid the word "cause" and use only that of "principle." This is the reason. "Principle" is more general than "cause," the latter being itself more general than element; in fact, the first term or even the first part of a thing is called the "principle" but not the "cause." But the more general a term, the more it can be used of God, for the more specialized names are, the more appropriate they are to the creature. So the word "cause" implies diversity of substance and a dependence of effect upon cause, which the name "principle" does not imply; for whatever be the kind of causality, there is always between cause and effect a kind of distance in perfection or in power. On the contrary, the word "principle" is used even when there is no such difference; it is enough that order is discernible. So we say that the point is the principle of the line, or even that the first part of a line is the principle of it.

ad. 3. It is true that the word "principle," considered etymologically, appears taken from a priority; however, it does not signify priority, but origin. Do not confuse the signification of the word with what was its origin or the occasion for its creation.

"Unbegotten" Signifies Relation
Summa of Theology I, q. 33, a. 4, ad. 3

. . . Since "begotten" implies relation in God, "unbegotten" belongs also to relation. Hence it does not follow that the unbegotten Father is substantially distinguished from the begotten Son, but only by relation, that is, as the relation of Son is denied of the Father.

All Things Spoken in the Word
Summa of Theology I, q. 33, a. 1, ad. 3

. . . For the Father, by understanding himself and the Son and the Holy Spirit and everything else comprised in this knowledge, conceives the Word; in this way, then, the whole Trinity is *spoken* in the Word; and likewise are all creatures also, just as the intellect of a man by the word he conceives in the act of understanding a stone, speaks a stone. . . . So only the person who utters the Word is *speaker* in God, although each person understands and is understood, and so is spoken by the Word.

"Word" Is Proper Name of Son
Summa of Theology I, q. 34, a. 2, c

"Word" used of God in its proper meaning is used personally, and is the proper name of the person of the Son; for it signifies an emanation of intellect, and the person who in God proceeds through intellect's emanation is called the Son; and this procession is called begetting. . . .

Word Is God's Being   *Summa of Theology* I, q. 34, a. 2, ad. 1

To be and to understand are in us not the same thing. So in us whatever has intellectual being does not belong to our nature. But in God "to be" and "to understand" are one and the same; thus the Word of God is not an accident in him or his effect but belongs to his very nature. Hence it has to be something subsistent, for anything in the nature of God subsists; and so Damascene says (*On Orthodox Faith* I, 18) that the "Word of God is substantial and has a hypostatic being; but other words (like ours) are activities of the soul."

Creatures Somehow within the Word   *Summa of Theology* I, q. 34, a. 3, c

Augustine says (*Eighty-three Questions*, 63) "the name 'Word' signifies not only relation to the Father, but also relation to those beings which are made through the Word by his operative power."

So "Word" implies relation to creatures. In knowing himself, God knows every creature. But the word conceived in thought expresses all that the subject knows in act; so in us there are as many different words as there are different things that we understand. On the contrary, God knows in one sole act himself and all things; his one Word does not only express the Father, but even all creatures. While with God the divine thought is pure knowledge, with creatures it is knowledge and cause; so the Word of God is a pure expression of the mystery of the Father, but it is expression and cause of creatures. Whence the Psalmist said (Ps. 32: 9): "He spake, and they were made," because in the Word is found the operative idea of what God makes.

Nontemporal Character of Relationship through the Word   *Summa of Theology* I, q. 34, a. 3, ad. 2

Since relations result from actions, some names carry a relation of God to the creature following from God's transitive actions, i.e., terminating at an extrinsic effect such as to create, to govern the world; names of this kind are attributed to God in time. But others carry a relation following from an action not passing into an extrinsic effect but remaining within the agent—as to know and to will. These are not applied to God in time, and this kind of relation to creatures is implied in the name of the Word. Nor is it true that all names relative to the created are attributed to God in time, but only those that imply a relation following upon a transitive action.

Requisites for Imaging   *Summa of Theology* I, q. 35, a. 1, c

Likeness belongs to the notion of image. Yet not any kind of likeness is sufficient for the notion of image, but only likeness of species, or at least of some specific sign. And in corporeal things the sign characteristic of the species is chiefly the figure. For we notice that the species of various animals are of various figures; but not of various colors. So if the color of a thing is placed upon the wall, we do not call this an image unless the figure is also pictured there. Moreover, more is needed for an image than likeness of species or figure, and this is origin; for, as Augustine says (*Eighty-three Questions*, 74): "One egg is not the image of another, because it is not derived from it." To be truly an image of another, it is necessary to proceed from it so as to resemble it in species or at least in a sign of the species. But the attributes that imply procession or origin in God are personal names. Hence the name "image" is a name of a person.

Summa of Theology I, q. 35, a. 2, c

Augustine says (*On the Trinity* VI, 2): "The Son alone is the image of the Father."

The Greek doctors usually say that the Holy Spirit is the image both of the Father and of the Son, but the Latin doctors attribute to the Son alone the name "image." For in the canonical Scripture it is only found as applied to the Son, as in the words: "Who is the image of the invisible God, the firstborn of creatures" (Col. 1: 15); and also: "Who being the brightness of his glory, and the figure of his substance" (Heb. 1: 3).

Summa of Theology I, q. 35,
a. 2, ad. 3

A thing may be an image in two ways. In one way as of the same specific nature, as the image of the king is found in his son. In another way as when it is something of a different nature, as the king's image on the coin. In the first way the Son is the image of the Father; in the second way man is called the image of God; and to express the imperfect character of the divine image in man, man is not merely called the image, but "to the image," whereby there is expressed a certain motion of tendency to perfection. But we cannot say that the Son of God is "to the image," because he is the perfect image of the Father.

Holy Spirit   *Summa of Theology* I, q. 36,
a. 1

. . . To signify the divine person who proceeds by way of love, this name "Holy Spirit" is suitable to him through scriptural usage. The appropriateness of the name is seen in two ways. First, because the person called "Holy Spirit" has something in common with the other persons. For, as Augustine says (*On the Trinity* XV, 17; V, 11): "Because the Holy Spirit is common to both, he himself is called that properly which both are called in common. For the Father also is a spirit and the Son is a spirit; and the Father is holy and the Son is holy."

Second, from the proper signification of the name. For in bodily things the name "spirit" apparently signifies impulse and motion; for we give the name "spirit" to breath and wind. Now, love moves and urges the lover's will toward the beloved. Moreover, holiness is attributed to whatever is directed to God. So because the divine person proceeds by way of the love by which God is loved, that person is most properly named the "Holy Spirit."

Suitability of the Term "Spirit"   *Summa of Theology* I, q. 36, a. 1, ad. 2

Although this name "Holy Spirit" does not indicate a relation, yet it substitutes for a relative term one suitable to signify a person distinct from the others by relation only. Yet one can see a relation in this term by considering the Holy Spirit as being breathed (*spiratus*).

Why the Holy Spirit Is Said to Be "from the Son"   *Summa of Theology* I, q. 36, a. 2, c

It must be said that the Holy Spirit is from the Son. For if he were not, he could in no way be distinguished from the Son. . . . the divine persons are distinguished from one another only by the relations. Now, relations cannot distinguish the persons unless they are opposite relations. . . . Now, there cannot be in God any relations opposed to each other except relations of origin. And opposite relations of origin are to be understood as of a *principle*, and of what is *from a principle*. So we must conclude that it is necessary to say either that the Son is from the Holy Spirit, which no one says, or that the Holy Spirit is from the Son, as we confess. . . .

Summa of Theology I, q. 36, a. 2, ad. 7

The Holy Spirit is distinguished personally from the Son insofar as the origin of one is distinguished from the origin of the other; but the difference itself of origin is found in the fact that the Son is only from the Father, but the Holy Spirit is from the Father and the Son; for otherwise the processions would not be distinguished from each other. . . .

Spirit Proceeding "through the Son" Also Valid Expression   *Summa of Theology* I, q. 36, a. 3

. . . Because it is from what the Son receives from the Father that the Holy Spirit proceeds from him, it can be said that the Father spirates the Holy Spirit through the Son or that the Holy Spirit proceeds from the Father through the Son, which means the same thing.

Summa of Theology I, q. 36, a. 4, c

Augustine says (*On the Trinity* XIV) that the Father and the Son are not two principles but one principle of the Holy Spirit.

The Father and the Son are one in everything when there is no distinction between them of opposite relation. Thus since there is no relative opposition between them as the principle of the Holy Spirit, it follows that the Father and the Son are one principle of the Holy Spirit.

Love as Notional Term   *Summa of Theology* I, q. 37, a. 1, c

. . . Insofar as love signifies only the relation of the lover to the beloved, "love" and "to love" are said of the essence, as "understanding" and "to understand"; but insofar as these words are used to express the relation to its principle, of what proceeds by way of love, and vice versa, so that by "love" is understood the "love proceeding," and by "to love" is understood the "spiration of the love proceeding," in that sense "love" is the name of the person and "to love" is a notional term, like "to speak" or "to beget."

Love, a Bond   *Summa of Theology* I, q. 37, a. 1, ad. 2, 3

ad. 2. Although "to know," "to will," and "to love" are used as verbs signifying actions passing to their objects [transitive verbs], they are really immanent actions, connoting within the agent itself a relation to the object. Likewise, even in us, love is something that remains within the lover, and the mental word is something remaining within the one who "speaks" it while connoting a relation to the thing expressed or loved. But in God, in whom there is nothing accidental, their condition is still better: the Word and love are there subsistent. So when we say that the Holy Spirit is the love of the Father *for* the Son or *for* anything else, we do not mean anything passing into another, but only the relation of love to the beloved, as also the Word connotes the relationship of the Word to the thing expressed in this Word.

ad. 3. We say that the Holy Spirit is the bond of the Father and the Son, inasmuch as he is love. In fact, it is by the one love (*unica dilectione*) that the Father loves both himself and the Son—and reciprocally; consequently it is as love that the Holy Spirit calls forth a reciprocal relationship between the Father and the Son, that of lover to the beloved. But from the fact that the Father and the Son love each other, their mutual love, in other words, the Holy Spirit, must proceed from both. If then we consider origin, the Holy Spirit is not in the middle but is the third person of the Trinity. But if we consider the relationship we are discussing, he is between the two other persons as the bond that unites them, while proceeding from each of them.

Creatures Grounded in Trinitarian Love

Summa of Theology I, q. 37, a. 2, c and ad. 3

. . . Since in God "to love" is understood in two ways, essentially and notionally, when it is understood essentially, it means that the Father and the Son love each other not by the Holy Spirit but by their essence. So Augustine says (*On the Trinity* XV, 7): "Who dares to say that the Father loves neither himself nor the Son nor the Holy Spirit except by the Holy Spirit? . . ."

If, on the contrary, the word "love" is understood in the notional sense, it only means "to spirate love"; just as "to speak" signifies "to produce a word," and "to flower," "to produce flowers." So then as we say that a tree flowers by its flowers, so we say, "The Father speaks by his Word or by the Son himself and the creature"; and we say, "The Father and the Son love themselves and us by the Holy Spirit or by the love that proceeds."

ad. 3. Not only does the Father love his Son by the Holy Spirit, but even himself and us; for, as we said, "to love" in the notional sense does not only connote the production of a divine person, it connotes the person produced by way of love; and love implies relationship to the thing loved. That is why, just as the Father speaks, by the Word that he begets, himself and every creature—since the Word begotten by him suffices to represent the Father and every creature, so also he loves himself and every creature by the Holy Spirit, since the Holy Spirit proceeds as love from that first goodness that is the reason for the Father loving himself as well as every creature.

So it is clear that relation to the creature is implied both in the Word and in the love that proceeds, although in a secondary way; for the divine truth and goodness are the principle of God's knowledge and love of the creature.

Personal Signification of the Term "Gift"   *Summa of Theology* I, q. 38, a. 1, ad. 1

The term "gift" implies a personal distinction, inasmuch as "gift" implies something belonging to another through its origin. Yet the Holy Spirit gives himself insofar as he is his own and can use or rather enjoy himself, as a free man likewise belongs to himself. And as Augustine says (on Jn. 29): "What is more yours than yourself?" Or we could more appropriately say that a gift should in a way belong to the giver. But this relationship of "belonging," "to be someone's" can be verified in many ways. First, by identity, as Augustine says, and in this sense "gift" is the same as "the giver," but not the same as "the one to whom it is given." The Holy Spirit in this sense gives himself. In another sense, something is another's as a possession, or as a slave, and "gift" in that sense is essentially distinct from "the giver." Understood this way, the gift of God is a created thing. In a third sense "this is someone's" only through its origin, and in this sense the Son is the Father's, and the Holy Spirit belongs to both. So inasmuch as in this sense "gift" signifies the possession of the giver, it is personally distinguished from the giver, and is a personal name.

Summa of Theology I, q. 38, a. 2, c

Understood in its personal sense in God, Gift is the Holy

Spirit's proper name. And for these reasons. According to the philosopher, there is properly a gift when there is a donation without return, i.e., when one gives without expecting any return; "gift" therefore implies a gratuitous donation. But love is the reason for a gratuitous donation: why do we give anything to anyone gratuitously? Because we wish them well. The first gift that we offer, therefore, is the love that makes us wish them well. We see then that love constitutes the first gift by virtue of which all gratuitous gifts are given. So, since the Holy Spirit proceeds as love, he proceeds as first Gift. Thus Augustine says (*On the Trinity* XV, 24): "By the gift which is the Holy Spirit, many particular gifts are distributed to the members of Christ."

Relations Are Realities *Summa of Theology* I, q. 39, a. 1, c

. . . It was shown previously (q. 3, a. 3) that the divine simplicity requires in God that essence be identical with *suppositum,* which is nothing else than person in intellectual beings. What is apparently difficult here is that with several persons, the essence keeps its unity. And as, according to Boethius (*On the Trinity* I), "relation multiplies the Trinity of persons," some considered that in God essence and person differ, since they thought of the relations as (*assistentes*) adjacent, seeing only in relation the notion of "reference to another," forgetting that relations are also realities.

But as previously shown, although in creatures relations inhere as accidents, in God they are the very divine essence. It follows that in God essence is not really distinct from person; and yet the persons are really distinguished from one another. For "person" . . . signifies relation as subsisting in the divine nature. But "relation," in reference to the essence, does not really differ from it, but only through our thinking about it; whereas in reference to an opposite relation, it is really distinct from it by virtue of the opposition. So there is one essence and there are three persons.

Relations Denote Individuals *Summa of Theology* I, q. 39,
a. 1, ad. 1, 3

ad. 1. . . . the relations themselves are not distinguished
from one another insofar as they are identified with the
essence.

ad. 3. Divine realities are named by us after the manner of
created ones. . . . So because created natures are individual-
ized by matter, which is the subject of the specific nature, it
follows that individuals are called "subjects," "supposita," or
"hypostases." So the divine persons are spoken of as "supposita" or "hypostases," but not because there really exists
any real supposition or subjection.

Scriptural Source of Trinitar- *Summa of Theology* I, q. 39,
ian Doctrine a. 2, ad. 2

Although in Holy Scripture we do not find the literal expression "three Persons of one essence," yet we find this
meaning there with the words: "I and the Father are one"
(Jn. 10: 30); and "I am in the Father, and the Father in
Me"; and in many similar texts.

Precision in Describing Pro- *Summa of Theology* I, q. 39,
cession a. 5, ad. 1

. . . As regards abstract names [standing for persons], a
certain order should be observed, inasmuch as what comes
from action is more nearly allied with the persons, since actions belong to *supposita*. So "nature from nature" and "wisdom from wisdom" are less incorrect than "essence from
essence."

Substantial Otherness Not Re- *Summa of Theology* I, q. 40,
quired in Subsistent Relations a. 2, ad. 4

Relation, when it is an accident, presupposes the distinction of subjects; but when it is subsistent, the relation does
not presuppose, but brings about the distinction; for when it
is asserted that the essence of the relation consists in being
toward another, the word "another" designates the correla-

tive, which is not prior but is simultaneous in the order of nature.

Relations Follow Notional Acts

Summa of Theology I, q. 40, a. 4, c

According to the view that properties do not distinguish and constitute the hypostases in God but only manifest them as already distinct and constituted, we must absolutely state that in our way of understanding, the relations come after the notional acts, so that without qualifying the phrase we can say, "because he begets, he is the Father." A distinction is necessary, however, when we allow that the relations distinguish and constitute the divine hypostases. For in God origin has both an active and passive signification—active, as generation is attributed to the Father, and spiration, taken for the notional act, is attributed to the Father and the Son; passive, as birth is attributed to the Son, and procession to the Holy Spirit. For, in the order of knowledge, origin in the passive sense absolutely precedes the personal properties of the person proceeding; since origin, as passively understood, signifies the way toward a person constituted by the property. Also, origin taken actively is prior in the order of knowledge to the nonpersonal relation of the person originating; as the notional act of spiration precedes in the order of knowledge the unnamed relative property common to the Father and the Son. The personal property of the Father can be considered in two ways: first, as a relation (and here in the order of knowledge it presupposes the notional act, since relation as relation is founded upon an act); second, inasmuch as it constitutes the person (and hence the notional act presupposes the relation, as an action presupposes a person acting).

Origin Designated by Acts

Summa of Theology I, q. 41, a. 1, c

Augustine says (Fulgentius, *De Fide ad Petrum* ii): "It is a property of the Father to beget the Son." But to beget is an act. Therefore, notional acts are to be found in God.

In the divine persons distinction is founded on origin. But origin can be properly designated only by certain acts. So in order to designate the order of origin in the divine persons, we must attribute notional acts to the persons.

God Called Power Only by Mental Distinction
Summa of Theology I, q. 41, a. 4, ad. 3

Power signifies principle; and "principle" implies distinction from that of which it is the principle. Now, we should observe a double distinction in things said of God: One is a real distinction; the other is a mental distinction only. God by his essence is really distinct from those things of which he is the principle by creation, just as one person is distinct from the other of which he is principle by a notional act. But in God the distinction of action and agent is a mental distinction only, or else action would be an accident in God. And so in respect to actions by which some things proceed as distinct from God, either personally or essentially, we may attribute power to God in its proper meaning as principle. And as we attribute to God the power of creating, so we may attribute the power of begetting and of spirating. But *to know* and *to will* are not such actions as to designate the procession of something distinct from God, either essentially or personally. We cannot, then, with regard to these actions, attribute power to God, strictly speaking; for we designate by different terms the intellect and the act of knowing in God, whereas in God the act of knowing is his very essence, which has no principle.

Divine Missions
Summa of Theology I, q. 43, a. 1, c

. . . So the mission of a divine person is appropriate as in one way signifying the procession of origin from the sender, and as signifying a new way of existing in another; so the Son is said to be sent by the Father into the world, since he began to exist visibly in the world by assuming our nature; whereas he was previously in the world (Jn. 1: 1).

Variety in Expressions
Summa of Theology I, q. 43, a. 2, c

There are some notable differences among the words expressing the origin of the divine persons. Certain words express only the relationship of emanation from the principle, as "procession" and "going forth." Others, in addition to this relationship to the principle, specify the term of the procession. Of these, some express the eternal term, like "generation" and "spiration"—for generation is a procession that puts the divine person in possession of the divine nature, and passive spiration expresses the procession of subsistent love. Others, along with the relation to the principle, express a temporal term, like "mission" and "gift." For a thing is only sent to be in something else, and is only given that it may be possessed. But for a divine person to be possessed by any creature or exist in it in a new way, is temporal.

So in God, mission and gift are used only as temporal attributes; generation and spiration only as eternal attributes. Finally, procession and going out have in God both an eternal and a temporal signification; for the Son may proceed eternally as God, but temporally by becoming man according to his visible mission or also by dwelling in man through his invisible mission.

Temporal Procession through Grace
Summa of Theology I, q. 43, a. 3, c

Augustine says (*On the Trinity* III, 4) that the Holy Spirit proceeds temporally for the creature's sanctification. But mission is a temporal procession. So because the creature's sanctification is by sanctifying grace, it follows that the mission of the divine person is only by sanctifying grace. . . .

For God is in everything by his essence, by his power, and by his presence as the cause existing in the effects that participate in his goodness. Above and beyond this common way, there is a special way, which is proper to the rational creature: in this way it is said that God exists as the known in the knower and the beloved in the lover. And because by its action of knowing and loving, the rational creature at-

tains to God himself, in this special way, God is said not only
to exist in the rational creature but also to dwell therein as
in his own temple. Thus outside of sanctifying grace there is
no other effect that can be the reason for the divine person's
existing in a new way in the rational creature. Thus the divine
person is sent and proceeds temporally only by sanctifying
grace.

Likewise we are said to possess only what we can freely
use or enjoy, and to have the power of enjoying the divine
person can only be through sanctifying grace.

However, in the very gift of sanctifying grace, it is the
Holy Spirit whom one possesses and who dwells in man.
Hence the Holy Spirit himself is given and sent.

Grace Prepares Indwelling of   *Summa of Theology* I, q. 43,
Persons   a. 3, ad. 2

ad. 2. Sanctifying grace disposes the soul to possess the di-
vine person, and this is signified when it is declared that the
Holy Spirit is given through the gift of grace. Yet the very
gift of grace is from the Holy Spirit, as these words mean:
"The charity of God is poured forth in our hearts by the Holy
Spirit."

Invisible Mission to Every   *Summa of Theology* I, q. 43,
Creature   a. 6, c

According to Augustine (*On the Trinity* III, 4; XV, 27),
the invisible mission is for the sanctification of the creature.
Since every creature having grace is sanctified, the invisible
mission is to every such creature. . . . Mission in respect to
the one to whom it is sent implies two things: the indwelling
of grace and a certain renewal by grace. . . .

Infused Gifts   *Summa of Theology* I–II, q.
                                  68, a. 1, c

And so in order to distinguish gifts from virtues we should
be sensitive to the way Scripture speaks, and there we find
that the term "spirit" rather than "gift" is used. Hence it is
written (Is. 11: 2): "The spirit . . . of wisdom and of under-

standing . . . shall rest upon him . . . ." From these words it is made clear that these seven gifts are there recorded as being in us by divine inspiration.

Now, inspiration signifies motion from without, for we should observe that man has a twofold principle of movement, one within—the reason; the other, external—God.

Now, it is evident that anything moved must be proportionate to its mover, and the perfection of a moved thing is to be found in a disposition whereby it is inclined to be well moved by its mover. So the more excellent the mover, the more perfect must be the disposition whereby the thing moved is made proportionate to its mover. For this reason a student needs a more perfect disposition to receive higher learning from his teacher.

It is quite evident that human virtues perfect man insofar as it is natural for him to be moved by his reason in his internal and external actions. Hence man needs even greater perfection to be disposed to be moved by God. These perfections are called gifts, not merely because they are infused by God but likewise because man is disposed by them to become responsive to the divine inspiration, as Isaiah (1: 5) says: "The Lord . . . hath opened my ear, and I do not resist: I have not gone back." Even the philosopher states in the chapter "On Good Fortune" in *Eudemian Ethics* that those who are moved by divine instinct need not take counsel from human reason but merely follow their inner promptings, because they are being moved by a principle above human reason.

3. SIN

Original Sin   *Summa of Theology* I–II, q. 81, a. 2, c

Good is more self-diffusive than evil. But immediate ancestors do not transmit their merits to their descendants. Much less would they transmit sins.

. . . Augustine proposes this question in *Enchiridion*

XLVI, XLVII, and leaves it unanswered. Yet a careful examination will show that neither the sins of immediate ancestors nor any sin other than that of our first parent can be transmitted by the way of origin. This is because man begets his like in species but not in individuals. Therefore whatever belongs directly to the individual such as personal actions and whatever affects them are not transmitted to their children by parents; for a grammarian does not transmit to his son the knowledge of grammar that he has gained by his own studies. On the other hand, whatever affects the specific nature is transmitted by parents to their children, unless some defect in nature occurs; so a man with eyes begets a son with eyes unless nature fails. And if nature is vigorous, even some individual accidents affecting the natural disposition are transmitted to the children, e.g., body speed, acuteness of intellect, etc.; but never those that are purely personal, as was asserted.

Now, just as something may pertain to the person as a person, and something through the gift of grace as well, so may something pertain to the nature as nature, e.g., whatever is caused by the principles of nature, and something through the gift of grace as well. In this way original justice, as asserted in I, q. 100, a. 1, was a gift of grace, given by God to all human nature in our first parent. By his first sin the first man lost this gift, so that as that original justice along with the nature was to have been transmitted to his posterity, so also was its disorder. Other actual sins, however, whether of the first parent or of others, do not corrupt the nature as nature, but only as that person's nature, i.e., in respect to tendency to sin; and therefore other sins are not transmitted.

Summary of Theology I–II, q.
81, a. 1

. . . All men born of Adam may be taken as one man since all have one nature, received from their first parents, in common, just as in civil affairs all the members of one community are considered one body and the whole community one man. In fact, Porphyry asserts that by participating in the same species, many men are one man. So the many men born of Adam are as so many members of one body. Wherefore a murder committed by the hand would not be charged to the hand in itself and apart from the body, but is charged to it as something belonging to man and moved by man's first moving principle. It is in this way that the disorder in any man born of Adam is voluntary not by his will but by his first parent's will, since by the movement of generation he moves all who originate from him just as the soul's will moves all the members to their actions. So the sin thereby transmitted by the first parent to his descendants is called *original*, just as the sin coming from the soul to the bodily members is called *actual*, and just as the actual sin committed by a bodily member is not that member's sin except insofar as that member is a part of man and is therefore called a *human sin*. So original sin is not any person's sin except insofar as this person receives his nature from his first parent, and for this reason it is called the sin of nature, as in Ep. 2: 3: "We . . . were by nature children of wrath."

> *Summa of Theology* I–II, q. 82, a. 3, c

A thing is placed in a species through its form; and it was said that the species of original sin is derived from its cause. So in considering the cause of original sin we should consider its formal element. Now, all contraries have contrary causes. So when considering the cause of original sin we should consider its contrary, original justice. Now, the entire order of original justice was in man's will being subject to God, and this subjection was primarily and principally in the will, whose function is the moving of all other parts to the end . . . , so that when the will was turned away from God, all other parts became inordinate. Hence the formal element in original sin is the privation of original justice in which the will was subject to God. All other disorder in the soul's powers is a sort of material element in original sin.

Now, the inordinateness of other powers of the soul chiefly consists in their turning inordinately to changeable good, and this inordinateness is given the general name of concupiscence. So original sin is formally privation of original justice, and it is only concupiscence, materially.

All Men Need Redemption   *Summa of Theology* I–II, q. 81, a. 3, c

According to the Catholic faith we must firmly believe that with the exception of Christ all men descended from Adam contract from him original sin; or else all would not require redemption, which is through Christ; but all do. From what has been asserted we may deduce the reasons for this, e.g., that original sin, through the sin of our first parent, is transmitted to all his posterity just as, through the soul's will, actual sin is transmitted to the bodily members by their being moved through the will. Now, it is clear that actual sin can be transmitted to all such members as have an innate aptitude to be moved by the will. Consequently, original sin is transmitted to all those who are moved by Adam through the movement of generation.

Redemption Is for All   *Summa of Theology* I–II, q. 81, a. 3, ad. 3

Just as Adam's sin is transmitted to all born of Adam corporeally, so is the grace of Christ transmitted to all begotten of him spiritually by faith and baptism. And this concerns not only the removal of the sin of their first parent, but the removal of actual sins and the attainment of glory.

Original Sin a Habit   *Summa of Theology* I, q. 82, a. 1, c

Habit is twofold. First, there is habit or durable disposition by which a power tends toward an act, and in this way science and virtue are called habits. But in this way original sin is no habit. The second kind of habit is the disposition of a complex nature by which the latter is well or ill disposed to something, mainly when this disposition has become like a second nature, as in the case of sickness or health. In this way is original sin a habit. It is a disordered disposition arising from the loss of harmony essential to original justice, as bodily illness is a disordered disposition of the body caused by loss of balance essential to health. So original sin is spoken of as the "languor of nature."

Adam, Principal Cause of Original Sin

Summa of Theology I–II, q. 83, a. 1, c

A thing can be in another in two ways. First, as in its cause, principal or instrumental; second, as in its subject. So the original sin of all men was in Adam certainly as in its principal cause, e.g. (Rm. 5: 12): "In whom all have sinned." But it is in the bodily semen as in its instrumental cause inasmuch as original sin, along with human nature, is transmitted to the child by the semen's active power. But original sin is only in the soul as its subject, in no way in the flesh.

This is because original sin is transmitted by our first parent's will to his posterity through a certain movement of generation, just as actual sin is transmitted by any man's will to his other parts. Now, in this transmission we should recognize that the character of sin is found in that part of man that is under the motion of the will consenting to sin when that part can in any way share in that guilt either as its subject or instrument. Hence from the will consenting to gluttony, the concupiscible power is charged with concupiscence of food, as both hand and mouth are with the partaking of food, for insofar as these are moved by the will, they are the instruments of sin. But the additional action stimulated in the nourishing power and the internal parts having no aptitude to be moved by the will is not characterized as guilt.

Consequently, because the soul is able to be the subject of guilt, whereas in itself the flesh cannot be, whatever comes to the soul through the corruption of the first sin has the character of guilt, whereas anything affecting the flesh has the character of punishment rather than of guilt. And so the soul rather than the flesh is the subject of original sin.

Original Sin in Souls

Summa of Theology I–II, q. 83, a. 2, c

That part of the soul to which the motivating cause of sin primarily belongs is principally the subject of the sin. So a concupiscible power is the proper subject of a sin whose motivating cause is sensual pleasure. Now, it is evident that original sin is caused by our origin. So original sin's primary subject is that part of the soul primarily reached by man's origin. But the origin reaches the soul as the term of generation, inasmuch as it is the body's form, a fact touching the soul's essence. . . . Thus the soul in its essence is the primary subject of original sin.

Original Sin Related to Soul's Powers   *Summa of Theology* I–II, q. 32, a. 3, c

There are two aspects of original-sin infection. First, its presence in its subject; and here it is related to the essence of soul. . . . Second, its inclination to act; and here it is related to the soul's powers. It is primarily related to that power wherein resides the first inclination to commit sin, and this is the will. . . . Therefore, original sin is related primarily to the will.

Original Sin in Certain Powers   *Summa of Theology* I–II, q. 83, a. 4, c

Corruptions naturally transmitted from one subject to another are called infectious, such as contagious diseases such as leprosy. . . . But the corruption of original sin is transmitted by the generative act. . . . So the powers taking part in this act are spoken of as primarily infected. Now, this act is in the service of the generative power insofar as it is ordered to generation, involving sense pleasure, the most powerful object of the concupiscible power. Whereas all in the soul is corrupted by original sin, these three are especially so.

Summa of Theology I–II, q. 83, a. 4, ad. 1

Original sin insofar as it inclines to actual sins pertains chiefly to the will. . . . Yet as transmitted to the children, it pertains to the aforementioned powers proximately and to the will remotely.

Tendency toward Virtue Less- *Summa of Theology* I–II, q.
ened 85, a. 1, c

A threefold good belongs to human nature. First, there are
the principles establishing nature and consequent properties,
such as powers of the soul. . . . 2. Because from nature man
tends to virtue, this tendency is called a good of nature. 3.
The gift of original justice given to all human nature in the
person of the first man may be spoken of as a good of
nature. . . .

So, because sin is opposed to virtue, because a man sins,
a decrease of that good of nature—the tendency toward virtue
—results.

Many Evils Caused by Origi- *Summa of Theology* I–II, q.
nal Sin 85, a. 5, c

A thing causes another in two ways: first, through itself;
second, accidentally. . . . A thing causes another accidentally if by removing an obstacle it causes it: hence we read
in *Physics* VIII, 32 that "by removing a pillar a man accidentally moves the stone resting on it."

In this sense our first parent's sin is the cause of death and
such defects in human nature, since by this sin there was removed that original justice whereby not only were the soul's
lower powers unified under reason's control without any disorder at all, but the entire body was likewise united in subjection to the soul with no defect . . . . so that when original
justice was lost through our first parent's sin not only did human nature suffer in the soul by disorder among the powers,
but because of the body's disorder, it became subject likewise to corruption.

But just like the removal of grace, the removal of original
justice has the character of punishment. Therefore, death
and all accompanying bodily defects are punishments for
original sin. And although the sinner never intended these defects, they are ordered through God's justice as punishments.

Death, Punishment for Sin *Summa of Theology* I–II, q. 85, a. 6, c

A corruptible thing has two aspects: first, its universal nature; second, its particular nature. A thing's particular nature is its own power of action and self-preservation. Every corruption and defect goes contrary to this nature, as asserted in *On the Heaven* II, 37, because this power tends to the existence and preservation of the being it belongs to.

On the other hand, the universal nature is an active force in some universal principle of nature, i.e., in some heavenly body, or else belonging to some higher substance, and in this sense God is referred to as the "nature who makes nature." This force intends the good and the preservation of the universe and requires in things alternate generation and corruption; and in this case corruption and defect in things are natural, not in respect to the tendency of the form or principle of being and perfection but in respect to the tendency of matter allotted proportionately to its particular form according to the judgment of the universal agent. And although every form intends perpetual existence as far as this is possible, yet no form of anything corruptible can achieve its own immortality except the rational soul, because the latter is not completely subject to matter as are other forms; in fact, it has its own immaterial action, as asserted (I, q. 75, a. 2). So, by his form, incorruption is more natural to man than to other corruptible things. But because this very form has a matter made of contraries, a corruptibility in the whole results from that matter's tendency. Thus man is naturally corruptible through the nature of his matter in itself but not through the nature of his form. . . .

. . . The form of man or the rational soul is through its incorruptibility adapted to its end which is everlasting happiness; but the human body, which is corruptible, is through its nature adapted in one way to its form and, in another way, it is not. For two aspects of matter are noticeable, one chosen by the agent and another not chosen but a natural condition of the matter. So that when a smith wishes to make a knife, he chooses a matter both hard and flexible so that it can be sharpened for use in cutting, and for this choice iron is best adapted for a knife; but that iron is breakable and tends to rust comes from iron's natural disposition, and it is not chosen by the workman who would eliminate this condition if possible, so that this disposition of matter is neither adapted to the workman's intention nor to the purpose of his art. In such a way nature chose the human body as a matter of mixed temperament suitable as an organ of touch and of the other sensitive and motive powers. But its corruptibility results from the condition of matter, not by nature's choice; in fact, if it were possible, nature would choose an incorruptible matter.

But God, to whom all nature is subject, supplied for nature's defect when he formed man, and through the gift of original justice, gave a certain incorruptibility to the body (I, q. 97, a. 1). In this sense it is said that *God made not death,* and that death is the punishment for sin.

4. CHRIST

Incarnation   *On the Union of the Incarnate Word*, q. 1, a. 1

The Mode of the Union of the Word incarnate.
State of the question.

1. The question concerns the mode of union of the Word incarnate. First, it is asked whether the union of the Word incarnate was accomplished in the person or in the nature. Indeed, it seems that it occurred in the nature. As Athanasius says (in the symbol of faith), just as the rational soul and flesh constitute one man, so God and man are one Christ. But the rational soul and flesh are united in one human nature; therefore, God and man are joined in the one nature of Christ.
2. Moreover, Damascene says in Book III, Ch. 3: This is the error of the heretics, that they call nature and hypostasis the same thing. But this does not seem false, for in anything

simple, and especially in God, the *suppositum* and the nature
are identical. Therefore do heretics speak falsely, because if
the union is accomplished in the person, is it not accomplished in the nature?

3. Moreover, Damascene says in Book III that the two natures are united without conversion, without alteration, but
on the contrary, as two natures. But the union of natures
seems to cause a natural union. Therefore, the union is accomplished in the nature.

4. Again, in all beings in which the *suppositum* has something besides the nature of the species (be it an accident or
an individual nature), it is necessary that the *suppositum* be
different from the nature, as is clear through the philosopher
(*Metaphysics* VII, c. 20, 21). But if the union of the human
nature to the Word is not accomplished in the human nature, it will not lie in the nature of the very species of the
Word. Therefore, it will follow that the *suppositum* of the
Word is something other than the divine nature. This conclusion is impossible. Therefore, it seems that the union occurred in the nature.

5. Moreover, a oneness follows upon a uniting. But since
oneness of the person of the Word is eternal, it is not subsequent to the union that is accomplished in the fullness of
time. Therefore the union is not accomplished in the person.

6. Again, the union achieves a certain additional something: thus union cannot be accomplished in anything that of
itself is consummate simplicity. But the person of the Word,
since he is truly God, is of consummate simplicity. Therefore,
union cannot be accomplished in the person of the Word.

7. Also, two things not of the same genus cannot be united
in one thing; from a line and whiteness one unity cannot be
made. But human nature differs from divine nature much
more than do things not of the same genus differ. Therefore,
the human and the divine natures cannot be united together
in one person.

8. Again, the person and the nature of the Word differ
only in the manner of being comprehended, inasmuch as the
relation of origin is attributed to the person of the Word, not
to the nature. But through the relation of origin, the Word is

not related to human nature, but to the Father. Therefore, in the same manner, the person of the Word and his nature are considered to be assumed to the human nature. If therefore the union was accomplished in the person, the union will be accomplished in the nature.

9. Again, the incarnation stimulates us to love God incarnate. But one ought not to love one divine person more than another; for the love should be equal for those whose goodness is the same. Therefore, the union of the incarnation was accomplished in the nature common to the three persons.

10. Moreover, according to the philosopher (*On the Soul* I, 37), to live is to be. But in Christ, life is twofold: the human and the divine. There are, therefore, two existences and consequently two persons: for "to be" (*esse*) is proper to the complete substance or the person. Hence the union is not accomplished in the person.

11. Again, as the form of a part is comparable to its matter, so the form of the whole is comparable to the complete substance. But the form of the part cannot exist except in its proper matter. Therefore, the form of the whole, which is its nature cannot exist except in its proper complete substance, which is the human person. Similar reasoning goes for the divine nature in a divine person. If two natures are present in this union, two persons are also present.

12. Moreover, what is truly predicated of anything is able to substitute for the thing itself. But divine nature is truly predicated of the person of the Word. Therefore nature is synonymous with person. If, therefore, the union is accomplished in the person, it can truly be said that the union is accomplished in the nature.

13. Moreover, whatever is united to anything is joined to it either essentially or accidentally. But human nature is not united to the Word accidentally, because in this way it would retain its own complete individuality, and there would be two persons: for a substance added to another retains its own singularity, as one clothed with a garment, as a rider on a horse. Therefore, it [the human nature] is united essentially to the essence or to the nature of the Word. Therefore, the union is accomplished in the nature.

14. Besides, nothing apprehended under one thing is ex-

tended beyond, for a thing bound by a place is not outside the place. But a complete substance of any nature is comprehended under that very nature, and the thing is said to be of the nature in question: for just as the species is comprehended under the genus, so the individual is comprehended under the species. Therefore, since the Word is a complete substance of divine nature, it cannot go beyond that nature to become a complete substance of another nature.

15. Moreover, nature is related to the complete substance as being more formal, more simple, more constitutive. But human nature cannot be in this way related to the person of the Word. Therefore the person of the Word cannot be a person of human nature.

16. Besides, action is attributed to a complete substance or to a person, because actions are from the individual, according to Aristotle (*Metaph.* I, 1). But in Christ there are two actions, as Damascene proves (III, 15). Therefore, there are two persons. Hence the union has not been accomplished in the person.

17. Moreover, "person" is defined as "nature of a special kind." If, therefore, the union is in the person, it follows that the union was accomplished in the nature.

Response: But on the contrary, as Augustine (Fulgentius) says (*On Faith*): "It remains true that there are in Christ two natures, but one person."

Moreover, to Orosious he says: "We recognize two natures in the one person of the Son."

I answer that to provide evidence for answering this question, we must consider: 1. what a nature is; 2. what a person is; 3. how the union of the incarnate Word is accomplished in the person, not in the nature.

It is necessary, therefore, to know that the term "nature" is taken from "a proceeding or originating"; hence, first of all, nature has been spoken of as something born, the very coming into being of living things, such as animals or plants; then the term has been applied to the principle of an interior movement like that spoken of in *Physics* II, 1—i.e., nature itself is a principle of motion from within and not from without. And because the natural motion, especially in generation, is terminated at the essence of the species, and further, the essence of the species that the definition specifies is called nature, whence it is that Boethius says in the book *On Two Natures* that "Nature is the specific difference that gives form to a thing," in this way nature is here understood. Moreover, to understand what a person is, it is necessary to consider this: If there is anything in which there is nothing other than the specific essence, that very specific essence will subsist individually on its own (per se); and so in a being of this kind, the complete substance and the nature will be in reality one same thing, differing only mentally insofar as the nature is considered the essence of the species, and the complete substance is said truly to subsist on its own. If, however, there should be something within the *res* besides the essence specified by the definition—whether it be other as an accident or individuating matter—then the complete substance will not wholly coincide with the nature, but will have something additional. This is especially evident in those things that are composed of matter and form. And what has been said about the complete substance must be understood of the person of rational nature, since a person is nothing other than a complete substance of a rational nature, as Boethius says in *On Two Natures:* that a person is an individual substance of rational nature.

Therefore what prevents something from being united not in nature but in person? For the individual substance of a rational nature has something not belonging to the specific nature, and this something is united to it personally, not naturally. In this way, therefore, must it be understood that the human nature is united to the Word of God in person, not in nature, for if the human nature does not belong to the person of the divine nature, it yet does belong to the person of the divine nature insofar as the person of the Word joined to himself a human nature by assuming it. But about the manner of this union we have doubt and disagreement.

Usually with created things one is joined to another in two ways, accidentally and essentially. Thus Nestorius, and before him Theodore, bishop of Mopsuestia [writings condemned by the Fifth General Council, 553] held that human nature was joined to the Word accidentally, as by an indwelling of grace. They held that the Word of God was united to the man Christ, dwelling in him as in his temple. But we see that any substance joined accidentally to another retains separately its own proper singularity of nature—for example, a garment on a man, or an inhabitant of a house. It follows then that the man would have his own proper singularity of nature, that is, his personality. Thus, according to Nestorius it followed that in Christ there was the person of the man distinct from the person of the Word; and that the one person was the son of man, and the other the Son of God. Wherefore, he did not confess that the Blessed Virgin was the mother of God but the mother of man. However, this is altogether absurd. First, certainly, sacred Scripture speaks in one way about men in whom the Word of God dwelt by grace, and in another about Christ. Of the former it says that the word of the Lord was spoken to such a Prophet; but of Christ it says: "the Word was made flesh," that is, man as if the very Word in Person became man. Again, the Apostle Paul in his second epistle to the Philippians calls the union the emptying of the Son of God. It is manifest, moreover, that the indwelling of grace does not satisfy the idea of emptying; otherwise, "emptying" should be attributed not only to the Son, but also to the Father and to the Holy Spirit, of whom the Lord spoke: "He shall abide with you and shall be in you"; and concerning himself and the Father (v. 23): "We will come to him, and will make our abode with him. . . ."

Therefore, on account of this and much else the aforesaid error was condemned in the Council of Ephesus. Some indeed, holding with Nestorius that human nature had accidentally come to the Word, wished to avoid a duality of persons which Nestorius had proposed; proposing that because the Word assumed a soul and body not mutually united, that a human person was not established from soul and body. But from this there followed a greater inconvenience; that Christ was not truly man, since the meaning of man consisted in the union of soul and body. And so this error was likewise condemned under Alexander III in the Council of Turonensi.

Others indeed took another position, arguing that human nature had come essentially to the Word, as though united in one nature or essence out of the divine nature and human nature. And towards this a certain Apollinaris of Laodicensis proposed three dogmas as Pope Leo declared in a certain letter to the men of Constantinople: the first of these was that the soul was not united in Christ, but the Word took its place; and so from the Word and the flesh there was made one nature, just as there are body and soul in us. In this teaching Apollinaris followed Nestorius. But because the Holy Scripture (Jn. 8: 18) speaks of Christ's soul: "I have the power to lay it down and I have the power to take it up again," a second teaching arose, which proposed a sensitive but not a rational soul to be in Christ; the Word was in the man Christ in the place of intellect. But this is inconsistent; for, according to it, the Word would not have assumed a human nature, but an animal nature, as St. Augustine argues in *Eighty-three Questions*, 80. His third teaching held that the flesh of Christ was not taken from woman but made from the Word, who was changed and turned into flesh. Yet this is in the highest degree impossible, because the Word of God insofar as he is truly God is altogether immutable. Hence in the Council of Constantinople Apollinaris was condemned for these doctrines; Eutyches, who held his third teaching, had been condemned in the Council of Chalcedon.

Again, if union is not accomplished in the person, but merely a habitation, as Nestorius holds, nothing new occurred in the incarnation of Christ. That the union was accomplished in the nature, as Apollinaris and Eutyches held, is wholly impossible since, in truth, species are like numbers in which additions or subtractions alter the unity of the species, as stated in *Metaph*. VIII. It is impossible for a complete nature to receive the addition of another nature; were it to receive the addition, it would no longer be the same nature, but another. However, divine nature is supremely complete; in fact, even human nature is complete as a species, so that the entrance of another nature cannot be allowed. If it were possible, what would be produced from both would be neither divine nature nor human. Thus Christ would be neither man nor God, which is inadmissible.

It remains, therefore, that human nature is united to the Word neither accidentally nor essentially, but substantially in the sense that substance signifies a rational single substance according to person, or personally. In created things there is no example of such union closer than that of the rational soul and body, as Athanasius points out (in his Creed). Nor certainly does he mean it in the sense that the soul is the form of the body (for the Word is not able to be the form of matter), but in the sense that the body is an instrument of the soul, not indeed extrinsic and adventitious, but innate and conjoined. Thus Damascene says (Book III, 15), "Human nature is the instrument of the Word." Still, there was something rather like this, as St. Augustine says in his treatise, *Against Feliciamus*, 12, if we may imagine, as very many wish to, that there is in the world a cosmic soul that makes the matter potential to various natures become one person with itself. However, all examples of this kind fall flat because instrumental union is accidental. But this incarnation is a unique union beyond all modes of union known to us. As God is goodness itself and is his own being, so also is he unity itself in his essence. Likewise his virtue is not limited to those modes of goodness and being that are in creatures, but he is able to make new modes of goodness and being not known to us. Furthermore, by his infinite power he has been able to make a new mode of union wherein the human nature is united to the person of the Word, yet not accidentally, although no satisfying example of this is found among creatures.

Whereupon, speaking of this mystery, Augustine says in a letter to Volusianus: "To one demanding reasons, let us admit that here we have a marvel! To one seeking precedents, admit that this is extraordinary. Let us grant that God can do something we cannot trace out; for in such things the whole explanation of the fact lies in the power of the Doer." Also, Dionysius says (*On the Divine Names*, 2): "Jesus as we consider him is a divine composition" (that is, union), "and unutterable in any word, unknown to any mind, even to the highest of the angels."

Answers to objections:

1. Analogy does not extend to the point of there being but one nature in man composed of soul and flesh, but to the point of one person's being constituted of both.

2. Granted that in divinity, nature and supposit or person

do not differ in reality, yet, they differ according to reason, as it is said. And, whereas there is the same subsistence in human nature and in the divine nature, nevertheless, the same essence is not united in both. Hence, union has been accomplished in the person to whose meaning it belongs to subsist; not, however, to the nature that expresses the essence of the thing.

3. The natures certainly are united in Christ—not, however, in the nature, but in the person. From this very fact it is clear that the natures are said to be united unchangeably and unalterably.

4. The heretics who say that the union has not been made in the person and may have been made in the nature did not weigh the truth that person is one thing, and nature another, both in reality and in reason. So they were deceived.

5. Strictly speaking, for union, one thing is said to be united to another; for unity, it is said to be one with it. Therefore, union is not understood to be directed to the divine person, for that person has been one within itself from eternity, but in time the person has been united to a human nature. Thus, in our consideration, union precedes the person, not as the person is one but as it is united.

6. Union is not said to be made in the divine person, as if that very person were made of two mutually united, for this is repugnant to supreme simplicity. But the union is said to have been made in the person, inasmuch as a simple divine person subsists in two natures, the divine and the human.

7. Two beings, different in genus, are not united in one essence or nature; nevertheless, nothing prevents them from being united in one supposit. For example, an essence is not made from string and whiteness, yet they are found in one supposit.

8. The person of the Son of God can be considered in a twofold manner: in one way, according to the usual understanding of "person" as it signifies a certain subsisting, and in this sense union was accomplished in the person according to the understanding of person, as we said above. In another way there can be considered in the person of the Son what is proper to the person of the Son: the relation of the Son to

the Father. For this meaning is not denoted by the hypostatic union of two natures.

9. As the incarnation adds no goodness to the divine person, so also it adds no lovableness; hence the person of the Word incarnate must not be loved more than the person of the eternal Word, strictly. He should be loved for another reason, that he is included under the universal goodness of the Word. Wherefore, it does not follow that since the union of the incarnation has been accomplished in one person and not in others that that person should be loved more than the other persons.

10. Being is characteristic both of the person subsisting and of the nature in which the person subsists as having being according to that nature. Therefore, the being of the person of the Word incarnate is one on the part of the subsisting person, but not, however, on the part of the natures.

11. Nature is not related to the complete substance as form to matter; for matter is constituted in being only through form, and for that reason, form requires determinate matter to be actual. But a complete substance not only is constituted by the specific nature but has other realities as well. Therefore, nothing prevents one nature's being possessed by a complete substance of another nature.

12. The divine nature is predicated of a divine person because of identity of being, but not according to strict logical requirements. Therefore, one term cannot be used interchangeably for the other in propositions. So we can say of God that a person begets, but we may not say that the divine nature begets.

13. Human nature is united to the Word neither accidentally, nor even essentially (as if belonging to the divine nature of the Word), but substantially, that is, according to substance, as if belonging to the substance or person of the Word.

14. The person of the Word is included in the nature of the Word, nor can it be extended to anything beyond it. But the nature of the Word by reason of its infinity includes every finite nature. Therefore, when the person of the Word assumed human nature, he did not extend himself beyond the divine nature, but rather took what is beneath him, as is

stated (Ph. 2: 6): "Who being in the form of God, thought it not robbery to be equal with God, but humbled himself." The greatness of God was not relinquished, but the lowliness of human nature was put on.

15. Just as the nature of the Word is infinite, so too is the person of the Word. Thus the divine nature of the Word corresponds equally to the very person of the Word as he is; the human nature, however, encounters the divine Word because the Word was made man. It does not follow that human nature, which makes a man to be human, is simpler and more formal than the human being, who is the Word made flesh.

16. Action comes forth from a complete substance according to its nature or form; hence, actions differ in accordance with the diversity not only of complete substance but also of nature and form. For example, in the case of one human being, seeing is one action, and hearing, another, because they come from different powers; wherefore in Christ there are two kinds of actions because of his two natures, although he is one person or hypostasis.

17. When person is defined as a distinctive (peculiar) nature, nature then means substance, and substance signifies not nature but hypostasis.

Articles of Faith, Art. 3

Third Article: "Who was conceived by the Holy Spirit, born of the Virgin Mary."

Not only should the Christian believe in the Son of God . . . but likewise in his incarnation. After St. John had discussed very subtle and difficult notions, he refers to the incarnation by saying: "And the Word was made flesh." Now, to understand anything about this, two examples will help.

Nothing is more like the Word of God, evidently, than the word we conceive in our mind but do not speak. Now, only he who conceives this interior word in the mind knows it, whereas it becomes known to others only when spoken. As long as the Word of God was within the Father, it was known only by the Father himself, but as soon as the Word became flesh—as a word becomes audible—it became manifest and known. "Afterward he was seen upon earth and conversed with men" (Ba. 3: 38).

Another example is found from the fact that the spoken word, although known through hearing, is nevertheless neither seen nor touched unless it is written upon paper. Likewise, as soon as the Word of God became flesh, he was made both visible and tangible. And just as the paper on which a king's word is written is spoken of as the word of the king, so likewise man, to whom the Word of God is united in one person (hypostasis), is called the Son of God. "Take thee a great book and write it with a man's pen" (Is. 8: 1). Therefore the holy Apostles stated: "Who was conceived by the Holy Spirit, born of the Virgin Mary."

Many errors arose around this point (Origen, Photius, Manichaeus, Ebion, Valentinus, Arius, Apollinarius, Nestorius), and to eliminate these errors the holy Fathers at the Council of Nicaea added a number of things in that other creed. . . .

Something is gained from all this:

1. Our faith is strengthened. For we would not believe someone who reported about a foreign land he had never visited to the extent that we would believe him had he been there. Now, the patriarchs and prophets and John the Baptist told something about God before Christ came into the world. But men did not believe them to the extent that they believed Christ, who was with God, or rather, was one with God. And so our faith is firmer with respect to what Christ himself tells us: "No one hath seen God at any time; the only-begotten Son who is in the bosom of the Father, he hath declared him" (Jn. 1: 18). Hence before the coming of Christ many mysteries of our faith were hidden from us, and these are now illuminated.

2. Our hope is uplifted. The son of man, in assuming our flesh, certainly did not come to us for any light reason, but for our very great benefit. For he, as it were, traded with us by assuming a living body and deigning to be born of the Virgin so that we may participate in his divinity. And so he became man in order to make man divine.

3. Our charity is stirred up. There is no clearer proof of divine charity than that God, the Creator of all, becomes a

creature, that Our Lord becomes our brother, and that the Son of God becomes the son of man: "For God so loved the world as to give his only-begotten Son" (Jn. 3: 16). Reflection upon all this should re-enkindle our love for God and inflame us.

4. We are led to preserve the purity of our souls. By its union with God our nature was exalted and dignified to the extent of being taken up into union with a divine person.

In fact, after the incarnation the angel would not allow St. John to adore him, although this was allowed to even the greatest patriarch; so that anyone who reflects upon this dignifying of his nature and is ever aware of it should scorn any cheapening or lowering of himself and his nature by sin. So St. Peter says: "By whom he hath given us most great and precious promises; that by these you may be made partakers of the divine nature; flying the corruption of that concupiscence which is in the world" (2 P. 1: 4).

Finally, our desire to come to Christ is intensified by reflection upon all this. If a king had a brother separated by a great distance from him, that brother would desire to come to the king to see him, be near him, and live with him. So likewise Christ is our brother, and we should desire to be with him and be united to him. "Wheresoever the body shall be, there shall the eagles also be gathered together" (Mt. 24: 28).

The Apostle desired "to be dissolved and to be with Christ" (Ph. 1: 23), and this desire increases within us as we meditate upon the incarnation of Christ.

Priesthood of Christ   *Summa of Theology* III, q.
                                    22, a. 1, c

It is proper to a priest to be a mediator between God and the people: namely, insofar as he bestows divine realities on the people, so that *sacerdos* (priest) signifies a giver of sacred things (*sacra dans*) (Mal. 2: 7): "They shall seek the law at his (i.e., the priest's) mouth"; and again insofar as he offers up the people's prayers to God and, in a way, makes satisfaction to God for their sins; hence, the Apostle says (Heb. 5: 1): "Every high priest taken from among men is ordained for men in the things that belong to God, that he may offer up gifts and sacrifices for sins." Now, this is most suitable to Christ, for through him are gifts bestowed on men (2 P. 1: 4): "By whom (i.e., Christ) he hath given us most great and precious promises, that by these you may be made partakers of the divine nature." Moreover, he reconciled the human race to God, (Col. 1: 19–20): "In him (i.e., Christ) it hath well pleased (the Father) that all fullness should dwell, and through him to reconcile all things unto himself."

Therefore, it is most fitting that Christ should be a priest.

Christ a Victim for Sin
Summa of Theology III, q. 22, a. 2, c

As Augustine says (*City of God* X, 5): "Every visible sacrifice is a sacrament, that is a sacred sign of the invisible sacrifice." Now, the invisible sacrifice is that by which a man offers his spirit to God (Ps. 50: 19): "A sacrifice to God is an afflicted spirit." So that whatever is offered to God with the purpose of raising man's spirit to him may be called a sacrifice.

Now, man should offer sacrifice for three reasons. First, for the remission of sin, which separates him from God. Thus the Apostle says (Heb. 5: 1) that it belongs to the priest "to offer gifts and sacrifices for sins." Second, that man may remain in the state of grace by cleaving to God, which constitutes his peace and salvation. . . . Third, so that the spirit of man may be perfectly united to God; this will be most perfectly achieved in glory. . . .

Now, these benefits were achieved for us by Christ's humanity. For, first of all, our sins were erased (Rm. 4: 25): "Who was delivered up for our sins." Second, through him we received the grace of salvation (Heb. 5: 9): "He became to all who obey him the cause of eternal salvation." Third, through him we have acquired the perfection of glory (Heb. 10: 19): "We have a confidence in the entering into the holies (i.e., the heavenly glory) through his blood."

Therefore, Christ himself as man was not only priest, but

also a perfect victim for sin, a victim for a peace-offering, and a holocaust.

Summa of Theology III, q. 22, a. 5, ad. 2

Although Christ's passion and death are not to be repeated, nevertheless the virtue of that victim lasts forever, since, as it is written (Heb. 10: 14): "By one oblation he hath perfected forever them who are sanctified."

Christ as Mediator   *Summa of Theology* III, q. 26, a. 1, c

Strictly speaking, a mediator is one who joins together and unites those between whom he mediates; for extremes are united in the mean. But to unite men to God belongs to Christ, through whom men are reconciled to God (2 Co. 5: 19): "God was in Christ reconciling the world to himself." And so only Christ is the perfect mediator of God and men, in that through his death he reconciled the human race to God. Thus the Apostle, after saying, "Mediator of God and man, the man Christ Jesus," added: "who gave himself a redemption for all."

But nothing stops others from being mediators in some fashion between God and man insofar as they collaborate in uniting men to God, either dispositively or instrumentally.

Function of Mediator   *Summa of Theology* III, q. 26, a. 2, c

We may reflect on the two aspects of a mediator: first, that he is a mean; second, that he joins together others. Now, by nature a mean is distant from each extreme, so that it unites by communicating to one what pertains to the other. Now, only as man and not as God can either of these aspects of the mean be applied to Christ. For as God he does not differ from the Holy Spirit in nature and ruling power, nor have the Father and the Holy Spirit anything not had by the Son, so that he should be able to communicate to others something belonging to the Father and the Holy Spirit but not to him.

But both can be applied to him as man. For as man he is distant both from God by nature and from man by dignity in respect to grace and glory. Moreover, it is proper to him as man to unite men to God by communicating to men both commandments and gifts, and by offering satisfaction and prayers to God for men. And therefore as man he is most truly spoken of as mediator.

Effectiveness of Christ's Passion
Summa of Theology III, q. 48, a. 1, c

Grace was given to Christ not only as an individual but insofar as he is head of the Church, so that it might flow over into his members; and so Christ's works are referred to himself and to his members, just as the works of any other man in a state of grace are referred to himself. But it is clear that whoever suffers for the sake of justice when in a state of grace thereby merits his salvation (Mt. 5: 10): "Blessed are they who suffer persecution for justice's sake."

Therefore, Christ by his passion merited salvation not only for himself, but likewise for all his members.

Atonement of Christ
Summa of Theology III, q. 48, a. 2, c

He atones appropriately for an offense who offers whatever the offended one equally loves, or loves more than he detested the offense. But Christ by suffering out of love and obedience gave to God more than was required to compensate for the offense of the whole human race. First, by reason of the tremendous charity from which he suffered; second, by reason of the dignity of his life, which he gave up in atonement, for this was the life of one who was both God and man; third, on account of the extent of the passion and the greatness of the sorrow suffered. . . . And so Christ's passion was not merely a sufficient but a superabundant atonement for the sins of the human race: according to "He is the propitiation for our sins; and not for ours only, but also for those of the whole world" (1 Jn. 2: 2).

Sacrifice of Christ   *Summary of Theology* III, q. 48, a. 3, c

A sacrifice, strictly speaking, is something done to give due honor to God in order to appease him, and so Augustine says (*City of God* X): "A true sacrifice is every good work done in order that we may cling to God in holy fellowship, yet referred to that consummation of happiness wherein we can be truly blessed." But, as is added in the same spot, "Christ offered himself up for us in the passion: and this voluntary enduring of the passion was most acceptable to God, as coming from charity." Therefore it is clear that Christ's passion was a true sacrifice. . . .

Cause of Salvation: Christ   *Summa of Theology* III, q. 48, a. 6, c

There is a twofold efficient agency: namely, the principal and the instrumental. Now, the principal efficient cause of man's salvation is God. But because Christ's humanity is the instrument of the Godhead, all Christ's actions and sufferings act instrumentally in virtue of his Godhead for the salvation of men. And so Christ's passion achieves man's salvation effectively.

Actions of Christ   *Summa of Theology* III, q. 19, a. 1, c

As was previously said (q. 18, a. 1), the aforementioned heretics who argued that there was one will in Christ argued that there was one action in Christ. Now, to clarify their wrong opinion, we should remember that wherever there are numerous mutually directed agents, the inferior is moved by the superior, as man's body is moved by his soul, and his lower powers by reason. And thus the inferior agent's actions and motions are acted upon rather than being actions; thus we speak of man's walking, which pertains to his feet, and touching, which pertains to his hand, as things exercised by the man—one exercised by the soul through the feet, the other through the hands. And because the same soul is acting in both cases, there is but one indifferent action on the part of that which is acting, namely, the first moving principle; but difference occurs through what is acted upon. Now, just as in a mere man, the body is moved by the soul, and the sensitive by the rational tendency, so the human nature in the Lord Jesus Christ is moved and ruled by the divine. So they said that there is one indifferent action of the acting God, but variety in what is acted upon, since Christ as God through himself did one thing, that is, by conserving all things through the Word of his power, and another thing through his human nature by walking in a body. Thus the Sixth Council quotes the statement of Severus the heretic: "Whatever things were done and wrought by the one Christ, differ greatly; for some are suitable to God and some are human, but to give strong steps to sickly limbs wholly unable to walk on the ground, is suitable to God. Yet one, i.e., the incarnate Word, wrought one and the other—neither was this from one nature, and that from another; nor can we justly affirm that because there are distinct things achieved there are therefore two acting natures and forms."

But in this they were mistaken, for whatever is moved by another has a double action—one from its own form—the other as moved by another; hence an ax's own action is to chop, but as moved by the carpenter, its action is to make benches. So the action belonging to anything by its form is proper to it, nor does it belong to the mover except in the measure that he uses the particular thing for his work: hence to heat is fire's proper action, but not a smith's, except in the measure that he uses fire to heat iron. But the action belonging to anything as moved by another is not distinct from the mover's action; so to make a bench is not the ax's action independent of the carpenter. Consequently, the mover's action must be distinct from the proper action of the moved whenever the mover and the moved have diverse forms or active powers; yet the moved participates in the mover's action, and the mover makes use of the action of the moved and, accordingly, each acts in communion with the other.

Hence in Christ human nature has its proper form and power whereby it acts, and so has the divine; so that human nature has its proper action distinct from the divine, and vice versa. Yet the divine nature makes use of the action of the human nature as of the action of its instrument; and likewise the human nature participates in the action of the divine nature as an instrument participates in the action of the principal agent. And this is what Pope Leo says (*Ep. ad Flavian*, 28): "Both forms (i.e., both the divine and the human nature in Christ) do what is proper to each in union with the other, i.e., the Word does what belongs to the Word, and the flesh does what belongs to flesh."

But if the action of the Godhead and manhood in Christ were only one, then we would have to say either that the human nature was without its proper form and power (for this could never be said of the divine), so that consequently there would be in Christ only the divine action; or we would have to say that one power resulted from the divine and human power. But both are impossible positions. The first would imply that the human nature in Christ is imperfect, and the second would imply a confusion of the natures. Thus with reason the Sixth Council (Act. 18) condemned this view, and stated this: "We confess two natural, indivisible, inconvertible, unconfused, and inseparable actions in the same Lord Jesus Christ our true God, i.e., the divine action and the human action."

Charity of Christ　　*Commentary on Epistle to Ephesians III, 5*

He says: "You ought to be so rooted and founded in charity, dearly beloved, *that you may be able to comprehend, with all the saints, what is the breadth and length and height and depth. . . .*"

Thus you may be able to comprehend in the sense of perfectly attaining to, with all the saints, what is the *breadth* with which your charity should extend even to enemies, what is the *length* during which it never ceases, its *height* in loving God for his own sake, and the *depth* of the divine predestination [from which it springs].

At this point it should be realized that it was within Christ's power to choose what type of death he wanted. And since he underwent death out of charity, he chose the death of the cross, in which the aforesaid four dimensions are present. The cross beam has *breadth,* and to it his hands were nailed, because through charity our good works ought to stretch out even to adversaries: "The Lord brought me forth into a broad place" (Ps. 17: 20). The trunk of the cross has *length* against which the whole body leans, since charity ought to be enduring, thus sustaining and saving man: "He who shall persevere unto the end, he shall be saved" (Mt. 10: 22). The projection of wood against which the head is thrown back has *height,* since our hope must rise toward the eternal and the divine: "The head of every man is Christ" (1 Co. 11: 3). The cross is braced by its *depth,* which lies concealed beneath the ground; it is not seen because the depth of the divine love, which sustains us, is not visible insofar as the plans of predestination, as was said above, are beyond our intelligence. . . .*

Christ's Passover Action: Death; Resurrection; Ascension *Summa of Theology* III, q. 50, a. 6, c

Christ's death may be considered in two ways: *in becoming* and *in fact.* Death is referred to as *in becoming* when anyone from natural or compulsory suffering tends toward death; and thus to speak of Christ's death is like speaking of his passion, so that Christ's death is in this sense the cause of our salvation in accord with what has been already said of the passion (q. 48). But death is considered in fact when the separation of soul and body has already occurred, and we are now speaking of Christ's death in this sense. In this sense it is not possible for Christ to cause our death through merit but only through causality, i.e., because the Godhead was not separated from Christ's flesh by death; and so even when the soul had left the flesh, whatever happened to Christ's flesh was on behalf of salvation in virtue of the united Godhead. But a cause's effect is properly judged according to its similarity to the cause. Therefore, because death is a kind of loss of one's own life, the effect of Christ's death is considered in reference to the withdrawal of impediments to our salva-

* Translated by R. F. Larcher, O.P.

tion: and these are the death of the soul and of the body. Thus in us Christ's death is said to have destroyed both the soul's death, caused by sin: "He was delivered up for our sins" (Rm. 4: 25) and the body's death, which is the withdrawal of the soul: "Death is swallowed up in victory" (1 Co. 15: 54).

The Risen Christ   *Summa of Theology* III, q. 53, a. 1, c

It was suitable for Christ to arise for five reasons. First, in the interest of divine justice, which appropriately exalts those who humble themselves for God's sake; "He hath put down the mighty from their seat, and hath exalted the humble" (Lk. 1: 52). Therefore, since Christ humbled himself even unto the death of the cross out of love and obedience to God, he was fittingly exalted by God to a glorious resurrection; thus in his person it is said: "Thou hast known, [i.e., favored] *my sitting down* [i.e., my humiliation and passion] and *my rising up,* [i.e., my glorification in the resurrection]" (Ps. 138: 2) as the gloss explains.

Second, for our instruction in the faith, because our belief in Christ's divinity is confirmed by his arising, since (2 Co. 13: 4): "Although he was crucified through weakness, yet he liveth by the power of God." And so it is written (1 Co. 15: 14): "If Christ be not risen again, then is our preaching vain, and our faith is also vain" and (Ps. 29: 10): "What profit is there in my blood?" that is, in the shedding of my blood, while I go down, as by various degrees of evils, into corruption? As though he were to answer, "None." "For if I do not at once rise again but my body be corrupted, I shall preach to no one, I shall gain no one," as the gloss explains.

Third, to raise our hope, because by seeing Christ our head rise again we hope that we also shall rise again. Thus it is written (1 Co. 15: 12): "Now, if Christ be preached that he rose from the dead, how do some among you say that there is no resurrection of the dead?" And (Jb. 19: 25): "I know [that is, with certainty of faith] that my redeemer, [i.e., Christ] liveth, having risen from the dead; and therefore in the last day I shall rise out of the earth: . . . . this my hope is laid up in my bosom."

Fourth, to bring order into the lives of the faithful (Rm. 6: 4): "As Christ is risen from the dead by the glory of the Father, so we also may walk in newness of life"; and farther on, "Christ rising from the dead dieth now no more; so do you also reckon that you are dead to sin, but alive to God."

Fifth, to bring the work of our salvation to perfection; for just as in dying he endured evil things to deliver us from evil, so was he glorified in rising again to perfect us with good things (Rm. 4: 25): "He was delivered up for our sins, and rose again for our justification."

Summa of Theology III, q. 53, a. 2, c

Christ's resurrection was needed for the instruction of our faith, but our faith with respect to Christ's divinity and humanity, for believing one without the other is insufficient. . . . Therefore, to confirm our faith in the truth of his divinity, he was required to arise speedily and not put off the resurrection until the world's end. But to confirm our faith with respect to the truth of his humanity and death, some interval between his death and arising was needed. . . .

Resurrection   *Letter to Archbishop of Palermo on Articles of Faith,* Art. 5

Fifth Article: "The third day he rose again from the dead."
    We can learn four things from this.
    1. First, let us try to arise spiritually from the soul's death, brought on by our sins, to that life of justice had through penance: "Rise, thou who sleepest, and arise from the dead; and Christ shall enlighten thee" (Ep. 5: 14). This is the first resurrection: "Blessed and holy is he who hath part in the first resurrection" (Jn. 20: 6).
    2. Second, let us not put off rising until our death, but do it now, since Christ arose on the third day: "Delay not to be converted to the Lord; and defer it not from day to day" (Ecc. 5: 8). When overcome by illness you will not be able

to attend to what is involved in salvation, and in addition you will by persevering in sin be unable to participate in all the good accomplished in the Church, and you will bring about many evils. In fact, the longer the devil possesses you, the harder it is to evacuate him, as St. Bede tells us.

3. Third, let us arise again to an incorruptible life so as never to die again, resolving to sin no more. "Knowing that Christ, rising again from the dead, dieth now no more. Death shall no more have dominion over him. . . . So do you also reckon that you are dead to sin, but alive unto God, in Christ Jesus Our Lord. Neither yield ye your members as instruments of iniquity unto sin; but present yourselves to God, as those who are alive from the dead" (Rm. 6: 9).

4. Fourth, let us again rise to a new and glorious life by avoiding everything that formerly was an occasion and cause of our death and sin: "As Christ is risen from the dead by the glory of the Father, so we also may walk in newness of life" (Rm. 6: 4). This new life is the life of justice renewing the soul and leading it to the life of glory.

Our Resurrection Rooted in Christ's   *Summa of Theology* III, q. 56, a. 1, c

As expressed in *Metaphysics* II, 4: "Whatever is first in any order is the cause of all that come after it." But Christ's resurrection was the first in the order of all resurrection. . . . Thus Christ's resurrection must be the cause of ours; and this the Apostle says (1 Co. 15: 20): "Christ is risen from the dead, the first fruits of them that sleep; for by a man came death, and by a man the resurrection of the dead."

And this is reasonable. For the principle of human life-giving is the Word of God, of whom it is said (Ps. 35: 10): "With thee is the fountain of life"; thus he himself says (Jn. 5: 21): "As the Father raiseth up the dead and giveth life, so the Son also giveth life to whom he will." Now, the divinely established natural order is that every cause acts first upon what is nearest to it, and through it upon others that are more remote, just as fire first heats the nearest air and through the air bodies that are more distant; and God himself first illuminates those substances closer to him, and through them others that are more distant, as Dionysius says (*Heavenly Hierarchy*, 13). Therefore, the Word of God first gives immortal life to that body naturally united with himself, and through it activates the resurrection in all other bodies.

Resurrection Grace Affects Soul and Body

Summa of Theology III, q. 56, a. 2, c

Christ's resurrection acts in virtue of the divinity. Now, this virtue extends not only to the resurrection of bodies, but also to that of souls; for from God it comes about that the soul lives by grace and that the body lives by the soul. Therefore, Christ's resurrection is instrumentally effective not only with respect to the resurrection of bodies but also with respect to the resurrection of souls. Likewise, it is an exemplary cause with respect to the resurrection of souls, since even in our souls we must be conformed with the rising Christ; as the Apostle says (Rm. 6: 4–11): "Christ is risen from the dead by the glory of the Father, so we also may walk in the newness of life: and as he, rising again from the dead, dieth now no more, so let us reckon that we are dead to sin, that we may live together with him."

Christ's Ascension

Summa of Theology III, q. 57, a. 1, c

The place should be suitable with whatever is within it. Now, through his resurrection Christ began an immortal and incorruptible life. But although our situation is one of generation and corruption, the heavenly situation is one of incorruption. And so it was not suitable for Christ to remain on earth after the resurrection, but it was suitable for him to ascend into heaven.

Effects of Ascension

Summa of Theology III, q. 57, a. 6, c

Christ's ascension is the cause of our salvation in two ways: first, on our part; second, on his.

It is on our part because through the ascension our souls are upraised to him, since his ascension promotes first, faith;

second, hope; third, charity; and fourth, our reverence for him is thus increased when we consider him no longer an earthly man but the God of heaven; hence the Apostle says (2 Co. 5: 16): "If we have known Christ according to the flesh—that is, as mortal, whereby we reputed him as a mere man," as the gloss explains the words, "but now we know him so no longer."

It is on his part in respect to what he did on ascending for our salvation. First, he prepared the way for our ascent into heaven, according to his own saying (Jn. 14: 2): "I go to prepare a place for you," and the words of Micheas (2: 13): "He shall go up that shall open the way before them." Because he is our head, the members must follow where the head has gone; thus he said (Jn. 14: 3): "That where I am, you also may be." To signify this he took the souls of the saints delivered from hell to heaven (Ps. 67: 19): "Ascending on high, he led captivity captive," because he took with him to heaven those who had been held captives by the devil, to heaven as to a place alien to human nature; captives certainly of a happy capture acquired by his victory.

Second, since as the high priest in the Old Testament entered the holy place to stand before God on behalf of the people, so likewise Christ entered heaven "to make intercession for us," as is said (Heb. 7: 25).

For the very manifesting of himself in the human nature in which he entered heaven is a pleading for us; so that because God so exalted human nature in Christ, he may take pity on them for whom the Son of God assumed human nature. Third, that once settled in his heavenly seat as God and Lord, he might pour down gifts upon men (Ep. 4: 10): "He ascended above all the heavens, that he might fill all things," that is, "with his gifts," according to the gloss.

Single Salvific Action
Summa of Theology III, q. 57, a. 6, ad. 2

Christ's passion is the cause of our ascending into heaven, strictly speaking, by withdrawing the obstacle that is sin, and also through merit. But Christ's ascension is the direct cause of our ascension through our beginning it in him, who is our head, and with whom the members have to be united.

Lordship of Christ   *Commentary on Epistle to Ephesians*, c. I, lect. 8

. . . The divine activity in Christ is the form and exemplar of the divine activity in us. . . . In Scripture we frequently read that we will be exalted in the likeness of Christ's exaltation. For example (Rm. 8: 17): "If we suffer with him, that we may also be glorified with him." . . .

The Apostle has previously dealt with the exaltation of Christ both from the viewpoint of his passing over from death to life (1: 20a), and from that of his exaltation to the highest glory (1: 20b–21). Now he treats of the immense power of his exaltation. . . .

He affirms that, with respect to the whole of creation, Christ has universal power, since God the Father hath subjected all things under his feet. . . .

He speaks of the relation of the Church to Christ, which is his body, inasmuch as she is subject to him, receives his influence, and shares the same nature with Christ. . . .

Since the Church was instituted on account of Christ, the Church is called the fullness of Christ. Everything that is virtually in Christ is, as it were, filled out in some way in the members of the Church; for all spiritual understanding, gifts, and whatever can be present in the Church—all of which Christ possesses superabundantly—flow from him into the members of the Church, and they are perfected in them. . . .

c. II, lect. 2

. . . When a man's love is caused from the goodness of the one he loves, then that man who loves does so out of justice, inasmuch as it is just that he love such a person. When, however, love causes the goodness in the beloved, then it is a love springing from mercy. The love with which God loves us produces goodness in us; hence mercy is presented here as the root of the divine love: "I will remember the tender mercies of the Lord. . . ."*

* ASC 2, translated by Matthew L. Lamb.

5. THE SACRAMENTS

Christ Active in the Sacra-   *Summa of Theology* III, q.
ments   19, a. 2, c and ad. 1

The power of achieving something is present both in the
instrument used and in the principal agent, but since it is
more perfectly in the latter, it is not present in both in the
same way. Now, our power of the keys is, like other sacramental powers, instrumental; but it is present in Christ as
principal agent in saving us, as God by authority and as man
by merit. The very idea of key connotes a power of opening
and closing, whether done by a principal agent or by an
instrument. Accordingly, we should conclude that Christ had
the key, but in a way superior to his ministers, so that he
is spoken of as having the key of *excellence*.

ad. 1. A "character" implies that one thing is derived from
another, so that the power of the keys that we receive from
Christ comes from that "character" whereby we are conformed to Christ, but in Christ it comes not from any character, but rather from the principal form.

Summa of Theology III, q.
64, a. 3, c

Christ as God and as man produces the interior sacramental effect, but not in the same way. As God, he acts by
authority in the sacraments, yet as man his action brings
about the interior sacramental effects meritoriously and efficiently but instrumentally. For it was affirmed that Christ's
passion, belonging to him by his human nature is, meritoriously and efficiently, the cause of justification—not as its principal cause, i.e., by his own authority, but as instrumental
cause, insofar as his humanity is the instrument of his Godhead, as declared previously.

Yet as instrument joined to the Godhead in the unity of
person, it possesses a certain headship and efficiency in rela-

tion to extrinsic instruments—the ministers of the Church and the sacraments themselves. . . . So Christ has the principal power of ministry, i.e., the power of excellence, just as he has as God the power of authority over the sacraments.

There are four aspects of this power of excellence. First, the merit and power of his passion act in the sacraments. And because the power of the passion is communicated to us by faith (Rm. 2: 25): "Whom God hath proposed to be a propitiation, through faith in his blood," and we proclaim this faith by calling upon the name of Christ, the second aspect is that the sacraments are sanctified by invoking his name. And inasmuch as the sacraments draw their power from their institution, the third aspect of the excellence of Christ's power is seen in the fact that the sacramental power comes from the one who instituted them. And since cause does not depend upon effect, but conversely, it pertains to the excellence of Christ's power that he could bestow the sacramental effect without conferring the exterior sacrament. . . .

Christ's Sacramental Sign   *Summa of Theology* III, q. 60, a. 1, c

. . . A thing may be spoken of as a sacrament either because it has a certain hidden holiness, and in this sense a sacrament is a sacred secret; or from having some relation to this holiness, that of a cause or of a sign or any other relation. But we are now referring to sacraments in a special way as implying a signifying disposition; and in this sense a sacrament is a kind of sign.

Meaning of Sacrament   *Summa of Theology* III, q. 60, a. 2, c

Signs are made to men for whom it is proper to learn the unknown from the known. So that strictly speaking, a sacrament is the sign of some sacred thing referring to man; so that a sacrament in the strict sense defined here is the *sign of a holy thing insofar as it makes men holy.*

Sacraments and Sanctification   *Summa of Theology* III, q. 60, a. 3, c

Strictly speaking, a sacrament is that which is directed toward signifying our sanctification. There are three aspects here: the cause itself of our sanctification, which is Christ's passion; the form of our sanctification, which is grace and the virtues; and the ultimate end of our sanctification, which is eternal life.

And all these are signified by the sacraments. Therefore, a sacrament is a sign that is both a reminder of the past, i.e., Christ's passion; an indication of what is achieved in us through Christ's passion, namely, grace; and a prognosis, that is, a prediction of future glory.

Sensible Signs Needed   *Summa of Theology* III, q. 60, a. 4, c

Divine wisdom provides for everything in accord with its manner of being; thus it is written (Wi. 8: 1): "She . . . ordereth all things sweetly." So also we are told (Mt. 25: 15): "She gave to everyone according to his own ability." Now, it is natural for man to gain knowledge of the intelligible from the sensible. But a sign is that whereby one gains knowledge of something else. Therefore, since the sacred realities signified by the sacraments are the spiritual and intelligible goods whereby man is sanctified, the sacramental signs consequently consist in sensible things. . . .

Sacraments Exist by Divine Choice   *Summa of Theology* III, q. 60, a. 5, c

There are two aspects in the use of the sacraments: the worship of God and the sanctification of man. The former has to do with man as related to God, and the latter has to do with God in respect to man. Now, no one may determine about what is in another's power, only about what is in his own. Since then the sanctification of man is within the power of God, who sanctifies, man should not decide what things must be used for his sanctification, but this should be de-

termined by divine institution. So that in the sacraments of
the New Law by which man is sanctified: (1 Co. 6: 11):
"You are washed, you are sanctified," we must make use of
those things determined by divine institution.

Words Suitably Added to Sacramental Signs
Summa of Theology III, q. 60, a. 6, c

The sacraments are used as signs for man's sanctification.
Therefore, they can be considered in three ways and in each
way it is suitable for words to be added to the sensible signs.
First of all, they can be considered in reference to the cause
of sanctification, which is the Word incarnate, to whom the
sacraments are somewhat conformed insofar as the word is
united to the sensible sign, just as the Word of God in the
mystery of the incarnation is united to sensible flesh.

Second, sacraments may be considered with reference to
the man who is sanctified and who is made up of soul and
body, to whom the sacramental remedy is suited insofar as
through the sensible element it touches the body, and through
faith in the words it reaches the soul. . . .

Third, a sacrament may be considered with reference to
the sacramental signification. Now, Augustine says (*On
Christian Doctrine* II), "words are the chief signs used by
men"; for words can be formed variously to signify diverse
mental ideas, so that we can through words express our
thoughts with greater precision. And so to make the sacramental signification perfect, it was required to determine the
signification of sensible things through definite words. For
water may signify both a cleansing on account of its humidity,
and refreshment by its coolness; but when we say, "I baptize
thee," it is clear that we use water in baptism to signify a
spiritual cleansing.

Definite Word Formula Needed
Summa of Theology III, q. 60, a. 7, c

. . . The words are as form and sensible things are as
matter in the sacraments. In everything made up of matter
and form, the determining principle is the form, which is,
so to speak, the end and the terminus of the matter. For

anything to exist, a determinate form is needed before there
is any need of determinate matter, which must be adapted to
the determinate form. Hence, because definite sensible things
are needed as sacramental matter in the sacraments, there is
greater need of a definite form of words.

Necessity for Sacraments   *Summa of Theology* III, q.
                                      61, a. 1, c

There are three reasons why sacraments are necessary for
man's salvation. The first is found in the human condition,
which is such that it must be brought to spiritual and intelligible reality through corporeal and sensible things. So divine
wisdom aptly provides man with salvific means in the corporeal and sensible signs called sacraments.

The second reason is in the situation of man whose sinning
subjected him to corporeal things by his affections. But any
healing remedy must be given to man so as to reach the part
affected by disease. So it was suitable for God to provide
man with a spiritual medicine through definite corporeal
signs; for if man were offered spiritual realities unhidden,
his mind distracted by the material world could not attend
to them.

The third reason comes from the fact that man tends to
direct his actions principally toward material things. To avoid
the difficulty of removing man completely from physical actions, bodily motions were made available to him in the sacraments, thereby disciplining him to avoid superstitious practices or the worship of demons and all destructive action or
sinful acts.

So that by the institution of the sacraments man in harmony with his nature learns through sensible things. He is
humbled by admitting that he is subject to corporeal things,
inasmuch as he gets help through them. And he is even preserved from physical harm through the healthy partaking of
the sacraments.

Sacraments, Instrumental   *Summa of Theology* III, q.
Causes of Grace   62, a. 1, c

We must then assert against this that an efficient cause is

twofold, principal and instrumental. The principal cause acts by the power of its form, to which the effect is likened, as fire through its own heat makes a thing hot. In this way only God can cause grace, for grace is no other than a participated likeness of the divine nature (2 P. 1: 4): "He hath given us great and precious promises that we may be partakers of the divine nature." But the instrumental cause acts not through the power of its form but only through the motion by which the principal agent moves it, so that the effect is not likened to the instrument but to the principal agent; for example, the bed is not like the ax, but like the art in the carpenter's mind. And in this way the sacraments of the New Law cause grace, for they are instituted by God to be used for the giving of grace. So Augustine says (*Against Faustus*, xix): "All these things [e.g., pertaining to the sacraments] are done and pass away, but the power [i.e., of God], which acts by them, remains forever." Now, strictly speaking, that is an instrument by which someone acts; so it is written (Tit. 3: 5): "He saved us by the laver of regeneration."

Special Sacramental Grace   *Summa of Theology* III, q. 62, a. 2, c

. . . Grace, in itself, perfects the soul's essence, since it is a certain participated likeness of the divine nature. And just as the soul's powers result from its essence, so certain perfections of these powers result from grace—namely, virtues and gifts perfecting the powers in relation to their acts. Now, the sacraments are directed to special effects needed for Christian life. Thus Baptism is directed to a certain spiritual rebirth, whereby man dies to vice and becomes a member of Christ, and this effect is a special addition to the actions of the soul's powers; and it is the same with the other sacraments. Therefore, just as the virtues and gifts give in addition to what is generally called grace a certain special perfection directed to the powers' proper actions, so does sacramental grace give something in addition to the grace of the virtues and gifts.

Sacraments Bring Virtue of   *Summa of Theology* III, q.
Passion   62, a. 5, c

Those who maintain that the sacraments cause grace only
by a certain coincidence deny that sacraments have a power
sacramentally effective, maintaining that the divine power
aids the sacraments and produces their effect. But if we hold
that a sacrament is an instrumental cause of grace, we must
admit in the sacraments a certain instrumental power of
achieving the sacramental effects. Now, this power is proportionate with the instrument, and so it is related to the complete and perfect power of anything as the instrument to the
principal agent. For an instrument . . . does not act unless
moved by the principal agent, which acts of itself. And so
the principal agent's power exists in nature completely and
perfectly; but the instrumental power has a being that goes
from one thing into another, and is incomplete, just as motion is an imperfect act passing from agent to patient.

. . . Christ delivered us from our sins chiefly by his passion, not only by way of efficiency and merit but also by way
of satisfaction. By his passion also he originated the rites of
the Christian religion by offering "himself—an oblation and
a sacrifice to God" (Ep. 5: 2). So it is clear that the sacraments of the Church receive their power especially from
Christ's passion, and the virtue of this is somehow united to
us when we receive the sacraments. In sign of this there
flowed from the side of Christ hanging upon the cross water
and blood, the former belonging to Baptism, the latter to the
Eucharist—and these are the leading sacraments.

Sacramental Character   *Summa of Theology* III, q.
                             63, a. 3, c

. . . Each of the faithful is destined to receive or to give
to others realities having to do with God's worship. And this,
strictly speaking, is the purpose of the sacramental character.
Now, the entire rite of the Christian religion is drawn from
Christ's priesthood. Therefore, it is evident that the sacramental character is specially the character of Christ, to whose
character the faithful are likened through the sacramental

characters, which are not other than certain participations of Christ's priesthood poured out from Christ himself.

Character Present in Powers   *Summa of Theology* III, q. 63, a. 4, c

A character is a kind of seal by which the soul is marked, enabling it to give or receive realities having to do with divine worship. Now, divine worship comprises certain actions, and the soul's powers are properly directed to actions, just as the essence is directed to existence. So a character inheres in the soul's power, not in its essence.

Priesthood of People   *Summa of Theology* III, q. 63, a. 5, c

In a sacramental character Christ's faithful participate in his priesthood; for as Christ has the full power of a spiritual priesthood, so his faithful are conformed to him by participating a certain spiritual power referring to the sacraments and to realities related to divine worship. Thus it is unsuitable for God to have a character, but his priesthood is related to a character as a complete and perfect reality is related to some participation in it. Now, Christ's priesthood is eternal (Ps. 109: 4): "Thou art a priest forever according to the order of Melchisedech."

Therefore, all sanctification effected by his priesthood is perpetual, lasting as long as the sanctified reality lasts. This is evident even with inanimate things; for the consecration of a church or of an altar lasts forever unless they are destroyed. Since then a character resides in the intellective part of the soul . . . it is evident that since the intellect is perpetual and incorruptible, a character cannot be eradicated from the soul.

Conferring of Character   *Summa of Theology* III, q. 63, a. 6, c

. . . But it [the Eucharist] contains within itself Christ, in whom there is not the character but the plenitude of the priesthood.

But it is the sacrament of Order that relates to sacramental agents. Through this sacrament men are charged with giving sacraments to others, whereas the sacrament of Baptism relates to recipients, since to man it gives the power to receive the other sacraments of the Church; so it is called the *door of the sacraments*. In a sense Confirmation is also directed to the same end. . . . Thus these three sacraments—Baptism, Confirmation, and Order—imprint a character.

Christ Acts in Sacraments: Man Is Minister   *Summa of Theology* III, q. 64, a. 1, c

There are two ways of producing an effect: first, as a principal agent, second, as an instrument. As principal agent only God produces the interior sacramental effect. . . .

In the second way the interior sacramental effect can be produced by man inasmuch as he acts as a minister. For a minister is of the nature of an instrument, since the action of both reaches something extrinsic, whereas the interior effect is produced through the power of the principal agent or God.

Summa of Theology III, q. 64, a. 2, c

. . . The power of the sacrament is from the sacrament's institutor. Thus since the power of the sacrament is from God alone, only God consequently can institute sacraments.

Ministers of Sacraments Act Instrumentally   *Summa of Theology* III, q. 64, a. 5, c

The ministers of the Church act instrumentally in the sacraments, for in a sense a minister is instrumental in nature. But . . . an instrument acts not through its own form but through the power of the one moving it. So that whatever form or power beyond being an instrument exists in an instrument is accidental to it: for example, that a doctor's body, the instrument of his soul where his medical art resides, is healthy or sickly; or that a pipe for the transmission of water is silver or leaden. Therefore, even when the ministers of the Church are evil, they can give the sacraments.

Intention of Church Required *Summa of Theology* III, q. 64, a. 8, ad. 1

An inanimate instrument has no intention with respect to the effect; but in the intention's place is the motion by which the principal agent moves it. But an animate instrument like a minister is not only moved but somehow moves himself, in that by his will he moves his bodily members to act. Therefore, it is required that he have the intention of subjecting himself to the principal agent—that is, it is necessary for him to intend to do that which Christ and the Church do.

Reason for Sacraments *Summa of Theology* III, q. 65, a. 1, c

The sacraments of the Church were instituted for two reasons: to perfect man in those things concerned with God's worship in accord with the religion of Christian life, and to be a cure for the evils caused by sin. For both these reasons, seven sacraments are suitable. . . .

The number of the sacraments can be gleaned also from their institution as a remedy against the evil caused by sin. For Baptism is intended to remedy the absence of spiritual life; Confirmation remedies the weakness of the recently born soul; the Eucharist remedies the soul's tendency to sin; Penance remedies the actual sin committed after Baptism; Sacrament of the Sick remedies the remainders of sins—of those sins not altogether removed by Penance, whether on account of negligence or ignorance; Order remedies divisions in the community; Matrimony remedies concupiscence in the individual and the numerical deficit brought about by death.

Other people see in the number of sacraments a certain harmony with virtues and evils and punishments for sin. They assert that Baptism harmonizes with faith and is directed to the cure of original sin; Sacrament of the Sick, to hope, directed against venial sin; the Eucharist, to charity, directed against the punishment of malice; Order, to prudence, directed against ignorance; Penance, to justice, directed against mortal sin; Matrimony, to temperance, directed against concupiscence; Confirmation, to fortitude, directed against weakness.

Eucharist   *Summa of Theology* III, q.
                                65, a. 3, c

Absolutely speaking, the sacrament of the Eucharist is the greatest of all the sacraments, as is evident in three ways. First, because it contains Christ himself substantially, while the other sacraments have a certain instrumental power that is a participation in Christ's power. . . . Now, that which is essentially such is always greater than that which is such by participation.

Second, this becomes evident when we examine how the sacraments are related to one another, for all the other sacraments seem to be directed to this one as to their end. Clearly the sacrament of Order is directed to the consecration of the Eucharist, and the sacrament of Baptism to the reception of the Eucharist; while man is perfected by Confirmation to remove the fear of approaching this sacrament. Penance and Sacrament of the Sick prepare man to receive the body of Christ worthily. And Matrimony, at least in its signification, affects this sacrament in that it signifies the union of Christ with the Church, and of this union the Eucharist is a figure, so that the Apostle says (Ep. 5: 32): "This is a great sacrament, but I speak in Christ and in the Church." . . .

Necessity of Sacraments for   *Summa of Theology* III, q.
Salvation   65, a. 4, c

Necessity of end is twofold, and we are now speaking of this. First, a thing may be so necessary that the end cannot be attained without it; thus is food necessary for human life. And this is simple necessity of end. Second, something is called necessary if the end is more suitably attained through it; in this way a horse is necessary for a journey. But this is not simple necessity of end.

In the first way, three sacraments are necessary for salvation. Two of them are necessary to the individual: Baptism, simply and absolutely; Penance, if mortal sin is committed after Baptism; whereas the sacrament of Order is necessary to the Church, because "where there is no governor the people shall fall (Pr. 11: 14).

But in the second way, the other sacraments are necessary; for Confirmation in a sense perfects Baptism; Sacrament of the Sick perfects Penance; whereas Matrimony preserves the numbers in the Church through propagation.

6. THE PEOPLE OF GOD

The Holy Spirit in God's People   *Letter to Archbishop of Palermo on Articles of Faith,* Art. 8

The Word of God is, as we said, the Son of God almost the way the word of man is the concept of his intellect. But often man has a word that is lifeless. This occurs, for example, when he conceives what he ought to do without willing to do it or when he believes but does not practice; then his *faith* is called *dead*, as St. James shows (Jm. 2: 17). Yet the Word of God is alive: "For the word of God is living" (Heb. 4: 12). There must therefore be both will and love in God. So St. Augustine declares: "The Word of God we intend to speak is knowledge with love" (*On the Trinity* IX, 10). Now, just as the Word of God is the Son of God, so God's love is the Holy Spirit. And so anyone loving God possesses the Holy Spirit: "The charity of God is poured forth in our hearts by the Holy Spirit, who is given to us" (Rm. 5: 5). . . .

The Holy Spirit brings us many gifts.

1. He releases us from our sins. This is because what anyone has made, he must remake. Now, the soul is made through the Holy Spirit, inasmuch as through him God has made all things; for by loving his goodness, God created everything: "Thou lovest all things that are, and hatest none of the things that thou hast made" (Wis. 11: 25). Hence Dionysius says: "Divine love did not allow him to be without offspring" (*On the Divine Names* IV). Consequently the hearts of men that were destroyed by sin had to be renewed through the Holy Spirit: "Thou shalt send forth thy Spirit,

and they shall be created; and thou shalt renew the face of the earth" (Ps. 103: 30). Nor should we be surprised that the Spirit releases from sin, because all sins are removed through love: "Many sins are forgiven her, because she hath loved much" (Lk. 7: 47). "Charity covereth all sins" (Pr. 10: 12). And likewise: "Charity covereth a multitude of sins" (I Pt. 4: 8).

2. The Holy Spirit enlightens the mind because whatever we know is known through the Holy Spirit: "But the Paraclete, the Holy Spirit, whom the Father will send in my name, he will teach you all things and bring all things to your mind, whatsoever I shall have said to you" (Jn. 14: 26). Also: "His unction teacheth you all things" (II Jn. 2: 27).

3. He aids us and to some extent insists that we keep the commandments. Unless one loves God, he cannot keep the commandments: "If anyone love me, he will keep my word" (Jn. 14: 23). Hence the Holy Spirit makes us love God: "And I give you a new heart and put a new spirit within you; and I will take away the heart of stone from within you and give you a heart of flesh. And I will put my Spirit in the midst of you; and I will cause you to walk in my commandments and to keep my judgments and do them" (Ezech. 36: 26–27).

4. He confirms the hope for eternal life in us since he is the pledge of our destiny: "You were signed with the Holy Spirit of promise, who is the pledge of our inheritance" (Ep. 1: 13). He is, so to speak, the guarantee of our eternal life. This is because eternal life is man's insofar as he becomes the son of God, which is accomplished by his being made like unto Christ, and this follows from his having the Spirit of Christ, who is the Holy Spirit: "For you have not received the spirit of bondage again in fear; but you have received the spirit of adoption of sons, whereby we cry: *Abba* (Father). For the Spirit himself giveth testimony to our spirit that we are the sons of God" (Rm. 8: 15). And likewise: "Because you are sons, God hath sent the Spirit of his Son into your hearts, crying: *Abba* (Father)" (Gal. 4: 6).

5. In our doubt he counsels us, teaching us what is the will of God: "He that hath an ear, let him hear what the Spirit saith to the churches" (Rv. 2: 7). Also: "I may hear him as a master" (Is. 1: 4).

The Apostles' Creed: Com-   *Letter to Archbishop of Pa-*
munion of Saints   *lermo on Articles of Faith,*
                              Art. 10

The Tenth Article: "The communion of saints, the forgiveness of sins."

As in our natural body one member's action works for the
good of the whole body, so likewise with a spiritual body
like the Church. Because all the believers are one body, the
good of one member is communicated to another: "And all
members one of another" (Rm. 12: 5). Hence that there is
a common sharing of good in the Church is among the articles of faith handed down by the Apostles. This is expressed
by the words, "the communion of saints." Among the
Church's many members, the principal member is Christ,
since he is the head: "He hath made him head over all the
Church, which is his body" (Ep. 1: 22). As the power of the
head is communicated to all the members, so Christ communicates his good.

This communication occurs through the sacraments of the
Church, wherein the merits of Christ's passion are active for
the giving of grace unto the remission of sins. These sacraments of the Church are seven in number. . . .

We should also realize that not only the power of the passion of Christ is communicated to us, but likewise the merits
of his life; and, in addition, all the good that all the saints
have done is communicated to all in the state of grace, since
all are one: "I am a partaker of all them that fear thee" (Ps.
118: 63).

Therefore, whoever lives in charity participates in all the
good that is done in the whole world; but since one man can
certainly make satisfaction for another, he for whom some
good work is done benefits in a special way.

There is then a twofold benefit from this communion. One
is that Christ's merits are communicated to all, while the
other is that each one's good is communicated to another.
Since those who are excommunicated are cut off from the
Church, they forfeit their share of all the good that is

done, and this is a far greater loss than that of all material things. . . .

Authority in the Church   *Summa of Christian Teaching*
                                              IV, 76

Now, all these orders are conferred with a sacrament . . . , and the Church's sacraments necessitate some ministers to confer them. So in the Church there must exist a higher power with a superior ministry conferring the sacrament of Order. Such is the episcopal power which, whereas it does not extend beyond the priest's power to consecrate the body of Christ, does extend beyond the priest's power in whatever concerns believers. For the priestly power itself comes from the episcopal power, and anything very specially difficult to be done on behalf of believers is reserved to the bishops; and by their authority priests are even authorized to do their own tasks. Thus, even in these tasks, priests use things consecrated by bishops; so, in the Eucharistic consecration, they use a chalice, an altar, and a pall consecrated by a bishop. It is therefore evident that part of the dignity of the bishops is their chief direction of the believers.

But it is likewise evident that, although people are situated in various dioceses and states, nevertheless, inasmuch as the Church is one, so must the Christian people be one. So that inasmuch as every special Church congregation requires one bishop as head of that Church, so the whole Christian people should have one who is head of the whole Church.

Moreover, the Church's unity requires agreement on the faith among all believers. But questions often arise about matters of faith. A difference in decrees would divide the Church unless kept in unity through the promulgation of one. So the unity of the Church requires one to be the head of the whole Church. In these needs Christ has clearly not forsaken the Church he loved and for whom he shed his blood, since even of the synagogue the Lord said: "What is there that I ought to do more to my vineyard that I have not done to it?" (Is. 5: 4). We should not therefore doubt that there is one who is the head of the whole Church, and this by Christ's command.

7. THE COMMANDMENTS

The Fourth Commandment   *Sermon on the Two Commandments of Charity and the Ten Commandments of the Law*

"Honor thy father and thy mother, that thou mayest be long-lived upon the land that the Lord thy God will give th..e" (Exod. 20: 12; Deut. 5: 16).

Man's perfection consists in loving God and neighbor. Now, the three Commandments written upon the first tablet refer to the love of God; with respect to the love of neighbor there were seven Commandments on the second tablet. But we should "love, not in word nor in speech, but in action and in truth" (I Jn. 3: 18). To love in this way a man must do two things: avoid evil and do good.

Some Commandments prescribe good acts, whereas others forbid evil acts. And we should realize that it is within our power to avoid evil, but we cannot do good to everyone. So St. Augustine tells us that we should love all, although we are not obliged to do good to all. But among those to whom we are obliged to do good are those in any way united to us. Hence, "if any man have not care of his own and especially of those of his house, he hath denied the faith" (I Tm. 5: 8). Now, there are no closer relatives to us than our father and mother. "We ought to love God first," states St. Ambrose, "then our father and mother." So God has given us the Commandment: "Honor thy father and thy mother."

The philosopher also cites another reason for honoring parents, inasmuch as we can make no equal return to our parents for the great benefits they have given us; and so an offended parent has the right to send away his son, but the son has no such right.

Parents, in fact, give their children three things. First, they brought them into existence: "Honor thy father, and forget not the groanings of thy mother; remember that thou hadst not been born but through them" (Ecclus. 7: 29). Second, they provide them with food and the support needed for life. For a child comes into the world naked, as Job says (1: 21), but he is provided for by his parents. The third is education: "We have had fathers of our flesh for instructors" (Heb. 12: 9). "Hast thou children? Educate them" (Ecclus. 7: 25).

Hence parents should not delay to educate their children, because "A young man according to his way, even when he is old, will not depart from it" (Pr. 22: 6). And again: "It is good for a man when he hath borne the yoke from his youth" (Lm. 3: 27). Now, the instruction given by Tobias to his son was: "Fear the Lord and resist sin." This is certainly contrary to those parents who condone their children's bad behavior. And so children receive from their parents birth, nourishment, and instruction.

Now, because we are indebted to our parents for our birth, we should honor them above every superior from whom we receive only temporal things. "He that feareth the Lord honoreth his parents, and will serve them as his masters that brought him into the world. Honor thy father in work and word and all patience, that a blessing may come upon thee from him" (Ecclus. 3: 10). And in so doing, you will honor yourself, since "The glory of a man is from honor of his father, and a father without honor is the disgrace of his son" (Ecclus. 3: 13).

Moreover, because in our childhood we receive food from our parents, in their old age we should support them. "Son, support the old age of thy father, and grieve him not in his life. And if his understanding fail, have patience with him; and despise him not when thou art in thy strength. . . . Of what an evil fame is he who forsaketh his father! And he is cursed of God who angereth his mother" (Ecclus. 3: 14, 15, 18). For the humiliation of those who act otherwise, Cassiodorus tells how young storks whose parents have lost their feathers by the onslaught of old age and cannot find suitable food, make the parent storks comfortable with their own feathers, bringing them food for their tired bodies. "And so by this affectionate exchange the young ones repay their parents for what they received when young" (Epist. II).

Because our parents have educated us, we should obey them. "Children, obey your parents in all things" (Col. 3: 20). This obviously excludes those things opposed to God. In such cases the only loyalty is to be cruel, says St. Jerome: "If any man hate not his father and mother . . . he cannot be my disciple" (Lk. 14: 26). This is really saying that in the truest sense God is our Father: "Is not he thy father who hath possessed thee, and hath made thee and created thee?" (Dt. 32: 6).

"Honor thy father and thy mother." Only this Commandment among them all has the added words: "that thou mayest be long-lived upon the land." This is because it is a natural obligation, and so it could be thought that honoring parents went unrewarded.

The first reward is grace for the present life and glory in the future life, and these certainly are greatly to be desired: "Honor thy father . . . that a blessing may come upon thee from God, and his blessing may remain in the latter end" (Ecclus. 3: 9). Exactly the opposite happens to those who dishonor their parents; in fact, they are cursed in the law by God (Dt. 27: 16). It is likewise written: "He that is unjust in that which is little, is also unjust in that which is greater" (Lk. 16: 10). But our natural life is as nothing when compared with the life of grace. Hence, if you do not admit the blessing of the natural life for which you are indebted to your parents, then you are unworthy of what is greater—the life of grace—and all the more unworthy of the life of glory, the greatest of all blessings.

The second reward is a long life: "That thou mayest be long-lived upon the land." For "he that honoreth his father shall enjoy a long life" (Ecclus. 3: 7). Now, a long life is a full life, and it is not measured by time but by action, as the philosopher notes. It is the life of virtue that is full; thus a man who is virtuous and holy enjoys a long life even if he dies young in respect to body: "Being perfect in a short space, he fulfilled a long time; for his soul pleased God" (Wi. 4: 23). So a good merchant is one who does in one day as much business as another would do in a year. And remember that it sometimes happens that a long life may lead to spiritual as well as bodily death, as with Judas. Hence a long life for the body is the reward for keeping this Commandment. But the contrary, i.e., death, is the fate of those who dishonor parents. From them we receive life, and just as soldiers owe loyalty to the king and lose their rights by treachery, so likewise those who dishonor their parents deserve to forfeit their lives: "The eye that mocketh at his father and that despiseth the labor of his mother in bearing him, let the ravens pick it out, and the young eagles eat it" (Pr. 30: 17). Here "the ravens" refer to officials of kings and princes, who are the "young eagles." But even if such are not bodily punished, they cannot escape death in respect to the soul. A father then should not give too much power to his children: "Give not to son or wife, brother or friend, power over thee while thou livest; and give not thy estate to another, lest thou repent" (Ecclus. 33: 20).

The third reward is to have in turn grateful and pleasing children. For a father naturally cherishes his children, but the reverse is not always so. "He that honoreth his father shall have joy in his own children" (Ecclus. 3: 6). Again: "With what measure you mete, it shall be measured to you again" (Mt. 7: 2).

The fourth reward is a good reputation: "For the glory of a man is from the honor of his father" (Ecclus. 3: 13). And again: "Of what an evil fame is he that forsaketh his father?" (Ecclus. 3:18).

The fifth reward is wealth: "The father's blessing establisheth the houses of his children, but the mother's curse rooteth up the foundation" (Ecclus. 3: 11).

Summary of the Ten Commandments   *The Ten Commandments*

Such are the ten precepts to which Our Lord referred when saying: "If thou wilt enter into life, keep the commandments" (Mt. 19: 17). The two main principles of all the Commandments are love of God and love of neighbor. A man who loves God must do three things:

1. He must have no other God. And to assist this we have the command: "Thou shalt not have strange gods."

2. He must totally honor God. And thus it is commanded: "Thou shalt not take the name of God in vain."

3. He must freely rest in God. Hence: "Remember that thou keep holy the Sabbath day."

But one must first of all love one's neighbor in order to love God worthily. Hence: "Honor thy father and thy mother." Then one must avoid harming one's neighbor by act. "Thou shalt not kill" refers to our neighbor's person; "Thou shalt not commit adultery" refers to the person united in marriage to our neighbor; "Thou shalt not steal" refers to our neighbor's external goods. We must also avoid injuring our neighbor by word, "Thou shalt not bear false witness," and by thought, "Thou shalt not covet thy neighbor's goods" and "Thou shalt not covet thy neighbor's wife."

8. RELIGIOUS LIFE

On the Perfection of the Spiritual Life

Because certain persons not acquainted with perfection have presumed to speak nonsense about the state of perfection, it is our intention to treat of perfection and to discuss the following points: What does it mean to be perfect? Which state is a state of perfection? Who can be said to be in a state of perfection? What type of work may be performed by those who adopt a state of perfection?

Chapter I. The Perfection of the Spiritual Life Consists Absolutely in Charity

Let us begin by recognizing that there are a number of ways in which we can speak of a thing's being perfect. For our purpose we shall speak of something being perfect either absolutely or in some respect. A thing is said to be perfect absolutely when it has acquired all those attributes that its nature implies. But when it has merely developed some attribute not necessarily implied in its nature, it is said to be perfect in some respect. For example, an animal is absolutely perfect as animal, when it is not missing anything required for the fullness of animal life; say, when it has the full number and proper arrangement of its limbs, organs, and parts, when it possesses its appropriate size and all that is required for the perfect functioning of animal life. But an animal is said to be in some respect perfect when it is outstanding in something outside its nature as animal; say, its whiteness or odor or something of that sort.

In like manner, in the spiritual life a man is said to be absolutely perfect when he is perfect in that in which the spiritual life principally consists; but he is perfect in some respect in the spiritual life when he is perfect in something other than the essential constituent of the spiritual life; say, knowledge of mathematics.

Now, the spiritual life consists principally in charity in such wise that if charity be missing, a man is considered to be spiritually *nothing*, as St. Paul says: "If I have prophecy and know all mysteries and all knowledge, and if I have all faith so as to remove mountains, yet do not have charity, I am nothing" (I Co. 13: 2). The blessed Apostle John, too, declares that the spiritual life consists in charity, for he writes: "We know that we have passed from death to life because we love the brethren. He that loveth not abideth in death" (I Jn. 3: 14). Therefore, only a person perfect in charity is absolutely perfect in the spiritual life.

Anyone perfect in some quality other than charity is said to be in some respect perfect. This is clear from the words of sacred Scripture. Thus St. Paul, writing to the Colossians, attributes perfection principally to charity, for he mentions a number of virtues: mercy, kindness, humility, and so on, but then adds: "Above all these things have charity, which is the bond of perfection" (Col. 3: 14). According to this doctrine, when someone is called perfect for having achieved intellectual greatness, it is not in such accomplishments that perfection lies. When St. Paul exhorts us to "be children in malice, but in sense be perfect" (I Co. 14: 20) and again in the same epistle, "be perfect in the same sense and in the same knowledge," he has not forgotten that earlier he had said that even though a person have perfect knowledge, if it be without charity, he is nothing. In the light of this doctrine, one should be careful to detect the meaning of the word "perfect" whenever a person is said to be perfect. Thus a person can be perfect "according to patience, which has a perfect work," as St. James says, or according to some other virtue. Indeed, one can be perfect in evil, as when someone is called a perfect thief or a perfect bandit. Even the Scriptures speak in this way, for it is written in Isaias (32: 6): "The heart of the fool will work iniquity to make his hypocrisy perfect."

Chapter II. Perfection Consists Both in the Love of God and in the Love of Neighbor

Since perfection consists chiefly in charity, it is easy to see in what the perfection of the spiritual life consists. For there are two precepts of charity: one pertains to loving God, the other to loving our neighbor. These two precepts are mutually related; for what must be principally loved through charity is God, the supreme good and source of man's happiness. After God we are obliged by charity to love our neighbor, to whom we are bound by special social ties due to our common vocation to happiness. What charity obliges us to love in our neighbor is this: that together we may attain to happiness. Our Lord shows that this is the sequence of the precepts when he says (Mt. 22: 37–39): "Thou shalt love the Lord thy God with thy whole heart and with thy whole soul and with thy whole mind. This is the greatest and the first commandment. And the second is like to this: Thou shalt love thy neighbor as thyself." The perfection of the spiritual life, therefore, consists first and principally in loving God. For this reason the Lord in speaking to Abraham says (Gen. 17: 1): "I am Almighty God: *walk* before me and be perfect." One walks before God not with steps taken by the feet but by the desires of the mind. But secondarily the perfection of the spiritual life consists in loving one's neighbor. Hence after Our Lord had said: "Love your enemies" and had added a number of examples regarding love of neighbor, he concluded (Mt. 5: 48): "Be ye therefore perfect as also your heavenly Father is perfect."

Chapter III. The Love of God as It Exists in God

In regard both to the love of God and to the love of neighbor, various degrees of perfection are found. The first and highest degree of loving God is found in God alone. We can understand why this should be so if we remember that love can be considered from the standpoint of the beloved and from the standpoint of the lover. I mean that the beloved should be loved with as much love as it is worthy and that the lover should love according to the maximum of which he is capable. Now, since a thing is lovable to the extent that it is good, and since the goodness of God is infinite, he is infinitely lovable. However, no creature is capable of loving God infinitely, because an infinite act is impossible to a finite power. Consequently, only God, whose power to love matches his goodness, can love himself perfectly according to the first degree of perfection.

Chapter IV. The Love of God as It Exists in the Blessed

As far as the rational creature is concerned, the only way of perfectly loving God that is open to him is from the standpoint of the one loving, i.e., to love God according to the maximum of his capacity. This is clearly expressed in the very precept of divine love. For it is said in Deuteronomy: "Thou shalt love the Lord thy God with thy *whole* heart and with thy *whole* soul and with thy *whole* strength" (Dt. 6: 15). To this the Gospel according to St. Luke adds: "and with thy whole mind" (Lk. 10: 27). This commandment is such that "heart" refers to the intention, "mind" refers to knowledge, "soul" refers to the affections and desires, and "strength" refers to external performance, for all these powers and actions must be employed in loving God. But bear in mind that this commandment can be fulfilled in two ways. For since "whole" and "perfect" apply only to things that have nothing missing, God will be loved with one's whole heart and soul and strength and mind as long as nothing in these powers ever misses being actually converted to God. This degree of love is found in the blessed and is not expected of those who are struggling heavenward. That is why St. Paul writes: "Not as though I had already attained, or were already perfect; but I follow after, if I may by any means apprehend" (Ph. 3: 12). These are the words of one expecting perfection when he shall have apprehended, i.e., when he shall have obtained the palm of beatitude. Since that beatitude consists in the enjoyment of God, both the intellect and the will of the rational creature will be continuously and actually always centered upon God. Indeed, it will not be an interrupted series of acts but entirely continuous. Then the rational creature will cleave to God as to its ultimate end, the supreme truth. And since all that one does is directed to the ultimate end through one's intention and all one's acts are disposed in accordance with the ultimate end, it will come to pass that when he is in the state of eternal beatitude, the rational creature will be loving God with his whole heart as long as his intention directs every thought and every love and every desire and every action to God. He will be loving God with his whole mind, as long as his mind is always actually sunk in God by seeing him always and all else in him and by judging all things according to his truth. He will be loving God with his whole soul, as long as all his affections are borne toward loving God *continuously* and loving all else for his sake. He will be loving God with all his strength or with all his powers, as long as the motive behind all his outward actions will be the love of God. This is the second way in which the love of God is possible, and it is peculiar to the blessed.

Chapter V. The Degree of Perfection to Which All in This Life are Obligated in Order to Be Saved

In a lesser degree we love God with our whole heart and mind and soul and strength if there is nothing in our love that is not either actually or habitually referred to God. Such perfection is laid upon us by God's commandment and can be described in the following way.

First, a man must refer all to God as to his end, as the Apostle says: "Whether you eat or drink or whatsoever else you do, do all to the glory of God" (1 Co. 10: 31). One fulfills this command when he directs his life to the service of

God in such a way that everything he does is virtually ordained to God, excepting, of course, what of its very nature turns one away from God, such as sin. Thus does a man love God with his whole heart.

Second, a man must bow down his intellect to God by believing what has been divinely revealed: "bringing into captivity every understanding unto the obedience of Christ" (2 Co. 10: 5). Thus does a man love God with his whole mind in this life.

Third, one must love God in such a way that whatever he loves, he loves in God and that he relates all his desires and affections to God. St. Paul describes it thus: "For whether we be transported in mind, it is to God; or whether we be sober, it is for you. For the charity of God presseth us" (2 Co. 5: 13). Thus does one love God with his whole soul.

Fourth, one must love God in such a way that all his outward actions, words, and works be tempered with the love of God. St. Paul speaks of this: "Let all that you do be done in charity" (1 Co. 16: 14). Thus is God loved with one's whole strength.

This, therefore, is the third kind of perfect love of God, and to it every man is obligated by a necessity of precept. The second kind is not possible to anyone in this life, unless he be both a viator and a comprehensor, as was Our Lord, Jesus Christ.

Chapter VI. The Perfection of Divine Love That Falls under Counsel

After St. Paul had written: "Not as though I had already attained or were already perfect," he added: "but I follow after, if I may by any means apprehend," and finally: "Let us, therefore, as many as are perfect be thus minded." From these words it is plain that even though the perfection of the blessed is not possible to us in this life, yet we ought to strive after a likeness of that perfection as far as possible. It is in this that the *perfection* of the wayfarer's life lies, and to it we are invited by the counsels. For it is plain that the human heart will tend more intensively toward one object the more it turns away from the many other things it can love. Consequently, man's spirit will be borne more perfectly toward loving God to the extent that his affections are turned from the love of temporal things. For this reason St. Augustine declares that the hope of obtaining or of retaining temporal things is the poison of charity; whereas, the increase of charity depends on lessening cupidity, and the perfection of charity will consist in no cupidity. Therefore, all the counsels, by which we are invited to perfection, aim at the one objective of turning the spirit of a man from attraction to temporal things, so that his mind may the more freely tend to God by contemplating him, by loving him, and by fulfilling his will.

Chapter VII. The First Road to Perfection Consists in Renouncing Temporal Goods

The first temporal goods that suggest themselves for renunciation are the external goods called riches. Our Lord counsels this when he says: "If thou wouldst be perfect, go sell what thou hast and give to the poor and thou shalt have treasure in heaven, and come follow me" (Mt. 19: 21).

The usefulness of this counsel will now be shown. First, we shall appeal to the evidence of the fact. For when the young man who had asked about the way of perfection heard this, he went away sad. The reason for this sadness is given by St. Jerome. He says that this youth had great possessions, i.e., thorns and thistles, which choked the flower of Our Lord's teaching. St. Chrysostom, explaining this interview between the rich young man and Our Lord, declares that those who have little and those who have much are *slowed up* in different ways because the possession of riches kindles a stronger flame and engenders a more violent type of covetousness. Moreover, St. Augustine, in an epistle to Paulinus, writes that when earthly things are loved overmuch, possessions already acquired create stronger fetters than those that are merely desired, for what caused that youth to go away sad if it was not that he had great possessions? For it is one thing not to covet what one does not yet have and another thing to lay aside what is already in one's treasure; the former are forsaken as something foreign, the latter are removed as friendly members.

Second, the usefulness of the counsel to abandon riches is manifested by the words of Our Lord that it is with difficulty that a rich man enters the kingdom of heaven. The reason, says St. Jerome, is that riches already in one's possession are difficult to despise. Our Lord did not say that it is impossible for a rich man to enter the kingdom of heaven, but that it is *difficult*. To say it is difficult does not imply that it is impossible but that it is rare. But as St. Chrysostom comments, Our Lord almost goes so far as to say that it is impossible when he declares that it is easier for a camel to pass through the eye of a needle than for a rich man to enter the kingdom of heaven. From these words St. Augustine tells us the disciples took Our Lord to mean that *all those who covet riches* are included in the term "rich man." Otherwise, knowing how few rich men there are in comparison with the great number of the poor, would they have asked: "Who then can be saved?"

From these two declarations of Our Lord it is clearly shown that those who possess riches have difficulty in entering the kingdom of heaven because, as Our Lord says elsewhere, "the solicitude of this world and the deception of riches choke the word of God and prevent it from bearing fruit." Indeed, for those who love riches inordinately, it is less likely for them to enter the kingdom of heaven than it is for a camel to pass through the eye of a needle. The latter is impossible because it is contrary to nature; the former is impossible because it is contrary to divine justice, which is more powerful than all nature. From all this can be gathered the reason for Our Lord's counsel. For counsels deal with matters that are of greater utility, as St. Paul says: "And herein I give my advice: for this is more useful to you" (2 Co. 8: 10). To gain eternal life it is more useful to spurn riches than to possess them, because the rich have difficulty in entering the kingdom of heaven due to the fact that it is difficult not to be held fast by the love of riches, and it is that which makes it impossible to enter the kingdom of heaven. Consequently, it was with an eye to our advantage that Our Lord counseled it as being more useful that riches be abandoned.

It can be objected that Matthew, Bartholomew, and Zaccheus all had riches, and yet they entered the kingdom of heaven. But St. Jerome answers that "they had ceased being rich at the time they entered." Nevertheless, it can still be observed that since Abraham had never ceased being rich and even died amidst plenty, it would seem that according to Our Lord's teaching Abraham was not perfect even though God had said to him: "Be perfect" (Gn. 17: 1). This question could not be settled if the perfection of the Christian life consisted in the very putting aside of riches. If it did, then anyone who possessed riches could not be perfect. But if the words of Our Lord are studied closely, he does not make perfection consist in the putting aside of riches, but he shows that such an act is a sure *way* to perfection, as his very words testify: "If thou wouldst be perfect, go sell what thou hast and give to the poor and *follow Me*." It is in the following of Christ that perfection consists, wherefore the putting aside of riches is a *way* to perfection. Hence St. Jerome, preaching on a passage from St. Matthew, says: Because it is not enough merely to abandon riches St. Peter adds what is perfect; namely, "and we have followed thee." Origen, too, has this to say: "If thou wouldst be perfect . . . ." does not mean that at the time a person gives all his goods to the poor he becomes completely perfect; rather, from that time his concentration on God will lead him to all virtue. It can happen, therefore, that a rich man be perfect if his spirit is not trapped by riches but is totally joined to God. This was indicated in God's word to Abraham: "Walk before me and be perfect." By these words he showed that his perfection would consist in walking before God, i.e., in loving God to the extent of despising himself and all he loved or owned. He showed this by his willingness to immolate his son, for which God said to him: "Because thou hast done this thing and hast not spared thy only begotten son for my sake, I will bless thee" (Gn. 22: 16).

This should not lead anyone to suppose that the counsel of Our Lord about riches is useless, seeing that Abraham became perfect even though he was wealthy. For Our Lord did not give this counsel because the rich could not become perfect or could not enter the kingdom of heaven but because they *could not do so without difficulty*. Let us rather admire the (greatness) of Abraham's virtue who, in spite of his riches, kept his spirit detached from them, just as Samson's power was great in slaying his enemies with no weapon other than the jawbone of an ass. Certainly Samson's example does not make useless the advice given to soldiers that in battle they should have arms to conquer their enemies. Neither does the example of Abraham arriving at perfection in spite of riches make useless Our Lord's advice that those who desire perfection should abandon riches.

Such marvels are not to be carried too far, because the weak are more capable of admiring and praising them than of imitating them. Thus it is said in Ecclesiasticus 31: 8: "Blessed is the rich man that is found without blemish; and that hath not gone after gold nor put his trust in money nor in treasures." Herein is described a rich man of great virtue with perfect charity fixed upon God. He has contracted no stain of sin from a love of riches; his desires have not wandered after gold, nor has he put such trust in riches as to account himself better than others. Hence, St. Paul says to Timothy: "Charge the rich of this world not to be highminded nor to trust in the uncertainty of riches" (1 Tm. 6: 17). But as we advance up the scale of virtue, the higher we go the fewer is the number of the rich possessing such virtue. Wherefore it is said: "Who is he and we will praise him? For he hath done wonderful things in his life." It is a real wonder not to sink one's heart in the riches one possesses, and anyone who is such is without doubt proved to be perfect. Wherefore we read further: "Who hath been tried therein," i.e., in this, that he has riches but no sin, "and has been found perfect," as if to say, it is something rare, "and he shall have glory everlasting." This agrees with the words of Our Lord that it is difficult for a rich man to enter the kingdom of heaven.

This therefore is the first way of arriving at perfection: to abandon riches and embrace poverty in order to follow Christ.

Chapter VIII. Of the Second Way of Perfection, Which Is to Give Up Bodily Pleasures and Marriage

To point out the second way of perfection let us begin with a statement of St. Augustine: "The less we love our own good, the more apt we are to cling to God." Therefore, according to the value of the goods that a man sacrifices for the love of God we can judge the value of what leads to perfect union with God. For the first things we give up are those that are less intimate to us; hence the first things we give up are external goods, since they are separate from our nature. After that it occurs to us to give what is very close to us and to our nature. Hence Our Lord says: "If anyone comes to me and does not hate his father and mother and wife and children and brothers and sisters, he cannot be my disciple" (Lk. 14: 26).

Now, one naturally wonders how we, who are commanded even to love our enemies, can now be told that we must hate our parents and relatives. But if we ponder the force of these commandments we can wisely observe both; for when anyone who is bent upon things of the flesh suggests to us what is base, we are said to love him as it were through hatred if we pay no attention to him. Similarly we must show our neighbors a holy hatred by loving them for what they are and hating whatever there is in them that blocks our way to God. For whoever is zealous for eternal things ought to enter into the cause of God by existing outside father and mother and wife and children and relatives and outside even oneself. Indeed, God is known more truly the more no one else gets in the way. For it is evident that many carnal affections distract the attention of the mind and dull its acuity. Among all human affections the human spirit is especially held fast by married love, so much so that our first parent said: "A man shall leave father and mother and cling to his wife" (Gn. 2: 24). Consequently the marriage bond is to be avoided at all costs by those tending to perfection, because this bond entangles a person in worldly cares. This is the very reason that St. Paul assigns for giving the counsel to observe continence: "He that is without a wife is solicitous for the things that belong to the Lord, how he may please God. But he that is with a wife is solicitous for the things of the world" (1 Co. 32–33). Hence in order that a man may more freely give himself to God and adhere to him more perfectly, the second way of perfection is the perpetual observance of chastity.

Continence is in a special way adapted to obtaining perfection. For man's spirit is prevented from freely giving himself to God not only by the love of external goods but much more by the intensity of the passions. And of all the passions the most absorbing is the concupiscence of the flesh and sexual indulgence. Of this St. Augustine says: "I consider that there is nothing more calculated to cast a man's spirit down from the citadel of virtue than the blandishments of a woman and that bodily union without which a wife cannot be had, and therefore the way of continence is especially necessary to attain perfection. This way the Apostle counsels when he says: "Now, concerning virginity I have no commandment of the Lord; but I give counsel, as having obtained mercy of the Lord, to be faithful" (1 Co. 7: 25). The usefulness of this way is shown in the Gospel according to St. Matthew. There it is recorded that when the disciples said to Christ, "If the case of a man with a wife be so, it is not expedient to marry," he answered: "All men take not this word, but they to whom it is given" (Mt. 19: 10–11). This answer shows how difficult this way is. Indeed, when we consider that the ordinary virtue of men cannot persevere on this way and that it cannot be reached without a gift of God, it is no wonder that the wise man says: "I knew that I could not otherwise be continent except God gave it, and this also was a point of wisdom, to know whose gift it was" (Wis. 8: 21). This agrees with the words of St. Paul: "I would that all men were even as myself (i.e., in observing continence) but everyone has his own gift from God; one after this manner and another after that" (1 Co. 7: 7). But lest it be supposed that it is a gift of God that requires no effort on man's part, Our Lord hastens to exhort us to make this effort, first by an example, when he says: "There are eunuchs who have made themselves such," not by mutilation but by forestalling evil thoughts; second, by suggesting the reward: "For the kingdom of heaven." Wherefore it is written in the Book of Wisdom: "The chaste generation triumpheth crowned forever, winning the reward of undefiled conflicts" (Wis. 4: 2). Third, Our Lord actually extends an invitation: "He that can take, let him take." This, says St. Jerome, is the voice of the Lord exhorting and encouraging his soldier to struggle for the reward of chastity, as though saying: "He who can fight, let him fight and overcome and be victorious."

If anyone alleges against this teaching, the example of

Abraham, who was perfect, or of other just patriarchs, who did not abstain from marriage, let him hear an answer from St. Augustine. In his book, *De Bono Conjugali*, he says: "Continence is not a virtue of the body but of the soul. Virtues of the soul sometimes reveal themselves in external actions; sometimes they remain hidden in the soul. Hence just as the merit of patience was not less in John, who did not suffer, than in Peter, who did, so the merit of continence in Abraham, who begot children, was not unequal to that of John, who never married. According to the times in which they lived, both the celibacy of John and the marriage of Abraham served the purposes of Christ. Therefore, let him who is faithful in his continence say: "I am not in the law better than Abraham; although the charity of the chaste is better than the chastity of the wed, of the two Abraham kept one in use and the other in reserve. For he lived chastely as a married man, and he could have lived chastely without marriage, but the time was not fitting. But it is easier for me not to make use of marriage, which Abraham made use of, than to make such use of it as Abraham did; and, therefore, I am better than those who through continence cannot do what I can, but I am not better than those who on account of the age in which they lived did not do what I do. For what I now do they would have done better if their times called for it." This answer of St. Augustine harmonized with what was said above about observing poverty. Abraham possessed such a degree of perfection that neither great possessions nor the use of marriage shook his mind from perfect love of God. But if anyone lacking this strength of mind attempted to arrive at perfection saddled both with riches and with marriage, he would be guilty both of a presumptuous error and of making light of Our Lord's counsels.

Chapter IX. *Helps to Preserving Chastity*

To enter the way of continence is so arduous that Our Lord said that not all take this word but that it is obtained by the gift of God. Accordingly, it behooves anyone who desires to enter this way to avoid whatever can impede a successful journey. Immediately three obstacles to continence appear:

one from the body, a second from the soul, and a third from the persons and things outside a person.

St. Paul speaks of the obstacles that arise from the body when he says: "The flesh lusteth against the spirit" (Ga. 5: 17). And he lists the works of the flesh as fornication, uncleanness, immodesty, and things of this kind. This lust of the flesh is the law of which he says: "I see another law in my members fighting against the law of my mind" (Rm. 7: 23). The more the flesh is indulged by excess of food and by the softness of pleasures, the more this lust grows. Wherefore St. Jerome says: "The stomach that is overheated with wine quickly belches forth lust." Likewise in the Book of Proverbs we read: "A luxurious thing is wine" (Pr. 20: 1). And in the Book of Job it is said of Behemoth (through whom the devil is signified) that "he sleepeth under the shadow in the covert of the reed and in the moist places" (Jb. 40: 16). St. Gregory explains that the moist places are lustful acts. For the feet do not slip when they are planted on the dry earth, but on an oily surface they can scarcely stay put. Hence a man who cannot stand erect in righteousness is making his journey through life in moist places.

Consequently those who would enter the way of continence must chastise their flesh by abstinence from pleasures and exercise themselves by fasts and vigils and things of this sort. St. Paul gives us an example of this: "Everyone that strives for the mastery refrains himself from all things," and then adds: "I chastise my body and bring it into subjection; lest perhaps when I have preached to others I myself should become a castaway" (1 Co. 9: 25, 27). In this matter St. Paul's words matched his deeds, for he wrote to the Romans: "not in rioting and in drunkenness" and added: "make no provision for the flesh in its concupiscences" (Rm. 13: 13, 14). Well does he say "concupiscences" and not "necessities," because provision must be made for the necessities of the flesh. For that reason he writes to the Ephesians: "No man ever hated his own flesh, but nourisheth and cherisheth it" (Ep. 5: 29).

The resolution to be continent runs into obstacles placed by the soul when one lingers upon impure thoughts. Hence God, speaking through the prophet, commands us: "Take

away the evil of your devisings from my eyes" (Is. 1: 16).
For evil devisings frequently lead to evil actions, as Micheas
says: "Woe to you that devise that which is unprofitable and
work evil in your beds" (Mi. 2: 1).

In the realm of evil thoughts none induces to sin as much
as do thoughts that concern the pleasure of the flesh. This was
known also to the philosophers, who gave two good reasons
explaining the fact. The first reason is that since such pleasure is most natural to man and grows up with him from
childhood, it is easy to desire it when the thought of it is in
the mind. Hence Augustine says that it is not easy to think
about pleasure without desiring it. The second reason is that
pleasures in the concrete have more power to attract than
they do when they are present in abstract speculation. For it
is plain that through sustained thought we are apt to get
down to particulars, so that prolonged cogitation of certain
matters is apt to beget a strong desire for them. For this reason St. Paul says to the Corinthians: "Fly from fornication"
(1 Co. 6: 18) because as a gloss comments: "With respect
to other vices we can expect to be engaged in battle but fly
from this, lest it get near, for this is the only way to overcome
this evil."

A number of remedies are effective against this obstacle.
The first and chief remedy is to keep the mind occupied with
prayer and the contemplation of divine things. Wherefore
St. Paul says: "Be not drunk with wine wherein is luxury;
but be ye filled with the Holy Spirit, speaking to yourselves
in psalms and hymns and spiritual canticles"—which seems
to pertain to contemplation—"singing and making melody in
your hearts to the Lord"—which seems to refer to prayer (Ep.
5: 18–20). In like vein Our Lord, speaking through the
prophet, says: "For my praise I will bridle thee, lest thou
shouldst perish" (Is. 48: 9). Praising God is a special bridle
that keeps the soul from the distraction of sin.

The second remedy against dangers that arise from the
soul is the study of the Scriptures, as St. Jerome wrote to the
monk, Rusticus: "Love to study the Scriptures and you will
not love the vices of the flesh." Similarly, St. Paul has said to
Timothy: "Be thou an example to the faithful in word, in

conversation, in charity, in faith, in chastity," immediately adding, "till I come, attend to reading" (1 Tm. 4: 12–13).

The third remedy is to keep the soul occupied with any type of wholesome thought; hence, St. Chrysostom, explaining a certain passage of St. Matthew's gospel, says that mutilation does not suppress temptations and bring peace, as does the bridling of one's thoughts. This explains why St. Paul tells the Philippians: "For the rest, brethren, whatsoever things are true, whatsoever modest, whatsoever just, whatsoever holy, whatsoever lovely, whatsoever of good fame, if there be any virtue, if any praise of discipline, think on these things" (Ph. 4: 8).

The fourth remedy is to avoid idleness, even if that involves bodily work, for it is written: "Idleness has been the teacher of much evil" (Eccles. 33: 29). Indeed, because idleness is an incentive to carnal vices, Ezechiel writes: "Behold this was the iniquity of Sodom, thy sister: pride, fullness of bread, and abundance and her idleness" (Ezech. 16: 49). Accordingly, St. Jerome writes to Rusticus: "Do some kind of work so that the devil will always find you occupied."

The fifth remedy is against the concupiscence of the flesh, and it consists in enduring disturbances of the mind. In the Epistle to Rusticus, St. Jerome recounts an incident that took place in a certain monastery where lived a youth who in spite of continual abstinence and enormous bodily toil could not extinguish the flame of concupiscence. But the abbot of the monastery helped him out of his danger by the following ruse. He ordered one of the more serious members of the community to hound this youth with insults and affronts, and after starting a quarrel, to be first to complain to the abbot; even the witnesses who were summoned took sides against the youth. Only the abbot opposed them, lest the youth be overcome with excessive sadness. After a year of this treatment the youth was asked about his previous troublesome thoughts. He replied: "Father, the community hardly leaves me a moment of peace; how can I be troubled with such thoughts?"

On the part of external things, the greatest temptations against chastity arise from gazing upon and frequent conversations with the opposite sex. Wherefore it is written in the Book of Ecclesiasticus: "Look not upon a woman that hath a mind for many, lest thou fall into her snares. Use not much the company of her that is a dancer and hearken not to her, . . . lest her beauty be a stumbling block to thee" (Ecclus. 9: 3–5). Again it is commanded: "Behold not everybody's beauty; and tarry not among women. For from garments cometh a moth, and from a woman the iniquity of a man" (Ecclus. 42: 12–13). Wherefore, St. Jerome, writing against Vigilantius, says the monk who knows his own feebleness and the frailty of a vessel that he might be carrying fears to stumble lest it be struck and fall and break; in like manner, let him avoid the sight of women, especially those that are young, for fear that the eye of a harlot captivate him and the beauteous form incite him to unlawful embraces.

It follows from this that as the Abbot Moses says in the *Conferences of the Fathers:* "For the sake of preserving purity of heart, seek solitude. And remember that we accept the privations, fasting, vigils, bodily labors, insufficiency of warm clothing, reading, and the product of other virtues in order that through these things we may preserve our heart from all harmful passions, for each of these things is a special rung up the ladder of the perfection of charity." Special works of this kind are enjoined in the rule of every religious community, not because perfection principally consists in them, but because they are means to perfection. Hence, Abbot Moses continues: "Therefore, fasts, vigils, privations, meditation on Scripture, insufficient clothing and supplies are not perfection, but instruments of perfection; for the objective of this training does not lie in them, but through them one arrives at the objective."

Do not be led astray by the claim that a man can acquire perfection without fasts and vigils and so on by appealing to the description of Our Lord given by St. Matthew: "The son of man came, eating and drinking" (Mt. 11: 19) or by alleging that Jesus' disciples did not fast as did the Pharisees and the disciples of John. For the reason why John took no wine or strong drink is that abstinence increases merit, and that is something that no power of nature can do. Moreover, why should Our Lord, who can forgive sin, have stayed away from sinners who did not fast when he could have made them more just than those who fasted? Therefore, the disciples of Christ had no need of fasting because the presence of the bridegroom afforded them more strength than the disciples of John obtained through their fast. But it must be remembered that Our Lord also said: "The days will come when the bridegroom will be taken away from them and then they shall fast." Explaining this passage, St. John Chrysostom says: "To fast is not a natural cause of sadness except for those who are yet too feebly disposed; for those who desire to contemplate wisdom, fasting is a delight. As long as the disciples were weak, it was wiser to wait until they became stronger. This shows that it was not an invitation to gluttony but a recognition of their weakness."

That fast and vigils, etc. are aids against sin and helps to perfection is expressly declared by St. Paul: "Giving no offence to any man that our ministry be not blamed; but in all things let us show ourselves as the minister of God, in much patience, in tribulation, in necessity, in distresses, in stripes, in prisons, in seditions, in labors, in watchings, in fastings, in chastity" (2 Co. 6: 3–6).

Chapter X. The Third Way of Perfection, Which Is to Abandon One's Will

In order to attain to the perfection of charity it is necessary for man not only to forsake external goods but also in some way to forsake himself. For St. Denis in *The Divine Names* asserts that divine love produces ecstasy, i.e., it puts one outside of oneself by not allowing a man to be fixed upon self but upon that which is loved. St. Paul proposes himself as an example of this: "I live, now not I, but Christ liveth in me," (Ga. 2: 20), as though he regarded his life not his own but Christ's, for he despised what was his own in order to cleave entirely to Christ. He was aware that others, too, were like him, for he writes: "You are dead and your life is hidden with Christ in God" (Col. 3: 3). Others he exhorts to strive after this, saying: "Christ died for all that they also who live may not now live to themselves but unto him who died for them and rose again" (2 Co. 5: 15). All this rests upon the teaching of Our Lord, who after declaring, "If any man come to me and hate not his father and mother and wife and children and brethren and sisters," and then, as though adding something very important continues, "yea, and his own life also, he cannot be my disciple" (Lk. 14: 26). Our Lord teaches the same thing in the Gospel according to St. Matthew: "If any man will come after me, let him deny himself and take up his cross and follow me" (Mt. 16: 24).

This salutary self-denial and charitable hatred of self is partly necessary to salvation—indeed, it is found in all the just—and partly the crown of perfection. For as the aforementioned teaching of St. Denis points out, it is of the very nature of divine love that the lover be fixed not on self but on the beloved. Hence, this salutary self-denial and charitable hatred will vary with each degree of divine love. As was already pointed out, it is necessary for salvation to love God in such a way as to make him the end of one's intention and to accept nothing that is contrary to the love of God. Consequently, both hatred and self-denial are necessary for salvation, as St. Gregory says: "We have forsaken and abandoned ourselves when we avoid what pertains to the old life and strive to fulfill what the call of the new life demands." In another place he writes: "We hate our life properly when we do not acquiesce to its carnal desires, when we bridle its appetites and struggle against its inclinations to pleasure." On the other hand, perfection requires that the love of God prompt a man to abandon even what was lawful so that he may more freely give himself to God. Hatred and self-denial on this level pertain to perfection. For just as the words: "If thou wouldst be perfect, go, sell what thou hast and give to the poor" lay no necessity upon anyone but leave the matter up to one's will, so when Jesus says: "If anyone will come after me, let him deny himself and take up his cross and follow me," he does not force anyone, because he does not say "willy-nilly, you must do this." Similarly, Our Lord said: "If anyone comes to me and does not hate his father . . . ." and immediately added: "For which of you having a mind to build a tower does not first sit down and reckon the charges that are necessary whether he have the wherewithal to finish it?" (Lk. 14: 28). St. Gregory explains this by saying that "because lofty precepts were being given, he uses a comparison about building a tower." Farther on, St. Gregory continues: "The rich man who went away sad after hearing that he must do more than keep the commandments is an example of one who could not pay the expense of building."

From the above it is clear that these matters pertain in some way to the counsel to perfection. This counsel was fulfilled most perfectly by the martyrs, of whom St. Augustine says that no one gives as much as the one who gives himself. The martyrs of Christ, however, are the ones who in a sense hated the present life for the sake of Christ by denying themselves; because, as St. John Chrysostom says: "He that denies another, for example, his own brother or his servant or someone else, will not come to his assistance even though he sees him being whipped or ill-treated. In like manner Christ wants us not to spare our body even though it be scourged or maltreated." And lest you suppose that self-denial should go no farther than enduring misuse and contumely, Our Lord said: "And let him take up his cross and follow me," to show that self-denial goes as far as enduring death, even the shameful death of the cross. Such self-denial is entirely perfect because for the love of God the martyrs forsook their own lives, the lives for which men labor to acquire temporal things, the lives for which a person will sacrifice everything else. For a man would prefer to lose all his wealth and friends and the health of his being and even undergo slavery rather than lose his life. Even in war it is thought to be a gesture of kindness to spare the lives of the vanquished and make them slaves. Hence, Satan said to the Lord: "Skin for skin and all that a man hath he will give for his life" (Jb. 2: 4).

The more we naturally love something, the more perfect it is to sacrifice it for Christ. Now, nothing is more loved by man than the freedom of his own will. For through his will a man is master of others; through it he can use and enjoy things; and through it he is even master of his own actions. Hence just as a man, when he forsakes riches or his loved ones, denies them; so when he gives up the right to choose according to his own will through which he is master of himself, he truly denies himself. Next to death there is nothing more naturally disagreeable to man than servitude; indeed, next to dying for another, the greatest benefit that a person can confer is to become his slave. This is implied in the words of young Tobias to the angel: "If I should give myself to be thy servant, I should not make a worthy return for thy care" (Tb. 9: 2).

Now, some abandon this freedom of will on one or another point when they make a vow to do or to omit this or that. For a vow lays a type of necessity upon the one who vows so that he no longer can lawfully do what previously was lawful; rather, he is bound by some necessity to fulfill the vow. Hence David says: "I will pay thee my vows, which my lips have uttered" (Ps. 65: 13); again, in the Book of Ecclesiastes, we are told: "If thou hast made a vow to God, make haste to pay; for a faithless and foolish promise is an abomination to him" (Ecc. 5: 3).

Others sacrifice the freedom of their will totally, by subjecting themselves to others for the love of God through the vow of obedience, of which we have the chief example in Christ. Of him St. Paul writes: "As by the disobedience of one man many were made sinners; so also by the obedience of one, many shall be made just" (Rm. 5: 19), and to the Philippians he says: "Christ humbled himself, becoming obedient unto death, even to the death of the cross" (Ph. 2: 8). This obedience of Christ consisted in the denial of his own will; hence, he prayed: "My Father, if it be possible, let this chalice pass from me. Nevertheless, not as I will, but as thou wilt" (Mt. 26: 39). Again, according to St. John, he said: "I came down from heaven not to do my own will but the will of him who sent me". (Jn. 6: 38). Thus Christ has given us an example that just as he denied his own human will by subjecting it to the divine will, so we should submit our will totally to God and to men who are set over us as the ministers of God. Wherefore St. Paul says: "Obey your prelates and be subject to them" (Heb. 13: 17).

Chapter XI. The Three Ways Constitute the State Called Religion

Hand in hand with the three ways of perfection that are trod in the religious state are found the three vows of poverty, chastity, and obedience unto death. Through the vow of poverty, religious enter upon the first way of perfection by renouncing all property. Through the vow of chastity they take the second way by renouncing marriage forever. Through the vow of obedience they enter the third way by renouncing their own will. These three vows are peculiarly suited to religion. For as St. Augustine says in *The City of God:* "Religion seems to denote not just any worship but precisely the worship of God." Wherefore even Cicero says in the *Rhetoric* that "Religion is a virtue that offers worship and ceremony to the superior nature that we call divine." Now, the worship that is due to God alone is exemplified by the offering of sacrifice, whether it be of external things of one's own body or of one's spirit. A sacrifice of external things is offered to God whenever someone distributes them for the love of God, as St. Paul teaches: "Do not forget to do good and to impart; for by such sacrifices God's favor is obtained" (Heb. 13: 16). The sacrifice of one's body is offered to God when "those who are Christ's crucify their flesh with its vices and concupiscences" (Ga. 5: 24). But it is a sacrifice most acceptable to God when one offers his very spirit to God, according to the Psalmist: "A sacrifice to God is an afflicted spirit" (Ps. 50: 19).

As St. Gregory points out, there is this difference between a sacrifice and a holocaust: Every holocaust is a sacrifice, but not every sacrifice is a holocaust. For in a sacrifice only part of an animal is offered, but in a holocaust the entire animal is offered. When, therefore, anyone vows something of his own to God and does not vow something else of his own, it is a sacrifice. But when he vows to Almighty God all that he has, all that he lives for, and all that is pleasurable, it is a holocaust. Such a holocaust is offered through the three vows. Hence it is evident that persons who make these vows deserve to be called religious in a special sense on account of the excellence of the holocaust.

In the Old Law it was commanded to offer sacrifice in order to satisfy for sin. This is expressly commanded in Leviticus. Again, in Psalm 4: 5, King David after saying: "The things you say in your hearts, be sorry for them upon your beds," immediately enjoins sacrifice: "Offer up the sacrifice of justice and trust in the Lord." This means: "Do just works to crown the sorrow of repentance." Therefore, just as a holocaust is a perfect sacrifice, so by the three vows man makes perfect satisfaction to God when he offers a holocaust of external things, of his own body and of his own spirit. From this it is evident that the religious state contains not only the perfection of charity but the perfection of penance as well, so much so that there are no sins so grave that entering religion would not be a suitable satisfaction for them; for the religious state transcends all satisfaction. Hence Astulphus, who had murdered his wife, was advised to enter a monastery as something better and more lenient; otherwise, he would have to undergo a very severe penance.

Of the three vows that pertain to the religious state the chief is the vow of obedience. It is easy to see why. First of all, the vow of obedience offers to God one's own will, whereas the vow of chastity offers him a sacrifice of one's body and the vow of poverty one of external things. Now, just as one's body is preferred to external goods, thus making the vow of chastity of more account than the vow of poverty, so the vow of obedience is of more value than the other two. Second, a man employs external goods and his body in the service of his will. Consequently, to give one's will to God is to give all. No matter how you look at it, the vow of obedience is more extensive than chastity and poverty; indeed, in a sense it includes them. Hence, Samuel prefers obedience to all sacrifice, saying: "Obedience is better than sacrifice" (1 K. 15: 22).

Chapter XII. Refutation of Those Who Presume to Belittle the Merit of Obedience or of Vows

The devil in his envy of human perfection has constantly

raised up masters of deception and of empty talk to attack the aforementioned ways of perfection. The first way of perfection was assailed by Vigilantius, whom St. Jerome answered by saying: "When Vigilantius exhorts that one who continues using his wealth while giving bit by bit of the fruit of his possessions to the poor is better than one who sells his possessions and distributes them all at once, it is not I but the Lord who answers: 'If thou wilt be perfect, go, sell all that thou hast and give to the poor and come, follow me.' He is speaking to one who wants to be perfect, to one who with the Apostles leaves father and ship and nets. The degree that you praise is second or third; we likewise praise it, but know at the same time that the first is preferable to the second and third." Furthermore, it was in order to crush this error that the *Book of Ecclesiastical Dogmas* says: "It is good to give to the poor what is acquired by good management, but it is better to give all at once with the intention of following the Lord, and being freed of anxiety, to suffer want with Christ."

The second way of perfection was attacked by Jovinian, who made marriage the equal of virginity. St. Jerome refuted him in the special book dedicated to answering Jovinian. St. Augustine also answered him, in his book, *Retraction,* saying: "The heresy of Jovinian attempted to make the merit of conjugal chastity equal to that of the holy virgins; as a result it is said that certain dedicated virgins of whose chastity there was never any doubt have entered marriage. Our holy mother the Church most faithfully and firmly has opposed this, as we can see in the *Book of Ecclesiastical Dogmas,* where it is written that the teaching that makes marriage the equal of virginity consecrated to God or that declares that no merit is obtained by abstaining from wine or meat in order to chastise the body is not Christ's but Jovinian's doctrine."

In our own times the devil, not content with the damage he wrought by his past wiles, is said to have raised up certain advocates who impugn not only the vow of obedience but all vows in general by teaching that it is more praiseworthy to do good works without a vow or without obedience, as though a vow or obedience forces a man to do these good works. Indeed, the madness of some is said to have reached the point of exhorting that a vow to enter religion can be ignored without any danger to salvation. The teachers of this error are said to support it with foolish and frivolous arguments. For they argue thus: "A work is more praiseworthy and of more merit the more voluntary it is. But the more necessary it is, the less voluntary. Therefore, it seems to be more praiseworthy and more meritorious to do good works according to one's own desires and without the necessity of a vow or of obedience than to do them under the compulsion of vow or of obedience." They are said to support this reasoning by adducing what Prosper says in the second book on the contemplative life: "We ought to fast and abstain but not in such wise as to be subjected to the necessity of fasting lest being no longer devout but reluctant we do it unwillingly." Yet they forget that St. Paul said: "Everyone as he has determined in his heart, not with sadness, or of necessity; for God loveth a cheerful giver" (2 Co. 9: 7). It will be our task both to show in detail the falseness of their conclusions and to puncture the flimsy reasons they allege.

To make clear wherein lies the falseness of this error, we appeal to what the Psalmist says: "Vow ye, and pay to the Lord, your God" (Ps. 75: 12). A gloss on this passage has this to say: "Observe that there are some vows that are common, i.e., pertaining to matters without which there is no salvation: for example, to vow faith in baptism and like things that must be done even if we do not promise. Of such things everyone is commanded: "Vow and pay." There are other vows that are personal, such as chastity, poverty, and things of that kind. God invites us to vow these; he does not command us to vow, but he does command us to pay if we vow. Whether or not to vow is up to one's will, but after the vow is made, it is necessary to fulfill it. Therefore, some vows are commanded, some are counseled. In either case it is necessary to conclude that it is better to do a good work with a vow than without a vow. For it is evident that everyone is bound by God's commandment to do what is necessary for salvation, and no one can safely hold that any of God's commands are without a purpose, for "the end of each commandment is charity" (2 Tm. 1: 5). Now, it would be in vain to give a command to do something if it did not pertain more to charity to do it than not to do it. But there are commands not only to believe or not to steal but also to vow these things. Therefore, to believe as a result of vowing or to abstain from stealing as a result of vowing and so on pertain to charity more than if they are done without a vow. However, what pertains more to charity is more praiseworthy and more meritorious. Therefore, it is more praiseworthy and more meritorious to do something under a vow than without a vow.

Again, Scripture gives counsel not only about preserving virginity or chastity but also about vowing. This is evident from the gloss quoted above. Now, a counsel always concerns a better good. Therefore, it is better to preserve virginity with a vow than without a vow, and the same is true of other cases. Likewise, in the list of good works it is virginity that is especially commended. Our Lord counsels it when he says: "He that can take, let him take it" (Mt. 19: 12). But when virginity is preserved under vow it becomes commendable. For St. Augustine says in the *Book Concerning Virginity:* "Virginity is held in honor not because it is virginity but because it is consecrated to God. It is the virtue of piety that vows and preserves it." Later he says: "We do not extol virgins because they are virgins but because they are dedicated by the pious virtue of virginity." Much more, therefore, other works are rendered more laudable by being directed to God by a vow. Again, any finite good added to another good becomes better. But there is no doubt that to promise a good is good, for as soon as you promise a person something, you seem already to have conferred a good upon him, and he even thanks you for the promise. Now, a vow is a promise made to God, as is evidenced from the Book of Ecclesiastes (5: 3): "If thou hast vowed anything to God, defer not to pay it; for an unfaithful and foolish promise displeaseth him." Therefore, it is better to vow and do than just to do without a vow. Further, the more you give to someone, the more you deserve from him. Now, when you do something without a vow you merely show that you are doing it out of love for him, but when you not merely do but vow to do, you not only give him what you do but also the vow by which you do it. For the vow puts you in a position of not being able not to do what previously you could lawfully have omitted. Therefore, it is of greater merit before God to do something as a result of a vow than without a vow. Furthermore, one of the reasons why a good work is laudable is that the will is firmly entrenched in the good, just as a sin is more grievous on account of the will being settled in evil. Now, it is evident that a vow fixes the will on that which is vowed, so that when the vow is fulfilled, the act comes from a will that is fixed. Therefore, just as the firm purpose of doing evil makes a sin graver, so it is an added merit to do a good work under the influence of a vow. Likewise, the higher the virtue from which a good work proceeds, the more praiseworthy it is, since all the praise due to a good work stems from the virtue. Now, it can happen that an act of an inferior virtue be commended by a higher virtue, e.g., when someone performs an act of justice out of charity. It is, therefore, much better to perform the good work of an inferior virtue under the impetus of a higher virtue, just as an act of justice is better if it is done through charity. Bearing this in mind, it is easy to see the value of a vow. For many of the good works that we do pertain to the inferior virtues; for instance, to fast pertains to the virtue of abstinence; to be continent pertains to the virtue of chastity. But to vow is an act of the virtue of latria, which is undoubtedly a greater virtue than chastity or abstinence or any such virtues, for it is better to render worship to God than to be virtuous toward one's neighbor or toward oneself. Therefore, the works of abstinence or chastity and like virtues that are below latria are more laudable when they are done under vow. The pious zeal of the Church recommends this when it invites men to vow and when it grants indulgences and privileges to those who vow to go to the Holy Land or elsewhere in defense of the Church. The Church would not extend an invitation to make such vows if it were better to do such works without a vow. Indeed, it would be against the exhortation of St. Paul: "Be zealous for the better gifts" (1 Co. 12: 31). For if it were better to act without vows, the Church would not invite the faithful to make vows; rather, she would discourage vows by prohibiting or at least advising against them. Similarly, since it is the intention of the Church to improve the status of the faithful, she would absolve all men from vows so that their works would be rendered more praiseworthy. Hence, it is most clear that the position of our opponents is contrary to what the Church teaches and does; wherefore they must be rejected as heretical.

Now, as to the reason alleged in support of their position, any number of answers can be given. For the assertion that a good work done under vow is less voluntary is not universally and in all cases true. As a matter of fact, there are many persons who fulfill with such promptitude what they vow that even had they not vowed, they would not only do the good work but would vow to do it.

Second, granted that some good work done under vow or under obedience is, simply speaking, involuntary and is done from the necessity of the vow that he does not wish to violate, yet as long as he does it, it is more laudable and more meritorious than if it were done with the greatest promptitude without a vow. For although the keen desire to fast may be lacking, yet the prompt will to fulfill the vow or to obey is more meritorious than fasting and makes the act better than if it were done without a vow. Indeed, the willingness to keep a vow or to obey is judged to be the more prompt as the act done for the sake of obedience or the vow is repugnant to the will. Hence, St. Jerome says to the monk Rusticus: "Through all these things my prayer is simple; to teach you that you shall not be left to your own judgment. You will not do what you wish; you will eat what you are commanded; you will take what you get; you will put on what is given to you; you will turn in the salary for your work; you will obey a person you may not desire to obey; though tired, you will continue toward your journey's destiny; you will nap as you walk and you will be compelled to rise even though you have not finished sleeping." This shows that the merit of good work increases when someone does or suffers for God what he would not will for its own sake; for we can recognize that a will is more enkindled by the fire of divine love, the more opposed to our will are the things we do or suffer for God. It is for that reason that martyrs are the more commended for having endured for the love of God things that are more hateful to their wills. Hence, when Eleazar was being tortured, he said: "I suffer grievous pains in body;

but in soul I am well content to suffer these things because I fear thee" (2 Mach. 6: 30).

Third, supposing that someone no longer has the intention of keeping his vow or of obeying, is it not God who judges the heart, and will it not be before God that he will be considered a breaker of the vow or a violator of obedience? Or if such a person fulfills what he has vowed or what is commanded of him merely from human fear or shame, he obtains no merit before God because he is not acting with the intention of pleasing God but under the force of human necessity. Yet even in this case it was not useless to have vowed if it was originally done out of charity, for he merits more by vowing than one does by just fasting, and this merit will be restored to him if he repents.

This last response suggests also an answer to the authority adduced by our opponents: the authority that speaks of human necessity; for example, when someone does out of shame or human fear what he has vowed or sworn to do. They are not speaking of the necessity that arises from the end of divine love when someone, for example, does or suffers what is against his will in order to fulfill God's will. It is of this latter necessity that St. Paul speaks: "not with sadness or of necessity" (2 Co. 9: 7). For necessity begets a human sadness, but the necessity engendered of divine love terminates sadness or at least diminishes it. This is also evident from the words of Prosper, whom our opponents quote: "Lest lacking devotion and being unwilling, we act not voluntarily." For the necessity that proceeds from divine love does not lessen love, it increases it. Indeed, St. Augustine declares that such necessity is praiseworthy and should be sought, for in a letter to Armentarius and Paulina, he writes: "As you have now made the vow, as you have now bound yourself, you are not free to do anything else. Before you incurred the obligation of the vow, you were free to choose the less perfect way, although such liberty deserves no credit when what is not owed is paid, to one's own gain. But now that your promise binds you before God, I do not invite you to great perfection, I warn you to avoid a great sin. If you do not keep what you have vowed, you will not be the same as you would have been if you had not made the vow. For, in that case, you would have been less perfect, no worse; whereas now—which God forbid!—you will be as much worse off if you break your word to God as you will be more blessed if you keep it. So, then, do not regret having made the vow; rather, rejoice that you are no longer free to do what you might have done to your own great harm. Go forward boldly, then, and turn your words into deeds; he who inspired your vow will help you. Happy the necessity that forces us to better things!"* These words manifest the error of saying that a person is not bound to fulfill a vow to enter religion.

9. PRAYER AND PRAYERS

On Prayer   *Exposition of the Lord's Prayer*

"Our Father, who art in heaven." The Lord's Prayer is the best of all prayers. All prayer requires five excellent qualities, which are found here. A prayer should be *confident, ordered, suitable, devout,* and *humble.*

It should be *confident:* "Let us, therefore, approach with confidence the throne of grace" (Heb. 4: 16). It should not lack faith, as is stated: "But let him ask in faith, nothing wavering" (Jm. 1: 6). It is reasonable to trust in this prayer because he who is our advocate and most wise petitioner for us composed it: "In whom are hid all the treasures of wisdom and knowledge" (Col. 2: 3), and of whom it is said: "For we have with the Father an advocate, Jesus Christ the just one" (1 Jn. 2: 1). So St. Cyprian says: (on the Lord's Prayer) "Since we have Christ as our advocate with the Father for our sins, when we pray on account of our faults, we use the very words of our advocate."

Moreover, we have all the more confidence in this prayer because he who taught it to us graciously hears our prayer along with the Father, as declared in the Psalm: "He will cry to me, and I shall hear him" (Ps. 90: 15). Thus St. Cyprian states: (on the Lord's Prayer) "It is a friendly, familiar, and

* Translated by R. F. Larcher, O.P.

devout prayer to beseech the Lord in his own words." And so no one ends this prayer without fruit. St. Augustine says that our venial sins are forgiven through it (*Enchir.* 78).

Furthermore, our prayer should be *suitable* so that God is asked in prayer for what is suitable to the one praying. St. John Damascene says: "Prayer is the asking of what is right and appropriate from God" (*On Orthodox Faith* III, 24). Our prayer is often not heard when we ask for something not good for us: "You ask and you do not receive because you ask amiss" (Jm. 4: 3). It is very difficult to know what to pray for, since it is difficult to know what to desire. Whatever is rightly sought in prayer is rightly desired; so the Apostle says: "For we know not what we should pray for as we ought" (Rm. 8: 26). Christ is himself our teacher; he teaches us what we should pray for, and to him the disciples said: "Lord, teach us to pray" (Lk. 11: 1). Whatever he has taught us to pray for we should properly ask for. "Whatsoever words we use in prayer," says St. Augustine, "we cannot but repeat what is found in Our Lord's Prayer, if we pray suitably and worthily" (*Epist.* 130).

Just as our desires should be *ordered,* so should our prayer be, since prayer is only the expression of desire. Now, the correct order is to prefer spiritual to bodily things, and heavenly things to merely earthly ones. This is in accord with what is written: "Seek ye first the kingdom of God and his justice, and all these things shall be added unto you" (Mt. 6: 33). Here Our Lord indicates that we should first seek heavenly things and then material ones.

Our prayer should be *devout* because a rich amount of piety makes the sacrifice of prayer acceptable to God: "In thy name I will lift up my hands. Let my soul be filled with marrow and fatness" (Ps. 62: 5). Often devotion cools with the length of prayers, so that Our Lord taught us to avoid wordiness in our prayers: "When you are praying, speak not much" (Mt. 6: 7). And St. Augustine says: "Do not drag out your prayer, but as long as fervor is there, let the prayer continue" (*Epist.* 130). This is why the Lord made his prayer short. Devotion in prayer arises from charity, which is our love of God and neighbor, and in this prayer both are evident. Our love for God is apparent when we call God "our

Father"; and our love for our neighbor is apparent when we say: "Our Father . . . . forgive us our trespasses," and this leads us to love of neighbor.

Prayer should be *humble:* "He hath had regard for the prayer of the humble" (Ps. 101: 18). This is obvious in the parable of the Pharisee and the Publican (Lk. 18: 9–15), and likewise in the words of Judith: "The prayer of the humble and the meek hath always pleased thee" (Jdt. 9: 16). This same humility is found in this prayer, for when a person does not presume upon his own powers but expects everything he asks for from the divine strength, he has true humility.

We should be aware that three good things result from prayer. First, prayer is effective and useful as a remedy for evils. Hence, it frees us from the sins we have committed: "Thou hast forgiven the wickedness of my sin. For this shall all who are holy pray to thee in a seasonable time" (Ps. 31: 5). On the cross the thief prayed and was forgiven: "This day thou shalt be with me in paradise" (Lk. 23: 43). The Publican likewise prayed and "went down to his home justified" (Lk. 18: 14). One who prays is delivered from fear of future sin as well as from trials and sadness of soul: "Is any one of you sad? Let him pray" (Jm. 5: 13). It also delivers one from persecutors and enemies: "Instead of making me a return of love, they detracted me, but I gave myself to prayer" (Ps. 18: 4).

Second, prayer is useful as well as effective in granting every desire: "All things whatsoever you ask when you pray, believe that you shall receive" (Mk. 11: 24). If our prayers are not answered, this is because we do not persevere in prayer, although "we ought always to pray, and not to faint" (Lk. 18: 1), or because we are not asking for what most leads to our salvation. "Our good Lord often does not give us what we wish," St. Augustine declares, "because it would really be what we do not want." St. Paul is a good example of this insofar as he thrice prayed that the sting of his flesh be withdrawn from him, and his prayer was not heard" (2 Co. 12: 7).

Third, prayer is profitable inasmuch as through it we become friends of God: "Let my prayer be directed as incense in thy sight" (Ps. 140: 2).

Prayers   *Commentary on Epistle to Romans V*

Prayer of Our Lord in the Garden

1. "And going a little farther, he fell upon his face, praying and saying: 'My Father'" (Mt. 26: 39).

Our Lord here recommends to us three conditions to be observed when we pray.

a. Solitude: because going a little farther he separated himself even from those whom he had chosen. "When thou shalt pray enter into thy chamber, and having shut the door pray to thy Father in secret" (Mt. 6: 6). But notice that he went not *far* away but *a little farther,* that he might show that he is not far from those who call upon him, and also that they might see him praying and learn to pray in like fashion.

b. Humility: He *fell upon his face,* giving thereby an example of humility. This because humility is necessary for prayer and because Peter had said: "Yea, though I should die with thee, I will not deny thee" (Mt. 26: 35). Therefore did Our Lord fall, to show us that we should not trust in our own strength.

c. Devotion, when he said, "My Father." It is essential that when we pray we pray from devotion. He says "My Father" because he is uniquely God's Son; we are God's children by adoption only (in Mt. 26).

2. "If it be possible, let this chalice pass from me. Nevertheless, not as I will, but as thou wilt" (Mt. 26: 39).

Here we consider the tenor of prayer. Christ was praying according to the prompting of his sense nature, insofar, that is, as his prayer as advocate for his senses was expressing the inclinations of his senses, proposing to God, by prayer, what the desire of his senses suggested. And he did this that he might teach us three things:

a. That he had taken a true human nature with all its natural inclinations.

b. That it is lawful for man to will, according to his natural inclination, a thing that God does not will.

c. That man ought to subject his own inclination to the divine will. Whence St. Augustine says: "Christ, living as a man, showed a certain private human willingness when he said, 'let this chalice pass from me.' This was human willingness, a man's own will and, so to say, his private desire. But Christ, since he wills to be a man of right heart, a man directed to God, adds, 'Nevertheless, not as I will, but as thou wilt.'"

And in this he teaches by example how we should arrange our tendencies so that they do not come into conflict with the divine rule. Whence we learn that there is nothing wrong in our shrinking from what is naturally harmful, so long as we bring our emotion into line with the divine will.

Christ had two wills, one from his Father insofar as he was God and the other insofar as he was man. This human will he submitted in all things to his Father, giving us in this an example to do likewise. "I came down from heaven, not to do my will, but the will of him who sent me" (Jn. 6: 38).

"God commendeth his charity toward us: 'because when as yet we were sinners, according to the time, Christ died for us'" (Rm. 5: 8–9).

1. Christ died for the ungodly (ibid., 6). This is a great thing if we consider who it is who died, a great thing also if we consider on whose behalf he died. For scarcely for a just man will one die, i.e., you will hardly find anyone who will die even to set free a man who is innocent, nay, even it is said, "The just perisheth, and no man layeth it to heart" (Is. 57: 1).

Rightly therefore does St. Paul say that scarcely will one die. There might perhaps be found one, some one rare person who out of superabundance of courage would be so bold as to die for a good man. But this is rare, for the simple reason that so to act is the greatest of all things. "'Greater love than this no man hath,'" says Our Lord himself, "'that a man lay down his life for his friends'" (Jn. 15: 13).

But the like of what Christ did himself, to die for evildoers and the wicked, has never been seen. Wherefore rightly do we ask in wonderment why Christ did it.

2. If in fact it be asked why Christ died for the wicked, the answer is that God in this way commends his charity to-

ward us. He shows us in this way that he loves us with a love that knows no limits, for while we were as yet sinners Christ died for us.

The very death of Christ for us shows the love of God, for it was his Son whom he gave to die that satisfaction might be made for us. God so loved the world as to give his only begotten Son (Jn. 3: 16). And thus as the love of God the Father for us is shown in his giving us his Holy Spirit, so also is it shown in this way, by his gift of his only Son.

The Apostle says that God commendeth, signifying thereby that the love of God is a thing that cannot be measured. This is shown by the very fact of the matter, namely, the fact that he gave his Son to die for us, and it is shown also by reason of the kind of people we are for whom he died. Christ was not stirred up to die for us by any merits of ours when as yet we were sinners. God (who is rich in mercy) "for his exceeding charity wherewith he loved us, even when we were dead in sins, hath quickened us together in Christ" (Ep. 2: 4).

A Prayer Before a Picture of Christ

Most merciful God, let me ardently desire what pleases you, prudently seek, truly learn, and faithfully fulfill all to the praise and glory of your name. Order my day so that I may know what you want me to do, and for my soul's good, help me to do it. Let me not be elated by success nor cast down by failure, neither puffed up by the former, nor depressed by the latter. I want only to take pleasure in what draws me to you, only to grieve for what displeases you. I want neither to please nor fear to displease anyone but you. For love of the eternal I would forgo the things of time. May all the joys in which you have no part weary me. Work done for you is pleasure, relaxation apart from you, tedium. Teach me to turn my thought to you often and with firm purpose of amendment to feel contrite when I have failed to do so. Make me obedient without cavil, poor without repining, pure without corruption, patient without murmuring, humble without pretense, cheerful without dissipation, sorrowful without dejection, serious without solemnity, gay without levity, truthful without deceit. Let me fear you without despairing, do good without presuming, correct my neighbor without arrogance, edify him by word and action without hypocrisy.

Give me, O Lord, a vigilant heart lest vain thoughts take me from you, a noble heart that no unworthy affection can debase, an upright heart that no bad intention can degrade. Give me a strength that will withstand any trial, a liberty of spirit that no violent passion can overcome.

Grant me, O Lord my God, a mind to know you, a heart to seek you, wisdom to find you, conduct pleasing to you, faithful perseverance in waiting for you, and a hope of finally embracing you.

Here I accept trials as penance, your favors as grace for the way, your joys especially as pledge of glory in heaven.

Prayer Before Holy Communion

All-powerful, everlasting God, I am about to receive the sacrament of your only begotten Son, Our Lord Jesus Christ. I come as one sick, for life-giving medicine; as unclean, to the fountain of mercy, as blind, to eternal light; a needy beggar to the lord of heaven and earth.

I implore you in your abundant kindness to cure my sickness, to cleanse my impurity, to enlighten my blindness, to enrich my poverty, to clothe my nakedness. May I encounter the king of kings and lord of lords with such reverence and humility, such contrition and devotion, such purity and faith, and with so right an intention as to obtain salvation.

Grant, I implore you, that I may receive not only the sign but also the reality and power of the sacrament. O kindest God, let me so receive the body of your only Son, Our Lord Jesus Christ, which he took from the Virgin Mary, that I may be incorporated into his mystical body and be included among his members. Most loving Father, grant that your beloved Son, whom I now receive veiled, I may one day behold face to face forever, who together with you and the Holy Spirit lives and reigns. Amen.

Prayer After Holy Communion

Thank you, all-powerful Father and eternal God for allowing me, a sinner and unworthy child, to receive the precious body and blood of your Son, Our Lord Jesus Christ, and this solely through your mercy, and unmerited by me. I implore that this holy communion may not bring judgment upon my wretchedness but be a salutary plea for pardon. May it be the armor of faith, a shield of good will; may it quench vice, cast out evil desires and concupiscence, give an increase of charity, patience, obedience, humility, and other virtues. May it be a firm defense against enemies, visible and invisible. May it subdue carnal as well as spiritual inclinations, unite me closely to you, the true and only God, and at life's end bring me happily to bliss everlasting. I implore you to lead me to that ineffable banquet where together with your Son, the Holy Spirit, and all the saints you are the true light, complete contentment, supernal joy, complete delight, and perfect happiness.

Prayer to the Blessed Virgin Mary

Most holy and sweetest virgin, mother of God, daughter of the sovereign king, queen of angels, mother of the Creator, I commend to your mercy, this day and all the days of my life, my soul and body, thoughts, words, deeds, and desires, and my life and its ending, so that through your prayers all may be ordered according to the will of your beloved son, Jesus Christ, Our Lord. Be to me, most holy mother, a help, a consoler against the snares and deceits of the evil one and of all my enemies. Ask for me from your beloved son the grace to resist temptations of the world, the flesh, and the devil, to resolve to sin no more but to persevere in the service of your divine son.

I also beg, most holy lady, that you obtain for me perfect obedience and humility of heart so that I may truly know myself for the wretched sinner that I am, unable of myself to do anything good or to resist temptation without the grace and help of my Creator and by your holy prayers.

Likewise obtain for me, dearest lady, perfect purity of soul and body that I may serve your beloved son and you with a chaste body and a pure heart. Obtain from him the grace to accept voluntary poverty with a patient and calm mind so that I may be able to endure the labors of this order, working for my own salvation as well as that of my neighbor.

I implore you, lady, to obtain for me true charity, that with all my heart I may love your most holy son, Our Lord Jesus Christ and, after him, you above all things. Grant me to love my neighbor for his sake so that I may be glad for what is good in him and grieve for what is evil, never condemning nor judging rashly, nor interiorly preferring myself to anyone. May I always fear and love your son, ever thankful for so many favors given through his bounty with no merit on my part. May I sincerely confess my sins, do real penance, and merit his mercy and pardon. Do thou, gate of heaven and refuge of sinners, see to it that at the end of my life I do not swerve from the Catholic faith. In your kindness and mercy succor me from the evil spirits, and through the merits of his glorious passion and my hope in your intercession, obtain his pardon for my sins so that you will lead me, dying in his and your love, to salvation. Amen.

Prayer for the Remission of Sins

O God, fountain of mercy, I, a sinner, approach you. Cleanse me, sun of justice, enlighten my blindness. Eternal physician, heal my wounds. King of kings, repair my losses. Mediator between God and man, reconcile me. Good shepherd, lead back this wandering sheep. O God, show mercy toward a wretch, indulgence toward a sinner. Give life to one dead, reinstate a wrongdoer. Soften a heart closed to grace. O most merciful God, call me back when I flee from you, draw me when resisting you. Lift me up and support me when I rise. Guide my steps. Do not forget one who has forgotten you, nor abandon one who has abandoned you, nor despise a sinner.

In sinning I have offended you, hurt my neighbor, and harmed myself. Through weakness I have sinned against you, omnipotent Father; through ignorance against you, all-

wise Son; through malice against you, Holy Spirit. And so I
have offended the most Holy Trinity. What a wretch I am!
How often and how much have I sinned! What evil deeds I
have committed! Attracted by evil, I have turned from you.
So doing, I have chosen to lose you rather than give up what
I loved; to offend you rather than turn from what I should
have feared. How often have I sinned—secretly, openly, and
boldly, in word and deed! Therefore in my misery I entreat you not to look upon my iniquity but upon your immense goodness. Graciously forgive all I have done. Grant
me sorrow for the past, and for the future, a wise vigilance.
Amen.

Prayer Before Writing or Preaching

O ineffable Creator, who has wisely appointed nine choirs
of angels, setting them above the heavens in marvelous order, who has wonderfully established the parts of the universe, who is the fountain of light and wisdom, the First
Cause, shed upon the darkness of my mind the light of your
love and remove from me the twofold darkness of sin and
ignorance in which I was born. You who make eloquent the
tongues of babes, instruct my tongue, pour the grace of your
blessing upon my lips. Give keenness in understanding, re-
tention in memory, facility in preaching and interpreting
sublime realities, and a wide vocabulary as well. Inspire my
beginning, direct my progress, bring all to an end, you who
art true God and man, who livest and reignest one God,
world without end. Amen.

Contemplative Prayer

I entreat you, God of consolation, you who see nothing in
us but what is of your own giving, that at the end of my life
you will grant me knowledge of primal truth, enjoyment of
the highest good. To my body also, most generous bene-
factor, be pleased to give a radiant beauty, agility, subtlety
and impassibility. Add to these abundant riches an influx of
delight, a convergence of every good so that I may delight
above all in your consolation—below me through the pleas-

antness of the place, within me through the glorification of body and soul, and around me through the close community of angels and men.

Near you, most merciful Father, may I praise the power of reason, the light of wisdom, the satisfaction of all desire, with lower emotions pacified. For in your presence there is no fear of danger, but only blessed security, harmony of wills, the loveliness of spring, the brightness of summer, the abundance of autumn, and the repose of winter.

Grant, O Lord God, life without death, joy without sorrow, for with you there is the greatest freedom, free security, secure peace, joyful happiness, happy eternity, eternal happiness, a vision of truth, and praise. Amen.

Verbum Supernum Prodiens*

The only Word of God went forth,
still held in the Father's right hand,
To his appointed task descended
bringing light to a darkened land.

The traitor's kiss he well foreknew—
it could in no wise hold him back.
The gift of self his one intent
without reserve, nor want, nor lack.

Under two species, to us men
his perfect, whole, divine manhood
He hid in twofold substance oned—
the wine, his blood; his flesh, the food.

Being born, he gave himself to men,
he lived man's life, a brother, friend
And died for them on Calvary's hill
because he loved, loved without end.

O Victim, saving those who plead
for gates of heaven opened wide,
Give us your grace, your strength bestow
to conquer foes on every side.

To you, may endless glory be
blessed and eternal God adored.

* Translated for this volume by Jane Wynne Saul, R.S.C.J.

O give to us, in endless bliss
a home with you, our Triune Lord.   Amen.

Pange Lingua*

Sing, my tongue, sing out the glory
of that sacred body, sprung
with the blood beyond all pricing
from the spotless mother's womb:
Of this body, blood, in fullness
Man's redemption's price is wrung.

Born to us of Mary, virgin,
homed here on earth a little while,
spoke as man to man, free giving
a warning of that night of woe
which, the Father's will ordaining,
men redeemed in sweat of brow.

On that night unlike all other
resting quietly with his own,
every law fully accomplished,
Paschal lamb with them consumed,
his own body then he handed
them as food—his chosen band.

Through his word, from seed-sown field—
plowed and reaped by lowly sower,
the golden wheat became his flesh,
Wine of the grape his sacred blood.
How could this be done, dear master?
Faith alone can understand.

Come, let us worship and draw near
to this great sacrament divine;
Faith for all our doubts supplying,
in simple rites discern sublime,
Adore, though all our senses fail;
Believe, as our God we hail.

* Translated for this volume by Jane Wynne Saul, R.S.C.J.

To the Father everlasting
Let glory be through endless days;
To the Son in equal measure
loud songs in adoration raise,
and Holy Ghost from both proceeding
To Triune God, eternal praise.   Amen.

Adoro Te Devote*

Godhead here in hiding, whom I do adore
Masked by these bare shadows, shape and nothing more,
See, Lord, at thy service low lies here a heart
Lost, all lost in wonder at the God thou art

Seeing, touching, tasting are in thee deceived;
How says trusty hearing? that shall be believed;
What God's Son has told me, take for truth I do;
Truth himself speaks truly or there's nothing true.

On the cross thy godhead made no sign to men;
Here thy very manhood steals from human ken:
Both are my confession, both are my belief,
And I pray the pray'r made by the dying thief.

I am not like Thomas, wounds I cannot see,
But can plainly call thee Lord and God as he:
This faith each day deeper be my holding of,
Daily make me harder hope and dearer love.

O thou our reminder of Christ crucified,
Living bread the life of us for whom he died,
Lend this life to me then: feed and feast my mind,
There be thou the sweetness man was meant to find.

Bring the tender tale true of the pelican;
Bathe me, Jesus Lord, in what thy bosom ran
Blood that but one drop of has the world to win
All the world forgiveness of its world of sin.

Jesus whom I look at shrouded here below,
I beseech thee send me what I thirst for so,

* Translated by Gerard Manley Hopkins.

Some day to gaze on thee face to face in light
And be blest forever with thy glory's sight.   Amen.

10. OFFICE FOR THE FEAST OF ST. AUGUSTINE, BISHOP, CONFESSOR, AND DOCTOR OF THE CHURCH*

At Vespers

Super Psal. Antiph. Rejoice, Jerusalem, our mother, for your king has restored to you from the bondage of Babylon, Augustine, a wise administrator and a most faithful citizen. Ps. *Laudata cum ceteris.*

Hymn

Great Father, Augustine
Listen to our prayers
Through them render us
Pleasing to our Maker
Rule your flock as becomes
A most worthy Shepherd

Lover of poverty
The Poor extol you
Judges of the true
Love you, Defender of truth
Discoursing of the Scriptures
You feed us honey from the hive

Things once obscure
You make plain to us
From the Saviour's words

* Translated by H. Moclair, R.S.C.J. for this volume. This office is printed in the Parma Edition of St. Thomas's works. It is not mentioned in Father Eschman's list of authentic works. For it as well as for the prayers we claim only probable authorship.

You break sweet bread
And from the nectar of the Psalms
You offer us the elixir of life

For the life of clerics
You wrote a holy rule
Those who love and follow
Walk a royal road
Led by your holy example
They reach the fatherland

Salvation, life to the king of kings
Glory and power
Praise and honor to the Trinity
Forever and ever
That has enrolled us
As fellow citizens of the saints.   Amen.

V. Pray for us Blessed Augustine.
R. That we may be worthy of the promises of Christ.

Prayer

Almighty God, listen to our pleading; and as you allow us to
hope in your goodness, according to your wonted mercy,
grant our request, Augustine interceding, through Our Lord
Jesus Christ . . . .

At Matins

Invitat. Great God, worthy of all praise, who called Augustine from the darkness of paganism to the light of your
Church

Ps.   Venite
Hymn   Magne Pater

First Nocturne

Antiph. Augustine opened the Gospel and casting his eye on
the first heading read: "Put you on the Lord, Jesus
Christ; and at once, as if a light of conviction infused

his soul, all shadow of doubt was dispelled.   Ps. Beatus.

Antiph. Through letters he introduced himself to the holy man, Ambrose, expressing the wish that he would advise him as to what books of Holy Scripture he should read to become more receptive and better prepared for the grace of Christianity.   Ps. Quare.

Antiph. Ambrose bade him read the Prophet Isaias, for even before the other Evangelists he was a clearer foreteller of the call of the Gentiles.   Ps. Domine *quid.*

V. He loved him . . . .

Lesson 1

Augustine was born in Tagaste, a city in Africa; his worthy parents belonged to the ruling class; his father was a pagan, a worldly man; his mother, Monica, was a Christian. The boy was carefully raised, and well taught at home until he was sent to school to complete his education. However, one day he was stricken with a serious stomach disorder, and suffered much.

R. Augustine found himself far from God in quite another world. It was just as if he heard a voice from on high saying: "I am the food of grown men. Grow, and you shall eat me; you shall not change me into you (as bodily food), but you shall be changed into me. Grow."

Lesson 2

His good mother urged him to be baptized; but his pagan father objected, and his baptism was put off. Meanwhile, by the mercy of God the pain quieted, and he was cured. Baptism was still delayed, almost necessarily, for if he should live as he had been living up to now, his sin would be the greater. He hated the study of Greek, but loved Latin.   *Tu autem.*

R. He then saw and realized that it is not surprising that to the unhealthy palate bread is distasteful which to the healthy one is sweet and that to a diseased eye light is unbearable which to a whole eye is agreeable.

V. On account of his iniquity thou hast rebuked man and hast made his soul waste away as sand. . . .

Lesson 3

Meanwhile, he found a book of Cicero that contained an exhortation to philosophy. This book so affected him that he turned his prayers and thoughts to God and made his desires quite other. Suddenly every vain desire became vile to him, and with incredible ardor he longed for the immortality of wisdom and rose up to begin a return to God. He was now almost nineteen years old, and his father had been dead for two years.   *Tu autem.*

R. Then he saw the invisible things of God through the visible creation, but not with any fixed validity. . . . Rather was it only a loving memory, somewhat like the pleasant odor of food he could not yet eat.

V. As to his attitude toward the sacrament: The Word was made flesh; he could not conceive it.   *Quia. Gloria Patri.* . . .

Second Nocturne

Antiph. In fact, not understanding his first reading, so he thought the whole would be equally obscure; he set himself to acquiring greater skill in the school of rhetoric.   Ps. *Cum invocarem.*

When the time came that he must consult someone, leaving reluctantly, he returned to Milan. He was baptized by Ambrose. He dropped all concern with the passing things of life.   Ps. *Verba mea.*

Antiph. Nor did he ever tire during those days pondering, with marvelous sweetness, the depth of the divine plan for the salvation of the human race.   Ps. *Domine Deus.*

V. He led the just . . . .

Lesson 4

One thing alone delighted him in that exhortation of Cicero, it was not the manner of living, but that he should love, see, win, and hold wisdom itself. And only this was lacking: the name of Christ. This name of the savior he had drunk in with his mother's milk. He had taken it into his infant heart and still held it deep down in it. And whatever lacked that name, however learned and polished the style, it could not wholly win him.

R. He therefore began to read St. Paul avidly, even before the other Evangelists, and the text dispelled those doubts that seemed to him contrary to the law and the prophets.

V. It seemed to him a form of the purest eloquence, and with trembling he learned . . . .

Lesson 5

However, he was still led to believe in the nonsense that a fig wept milky tears when torn from the mother tree. His mother wept much for him before the Lord. She saw herself standing on a certain wooden ruler, and a radiant youth coming toward her, bright and smiling, while she herself was sorrowful and worn out with grief. He asked her why she was weeping; she answered him saying: "I weep over the ruin of my son, Augustine."   *Tu autem.*

R. The Lord had inspired her, and it seemed good to her, to go to Simplicius, who appeared to be a good servant of God, for the light of divine grace shone in him.

V. For she had heard that from his youth he had lived for God. And it was so. . . .

Lesson 6

Then he commanded her to be quiet, to look and see that where she stood her son also would stand. And when she looked she saw him too standing on the same ruler. When she told her dream to her son, he tried to make it out that she would one day be where he was. But she was unshaken and replied without hesitation, "No, not so, he did not say to me, 'Where he is you will be,' but 'Where you are, there he will be.'"

R. Fervor made him want to bring together his own that he might find who was as eager for this manner of living as he

himself was, for walking in the way of God. One would be
an example to the other.

V. It irked him to engage in worldly matters, preferring
rather to dwell with the sweetness of God and the beauty of
his house, which he loved.   I. *In Gloria Patri*. In.

Third Nocturne

Antiph. He wept much in hymns and canticles, being very
    strongly moved by the pleasing harmonies of Church
    music.   Ps. *Domine quis*.

Antiph. Joined by Nebridius and Evodius he was returning to
    Africa seeking for what he considered a more suitable
    place for them to live in; but when he was at Ostia, his
    dear mother died.   Ps. *Domine est terra*.

V. Justus et palma . . . .

Lesson 7

Nine years passed during which she hoped, and with tears
and sighs never ceased pleading before God in her hours of
prayer for her son. Her prayers were present to his sight, but
up to now he, her son, was turning this way and that in a fog
of heresy.

But God gave a profound answer through a certain bishop,
who when the mother asked that he would deign to speak to
her son, and refute his error, he, unwilling, said that her son
was not yet docile but was puffed up with the novelty of his
heresy.   *Tu autem*.

R. The love of Christ wounded his heart, and Christ's words
struck his innermost being like sharp arrows. And the examples of the servants of God, which raised the dead to life,
struck him as like ravaging fire.

V. To those coming up from the valley of tears, and to those
singing a gradual song.

Lesson 8

Then the bishop said to her: Let him alone, but pray to
the Lord for him. By reading he will himself find out his error and the extent of his impiety. She was not willing, and by

entreaties and floods of tears besought him to see and argue with him. Vexed at her importunity he said: "Go, God bless you, the child of so many tears cannot perish," which word she received as if it had come from heaven.

R. Having been baptized, he settled at Ostia with his mother. There they held sweet converse and drank equally of the waters of the supernal fountain of life. And compared with these delightful discourses this world seem vile.

V. Then she said to her son: Now I no longer find delight in this life, since I see that you, despising earthly things, are a servant of Christ.   *Vilescebatque.*

Lesson 9

Afterward he decided to go to Rome, preferring to teach there what he was teaching at Carthage. This thought was in truth a dispensation of God. When he set out, his mother followed him to the seacoast. But Augustine deceived her as she clung to him passionately, that either he should return with her or take her with him. . . . He pretended that he would not set sail until there was a favorable wind. He lied to his mother. When she had left him for a little while, he secretly that night took ship. But she remained the whole night praying and weeping, begging that something might prevent the ship from sailing. But God would have it otherwise.   *Tu autem.*

R. He preached the word of God uninterruptedly, forcefully with good sense and wise counsel up to the time of his illness. With all his bodily organs intact, sight and hearing unimpaired, in presence of his brethren surrounding him, he slept with his fathers.

V. He made no will for he had made himself poor for Christ's sake and had nothing to leave.   *Gloria Patri.*

At Lauds

Antiph. After the death of his mother, Augustine returned to his own fatherland. There with his friends, mortifying themselves with fasting and prayer, he wrote books and taught the ignorant.

Antiph. But his fame spread abroad. Blessed Valerius, bishop

of Hippo, invited him to come to visit him, and seized
the opportunity to induce him to become a priest.

Antiph. Therefore, having become a priest, he soon founded
a monastery for clerics and began to live according to a
rule.

Antiph. Valerius, who had ordained him, was exceedingly
happy that such a man was given to him, who in sacred
doctrine would be a fitting instrument to edify the
Church.

Antiph. At the same time, Fortunatus, a deacon, was leading many astray by the doctrines of the Manichees;
over whom St. Augustine, disputing in a public assembly, won the victory.

Hymn

Ye heavenly throngs exult
And brethren join the song
Rejoicing for our Father's feast
Throughout the day prolong

That which our tongues now utter
Our hearts most deeply move
Nor hesitate to imitate
That which our minds approve

He having run his earthly course
With his faithful rests at length
For the crown with which God crowned him
Let us strive with all our strength

To our prayers with his united
Grant most generous Father this
That through Augustine's merits
We may taste celestial bliss

V. The just will flourish etc.

At the Benedictus: Antiph. In his day the city of Hippo was
besieged by an army of barbarians. During this calamity
tears were Augustine's bread, day and night. And in
these circumstances, his last hour having come, he died.

At the Magnificat: Antiph. Today, the glorious Father Augustine, released from this human habitation, entered a celestial abode, not made with hands, which he by co-operation with the grace of God had built on earth by his works and preaching. And there now what he thirsted for he enjoys forever, clothed in a robe of glory and safely at rest.

Through the octave of the feast of St. Augustine, when there is an octave (not on Sunday):

Invitat. Regem Confessorum. The following antiphons are said at Benedictus and at the Magnificat or at the Mementos.

At the Benedictus: His most devoted mother, who in flesh had brought him forth into the world, afterward through the seed of many tears gave him birth in Christ.

At the Magnificat: Antiph. Rejoice, our mother (found above in first vesper ps..)

BIBLIOGRAPHY

VIVES	D. Thomae Aquinatis *Opera Omnia* (ed. S. E. Frette and P. Mare), 32 vols. (Paris: L. *Vives,* 1871–80).
PARMA	S. Thomae *Opera Omnia,* 25 vols. (Parma: Ficcadori, 1852–73). Photographic reproduction by Musurgia Publishers, New York, 1948–49.
LEONINE	S. Thomas Aquinatis *Opera Omnia* iussu Leonis XIII, edita, 22 vols. to date. (Rome: 1882–1972).
MANDONNET	S. Thomae Aquinatis *Opuscula Omnia* (ed. P. Mandonnet), 5 vols. (Paris: 1927).
PERRIER	S. Thomae Aquinatis *Opuscula Omnia necnon Opera Minora,* tome I (ed. J. Perrier) (Paris: 1949).
TAURIN PHILOSOPHY	D. Thomae Aquinatis *Opuscula Philosophica* (ed. R. M. Spiazzi) (Torino-Rome: 1954).
TAURIN THEOLOGY	D. Thomae Aquinatis *Opuscula Theologica* (ed. R. A. Varardo, R. M. Spiazzi, *et al.*), 2 vols. (Torino-Rome: 1954).
TAURIN	*Editio Tauriensis:* various editions of Cas Marietti (Torino-Rome).

All these editions depend upon the *Editio Princeps,* the Piana or Roman edition of 1570–71 issued under Pope Pius V. The *Piana* edition was itself derived from earlier printings.

Classifications

Reverend Peter Mandonnet, who died in 1936, and Monsignor Martin Grabmann, who died in 1949, are to be credited with the immense task of solving difficult problems of authenticity in the works of Thomas Aquinas. Nor may we say that the task is finished. Yet their classifications are the standard classifications recognized by scholars today.

The works of Thomas Aquinas were thus classified by Mandonnet:

I. *Philosophy:* a. Commentaries on Aristotle
b. Various works

II. *Scripture:* a. Old Testament
b. New Testament

III. *Theology:* a. General theology
b. Dogmatic theology
c. Moral theology

IV. *Apologetics*

V. *Canon Law*

VI. *Discourses*

VII. *Liturgy*

P. Mandonnet, *Des écrits authentiques de S. Thomas d'Aquin,* 2nd ed. (Fribourg: Imprimerie de l'Oeuvre de Saint-Paul, 1910).

M. Grabmann, *Die Werke des Hl. Thomas von Aquin,* 2nd ed. Beitrage zur Geschichte der Philosophie und Theologie des Mittelaters, Band XX, 1–2 (Munster: Aschendorff, 1931).

An annotated catalogue of St. Thomas's writings compiled by I. T. Eschmann, O.P. may be found in Gilson, E. *The Christian Philosophy of St. Thomas Aquinas* (New York: Random House, 1956). This catalogue does not claim to be definitive and admits that some items are debatable. To each number a note is appended explaining the nature of the work, the condition of its known text, the chronology, the available editions, and English translations.

WRITINGS OF ST. THOMAS AQUINAS

Syntheses

On the Four Books of the Sentences (of Peter Lombard)	Scriptum super libros sententiarum
Summa of Christian Teaching (in dialogue with philosophical and theological non-believers)	Summa contra Gentiles Leonine 13–15
Summa of Theology	Summa theologiae Leonine 4–12

Academic Debates

Debated Questions: Special Topics	*Quaestiones disputatae*
On Evil	De malo
On the Power of God	De potentia
On Spiritual Creatures	De spiritualibus creaturis
On the Soul	De anima
On Truth	De veritate Leonine 22
On the Union of the Incarnate Word	De unione verbi incarnati
On the Virtues	De virtutibus
Quodlibetal [General] Debates I–XII	*Quaestiones de quodlibet I–XII* Marietti
On the Admission of Boys into Religion	De pueris in religionem admittendis
On the Meanings of Holy Scripture	De sensibus s. Scripturae
On the Divine Attributes	De attributis divinis
On the Manual Work of Religious	De opere manuali religiosorum
On the Immortality of the Soul	De immortalitate animae

On Memory and Recall	Sententia libri De memoria et reminiscentia Marietti
On the Metaphysics	Sententia libri Metaphysicorum Marietti
On Meterology	Sententia libri Meterologicorum
On the Nicomachean Ethics	Sententia libri Ethicorum Leonine 47
On the Physics	Sententia libri Physicorum Leonine 2
On the Politics	Sententia libri Politicorum Leonine 48
On the Posterior Analytics	Sententia libri Posteriorum Analyticorum Leonine 1
On Sensation	Sententia libri De sensu et sensato Marietti
On the Soul	Sententia libri De anima Marietti

Other Commentaries

On Boethius' treatise: *"How Substances, insofar as they are, are good."*	Super Boethium *De hebdomadibus* Marietti
On Boethius' *On the Trinity*	Super Boethium *De Trinitate*
On Dionysius' *On the Divine Names*	Super Dionysium *De divinis nominibus* Marietti
On [Proclus'] *The Causes*	Super librum *De causis*

Polemical Writings

| Against Those Attacking the Worship of God and Religion (Apologia for Religious Orders) | Contra impugnantes Dei cultum et religionem
Leonine 41 |

On a Common Intellect, against Averroists	De unitate intellectus, contra Averroistas Marietti
Against the Destructive Doctrine of Those Who Would Deter Boys from Entering Religious Life (Apologia for Religious Orders)	Contra pestiferam doctrinam retrahentium pueros a religionis ingressu Leonine 41
On the Eternity of the World	De aeternitate mundi Marietti
On the Perfection of Religious (Spiritual) Life	De perfectione vitae spiritualis Leonine 41

Treatises on Special Topics

On Being and Essence	De ente et essentia
On the Combining of the Elements	De mixtione elementorum Leonine 3
On the Commendation and Division of Sacred Scripture; on the Commendation of Sacred Scripture	Duo principia de commendatione Sacrae Scripturae; De commendatione et partitione sacrae scripturae; De commendatione sacrae scripturae Marietti
A Compendium of Theology (Treatise on Faith, Hope, Charity)	Compendium theologiae ad fratrem Reginaldum socium suum carissimum Marietti
On Fallacies	De fallaciis ad quosdam nobiles artistas Marietti
On Kingship, to the King of Cyprus	De regno (De regimine principum) ad regem Cypri Marietti
On Modal Propositions	De propositionibus modalibus
On the Principles of Nature	De principiis naturae ad fratrem Sylvestrum
On Separate Substances	De substantiis separatis Leonine 40

Opinions Rendered

On the Form of Absolution	De forma absolutionis Leonine 40
Against the Errors of the Greeks	Contra errores Graecorum, ad Urbanum IV Pontificem Maximum Leonine 40
On Secrecy	De secreto
Reply to Brother John of Vercelli on CVIII Articles Extracted from the Work of Peter of Tarentasia	Responsio ad fr. Joannem Vercellensum, Generalem Magistrum O.P. de articulis CVIII ex opere Petri de Tarentasia Marietti
Reply to Brother John of Vercelli on XLII Articles	Responsio ad fr. Joannem Vercellensum, Generalem Magistrum O.P. de articulis XLII Marietti

Letters

On the Articles of Faith and the Sacraments of the Church	De articulis fidei et Ecclesiae Sacramentis
On Buying and Selling on Credit (Usury)	De emptione et venditione ad tempus
An Exposition on the First Decretal "On Catholic Faith and the Holy Trinity," and on the Second Decretal "On Damnation"	Expositio super primam decretalem "De fide catholica et sancta Trinitate" et super secumdum "Damnamus autem" Leonine 40
On Governing Jews	De regimine Judaeorum Marietti
On the Hidden Operations of Nature	De occultis operationibus naturae Marietti
On How to Study	De modo studendi Marietti

On Judgments by the Stars [Astrology]	De iudiciis astrorum Marietti
On the Movement of the Heart	De motu cordis Marietti
On the Reasons for the Faith —to Saracens, Greeks, Armenians	De rationibus fidei contra Saracenos, Graecos, Armenos Leonine 40
Reply to Bernard, Abbot of Monte Cassino	Ad Bernardum, abbatem Cassinensem
Reply to the Lector at Besançon on VI Articles	Responsio ad lectorum Bisuntinum de articulis VI Marietti
Reply to the Lector at Venice on XXXVI Articles	Responsio ad lectorum Venetum de articulis XXXVI
On Casting Lots	De sortibus ad Dominum Jacobum Marietti

Liturgical Pieces and Sermons

On the Angelic Salutation	Devotissima expositio super salutatione angelica
On the Apostles' Creed	Devotissima expositio super symbolum apostolorum Marietti
On the Lord's Prayer	Expositio devotissima orationis dominicae Marietti
Office of the Feast of Corpus Christi	Officium de festo corporis Christi, ad mandatum Urbani Papae IV Marietti
Prayers: Adoro Te and Others	Adoro te devote Marietti
Sermons	Sermones (cf. I. T. Eschmann, O.P., *A Catalogue of St. Thomas's Works* in E. Gilson, *The Christian Philosophy of St. Thomas Aquinas*) (New York, Random House, 1956, pp. 425–28).

On the Two Precepts of Charity and the Ten Precepts of the Law	De duobus praeceptis caritatis et decem legis praeceptis Marietti

Works of Uncertain Authenticity

On Demonstration	De demonstratione Marietti
On the Four Opposites	De quattuor oppositis Marietti
On Instants	De instantibus Marietti
On the Nature of Accidents	De natura accidentium Marietti
On the Nature of Genus	De natura generis Marietti
On the Nature of the Intellect's Word	De natura verbi intellectus Marietti
On the Nature of Matter	De natura materiae Marietti
On the Principle of Individuation	De principio individuationis Marietti
Office of the Feast of St. Augustine	Officium de festo Sancti Augustini

N.B. Any work in the above list which is not specified to be in the Leonine edition or the Marietti, Turin edition can be found in the Parma edition. The Parma edition also lists about fifty works at one time attributed to Thomas Aquinas.

The Editor wishes to thank James A. Weisheipl, O.P., and Justin Hennessey, O.P., for their kind help in preparing this section.

Contemporary English Translations

Theological Syntheses

Compendium of Theology (Compendium Theologiae)	Rose Brennan (St. Louis, Mo.: Herder, 1946); L. Lynch (New York: McMullen, 1947); C. Vollert (St. Louis: Herder, 1957).
On the Truth of the Catholic Faith (*Summa contra Gentiles*)	A. C. Pegis, J. F. Anderson, V. J. Bourke, C. J. O'Neil (Garden City, New York: Doubleday Image Books, 1955–57).
Summa against the Gentiles (*Summa contra Gentiles*)	English Dominican Fathers, 5 vols. (London: Burns, Oates, 1924; Benziger, 1928–29).
Summa Theologica (*Summa Theologiae*)	L. Shapcote and English Dominicans, 22 vols. (London: Burns, Oates, 1912–36; American edition, 3 vols. (New York: Benziger, 1947–48).
Summa Theologiae	T. Gilby, O.P. (general editor) (Cambridge, England: Eyre and Spottiswoode Ltd., 1966; 60 volumes projected, 37 published; New York: McGraw-Hill).
Volume 1—*The Existence of God;* Part I: Questions 1–13; Volume 2—*The Mind and Power of God;* Part I: Questions 14–26	Questions 1–26 (New York: Doubleday Image Books, 1969).

Academic Discussions

On the Eternity of the World (*De Aeternitate Mundi, contra Mumurantes*)
C. Vollert, L. Kenzierski, and P. M. Byrne (Milwaukee: Marquette University Press, 1964).

On the Power of God (*De Potentia Dei*)
L. Shapcote, English Dominican Fathers, 3 vols. (London: Burns, Oates, New York: Benziger, 1932–34; Westminster, Md.: Newman, 1952, 1 vol.).

On the Soul (*De Anima*)
J. P. Rowan (St. Louis: Herder, 1949).

On Spiritual Creatures (*De Spiritualibus Creaturis*)
M. C. Fitzpatrick and J. J. Wellmuth (Milwaukee: Marquette University Press, 1949).

On Truth (*De Veritate*)
R. W. Mulligan, J. V. McGlynn, and R. W. Schmidt (3 vols.) (Chicago: Regnery, 1952–54).

Unicity of the Intellect (*De Unitate Intellectus, contra Averroistas*)
R. E. Brennan (St. Louis: Herder, 1946); B. H. Zedler (Milwaukee: Marquette University Press, 1968).

On Special Topics

On Being and Essence (*De Ente et Essentia*)
C. C. Reidl (Toronto: 1934); A. Maurer (Toronto: PIMS, 1949); G. Leckie (New York: Appleton-Century-Crofts, 1957).

On Buying and Selling (*De Emptione et Venditione ad Tempus*)
A. O'Rahilly (*Irish Ecclesiastical Record*, 1928).

On Charity (De Caritate)	L. H. Kendzierski (Milwaukee: Marquette University Press, 1960).
On Kingship (De regno—De regimine principum)	G. B. Phelan and I. T. Eschmann (Toronto: PIMS, 1949).
On Nature and Grace	A. M. Fairweather, (tr. and ed.) Vol. 11, (Philadelphia: Library of Christian Classics, Westminster Press, 1954).
Political Ideas (selections)	D. Bigongiari (New York: Hafner, 1953).
Political Writings (selections)	A. P. D'Entreves (ed.), tr. J. G. Dawson (New York: Barnes & Nobles, 1959; Macmillan, 1960).
On Principles of Nature (De Principiis Naturae)	R. Henle-V. Bourke (St. Louis: 1947); Kocourek (St. Paul: 1948); P. H. Conway, O.P. (Columbus, Ohio: Alum Creek Press, 1964).
Providence and Predestination (De Veritate, questions 5 and 6)	R. Mulligan (Chicago: Regnery).
On Religious Life (De Perfectione vitae spiritualis)	F. R. Larcher, O.P., unpublished manuscript.
Religious Orders: An Apologia (Contra impugnantes Dei cultum et religionem; Contra pestiferam doctrinam retrahentium pueros a religionis ingressu)	J. Procter (London: Sands, 1902; Westminster, Maryland, 1950).
On Separate Substances (De substantiis, seu de angelorum natura)	F. J. Cescoe (West Hartford, Connecticut: St. Joseph's College, 1959).

On Studying (De modo studendi) The Teacher, Mind and Truth (De Veritate, 10–11) Treatise on God (Summa Theologiae, Part 1, selections)
V. White, Blackfriars (December 1944, Supplement). J. V. McGlynn (Chicago: Regnery, 1959). J. F. Anderson (Englewood Cliffs, New Jersey: Prentice-Hall, 1963).

Treatise on Happiness (*Summa Theologiae*, selections)
John A. Oesterle (Englewood Cliffs, New Jersey: Prentice-Hall, 1964).

Treatise on Man (*Summa Theologiae*, selections)
J. F. Anderson (Englewood Cliffs, New Jersey: Prentice-Hall, 1966).

Treatise on the Virtues
John A. Oesterle (Englewood Cliffs, New Jersey: Prentice-Hall, 1966).

Commentaries on Holy Scripture

Gloss on the New Testament (*Expositio continua in Mattaeum, Marcum, Lucam, Joannem; Catena aurea*)
John Henry Newman, ed. (London: Oxford, Parker, 1841–45).

On the Gospel of St. John
R. F. Larcher, O.P. (Albany, New York: Magi Books, 1970).

On St. Paul's Epistle to the Ephesians
M. L. Lamb, O.C.S.U. (Albany, New York: Magi Books, 1966).

On St. Paul's Epistle to the Galatians
R. F. Larcher, O.P. (Albany, New York: Magi Books, 1966).

On St. Paul's Epistle to the Philippians and First Thessalonians
R. F. Larcher, O.P. (Albany, New York: Magi Books, 1969).

Commentaries on Aristotle's Works

On Generation and Corruption (*In libros de generatione et Corruptione Expositio*)	P. Conway and W. H. Kane (Columbus, Ohio: Alum Creek Press).
On the Heavens (*In Libros de Caelo et Mundo Expositio*)	P. Conway, R. F. Larcher, (Columbus, Ohio: Alum Creek Press).
On Interpretation (*In Libros Perihermeneias*)	J. T. Oesterle (Milwaukee: Marquette University Press, 1962).
On the Metaphysics (*In Duodecim Libros Metaphysicorum Expositio*)	John P. Rowan (Chicago: Regnery, 1961).
On the Nicomachean Ethics (*In decem libros Ethicorum Expositio*)	C. I. Litzinger (2 vols.) (Chicago: Regnery, 1964).
On the Physics (*In Octo Libros Physicorum Expositio*)	R. J. Blackwell, R. J. Spath, W. E. Thirkel (New Haven: Yale University Press, 1963).
On the Posterior Analytics (*In Libros Posteriorum Analyticorum Expositio*)	P. H. Conway, O.P. and W. H. Kane (Albany, New York: Magi Books, 1969).
Prologues and First Lectures of Commentaries	P. H. Conway, O.P. and R. F. Larcher, O.P. (Columbus, Ohio: Alum Creek Press, St. Mary of the Springs).
On the Soul (with Aristotle's *De Anima*) (*In libros de anima expositio*)	K. Foster and S. Humphries (London: Routledge and Kegan Paul, 1951; New Haven: Yale University Press, 1951).

Other Commentaries

On the Trinity (*Expositio super Librum Boethii de Trinitate*) — R. Brennan (St. Louis: Herder, 1946).

General Collections of Texts

Basic Writings of St. Thomas Aquinas — A. C. Pegis (ed.), 2 vols. (New York: Random House, 1945).

An Introduction to the Metaphysics of St. Thomas Aquinas — J. F. Anderson (Chicago: Regnery, 1953).

Introduction to Saint Thomas Aquinas — A. C. Pegis (ed.) (New York: Random House, 1948).

Philosophical Texts — T. Gilby, O.P. (London: Oxford University Press, 1951).

The Pocket Aquinas — V. Bourke (New York: Washington Square Press, 1960).

Selected Writings of St. Thomas Aquinas — R. P. Goodwin (Indianapolis: Bobbs-Merrill, 1965).

Theological Texts — T. Gilby, O.P. (London: Oxford University Press, 1951).

Wisdom and Ideas of St. Thomas Aquinas — E. Freeman and J. Owens (eds.) (New York: Fawcett World, 1970).

A SELECTED BIBLIOGRAPHY
ON AQUINAS

The Man

Bourke, Vernon J.	*Aquinas' Search for Wisdom* (Milwaukee: Bruce, 1965).
Chesterton, G. K.	*St. Thomas Aquinas* (New York: Sheed & Ward, 1933; Doubleday Image Book, 1956).
D'Arcy, M. C.	*Thomas Aquinas* (Westminster, Maryland: Newman Press, 1953).
Foster, K.	*The Life of St. Thomas Aquinas* (Baltimore: Helicon, 1959).
Grabmann, M.	*Thomas Aquinas, His Personality and Thought* (New York: Longmans, 1928).
Maritain, J.	*St. Thomas Aquinas* (New York: Meridian, 1958, rev. 1964).
Petitot, H.	*The Life and Spirit of Thomas Aquinas* (Chicago: Priory Press, 1966).
Pieper, J.	*St. Thomas Aquinas* (trans. D. MacLaren) (New York: Sheed & Ward, 1948).
Sertillanges, A. D.	*St. Thomas Aquinas and His Work* (London: Burns, Oates, 1932).
Vann, G.	*St. Thomas Aquinas* (London: Hague & Gill, 1940).
Walz, A.	*St. Thomas Aquinas* (Westminster, Maryland: Newman, 1951).
de Wohl, L.	*The Quiet Light* (Philadelphia: Lippincott, 1950). A novel.

Metaphysics and the World

Anderson, J. F.	*The Cause of Being* (St. Louis: Herder, 1952).
Gilson, E.	*Being and Some Philosophers* (Toronto: Pontifical Institute of Medieval Studies, 1949).

—— *Elements of Christian Philosophy* (New York: New American Library, 1965).

—— *God and Philosophy* (New Haven: Yale University Press, 1941).

Hart, C. A. *Thomistic Metaphysics* (Englewood Cliffs, New Jersey: Prentice-Hall, 1959).

Kenny, A. *The Five Ways* (New York: Schocken, 1969).

Klubertanz, G. *St. Thomas Aquinas on Analogy* (Chicago: Loyola University Press, 1960).

Lynch, L. *A Christian Philosophy* (New York: Scribner, 1968).

Maritain, J. *Seven Lessons on Being* (Paris: Teque, 1934).

—— *Preface to Metaphysics* (New York: Sheed & Ward, 1939).

de Raeymaeker *Philosophy of Being* (trans. E. H. Zeigelmeyer) (St. Louis: Herder, 1954).

Sillem, E. *Ways of Thinking about God* (London: Darton, Longman & Todd, 1961).

Sweeney, L. *Metaphysics of Authentic Existentialism* (Englewood Cliffs, New Jersey: Prentice-Hall, 1965).

Taylor, E. S. *St. Thomas and Natural Science* (Oxford: Blackfriars, 1945).

Man

Dhavamony, M. *Subjectivity and Knowledge in the Philosophy of St. Thomas Aquinas* (Rome: Lib. ed. Pontificia Univ. Gregoriana, 1965).

Donohue, J. W. *Thomas Aquinas and Education* (New York: Random House, 1968).

Hislop, Ian — *Anthropology of St. Thomas* (Oxford: Blackfriars, 1950).

Hoenen, P. — *Reality and Judgment According to St. Thomas* (tran. H. F. Tiblier) (Chicago: Regnery, 1952).

Joly, R. P. — *The Human Person in a Philosophy of Education* (New York: Humanities, 1965).

Klubertanz, G. — *The Discursive Power-Sources and Doctrine of the Vis Cogitativa According to St. Thomas Aquinas* (St. Louis: Modern Schoolman, 1952).

Marty, F. — *La perfection de l'Homme selon St. Thomas d'Aquin* (Rome: Presses de l'université gregorienne, 1962).

Regis, L. M. — *Epistemology* (New York: Macmillan, 1959).

Rousselot, P. — *Pour l'histoire du problème de l'amour au moyen âge* (Munster: Beitrage, 1908).

Schmidt, R. W. — *The Domain of Logic According to St. Thomas Aquinas* (The Hague: Nijhoff, 1966).

Man as Ethical and Political

Armstrong, R. A. — *Primary and secondary precepts in Thomistic Natural Law Teaching* (The Hague: Nijhoff, 1966).

Bourke, V. J. — *Ethics* (New York: Macmillan, 1951).

D'Arcy, E. — *Conscience and its Right to Freedom* (New York: Sheed & Ward, 1961).

—— — *Human Acts* (Oxford: Clarendon, 1963).

Eschmann, I. T. — "Studies in the Notion of Society in St. Thomas Aquinas," *Medieval Studies* XVIII (1946), 1–42; IX (1947), 19–55.

Gilby, T.   *The Political Thought of Thomas Aquinas* (Chicago: University of Chicago Press, 1958).

Gilson, E.   *Moral Values and the Moral Life* (tran. L. Ward) (St. Louis: Herder, 1931).

Leclerq, J.   *La philosophie Morale de St. Thomas, devant pensée contemporaine* (Louvain: Publications universitaires de Louvain, 1955).

Lottin, O.   *Le droit naturel chez S. Thomas et ses prédecesseurs* (Bruges, Belgium: Beyaert, 1926; 2nd ed., 1931).

Maritain, J.   *Man and the State* (Chicago: University of Chicago Press, 1951).

——   *The Person and Common Good* (New York: Scribner's, 1947).

Michel, G.   *La notion thomiste du bien commun* (Paris: 1932).

Oesterle, J. A.   *Ethics* (Englewood Cliffs, New Jersey: Prentice-Hall, 1957).

Roland-Gosselin, B.   *La doctrine politique de St. Thomas d'Aquin* (Paris: Rievere, 1928).

Sertillanges, A. D.   *La philosophie morale de St. Thomas d'Aquin* (Paris: Aubier, 1942).

Simon, Y.   *The Nature and Functions of Authority* (Milwaukee: Marquette University Press, 1940).

Vann, G.   *Man and Morality* (New York: Sheed & Ward, rev. ed., 1960).

Aesthetics

Gilson, E.   *Painting and Creating* (New York: Pantheon, 1957).

Maritain, J.   *Art and Scholasticism* (New York: Scribner, 1930).

——   *Creative Intuition in Art and Poetry* (New York: Pantheon, 1953).

Man as Religious

Gillemann, G.
Primacy of Charity in Moral Theology (Westminster, Maryland: Newman, 1959).

Malet, A.
Personne et Amour dans la théologie trinitaire de St. Thomas d'Aquin (Paris: J. Vrin, 1956).

Pepler, C.
The Basis of the Mysticism of St. Thomas (London: Blackfriars, 1953).

Plé, A.
Chastity and the Affective Life (New York: Herder and Herder, 1966).

Thomism

Copleston, F. C.
Aquinas (Baltimore: Penguin Pelican, 1955).

Gilson, E.
Le Thomisme (Paris: J. Urin, 4th ed., 1942; 5th ed., 1947).

——
The Christian Philosophy of St. Thomas Aquinas (New York: Random House, 1956).

Grenet, Paul (tran. James F. Ross)
Thomism (New York: Harper & Row, 1967).

McInerny, R. M.
Thomism in an Age of Renewal (Garden City, New York: Doubleday, 1966).

Roensch, F. J.
The Early Thomistic School (Chicago: Priory Press, 1954).

Stockhammer, M. (ed.)
Thomas Aquinas Dictionary (New York: Philosophical Library, 1965).

CONTEMPORARY THOMISM

Brunner, A.   *Fundamental Questions of Philosophy* (tran. S. A. Raemers) (St. Louis: Herder, 1937).

——   *La Personne incarnée* (Paris: Beauchesne, 1947).

Cirne-Lima, C.   *Personal Faith* (New York: Herder and Herder, 1965).

Coreth, E.   *Metaphysics* (tran. J. Donceel; critique, B. J. F. Lonergan) (New York: Herder and Herder, 1968).

Fabro, C.   *La Nozione Metafisica di Partecipazione secondo S. Thommaso d'Aquino*, 3rd ed., rev. (Torino: Societa Editrice Internazionale, 1938, 1963).

——   *Participation et Causalité selon S. Thomas* (Louvain: Publications universitaires de Louvain, 1961).

de Finance, J.   *Etre et agir dans la philosophie de saint Thomas* (Paris: Beauchesne, 1942; 2nd ed., 1945).

——   *Existence et liberté* (Paris: Vitte, 1955).

——   *Essai sur l'agir humain* (Rome, Presses de l'Université gregorienne, 1962).

Forest, A.   *La structure métaphysique du concrèt selon S. Thomas d'Aquin* (Paris: J. Vrin, 1931, 1956).

Geiger, L. B.   *La participation dans la philosophie de S. Thomas d'Aquin* (Paris: J. Vrin, 1942; 2nd ed., 1952).

Hayen, A.   *L'intentionel selon St. Thomas* (Bruges, Belgium: 1954).

———— La Communication de l'être d'après St. Thomas d'Aquin (Paris: Desclée de Brouwer, 1957).

———— S. Thomas d'Aquin et la vie de l'Eglise (Louvain: Nauwelaerts, 1952).

John, H. J.   The Thomist Spectrum (New York: Fordham University Press, 1967).

Lonergan, B. J.   Insight: A Study of Human Understanding (New York: Philosophical Library, 1958).

———— Verbum: Word and Idea in Aquinas (Notre Dame, Ind.: University of Notre Dame Press, 1967).

Lotz, J. B.   Ontologia (Barcelona and Frieburg in Breisgau: Herder, 1963).

———— Le jugement de l'être; les fondements de la métaphysique, tran. R. Givord (Paris: Beauchesne, 1965).

Marc, A.   L'Idée de l'être chez S. Thomas et dans la scholastique posterieure (Paris: Beauchesne, 1933).

Maréchal, J.   Le point de départ de la métaphysique, c. 5 (Paris: Alcan, 1927).

Maritain, J.   Existence and the Existent (New York: Pantheon, 1948).

Mascall, E. L.   He Who Is (London: Longmans-Green, 1943).

Metz, J. B.   Christliche Anthropocentrik (Munich: Kosel, 1962).

Rahner, K.   Inquiries (New York: Herder and Herder, 1964).

———— Theological Investigations, Vols. I and II (New York: Herder and Herder, 1961, 1964).

———— Nature and Grace (New York: Sheed & Ward, 1963).

———— Spirit in the World (New York: Sheed & Ward, 1968).

——— *Hearers of the Word* (tran. M. Richards) (New York: Herder and Herder, 1969).

Rousselot, P.   *Intellectualism of St. Thomas* (tran. J. E. O'Mahoney) (London: Sheed & Ward, 1935).

Shine, D.   *An Interior Metaphysics* (Weston, Mass.: Weston College Press, 1966).

Vann, G.   *On Being Human* (London: Sheed & Ward, 1933).

——— *The Heart of Man* (New York: Longmans, Green, 1945; Doubleday Image, 1960).

INDEX